C000230425

THE HOUSE ON
THE SACRED LAKE

By the same author:

The Administration of International Development Aid, The Maxwell School of Citizenship and Public Affairs, Syracuse University, 1969

Gate of the Sun: A Prospect of Bolivia, Longmans, 1970

Bolivia: Gate of the Sun, Erikson, New York, 1971

Africa and the World, A Haile Selassie Prize Trust Symposium,, edited jointly with R.K.A. Gardiner and C.L. Patterson, OUP 1970

Report for the UN Conference on Trade and Development on Technical Assistance Needs of Developing Countries, UNCTAD, 1994

Desarrollo Diferente para un Pais de Cambîos: Salir del Circulo Vicioso de La Riqueza Empobrecedora, Final Report of the Pilot Mission on Economic and Social Reform in Bolivia, Inter-American Development Bank, 1995

Orphan of the Cold War: The Inside Story of the Collapse of the Angolan Peace Process 1992–3, Macmillan Press, London, St Martin's Press, New York, 1996

Portuguese edition: Orfão da Guerra Fría: Radiografía do Colapso do Proceso de Paz Angolano 1992–3, Campo das Letras, Oporto, 1997

Never Learn to Type: A Woman at the United Nations, John Wiley & Sons Ltd, 2003

Bolivia is a relatively unknown but important and intriguing nation, and this book by Dame Margaret gives an insight that is long overdue into the lives of its people.
Jimmy Carter, former President of the United States of America

Margaret Anstee brings a unique combination of experience and perspectives in writing of Bolivia across more than fifty years and many political vicissitudes. She has known Bolivia as an international civil servant, has fought valiantly for better development policies across decades, and has made a home high on the shores of Lake Titicaca. She writes with love and understanding of the life and traditions of the high, dry Altiplano, with an insider's knowledge of international policy and with sadness and realism of the missed opportunities and political failures that have stood in the way of change. Nobody else could have written this book, or written it so well.
Professor Onora O'Neill (The Rt. Hon. The Baroness O'Neill of Bengarve CBE, former President of the British Academy and Principal of Newnham College, Cambridge)

No one who has ever spoken to Margaret Anstee about Bolivia can doubt the depth of her affection for the country and its people. This book is a fascinating account of how her life and that of Bolivia came to be so closely intertwined. It picks its way elegantly and informatively through Bolivia's modern history and the story of the author's house on the shore of the idyllic Lake Titicaca (whose inhabitants sometimes mistook her for Margaret Thatcher). Like many love affairs, it ends on a note of disillusion. But anyone who wants to get a feel for this most beautiful, little known and poverty-stricken country would do well to read this book and share the author's triumphs and tribulations.
The Rt. Hon. The Lord Hannay of Chiswick GCMG, CH, DLitt (David Hannay, former UK Ambassador and Permanent Representative to the United Nations)

In this book Margaret Anstee, who has worked tirelessly for decency and justice around the world during her long record of service with the United Nations, tells the fascinating tale of living in a poor Andean community on the shores of Lake Titicaca. She skilfully interweaves local happenings, roadblocks and other travel adventures with dramatic events in high places in which she found herself involved as she simultaneously advised successive

Bolivian governments during the turbulent times of change that led to the election of President Evo Morales. This moving story of the evolving struggle for indigenous power in an impoverished country, long overlooked by the world at large, has far wider implications in today's globalised world that deserve the attention of intelligent readers everywhere.

Redoubtable, indomitable, human rights and justice have long been her watchwords – and now this wonderful account of Margaret Anstee's Bolivian odyssey: a special book by a special person.

The Rt. Hon. Peter Hain MP, Secretary of State for Wales (Minister of State, Foreign and Commonwealth Office, 1999-2002)

Like most people who visit Bolivia, Margaret Anstee fell in love with that beautiful and delightfully eccentric country. She was enthralled by its deep and unique culture and its warm but sometimes baffling people. So she decided to devote much of her meteoric diplomatic career to helping Bolivia, and to build herself a dream house on the shore of Lake Titicaca. This book is an Andean version of *A Year in Provence*, with the tribulations and triumphs of creating a house and gaining the affection of local people. But this charming story is uniquely combined with high-level diplomacy in the United Nations and with successive Bolivian governments, culminating with that of the *campesino* Evo Morales. No one else could have written such a vivid portrait of Bolivia, from presidential palace to village market.

John Hemming, explorer and author, former Director and Secretary of the Royal Geographic Society

This fascinating memoir means we understand far more fully the formidable Margaret Anstee, who is admired and sometimes feared by so many around the world.

From the highest macro levels of global policy intrigue to the tiniest micro detail, we can appreciate much more about her, especially her devotion to the two communities in Bolivia and the Welsh Borders that she adores.

Margaret Anstee writes as bravely and robustly as her reputation.

She charts without restraint the never-ending twists and unexpected developments of Bolivian politics, even as they arrive alarmingly at her own front gate.

She is renowned as a formidable diplomat and latterly international activist who can make even the most powerful wilt under her persuasive powers. Yet privately, she is one of the most generous of hosts and friends, who can leave international intrigues at either of her front doors to engage in the most detailed discussion of her fabulous garden designs and flower beds.

How does she do it all? *House on the Sacred Lake* means we all now have a far better understanding.

Nik Gowing, international news presenter

This is the remarkable story of a country eloquently told through that of a house. Margaret Anstee evocatively entwines the story of retiring to her dream home in Bolivia on the shores of Lake Titicaca with a professional lifetime of optimistic involvement in that country's dramatic and often tragic political and economic history. In the Andes, a reader might conclude, dreams are the stuff of life but fate is harder.
The Rt. Hon. The Lord Malloch-Brown KCMG PC (Mark Malloch Brown, formerly Minister for Africa, Asia and the United Nations, Administrator of the UN Development Programme and UN Deputy Secretary-General)

Britain's most distinguished woman diplomat engagingly explains her life-built affection for the people of Bolivia and her intense interest in their problems, and is delighted to focus on Lake Titicaca as the most attractive and welcoming Andean resting-place. A most alluring read.
The Rt. Hon. The Lord Howe of Aberavon CH QC (Geoffrey Howe, former Chancellor of the Exchequer, Foreign Secretary and Deputy Prime Minister)

In this compelling and beautifully written account of building her dream house on the remote and stunningly lovely sacred Lake Titicaca in the Bolivian Andes, Margaret Anstee captures the delights, frustrations, humour and tragedy of Bolivia, the country she has come to love.
The Rt. Hon. Professor Shirley Williams (former leader of the Liberal Democrats in the House of Lords)

Dame Margaret Anstee is one of the world's most distinguished civil servants, and has worked tirelessly for international development all her life. She has now shown us that she is also a gifted writer. *The House on The Sacred Lake* is the delightful, absorbing account of her work in the country she loves most – Bolivia – and the joys and sorrows of trying to build her home on its sacred lake. It's a joy to read.
William Shawcross, author of many books, including *Deliver Us From Evil: Warlords, Peacekeepers and a World of Endless Conflict.*

THE HOUSE ON
THE SACRED LAKE

and Other Bolivian Dreams – and Nightmares

Margaret Joan Anstee

Book Guild Publishing
Sussex, England

First published in Great Britain in 2009 by
The Book Guild Ltd
Pavilion View
19 New Road
Brighton, BN1 1UF

Copyright © Margaret Joan Anstee 2009

The right of Margaret Joan Anstee to be identified as the author of
this work has been asserted by her in accordance with the
Copyright, Designs and Patents Act 1988.

All rights reserved. No part of this publication may be reproduced,
transmitted, or stored in a retrieval system, in any form or by any
means, without permission in writing from the publisher, nor be
otherwise circulated in any form of binding or cover other than
that in which it is published and without a similar condition being
imposed on the subsequent purchaser.

Typesetting in Times by
Keyboard Services, Luton, Bedfordshire

Printed in Great Britain by
Athenaeum Press Ltd, Gateshead

A catalogue record for this book is available from
The British Library

ISBN 978 1 84624 354 7

For all the people of Bolivia
May they find 'Unity in Diversity'

El Condor Pasa

O mighty Condor, owner of the skies,
Take me home,
Up into the Andes

Contents

Illustrations

Preface

According to an old Spanish proverb, '*Hay amores que matan*' – 'There are loves that kill'. Over the nearly half a century since I first landed in a DC4 at El Alto airport, then boasting only a rough and stony landing strip serviced by a few small huts, there have been moments when that phrase has seemed all too apposite to my long-standing relationship with Bolivia.

Yet in the end it has always been the love that triumphed. Bolivia is a country that arouses extreme passions, both among its own inhabitants and those who come from afar. You cannot remain indifferent. It either snatches your heart and holds you in thrall forever, or persuades you unequivocally that its peculiar delights are not for you.

It is hard to convey in words the fascination felt by those who succumb to the mysterious enchantment of this country, locked away in the high Andes at the very heart of South America. Simón Bolívar, the Liberator, after whom it was named, wrote to his general, José Antonio Sucre, the first President of Bolivia: 'This Bolivian Republic has a special enchantment for me. The more I think about the destiny of the country, the more it seems to me a tiny marvel.'

In the 180 years since then, Bolivia's history has been chequered and its destiny uncertain, but it still retains that same mysterious allure. In trying to capture the essence of its fascination, I am, perhaps fancifully, reminded of Shakespeare's description of Cleopatra:

Age cannot wither her nor custom change
Her infinite variety.

For if variety is held to be the spice of life, there is plenty to be had in Bolivia.

These qualities are enshrined in its very geography. My hero, Alcides d'Orbígny, the nineteenth-century French explorer, described it as 'the microcosm of the world'. And so it is: a vertical microcosm, cascading down from dizzy snow peaks that mock the tropical sky, through the steep gorges and high valleys which furrow the eastern side of the *cordillera*, and so away to the deep forests and wide tropical plains that sweep more gently down to the Amazon basin. You can choose any climate you have a mind for: the clear snows and biting crystalline air of the uplands at between 10,000 and 20,000 feet; the gentle, slumbrous warmth of the temperate valleys between 5000 and 8000 feet; or the steaming jungles and torrid plains in the north and east, as little as 300 feet above sea level.

Bolivia is a country with a fabled past, the centre of a succession of Andean civilisations, superimposed on one another and culminating in the apex of the Inca Empire. Its earlier history is steeped in mystery, and the descendants of the peoples who created these civilisations, the Aymaras and the Quechuas who till the harsh earth of the *altiplano* today, are ignorant of their remoter origins, which disappear in the mists of the legends and the mountains. Myth and speculation abound. Some say that the Garden of Eden was located somewhere on what is today the Bolivian *altiplano* and that this was the cradle of the human race; others believe that the word Andes comes from *antis*, and have detected a link with the lost continent of Atlantis; while others again trace descendants from Shem, the son of Noah, after the biblical deluge.

By the latest count (2008) just over nine million people inhabit the vast expanses of a country still as large as France and Spain combined, despite disastrous losses of large tracts of territory to Chile (including its sea coast), Brazil and Paraguay since independence from Spain was declared in 1825. Their ethnic and cultural composition is also enormously varied: descendants of invading Spanish *conquistadores* and of the Spanish *criollos* born in Bolivia who led the revolt against Spain nearly 200 years ago and who retain mainly European blood; *cholos* and *mestizos*, people of mixed ancestry, the product of unions between the invaders and the indigenous population; and the vast majority who trace their origins back to the original inhabitants of these lands. These indigenous majorities – some 60% of the nation – comprise many different ethnic groups, of whom the most important are the Aymaras and Quechuas, of Andean Indian stock, who inhabit the *altiplano* and the high valleys, and the Guaranis who live in the more tropical eastern plains and forests.

This diversity is reflected in the richness and variety of Bolivia's cultural heritage. Its music, dance and folklore, which interweave the myriad threads of influence and inspiration across the ages, are alive and vibrant today and need no artificial conservation. By some fluke the country has so far managed to resist the insidious competition of modern music. When you hear the sudden lilt of a *quena* – the Andean Indian flute – played by some solitary unseen shepherd in the vast empty spaces of the *altiplano*, or floating up from some hidden valley by the shores of Lake Titicaca, there is a cold clarity and purity about the sound that echoes the solitude and mystery of the high Andes and seems to enshrine the spirit of the Amerindian peoples who made them their ancestral home. When I hear even a passing phrase of that music I am transported back to the land of the condor.

To be sure, the *quena* has a melancholy, nostalgic tone enhanced when played with other indigenous instruments: the soft sonority of *tarkas* (a square wooden flute) and *zampoñas* (rather like the pipes of Pan) gives a sombre effect, while the *bombo* (a large bass drum) can beat out an underlying theme of sadness. But these are offset by the merry chords of the *charango* (a small stringed instrument carved out of an armadillo carapace). It is in essence resilient music, embodying in its buoyant rhythm the unquenchable spirit of man, still able to find beauty even in these harsh uplands, and translate it into song.

And I defy anyone, save the most turgid of souls, to resist being carried away by the spirited rhythms of the dances: the *huayño* on the *altiplano*, defiant in its demands despite the limitations of scant oxygen and thin air; the more romantic *taquiraris*, *bailecitos* and *carnavalitos* in the warmer valleys and plains; and everywhere the elegant *cueca*, a courtship dance imported from Spain but modified to suit less courtly surroundings, the delicacy of its subtle, flirtatious fluttering of handkerchiefs offset by the fierce and fast *zapoteada* at the end.

The *cueca* is an example of the syncretic tendencies that infuse all Bolivian life. So too is *diablada*, or devil's dance, performed in Oruro at carnival time, with its intricate mix of ancient pagan rites and pantheism and the religious fervour of Catholicism introduced at a later date. This is all part of the duality of Bolivian life, a duality expressed in extremes of geography and temperament. It is a duality which has its roots deep in history and the bifurcation that occurred with the Spanish conquest, when the Indian, formerly integrated into the fabric of an admittedly hierarchical Inca society but able to express himself within its highly stylised patterns, was crushed into subjection. But the personality of the race was too strong to be obliterated. Even in the worst times of Spanish domination its subtle but pervasive infiltration could be detected: in the baroque carvings and paintings of the colonial period, in which the deft fingers of Indian artists meticulously followed the artistic instructions of their Spanish masters, but smuggled into the European-inspired framework autochthonous motifs, revealed in small animals and flowers of unmistakeable American origin, or in the Amerindian cast of the features of some New World Madonna.

Against such a background it is perhaps not surprising that Bolivian politics are as froward as her fractured geography. In the first seventy-three years of her independence Bolivia experienced no fewer than sixty revolutions, and in the twentieth century her history was not much less chequered, a pattern that repeated itself in the first years of the new millennium. The great watershed was the 1952 revolution, which transformed the structures of Bolivian politics and society, aiming for the first time to incorporate the indigenous peoples fully into the political, economic and social life of the country. That led to great hopes and a period of relatively stable government until 1964. It was during that time that I first came to Bolivia and spent the six happiest years of my working life, in the process falling irrevocably in love with the country and its people.

Then came a coup in 1964 and eighteen years of military dictatorship. Democracy was restored in 1982 and, after a shaky start, showed encouraging signs of becoming steadily more consolidated. But these signs proved misleading, masking an increasing tide of unrest among the indigenous majority, frustrated by the failure to fulfil all the great aspirations of half a century before. Things came to a head as the new century dawned, leading to the overthrow of two democratically elected presidents in quick succession, although the trappings of constitutionality were preserved. Since January 2006 Bolivia has, for the first time, had an indigenous President.

In the 1960s I wrote a book called *Gate of the Sun: A Prospect of Bolivia* with the ambitious aim of trying to convey the essence of *bolivianidad* (literally 'bolivianness'). My thesis, greatly influenced by my heady experiences in the years soon after the 1952 revolution, was that, despite all the historical differences and difficulties, there was an emerging state of nationhood of a peculiarly Bolivian character. It was not a 'travel book', although it had some elements of that genre, but attempted to instil some deeper understanding of the country and its people, as seen through my eyes and my experiences, embracing the geography and landscape, the history and politics, the literature, culture and everyday life.

The present offering is not a 'travel book' either, though again parts of it fall into that category. In a way it brings the story up to date, although on the narrower canvas of the story of a house and my efforts to establish a home in the country I love, as well as of my attempts to help successive governments deal with an increasingly unmanageable situation, both internally and internationally. The tale shows all too clearly that my impressions of forty years ago were perhaps too rosy. But then I had no idea that military dictatorships were to continue for so long or that, especially in their later years, they would create such havoc.

Democracy, for sure, has not been destroyed in Bolivia, but has run riot. It is evident that the spirit of nationhood and the forging of a national identity and sense of collective responsibility, as well as of rights, still have a lot further to go than I imagined four decades ago. Many wrongs have to be righted, of course, but my faith in the resilience of the people of my adopted country and my affection for them is in no way diminished. Living among them is never dull!

Villa Margarita   April 2009
San Pedro de Tiquina

Acknowledgements

My first acknowledgments must be posthumous: to my parents who, by their sacrifices, made possible the education that enabled me to lead a fulfilling and adventurous life all over the world; to Professor J. B. Trend, who, at Cambridge, first opened my eyes to Latin America; and to my aunt, Christina, who bore so patiently with my long absences during the last years of her life.

I owe an immense debt of gratitude to my agent, Mandy Little, without whose unfailing enthusiasm and encouragement I would have given up the struggle long ago. Mandy persevered long and hard with a series of publishers who said they liked the book but declined to publish it on the grounds that there was no interest in Bolivia and therefore no market – yet another indication of the dominance of that criterion over all others in so many spheres of life today.

I am therefore all the more grateful to the Book Guild, particularly Carol Biss, Joanna Bentley and Janet Wrench, who took on the challenging task of bringing this story to a wider audience with enthusiasm and imagination. I hope that their confidence that it will be of interest to general readers will be rewarded.

Alberto Terán, the Bolivian artist who painted the mural in the swimming pool at Villa Margarita, kindly provided the original drawing which Jon Gregory of the Book Guild skilfully fashioned into the book jacket. I am equally indebted to Don Alberto for many of the line drawings of local scenes which decorate each chapter. Others of Tihuanacu and Bolivian folklore motifs were drawn by Myriam Bono for my earlier book on Bolivia, *Gate of the Sun*. My thanks also go to Margaret Fry who patiently typed and retyped the earlier versions of the manuscript.

Many of the photographs of the Bolivian landscape and its people I owe to the generosity of Tony Morrison of South American

Pictures, whom I first met many years ago in Bolivia and whom, by a happy coincidence, I introduced to Marion, then a member of my staff, who soon afterwards became his wife. Some of the others were kindly provided by Peter Johnson, who discovered Bolivia for the first time in 2008 and also fell under its spell. To both of them I extend my warm thanks.

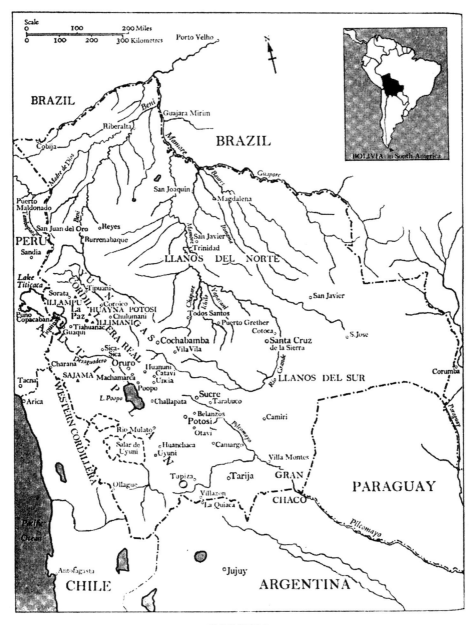

BOLIVIA

From Anstee, *Gate of the Sun*, Longman

XXV

PART ONE

The Dream

1

The Sacred Lake

I was a traveller bewitched by my first sight of the Sacred Lake, nearly a half a century ago. This book is the story of how, many years later, I came back to build a home on it shores. It is also the story of my continuing efforts, during the succeeding decades, to help Bolivia realise its long-cherished dream of development, and of achieving a better life for all its people. The two tales are intertwined, each with its share of disasters and triumphs, of dreams and nightmares.

If you look up Lake Titicaca in a reference book you will find it is an immense inland sea in the high Andes, shared between Peru and Bolivia, over 100 miles long and in some parts as much as 50 miles wide. At nearly 4000 metres above sea level, it also has the distinction of being the highest commercially navigable lake in the world. But dry statistics, imposing as they are, in no way convey the majestic grandeur of this vast expanse of water, fringed by the shimmering peaks of the Cordillera Real – the Royal Cordillera. It is a place of mystery and magic as well as beauty, enshrined in ancient myths and legends, and possessed of a strange telluric power.

For it is from the Sacred Lake that, according to local fable, and the sixteenth-century chronicler, Garcilaso Inca de La Vega, the Inca dynasty traced its supernatural origins. On the island of Titicaca (which means 'jaguar rock', the feline motif that became the symbol of the Incas) now called the Island of the Sun – *Isla del Sol* – the Sun God brought forth his son and daughter, Manco Capac and Mama Ojllo. They were to spread the arts of civilisation among the races of mankind who, at that time, were debased in ignorance and barbarism – a reference perhaps to the overthrow of the earlier empire of Tihuanacu. They were told to go forth and travel on until they reached the place where the golden staff carried by Manco Capac would sink into the ground of its own accord. The miracle took place at Cuzco, in what is now Peru, and it was there that the royal pair, following the behest of their father the Sun God, established the seat of their new empire.

No one quite knows when the small mountain state in the valley of Cuzco began to expand into the vast empire discovered by the Spanish conquistadores in the sixteenth century. By that time, their well-administered dominions extended over an area of 380,000 square miles, from the north of Ecuador to central Chile, a linear distance of 3000 miles.

Nor was this the only civilisation cradled by the Sacred Lake. There is even an Aymara myth that this was the original Garden of Eden, from which sprang all human life. More certainly, another prestigious empire, centred on Tihuanacu, preceded the Incas. Thirteen miles from the southern shores of the lake, present-day Aymaras graze their sheep and llamas among the ravaged but still imposing remains of its megalithic stone monuments, relics of a bygone civilisation of which no recollection, oral or intuitive, has come down to its modern descendants.

The significance of the surviving monuments is still largely unfathomed – the Gate of the Sun, beautifully carved and chiselled out of a solid piece of rock by people who knew neither the wheel nor the use of iron; its companion arch, known as the Gate of the Moon; the huge megalithic stairway; the crumbling terraces of the pyramid which forms the largest unit; and the fallen monolithic idols. The causes of the final fall of the civilisation, sometime in the ninth century, are as steeped in mystery as the influences which inspired its apogee.

In its heyday the bounds of Tihuanacu's empire must have been cast as widely as those of the Incas who followed them: traces of Tihuanacu culture have been found as far away as Colombia in the north, Argentina and Chile to the south, and the Peruvian coastlands to the west. Were these artistically talented and highly organised people the forebears of the Aymara peasants who today scratch out a bare subsistence on fragmented patches of often barren land? If so, they have retained no memory of their heritage. When the Spanish chronicler Pedro Cieza de León visited Tihuanacu in 1549 no one could explain the origin of these ancient buildings except in superstitious terms, claiming that they had appeared overnight.

The rise of Inca power marked the ascendancy of the Quechua culture over that of the Aymaras, but it is the Aymaras who today inhabit the region around the Bolivian side of the lake. They have their own legends centred on the lake: their world began with Virajocha – an anonymous god, for the term is a title meaning 'Creator Lord' and not a name – rising from the centre of Lake Titicaca. There is a close link with the legends woven round the enigmatic stones of Tihuanacu. According to one of these, Virajocha first created men of enormous size in a world without sun or warmth. These, however, incurred his displeasure and he destroyed them by a flood, and created a new world with sun, moon and stars, and peopled by a new race of men. A variation on this, according to some Aymara traditions, is that the giant human statuaries at Tihuanacu are made in the image of the first race of giants, whom Virajocha, in his anger, turned into stone. Yet another version affirms that these images were fashioned by Virajocha himself, as a grand design of the humanity he wished to create, and then served as prototypes for his disciples who, on his instructions, went forth and called the various peoples and tribes into being from rocks and caverns, rivers and streams.

The Cordillera Real, a constant backcloth, remote and awe inspiring, also has its place in Aymaran cosmogony. Each summit is a god with special attributes, the *achachila*, or ancestral spirit of the nearest valley or village. When an Aymara crosses a watershed and sees another *achachila* for the first time, he will kneel down in worship, doff his hat, and make an offering of the coca he is chewing by throwing it to the ground.

That Lake Titicaca should play a central role in all of these myths comes as no surprise to the traveller dazzled by the first glimpse of that cerulean vision, an oasis of light and colour amid the aridity and subdued half-tones of the surrounding high plateau. Neither does it seem strange that the region near the lake should have seen the mysterious rise, and equally mysterious decline, of a great and powerful civilisation that preceded the Incas, for this is the most fertile land, and enjoys the most benign climate to be found in all the bleak uplands of the *altiplano*. Over the centuries it has seen other conquerors come and go, and today bears silent witness to another dramatic interlude in the turbulent history of these mountains, the struggle of the descendants of their original, indigenous inhabitants to regain their ancient heritage.

5

Nor, then, is it surprising that I, who had known and loved Bolivia for many years, should come to love this place in particular and make my home here after a lifetime of wandering all over the world.

2

Why Bolivia?

'Why Bolivia?' That is the first question that everyone asks when they learn that I decided to retire here, after 41 years of peripatetic life all over the world with the United Nations. It is hard to answer in a few words. Some fascination with the country must go right back to my childhood in a distant rural Essex village in England. My parents, ever anxious to improve my general knowledge, bought me a huge jigsaw game called 'Mappa Mundi'. When we had at last assembled the large map of the world (which, in those far off days, was still largely coloured the imperial red of the British Empire), the game consisted of putting the names of the capitals in the correct countries. I won by being the only one of the family who identified La Paz as corresponding to Bolivia (I also got Antananarivo, but Madagascar never acquired significance in my life).

Both the makers of the game and I were wrong, of course. La Paz is not, and never has been, the legal capital of Bolivia. That honour has always gone to Sucre, the famous city of four names – Chuquisaca, Charcas, La Plata and Sucre. Founded as Chuquisaca by the Spanish conquistadores in 1538, in a benign and fertile valley in the eastern folds of the Andean Cordillera, in 1559 it became the centre of the Audiencia of Charcas, within the viceroyalty of Lima, holding sway over a vast region comprising most of modern Bolivia, southern Peru as far north as Cuzco, and the administrative districts of Buenos Aires, Tucumán and Paraguay, as well as the Atacama region on what is now the Chilean coast. It earned the title of the 'Athens of America', in competition with Bogotá, and was a centre of advanced liberal ideas. It was from Sucre that the first cry of freedom from the Spanish yoke rang out on 25 May 1809. Those ancient glories are long faded, reflected only in the town's splendid colonial architecture. Sucre is now a quiet backwater, lulled by a climate of perpetual spring, but still the legal capital and the seat of the Supreme Court. The seat of government is in La Paz, an altogether more austere and frugal city, huddled in a ravine gouged out of the harsh uplands of the *altiplano*.

All that knowledge came much later. My next encounter with Bolivia occurred during my undergraduate days at Cambridge, when I was Secretary of the University Spanish Society. The Spanish Faculty then was very small, but extremely lively. The Professor, J.B. Trend, a live wire if ever there was one, was the first among his fellow academics to appreciate the importance of Latin America. Among the numerous prominent speakers he invited to the Society was a Bolivian diplomat, just back from the first session of the United Nations General Assembly in London in 1946. Unusually tall for a Bolivian, he had the looks of a matinee idol, a striking combination of autocratic features inherited from Spain tinged with the dark mystery of some mingled Andean Indian blood. Needless to say all the women undergraduates, including myself, fell for him hook line and sinker. I am ashamed to say I have no recollection of what he talked about.

In the next phase of my life Bolivia figured in a less glamorous role. As one of the first women entrants to the Diplomatic Service, and presumably because I spoke Spanish (which astonishingly few people did in the Foreign Office in the late 1940s) I was assigned to the South American Department. Most of us young Third Secretaries had a starry-eyed view of our future careers. We envisaged ourselves moving in a charmed circle of diplomatic postings between London, Paris, Washington, Rome and Madrid. If Latin America hove into our sights at all, the vision did not go beyond Mexico, Rio de Janeiro, Buenos Aires and Santiago. I did not deal with Bolivia myself but it was a standing joke in the department that the two most abysmal postings on the continent were Tegucigalpa and La Paz. Any diplomat sent to either was being assigned to oblivion. When one of our Third Secretary colleagues had the misfortune to be despatched to La Paz we threw a huge party to commiserate with him and accompanied him en masse to the station to see him off on the boat train (in those more civilised days transfers were by sea). Little did I realise that I was to spend some of the happiest years of my life in what we then considered a benighted country, or that I would eventually choose it as my home.

8

That happened only when my aspirations had undergone a major sea change. I discovered that a diplomatic career in the most glittering capitals in the world no longer enticed me: what I wanted to do most was to work for the economic and social betterment of poor developing countries. In 1952 a benignly watchful fate had thrown me into the arms of the United Nations, quite by chance, in the Philippines where I found my true vocation. That work took me to my first Latin American post, in Colombia in 1956, and then in 1957 to Uruguay where I was to be the first woman Resident Representative of the UN Expanded Technical Assistance Programme (which later became the UN Development Programme – UNDP.) En route between these last two missions I hedgehopped my way across the continent, and visited La Paz for the first time.

It was love at first sight, on a brilliantly sunny winter day in May 1957, from the moment the DC4 bumped along the rough gravel airstrip, nearly 14,000 feet up in the Andes. Then the airport was a cluster of small huts, with little or no settlements around, a small island of life in the vast desert of the *altiplano*, with the silvery pinnacles of the Cordillera Real guarding the eastern horizon. One felt there must be some mistake, for there was no sign of any town or major habitation. But then, after a short drive between squat adobe huts, the missing city suddenly revealed itself, dramatically careening down a narrow defile between the mountains, a panorama given even greater depth and magnificence by the Illimani, last sentinel of the Cordillera Real, brooding with folded wings on the skyline like the legendary white condor of the Andes. The narrow streets of this hidden world throbbed with life: *cholitas* in provocatively poised bowler hats and brilliantly hued bell-skirts plied wares of every description, from exotic fruits grown in nearby tropical valleys to protective charms and fertility potions. There were donkeys and men heavily laden alike with everything imaginable: furniture, crates and sacks of flour and sugar. Beneath the mellow colonial facade of the San Francisco church, more bowler-hatted women gyrated on an ancient merry-go-round, babies on their backs, their russet faces impassive. I decided there and then that Bolivia must be my next post.

There was another reason for this besides the enchantment of my first brief visit. Uruguay, where I was bound, was a pleasant place, and a comfortable duty station but, in my still-youthful zeal, I longed to go to a country that was really poor and underdeveloped.

Bolivia certainly filled that bill – to begin with, there were only 500 kilometres of paved road in the whole country, and they did not start from La Paz. How I got there was due to another happy quirk of fate. Like my earlier colleagues in the Foreign Service, my UN colleagues had no desire to go to La Paz. In 1959 the subject of my future came up for discussion with my top boss in New York during a regional meeting with all our colleagues. The venue could not have been more bizarre: we were in a Venezuelan military plane on which we were bound for Lake Maracaibo, to visit oilfields there.

'How would you like to stay a couple more years in Uruguay?' he asked.

'I wouldn't,' I replied. 'I want to go to a really poor and underdeveloped country. Uruguay is too civilised for me.'

'But then you would have to go as Deputy Resident Representative,' my boss went on. 'It would be a much larger programme and you are still very young for so much responsibility.'

'I don't mind being deputy,' I said, 'so long as the work is really challenging and you put me under a boss from whom I'll learn a lot and not merely do his dirty work.'

It was then the bombshell came. 'What about Bolivia?' My boss was laughing and I could see he was not speaking seriously. Great was his surprise when I responded 'Done!' with great alacrity.

It all took time to work out, mainly because New York could find no one willing to take the top post. A compromise was eventually reached whereby the Resident Representative in Ecuador would be given the concurrent title in Bolivia, and would visit from time to time. As it turned out, he came for only a few days every two months, and nine months after I arrived in the country he was sent to the Congo operation. The Bolivian government then kindly asked that I be made titular Resident Representative and, since I had been running the programme virtually single-handed, UN Headquarters agreed.

After an initial visit at the end of 1959, I had taken up my official functions in Bolivia in January 1960. The journey from Montevideo, first by sea to Buenos Aires and then by ancient train up into Bolivia, turned into an odyssey of two weeks, instead of the planned four days and five nights. Beset by broken railway lines, floods, and attempted revolution I had many adventures along the way, resorting to any available mode of transport, including an overnight trip across the mountains in heavy rain on top of an open lorry and walking across the frontier between Argentina and Bolivia, pushing my belongings on a hand cart. There could hardly have been a fitter beginning to five and a half years of journeying, criss-crossing the length and breadth of Bolivia, and to many more memorable adventures. All of that is recounted in my book *Gate of the Sun: a Prospect of Bolivia* and in my autobiography *Never Learn to Type: A Woman at the United Nations*. Suffice to say here that those ineffable experiences served to transform love at first sight into a lifelong passion for the country and its people.

But it was not just the landscape and its inhabitants that entranced me. The country was going through a transcendental phase in its history and I felt myself to be part of it. Bolivia in the late 1950s and early 1960s was a heady place to be, and not simply because of the altitude. I felt, literally and figuratively, on top of the world.

In 1952 the country had undergone a profound political and social revolution, aimed at liberating the Andean Indian population from centuries of serfdom and oppression in order to integrate them fully into the political, economic and social life of the country. The sweeping reforms covered agrarian reform, universal suffrage, universal education, and nationalisation of the mines. There were many difficulties, and the only sources of external assistance then available were the United States and the United Nations, the latter preferred by the government, being considered less intrusive. With my UN team I worked in close and harmonious cooperation with Bolivian ministers and officials who were imbued with the spirit of the 1952 transformation. Together we prepared the first economic and social development plan for Bolivia (and indeed for anywhere in Latin America) and we undertook operational projects in rural development, mineral exploration, improvement of agricultural techniques, education methods, health services and many other areas.

It is hard to convey the enormous euphoria that swept us all up in its grip. We worked together enthusiastically, with no difference between Bolivian and international personnel. We were young and idealistic, full of energy, and inebriated by the unique opportunity that this special juncture of Bolivian history opened up. Our illusions did not go so far as to make us think we could change the world, but we believed we might play a modest part in making a difference in Bolivia, especially the lot of the poor. My first five and a half

11

years in Bolivia were the happiest and most satisfying of my working life.

But then there came a tragic turn of events. In November 1964 there was a military coup, the government of Víctor Paz Estenssoro was overturned, and much of our work was destroyed along with it. Eighteen years of successive military governments, each worse than the one before, were to follow until democracy was at last restored in 1982. I left in June 1965. Headquarters wanted to send me to Chile, but I was wedded to the Andes and preferred Ecuador. Since that post was not available, I asked for a transfer to Africa and was assigned to Ethiopia. It was there, in a little bungalow at the end of a cattle track, that I eased my nostalgia for Bolivia by writing *Gate of the Sun*, while African rain beat a tattoo on the corrugated iron roof.

Seven years and various assignments in other parts of the world were to intervene before I returned to Latin America. Then, in 1972, I was appointed head of the UN mission in Chile – an assignment that was to witness a far bloodier revolution – and from there I took the first opportunity to visit Bolivia. After the Pinochet coup on 11 September 1973, and the ransacking of my house by his secret police, I was transferred to New York in April 1974. In my first Headquarters post as Deputy Regional Director for Latin America of the UN Development Programme, and later as Assistant Secretary General of the UN Department for Technical Co-operation for Development, I visited Bolivia fairly often and continued to support development projects there.

When democracy was at last restored to Bolivia in late 1982, the elected president, Dr Hernán Siles Zuazo, inherited a derelict economy, virtually destroyed by years of military rule, especially in the latter period when dictators had succeeded one another in bewildering succession, corruption had flourished and the illegal production of drugs, a scourge from which Bolivia still suffers today, had been actively promoted by military leaders in order to enrich themselves. The country was impoverished and heavily in debt to foreign lenders, but no one knew exactly how much, to whom, or on what conditions. So unholy was the mess that the major international financial institutions, the International Monetary Fund and the World Bank, simply did not want to know, and were not prepared even to send a mission to investigate. So President Siles turned to the United Nations.

Hernán Siles Zuazo, like Víctor Paz Estenssoro, had been one of the three architects of the 1952 revolution that had changed the face of Bolivia forever, overthrowing the oligarchical and feudal structures that had characterised it for centuries, both before and after independence. The third was the labour leader, Juan Lechín Oquendo. Hernán Siles had good reason to remember the support that the UN alone had been ready to give the fledgling new government of the Movimiento Nacionalista Revolucionario, MNR – the Nationalist Revolutionary Movement – when it faced an initially hostile world. He had also been president during the first seven months of my mission in 1960, until Víctor Paz succeeded him in August of that year, and so knew me well.

President Siles, accompanied by some of his ministers, flew to New York in December 1982 to address the UN General Assembly and make a personal appeal to the Secretary General, then Javier Pérez de Cuéllar, a fellow Latin American who was just completing his first year in office. But first the president and his retinue came to see me – I was then Assistant Secretary General in the Department of Technical Co-operation, with world-wide responsibilities for operational programmes of economic and social development. They had hit on an entirely novel idea: that the Secretary General should appoint a Special Representative for Bolivia to assist the government in restoring order to the economy, reinstating its relations with the international financial community and mobilising donor assistance, all of which was considered indispensable for the consolidation of democracy, still in an immensely fragile state. They had also selected the person to whom they wished to entrust this onerous responsibility – myself. The Secretary General, who had happy memories of La Paz where he had served as a diplomat many years before, accepted the proposal with alacrity and within days I was despatched to Bolivia for my initial mission.

That was the beginning of a task that was to endure until my posting to war-torn Angola in early 1992 by Pérez de Cuéllar's successor, Dr Boutros Boutros Ghali. It was a job I had to do on top of my main functions, first as Assistant Secretary General in New York and, from 1987, as Under Secretary General and Director General of the UN office in Vienna. In the beginning the workload was very heavy indeed, involving almost monthly trips to La Paz, and the organisation of innumerable meetings, both in La Paz and New York, to try to drum up donor support, as well as lobbying visits to international institutions, heads of state and ministers. This was the time when the so-called Washington consensus was at its apogee and developing countries were obliged to introduce sweeping policies of economic liberalisation and structural adjustment in order to qualify for external assistance. The International Monetary Fund (IMF) and the World Bank (IBRD) were the main agents for implementing these strategies and it was with them that we had mainly to deal. Several times we were tantalisingly close to success in our negotiations but at the last minute social and political pressures within Bolivia, unleashed after long years of repression, and fuelled by unrealistic expectations that the return to democracy would improve living conditions overnight, always prevented the government from biting the IMF bullet. Without their seal of approval of Bolivia's economic policies no other donors would assist.

In the end President Siles, always a man of high principles and a patriot above all else, stepped down a year early. Víctor Paz Estenssoro was elected to succeed him in August 1985. Before the month was out the new government had adopted a swingeing programme of economic liberalisation and stabilisation that won the approval of the IMF and the World Bank, and so of the international community as a whole. Those decisions were unavoidable in the prevailing international economic and political climate, with its insistence on market economies. The social cost to the Bolivian people was very high, however, although partially offset by an emergency social programme of public works which we introduced soon afterwards, and for which we obtained external assistance.

As the situation stabilised my visits could become less frequent but they continued until 1992, a period of ten years in all. The economic policies introduced in 1985 were continued by succeeding, democratically elected governments, including those of different political persuasion, and continued to win international plaudits for their orthodoxy. But they failed to attract the expected levels of foreign private investment, or to improve the lot of the poorest strata of the population, mostly the *campesinos* who eke out a living on the barren *altiplano* or in the high valleys of the Andes. This was an issue that was addressed by an independent mission of the Inter-American Development Bank, headed by myself, in 1994 and is still unresolved. It was an incandescent topic on the electoral hustings in 2002, and in October 2003 widespread popular

14

movements toppled the democratically elected government and ousted the president. He was succeeded by his Vice President but in June 2005 he too fell, and, after an interim presidency, Evo Morales became the democratically elected Head of State in January 2006, the first indigenous person to occupy that position.

In 1985 President Paz Estenssoro awarded me the highest honour Bolivia has, making me *Dama Gran Cruz del Cóndor de los Andes* (Dame Grand Cross of the Condor of the Andes). That honour had first been proposed in 1965, but UN Headquarters had refused to approve my acceptance. This time it was presented as a surprise, and no one could object. Then, in 1990, President Jaime Paz Zamora offered to bestow Bolivian nationality on me, in recognition of my services to the country over thirty years, and signed a Supreme Decree to that effect.

As the years went by the prospect of retiring to settle down somewhere loomed. This is never an easy choice for anyone who has led an international life, moving from country to country every few years. It is especially hard for someone like myself, single, an only child whose parents were gone, and who had no near family left except a beloved aunt. Apart from a couple of brief spells I had not lived in the United Kingdom for over forty years and had lost most of my contacts there, and with them my roots. Bolivia seemed the obvious choice. I had lived there for more years than in any other place besides the land of my birth, had more friends there than anywhere else, and loved the country and its people. Moreover, I thought I could continue to help the country, in a personal and voluntary capacity, after leaving the UN.

So in the early 1980s I started preparing the ground for a permanent residence in Bolivia. That is the saga that unfolds in this book. It was not until late 1993, after my retirement, that I actually came here to live. My decision had by then become even clearer with the death in January 1991 of my long-time professional colleague and personal companion Sir Robert Jackson (Jacko) after three cruel years blighted by a severe stroke, and a year later by the loss in 1994 of my dearest friend from Cambridge days, Mary Gibson.

It is a story not without its vicissitudes, but also punctuated by moments of great happiness and often of hilarity. Like most things

15

in life it has not worked out entirely as planned, as this book will show. Because of commitments elsewhere in the world, and of developments in Bolivia itself, I have spent less time in my house on the Sacred Lake than I had intended. But it has always been, and remains, a haven of peace and tranquillity to which I return with a joyous sense of homecoming.

3

The Land

I knew that I wanted my Bolivian home to be on the *altiplano*, for I loved the vast distances and strange luminosity of that upland desert, set in its glittering palisade of snow-capped mountains. I felt myself to be irretrievably 'Kolla', as the austere natives of those frugal uplands are known, after the ancient kingdom of Kollasuyo, so different from the more easy-going 'Cambas' in the sultry lowlands of Santa Cruz.

Already in the 1960s I had fallen in love with a high valley not far from La Paz, hidden behind the serrated, eroded peaks of the Sierra de las Ánimas, and dominated by the towering bulk of the Illimani. I often walked there at weekends, and had christened it 'the valley of Cristina and Juan', after an encounter with a diminutive Andean shepherdess and her tiny black lamb, which she called Juan. No more than seven or eight years old, she was already dressed like a grown-up woman in a faded red *pollera*, the traditional Andean skirt, tattered blouse and shawl and an over-large bowler hat, green with age, that almost covered her large dark eyes. Those eyes were already clouded with grown-up cares, for she alone was responsible for a large flock of undersized sheep. Yet she was still a child at heart, whiling away the long hours by playing with tops that she had fashioned from berries and stiff stalks of *paja brava* grass, with the same fascination as would have gripped a more pampered child, born in kinder circumstances and given the latest mechanical toy. That was to be the first of many encounters until one day I no longer found Cristina pasturing her flock. Walking those same hills twenty years later I again had news of her – 'Married,' they said, 'and gone to live in another village in the next valley.'

Another regular of those weekend walks was Pablo, who would come flying down from a corralled adobe homestead, brandishing a rusty tin alarm clock for me to wind. It had always either stopped

17

or was hours wrong, and it seemed that I was the only one initiated into its mysteries. Perhaps it was some kind of esoteric status symbol, for it was difficult to explain in any other way this obsession with time in a timeless valley. Pablo's other obsession was education, and I still recall his anguish when the mud-walled, one-room school he attended in the next valley was closed for lack of a teacher. One day he arrived at less speed than usual, carrying his clock, but carefully cradling in his other hand an enormous duck's egg which, he shyly explained, was a special present for me. This was a gesture typical of the generosity of the poorest Bolivians that so endeared the country to me.

A place that had always fascinated me on those solitary walks was a deserted hacienda, abandoned since the agrarian reform, whose broken windows stared blindly at the Illimani and one of the most beautiful views in the world. It had become the local headquarters of the peasants' syndicate and visitors were not always welcome: on one occasion I was warned off by a churlish old man, brandishing an aged rifle.

Nonetheless, when I began my search in earnest for a site for my Bolivian home in the early 1980s, this was the place that came first to mind. I found the old hacienda even more dilapidated. No attempt had been made to renovate it, even to accommodate the syndicate, and the place had a deserted air. Farther up the hill, in my favourite village of Camiraya, I met a young *campesino* laboriously picking small stones out of barley ears before feeding them to the pigs. Pedro Mamani invited me into his tiny courtyard and gave me his low stool to sit on. We discussed the economic crisis, which we agreed was grave, and the harvest which (a rare admission) he conceded was reasonably good. The thought had occurred to me on the way up that the ruined hacienda might be just the place that I could renovate as my retirement home so, after these polite introductions, I asked him if he knew who owned it. It seemed that, while the hacienda's land had been divided among the local peasants under the agrarian reform programme of 1953, the old house itself had remained the property of the original family, who lived in La Paz. He did not know their name.

As we talked I was conscious of intense interest radiating from other occupants of the little compound: a small child's face peering round the corner of a hut and quickly disappearing, the greasy brim of an old man's hat and one sharp eye only momentarily glimpsed in a dark doorway. Pedro suddenly excused himself and went into the hut. A lengthy pause ensued in which I could hear an earnest debate being conducted within, too low even to distinguish whether it was in Spanish or Aymara, the local Indian language of that region. As I waited, crouched on my stool outside, a distasteful – and ignoble – thought occurred to me, sparked by recent experiences in the streets of La Paz: they were going to ask me for money. This was followed by swift panic, as I had left all my cash in the car, miles away. I was about to steal quietly away when, to my shame, Pedro emerged carrying an enamel plate full to the brim with *chairo* (the local soup made of vegetables, mostly potatoes – *chuño*, the frozen kind – and herbs), and a spoon obviously polished till it shone. I nearly wept on the spot – this was yet another example of the innate generosity and hospitality of rural Bolivians, despite their poverty.

I asked permission to enter the hut. It was the kitchen hut – they slept in another one – blackened and full of smoke from the adobe oven on which several pots were boiling, for there was no window or chimney. Pedro's wife, two small girls and his father-in-law were sitting on the dirt floor, also eating *chairo*, but from smaller plates than mine, together with dried broad beans which they also tried to press on me. From a hole under an adobe platform on one side came persistent scufflings and squeakings from a litter of young rabbits and a few guinea pigs. The meal the family shared with me was probably their only one that day. The next time I passed that way I left sweets and other goodies for the children.

I pursued my enquiries with the neighbours about the owners of the hacienda and was eventually rewarded with their name, but efforts to contact them in La Paz, with a view to purchasing their old home, proved fruitless.

This kind of dead end became par for the course. Eighteen months earlier I had taken advantage of a free Sunday, during one of my periodic visits, to drive to Lake Titicaca. It was meant to be a restful day out in beautiful surroundings, but at the back of my mind was the thought that I might spy a suitable spot for a house. Above all, I wanted somewhere with a spectacular outlook and a view of the Andes. Lake Titicaca certainly provided all that, but had not been high on my agenda because it was rather far from La Paz and, in my earlier days, reached only by an unpaved road.

I was driven by Víctor, my old UN chauffeur of twenty years before, with whom I had shared many rare adventures including some hairy experiences during the 1964 military coup. Also with us was Estela, my Bolivian housekeeper in New York, who was having a few weeks' leave. Now the road was paved as far as the Straits of Tiquina, though not in best repair.

The Straits of Tiquina are a narrow neck of water, a kilometre wide, connecting the huge Great Lake (Lago Mayor) – really an inland sea – with the misleadingly named Small Lake (Lago Menor), which is by any other standards immense in its own right. There the road abruptly stops and you have to cross to the other side by ferry. In the 1960s vehicles were transported on clumsy-looking pontoons, powered by enormous, ungainly sails, and by ragged urchins who poled and paddled with a variety of roughly hewn wooden implements. Huge lorries and buses were carried in this way, tilting tipsily in the swell, which can often be significant. Once I even saw a flock of llamas being ferried across, heads all pointing the same way, aristocratic noses high in the air, and on their faces a look of horrified disbelief. Once, too, in those years, a bus plunged to the bottom, luckily with no loss of life, but the property lost included all the material being sent to me for the celebration of United Nations Day, which an economy-conscious headquarters in New York, more versed in thrift than geography, had decided to send by surface means.

In the intervening twenty years there had been some progress. Sails had been replaced by small outboard motors, but the pontoons were still precarious, roughly made locally of timber, the decks of ill-fitting planks with huge gaps and water swirling below, ineffectually scooped out by small boys with tins. On the other side the road to Copacabana, the sanctuary of the legendary Virgen de la Candelaria (the Dark Virgin of the Lake) and a place of pilgrimage, was still unpaved in 1983. It had already dawned on me that a really good view of the Royal Cordillera was only possible on this side of the Straits of Tiquina, despite the inconvenience and perils of the crossing. Copacabana itself did not have such a view, and was a dirty little town, much at odds with the shimmering white *mudéjar* domes and brilliant blue tiles of the huge Moorish-style cathedral that dominates it.

Along the peninsula that links Tiquina with Copacabana there were many dramatic vistas but they were invariably in places where

20

the land dropped precipitously from the road edge to the lake far below without a handkerchief of space on which to build. I was ready to give up the search when, as we came back round the last curve of the hill down to Tiquina, Estela suddenly pointed excitedly to the right and said, 'What about that?'

Some way off the road the land sloped steeply down to a small rocky promontory, crowned with a few eucalyptus trees, and looking across the deep blue waters of the lake to the crenellated white peaks of the Cordillera Real. We got out and stumbled down several hundred yards along a rough stone-strewn footpath, past an abandoned graveyard with crumbling adobe crosses, and came to a small rocky plateau, fringed with a dozen eucalyptus. At nearly 14,000 feet the site was well above the tree-line, but eucalyptus manage to survive in the more benign micro-climate of the lake. The plateau was large enough for a small house. Below it the land fell away in a cascade of boulders and rocky outcrops, interspersed with colourful wild flowers and shrubs, to a stony beach at the water's edge, some eighty metres below.

The site had everything I had been looking for. There were just a few minor snags. We had no idea to whom the land belonged, much less whether the owners would be willing to sell. Dusk was already falling on a Sunday evening and in two days, already fully programmed, I would fly back to New York.

Had I known then what lay ahead I would probably have given up there and then (and indeed, very nearly did on several occasions thereafter) but I am a persistent soul, and back in La Paz I asked an old friend, Roberto Jordán Pando, for advice and help. I had first met him in 1960, when he was the secretary of Víctor Paz Estenssoro, at that time still a presidential candidate. After the latter's election in August 1960 Roberto had become a young and dynamic Minister of Rural Affairs and then the very first Minister of Development Planning. In both cases we had worked closely together and become fast friends. The 1964 military coup drove Roberto into exile, a state in which he remained intermittently during the succeeding eighteen years of military dictatorship. Every time he slipped back secretly into the country he was deported, his family threatened and at least once a bomb exploded at his home.

Abroad he had worked for international organisations and when democracy was at last restored in Bolivia in 1982, he became for

21

a while a prominent member of President Siles Zuazo's team, and again Minister of Planning. So, as the Secretary General's Special Representative, I found myself once more working closely with him. He, being very busy, co-opted a friend of his, another lawyer, whom I knew less well. I shall call him Antonio, not his real name, and sadly he died some years ago. I knew Antonio socially as a bon viveur and a great man to have at a party. He was the life and soul of every fiesta we had in the sixties. In those days there was little outside entertainment to be had in La Paz, and we made our own at home, with dancing and singing, enlivened by guitars, *quenas* and *charangos*. Antonio was gregarious and witty, always ready with amusing anecdotes and the latest political gossip. He came from one of those aristocratic families of Chuquisaca, who, in earlier centuries, had purchased princely titles in Europe, brought back collections of porcelain and pictures, and fine French furniture, and built phantasmagoric pseudo-castles and palaces, crowned with turrets and towers and set in Italianate gardens profuse in statuary and fretted gazebos. Antonio was a true scion of such a tradition, debonair and charming. I liked him a lot, but good sense and my knowledge of Bolivia should have warned me that he was not exactly cut out for the task in hand. Much later I discovered that he was an addicted gambler who would sometimes disappear for days on end to indulge his overwhelming passion for cards.

Nonetheless, Antonio leapt into action with an engaging show of enthusiasm and initiative, and was obdurate in his resistance to accepting any financial compensation for his labours, insisting that this was what friends were for. This extraordinary magnanimity, so characteristic of the Bolivian concept of friendship, concealed an enormous disadvantage: there was no way in which I could criticise him or goad him into speeding up the action. As the months went by without significant progress this drawback became increasingly evident. Each time I arrived in Bolivia, Antonio would cry reassuringly, '*No hay problema!*' ('No problems'). For anyone who knows Bolivia well this ominous phrase heralds all kinds of unimaginable shoals ahead, and warns that one must steel oneself to a long and frustrating struggle against the impalpable. He had, he continually assured me, been in touch with the owners of the land, of whom there appeared to be several, the agrarian reform having resulted in small parcels of land being shared by several families. But that was as far as it got, and there seemed no advance towards an offer of sale.

By 1986 I was becoming desperate and determined that I must take a firm decision soon. Roberto Jordán had tipped me off about a small house for sale in Chulumani, in the Yungas, the deep sub-tropical valleys cleft into the eastern slopes of the Cordillera Real that careen down to the hot plains of the Beni, and so to the Amazon basin. If a sub-tropical valley sounds a far cry from the barren frigidity of the *altiplano* where La Paz is situated, it should be explained that Yungas is reached quite quickly once one has climbed over the Cumbre, the high pass (over 5000 metres in altitude) through the mountains above the city. Quite quickly, that is, if the weather is good, but on the Saturday in April when I made the journey with the owner of the house the rainy season had made a comeback. There was snow on the pass and the narrow switchback road down the other side of the Cordillera, unpaved, was muddy and extremely slippery. In two or three places we nearly foundered in deep ruts or had to nose round landslides of rocks and tumbled earth. Thick clouds obscured the spectacular view of the eastern plains that normally unfolds at the topmost point of the Cumbre, and mist enveloped the thickening and increasingly tropical vegetation as we dropped lower in altitude. We had to go very carefully, for the road is a notorious death trap, dropping dizzily down in a succession of tight corkscrews. On one side vertiginous precipices plunge to invisible river valleys far below, fringed by crosses and fading plastic wreaths to warn the foolhardy of the fate of less fortunate travellers. On the other the mountain side rises in a sheer wall of unyielding rock. That day the air reverberated with the sound of torrential waters tumbling into the valleys far below. It took us four hours to get to our destination.

When at last we reached Chulumani, the sun was trying to pierce the warm mist, revealing the steep surrounding hills, each with a clustered white village clinging improbably to its perpendicular side, a soft, lush landscape in stark contrast to the harsh simplicity of La Paz. The property we were visiting had a panoramic view, and a large garden exotically overgrown with a profusion of brilliant tropical flowers and shrubs, and many kinds of fruit trees. But I did not care for the house, and the distance from La Paz, not to mention the precariousness of the road, clinched the argument against proceeding.

My spirits dented, but not yet quite daunted, I returned next day to Lake Titicaca, encouraged by Antonio that, at long last, negotiations were well advanced with the local *campesinos* and it was time to talk real business. Only a few weeks before disastrous rains and floods had caused the waters of the lake to rise to unprecedented levels, and scenes of devastation, of washed-out villages, and homeless people, were still all too evident. In San Pablo de Tiquina, the village on the La Paz side of the straits, the market building had collapsed, and the embarkation point for the pontoons, always rudimentary, was still under water. It was impossible to load the jeep and we crossed in a small boat, crammed with women, bowler-hatted and full-skirted, whose voluminous bundles of produce bade fair to sink the tiny craft to the bottom. Once on the other side we had to walk a kilometre or so uphill to my chosen site.

To my mystification, however, Antonio stopped half-way up, and started explaining about possible boundaries on a rocky piece of land on the wrong side of the road, with a scanty view of the lake and none at all of the Andes. The deal, he proudly declaimed, was virtually complete. It dawned on me with horror that, in one of these peculiarly Bolivian mix-ups, he had been negotiating all this time for the wrong plot of land!

My only accomplishment on that visit was to avert major disaster but once that little misunderstanding had been cleared up I saw my original choice for the first time on a really clear day. I was at least able to confirm, with joy, my supposition that from there one could see not only the 'Great Lake' beyond Tiquina, with its ancient islands of the Moon and the Sun, steeped in Inca legend, but also, in the other direction, the awesome sweep of the Royal Cordillera, culminating in the Illimani, standing in solitary magnificence apart from the rest and magically reflected in the waters of the 'Small Lake'.

The Sacred Lake is not so named in vain, and has its own secret enchantments. My dismay evaporated and resolve returned. The indisputable fact remained that, after three years, I was back at square one in my quest. Antonio, however, responded with his customary, if not always well-placed optimism. 'I now have all the local contacts,' he declared. 'It will be settled within a month.'

Not for the first time that prediction proved unattainable. At the end of 1986 there was still nothing to report, and 1987 was to be a difficult year in many respects. In March I was promoted to

Under-Secretary General and made Director General of the UN office in Vienna, the third headquarters of the UN. My worldwide responsibilities, again involving constant travel, covered all United Nations' programmes for narcotic drug control, crime prevention, and social development generally.

The move to Vienna was a major undertaking after thirteen years in New York. On top of this I was helping my aunt Christina with the reconstruction of the lovely home on the Welsh borders that she had just purchased, and selling my parents' home in Somerset. As a result of all these activities, as well as of the improving situation in Bolivia, I was not able to return to La Paz until November 1987, after an absence of nineteen months.

Fortunately, not everything had stood still meanwhile, and I had kept in touch with developments at long distance. This time my responsibilities in the field of narcotic drugs took me on a visit to the coca-growing fields in the Yungas and Chapare regions. I took part in a helicopter raid on illicit laboratories with the 'Leopardos', the specially trained drug traffic police, and helped incinerate 700 kilos of coca, which, or so I was informed, would have brought in 50 million dollars on the streets of New York. I also spent a weekend visiting the rural hospital that bears my name, a long drive south to Otavi in the Department of Potosí.

I only had time for a lightning visit to the lake. Antonio had identified the *campesino* owners of the land – several families of them – and they were anxious to sell. Unfortunately, new problems had arisen. I naturally wanted to seal the purchase strictly legally, and this had to be done through the procedures of the agrarian reform. But all the would-be sellers had lost their agrarian reform papers, nor could they be located in the government archives.

Once again I seemed to have hit a brick wall. Curiously, I found the solution in far-off Vienna. In June 1987 we had held there the ground-breaking UN International Conference on Drug Abuse and Illicit Trafficking which brought together ministers and senior officials from all over the world. One of the members of the Bolivian delegation was the Vice-Minister of the Interior and to him I appealed for help. He proved a tower of strength, located the documents and, when I visited Bolivia in November, arranged for me to be accompanied to the site by a senior government official and a topographer. I left at last beginning to feel confident that the red tape could finally be cut.

Even so the property did not become mine until September 1988. Antonio was no longer in the picture, but other UN and Bolivian friends had stepped in to help. It would be a mistake, however, to think that becoming a 'landowner' in Bolivia is simply a question of getting through all the bureaucratic hurdles, and paying over the money (insurmountable obstacles through these often appeared to be). Once you have come through this ordeal you have to 'take possession'.

I performed this rite on a Sunday morning, blessed with sunshine, the *altiplano* air as rare and sparkling as vintage champagne. Supported by friends and Victor we went first to San Pablo de Tiquina, on the La Paz side of the straits, to collect the 'Juez de Menor Cuantía' – a title that defies translation but roughly means a local judge who deals with minor matters. He had been apprised in advance of the need for his presence at the ceremony but was nowhere to be found. At length we ran him to earth, still at home, and with some difficulty extricated him from a crowd of bowler-hatted, bell-skirted ladies and poncho-clad men besieging his adobe house.

We hired a launch that took us diagonally across the lake to my new property. It was a very special feeling to leap from the boat onto my very own scrap of beach and then scramble up the steep path to the highest point of the rocky promontory above. As we breathlessly reached the small plateau at the top, the phrase 'silent upon a peak in Darien' inevitably sprang up in my mind.

This was not to be a silent occasion, however, for I was expected to perform some rites of possession that 'stout Cortes' never dreamed of. The Lake Titicaca region is divided into so many *minifundios* that my half-hectare of land belonged to several families of *campesinos* – hence the difficulty of arranging the purchase. The former owners, men and women, were all there in mass, supported by numerous hangers-on.

The ceremony began with a flowery speech by the judge, proclaiming me to be the new owner. He then invited me to 'take possession', which by Aymara tradition meant that I had to *revolcarme* – literally roll over and over on the ground that was to be mine. Forewarned, I had come prepared with an old poncho in which I enveloped myself before lowering myself gingerly onto the dusty earth. One should really roll over the whole area, a tall order in this case given the size of the plot, and an impossible one, in view of its topographical features. I thought honour was more than done by gyrating my supine form, in as dignified manner as was possible in these adverse circumstances, over the area of the small plateau.

The *campesinos* were not at all satisfied with this meagre performance. They stood over me shouting encouragement: '*Más lejos! señorita!*' – further, further – as I approached the edge of the precipitous rocky cliff down to the lake. The Aymara are often, and mistakenly, depicted as a dour and sombre race, when in fact they are endowed with a malicious sense of humour, as this incident showed. And who knows, perhaps they were inspired by the thought that in this way they could keep both the money and the land! Anyway, I decided discretion was the better part of valour and resisted their admonishments.

Once I had been helped to my feet, dusty and bedraggled, the next ritual was to *ch'allar*, that is, to offer a libation to the Pachamama, the Earth Goddess, to placate her as well as any evil spirits that might be hovering around, and ensure that good fortune accompanied my new enterprise. This involves sprinkling alcohol over as wide an area as possible while intoning traditional incantations in Aymara, in which I was prompted by the judge. We did it first with pure alcohol, and then with bottles of beer, all the assembled company having to perform the same ritual after me. Fortunately I had come prepared for this also, and there was more than ample beer left over for us to imbibe ample libations ourselves. Soon an al fresco party was in full swing, interspersed by increasingly loquacious and flamboyant declarations by some of the men. The Aymara – even those lacking in schooling – have an inherent gift of the gab that can reach the highest excesses of rhetoric.

Their bargaining power was not in any way minimised by inebriation, however. I was flabbergasted to discern, swathed in a great flow of oratory about my extraordinary virtues and the immense benefits I would bring as a neighbour and member of the community, some ominous words: 'Of course, most distinguished señorita, you must understand that you have bought only the earth of this plot, and not the trees that grow on it.' (The dozen or so prized eucalyptus that were a large part of the plot's charm.)

It was a good try but fortunately the judge came to my rescue, and with suitable grave demeanour and a bewildering display of recondite legal arguments dispelled this bizarre interpretation of my purchase by clarifying that the land included everything growing

27

upon it. I also won support by promising my neighbours that they could still grow crops on the land until I was ready with my own plans to develop it. One of the *campesinos* volunteered to be my watchman, but this was not a necessity at that point.

Our ceremony broke up in a happy, mutually congratulatory atmosphere, with embraces and declarations of eternal friendship all round. The sun was shining, striking diamonds of light from the lake and the distant white frieze of the mountains. Fate was smiling.

Next day I left Bolivia, continuing my mission northwards. The plane to Lima flew directly over the lake where, far below, I could just descry my tiny promontory. With an immense feeling of euphoria it finally sank into my consciousness that, after nearly five years of frustration and perseverance since I had first set eyes on it, I was at last the owner of a plot of land in Bolivia.

4

The House

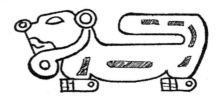

Had I but known, my real problems were only just beginning. While I had legal title to my land, its perimeters were not well defined in any visible manner and, given what is sometimes rather unkindly known as '*la malicia indígena*' (which might be roughly translated as 'native cunning') it was urgent to rectify this defect. Before leaving Bolivia in September 1988 I engaged the services of another old friend to build me a wall around the whole property.

I shall call this friend Lucho (not his real name) because the eventual dénouement of our relationship was not a happy one, either professionally or personally. I had known Lucho for nearly thirty years, from my first period in Bolivia. He had then been a young local technical expert on one of the UN projects. More recently he had become the owner of a construction firm. It seemed the most logical thing in the world to ask him to construct a wall and in March 1989 we signed the contract.

Ironically, the wall cost over twice as much as the land. It was only an adobe wall, built of mud bricks fabricated from my own soil – a gaping hole in the ground testified to this. But it was a very long wall, two and a half metres high, and traversed difficult terrain. One side of the property was bordered by the lake, so the wall was in the form of an open U, following the rocky contours of the promontory. At one end it could be built right to the water's edge; at the other it had to stop short, blocked by a tangled mass of boulders.

Once again I was not able to visit Bolivia for nearly a year, because of my commitments in Vienna. Early in August 1989 I made an Andes-hopping trip to La Paz to represent the Secretary General at the inauguration of a new president, on the traditional date of 6 August. It was a final and emotional, public farewell to Víctor Paz Estenssoro, now eighty-two years old, who had just completed his fourth and arguably most dramatic presidency. His firm leadership in introducing, in 1985 (when inflation was running at 24,000% annually), the harsh economic policies demanded by the international financial institutions as a condition for assisting Bolivia's desperate economy, and in maintaining those policies during the succeeding four years, undoubtedly saved his country from sinking into an abyss of anarchy, and consolidated the return of democracy. It cost him great personal sacrifices, both moral and physical: many of his new measures were in direct contradiction to the tenets of the 1952 revolution, of which he had been a principal leader; and almost at the onset of his presidency he had begun to suffer the first symptoms of Parkinson's disease, a fact he kept secret from all but a few persons. I had been among those with whom he shared this confidence, and I had admired his great fortitude.

The Bolivian people had also made great sacrifices, that they could ill afford. Nonetheless, the new president, Jaime Paz Zamora, although from a different party, the Revolutionary Movement of the Left (MIR), immediately declared his intention to maintain those same strict economic policies, as further successive governments of different political persuasions did until 2005. Now the validity of those policies is questioned, not only in Bolivia but almost the world over. But the fact remains – as I can attest as someone intimately involved in the process – that in 1985 a poor, developing country like Bolivia, struggling to restore democratic rule and totally dependent on outside aid, had no other choice but to conform to the prevailing international orthodoxy.

I stayed for ten days for talks with the new president and his cabinet, and was able to pay two visits to my plot of land on Lake Titicaca. The new wall, though of untreated adobe, was impressive. A fresh problem had arisen, however. My first adviser, Antonio, in the general euphoria of his negotiations to buy the land, had omitted to obtain access to it from the road higher up the hill. This was a serious omission, for which I shared responsibility. Some two hundred metres of scrub, rocks and tiny parcels of cultivation separated my plot from the rural road at the top of the hill, which was itself an offshoot of the main road to Copacabana. The only direct access was by water, to the beach below, followed by a tough scramble up the hillside, which was not going to be practical in the long term. Otherwise one had to leave one's vehicle on the top road and walk down.

Lucho had already told me about this rather fundamental difficulty. Had I bought a pig in a poke, I began asking myself. But Lucho was nothing if not ingenious in finding solutions, a boon on this occasion although it was a talent that was to prove highly disadvantageous later. Lucho joined me on my second visit, for which he had prepared the ground.

When we arrived on the road above, a small crowd was already assembled to greet us. We needed to negotiate the purchase of a strip of land three metres wide along the line of the existing footpath, where we could make an access road wide enough for a vehicle. Here the problem of ownership titles was even more of a nightmare. Most of the community of San Pedro de Tiquina had turned out, including the local judge, and the mayor and all his town councillors, these latter all identifiable by their trilby hats and ponchos. Quite a large part of the required strip, it transpired, belonged to the Town Council. The mayor made an eloquent speech, welcoming me as a neighbour and a new *tiquinense* (inhabitant of Tiquina) and thanking me profusely for raising local land values by purchasing the property! This immediately confirmed earlier suspicions in my mind that I had been grossly overcharged, as a supposed *gringa*. I consoled myself that it was worth it, given the extraordinary beauty of the place and the warmth of the welcome bestowed on me. The mayor went on to say that the council did not want me to pay cash for their part of the extra land I needed, preferring to receive compensation in kind, in a form to be determined later. This had an ominous ring about it; however, I had no choice but to agree, in a speech of thanks that I tried to make equally florid, though I was no match in eloquence for the *tiquinenses*.

The rest of the village conclave was not conducted in the same atmosphere of civic dignity and decorum. A series of scuffles broke out between the numerous contenders for minute scraps of the rest of the strip. There were no boundaries to mark any of it, not even the stone markers traditionally used on the *altiplano*. In the course of the skirmishes and heated discussions as to whose mini-plot ended where one poor old man, very fat and nearly blind, to judge by the magnification of his spectacles, was knocked into a bush, arising with his best black suit, obviously donned specially for this august occasion, liberally spattered with dust. Lucho appealed for calm, and assured everyone that matters would be sorted out, and due compensation paid to those who could prove legal title. Before

31

departing I left money to cover all this with Lucho, and was later assured that all was taken care of. Nonetheless, for years afterwards, one or two men and women would come knocking at the door claiming that they had not been paid for some tiny portion of land crossed by my entrance drive.

That Saturday in August 1989 seemed an especially auspicious day, a day of scintillating weather that showed off the rare panorama of mountains, lake and sky to perfection. When the crowd had dispersed and Lucho and I stood alone on my promontory, he suddenly said, 'Why don't you start building right away?'

That was far from my intention at that moment. I still expected to work in other parts of the world for some years, and to leave decisions about an actual dwelling until I retired and could come to Bolivia to supervise the work myself. But what little air there was at that elevation must have been intoxicating on that fateful day for I heard myself agreeing. Back in the hotel that night in La Paz I wondered if I was mad, a thought that has not too infrequently recurred since when I had to live with the consequences of building a home in a remote area, at long distance. But the die was cast.

As we walked down to the little port of San Pedro, to take the boat back across the straits of Tiquina, I passed a lady, conventionally attired in bowler hat and voluminous, many-layered skirts, carrying a heavy burden in a multi-coloured *aguayo*, or shawl, on her back. Behind her trotted her small daughter, similarly apparelled in miniature. In proper style, we gravely passed the time of day. And then the other woman's face broke into a flashing smile and she cried, 'Ah, but you [using the familiar version of *tu*] are the señora who lives over there...' – waving a hand in the direction of my little promontory, and oblivious of the fact that not even a tent had been erected on the site.

And as we passed through the market down in San Pedro a portly lady advanced from her stall and enveloped me in a crushing embrace. Her fortunes, I gathered, had prospered markedly from selling a small parcel of land to me.

All in all, I left with a pleasant feeling that the community had gathered me into its midst, and there was no going back.

Not very long after a letter arrived at my office in Vienna from the Town Council of San Pedro de Tiquina. It was smothered in official stamps and crests, and signed by all the members of the council, beginning with the mayor, each with the carnet number of the person concerned. In some cases there were thumbprints instead of signatures. The letter referred to our open-air encounter, and their request for compensation in kind for the land they would provide for my road. There had been a full discussion in a council session, they said, reaching the unanimous conclusion that, since a bulldozer would be needed to open up the road, that same bulldozer should be used to iron out San Pedro's community football pitch. At first sight it seemed an innocuous enough proposal and I instructed Lucho to accept it, on the understanding that this would represent full payment for the land in question. Little did I imagine what complications would arise!

Another prompt arrival in Vienna was a packet of five possible plans for the house itself. It was not easy to make a choice but eventually I selected a design. It was to be a modest adobe house, whitewashed outside, panelled with wood inside (one of the many original features that did not materialise) and a roof of colonial tiles (these did, but proved a disaster). The house was to have a living room and terrace, looking out on what for me is the most beautiful view in the world, two bedrooms and a small study, as well as the usual offices. I signed a second contract with Lucho for its construction.

It was about this time that I became all too tardily conscious of a few other details of major importance that had escaped my attention in my single-minded enthusiasm to buy the promontory. First, there was not a drop of water to be had on my rocky knob of land. Lucho proposed that we pump it up from the lake and purify it. Then there was the problem of electricity supply. It looked as though this would have to be provided by a generator, although the possibility of solar energy was to be explored as there is much sun on the *altiplano* during a large part of the year.

Lucho was never anything but upbeat about all these practical difficulties. Once the design was selected and I had advanced some money he actually said, in one of our many long-distance telephone conversations, that the house could probably be finished by Christmas 1989 – that is, in rather less than three months. Even my ingenuousness, at that stage of the game, would not extend to swallowing that, but I did expect that all would be in readiness by the time of my next visit.

That visit took place exactly twelve months later, in August 1990. In the meantime two other deadlines for the completion of the house had elapsed, in April and July, but it was still not finished. One major setback was that the building of the road had proved much more complicated and protracted than expected. In its absence, the workmen had to carry in all the materials – cement, tiles, pipes etc. – on their backs, with the exception of the adobe bricks which were made on site from the land itself, as for the perimeter wall.

We had not reckoned with the problem of getting a bulldozer on site to carve out the road. Unluckily for us, it transpired that a few years previously a bulldozer had sunk to the bottom of the lake while being transported across the Tiquina Straits on one of those rickety wooden ferries. No one would insure another such foolhardy venture unless we were ready to pay an astronomical premium nearly equivalent to the cost of the house. Nothing daunted, Lucho had pursued his enquiries. He discovered that there was a bulldozer on the right side of the water belonging to the Roads Maintenance Service. It had broken down many months since, and had been abandoned, conveniently near my property; the Roads Service did not have the spare parts to repair it. Lucho negotiated with them a typically Bolivian deal: we would purchase the spare parts in exchange for their doing the work on the approach road, *and* the levelling of the village football pitch that we had promised to do for the community. The Roads Service readily agreed, for this is a society traditionally based on barter. The needed spare parts had to be imported, however, and they had only just been received before my own arrival.

Nor had the football pitch saga run smoothly. With the passage of time my friends and neighbours in San Pedro de Tiquina had raised their sights. They had presented Lucho with an ambitious scheme that would involve moving half a hillside with the bulldozer, take several weeks and cost a fortune. Lucho demonstrated the usual creative genius with which he resolved every problem that came up. First he examined the proposition and the site judiciously with the local authorities. Then, addressing the mayor, he solemnly pronounced his verdict:

'Your project is an interesting one and both Señorita Margarita and I would like to help you. Of course, it is a considerable expansion of the original agreement, in which we were only required to level the football pitch. Nevertheless, I have examined the site

34

carefully. I do have to warn you that the school is in a very vulnerable position in the lee of the hillside that you want us to excavate. I am an experienced engineer, and I can assure you, Honourable Mayor, and all your councillors, that I will take every care. But with even the best of intentions in the world, I cannot lay my hand on my heart and guarantee that a mishap may not occur. Just in case, therefore, I should be grateful if you and the council could provide me with a certification that, were anything, by sheer mischance, to happen to the school – an eventuality that, I hasten to repeat, I would do everything in my power to avert – then both I and Señorita Margarita would be absolved from all responsibility.'

A deafening silence greeted this long and circumlocutory allocution. Then the Mayor and the Town Council retired for a private conclave. They did not deliberate for long. In very short order the Mayor returned to say that, after due (and remarkably brief) reflection, they thought it wiser to stick to the original arrangement.

So that hurdle was ingeniously overcome, but in the absence of the spare parts, the road had still not been built by August 1990. My visit again coincided with the Independence Day celebrations. In La Paz, National Day, Monday 6 August, was ushered in early with the banging of bells and the booming of brass bands. This was the day on which – clearly having been away from Bolivia for far too long – I had had the insane notion that I would be able to ch'allar my house, that is, inaugurate it with the traditional libations and incantations and a fiesta with my friends, music, dancing, and all the other jolly accompaniments of such celebrations. Instead, we set off in convoy to the lake with Lucho and his family and other friends, to inspect progress and enjoy an impromptu picnic, rustled together with purchases from the bowler-hatted ladies perched high on their mountains of fruit and vegetables in Camacho market, on our way out of La Paz.

It was another glorious day and we again hired a boat to take us over directly from San Pablo de Tiquina to my little beach. The building was fairly well advanced: the walls were up, and the colonial tile roof was in place. The tiles were old, and had been purchased, at Lucho's persuasion, from a tumbledown hacienda in Cochabamba (which, I was later given to understand, belonged to his own family before the agrarian reform). They then had to be transported hundreds of kilometres along the tortuous road through

35

the mountains. Much of that road was unpaved, and a goodly number of the tiles did not survive the journey. Those that did were to prove a serious liability, but of that I was still blissfully unaware.

In the event it was lucky that the construction was not finished for I discovered a number of defects. Some rooms were too small, but Lucho laughed these problems off. It was, it seemed, deceptively easy to knock down adobe walls and resurrect them a metre further out. So the downstairs rooms were extended at the back, as was my bedroom upstairs on the lake side, which we decided was to have a colonial-style wooden balcony looking out towards the Andes.

A more bizarre situation had arisen over the guest bathroom. There were to be two bathrooms, one upstairs en suite with my bedroom, the other downstairs next to the guest bedroom. Both were to have full bath and shower, but I had found out at long distance from Vienna that the guest bathroom, in error, was only being provided with a shower. 'No problem!' (that dread phrase) Lucho had assured me, 'it will be fixed!'

And so it had been, but in a very unexpected manner. Space had indeed been carved out for a bathtub, but as an extension to the kitchen, instead of to the adjoining guest bathroom. No convincing explanation of the thinking behind this curious arrangement was forthcoming. Dizzying images of guests bathing in full view while breakfast or dinner was being cooked alongside flitted before my horrified eyes. Lucho, as ever, was unfazed. It was just another wall to come down and be erected elsewhere. It also meant that the guest bathroom ended up a very curious shape, which it retains to this day.

I had asked Lucho to use local labour from the Tiquina area as far as possible. On my previous visit it had become clear that, now that the wall had been erected and construction materials for the house would begin to arrive, it was necessary to have a caretaker and night watchman. Lucho had recommended one of the workers who, he said, had performed well on the building of the wall.

'There's just one thing,' he said. 'He's only got one arm, but that makes his efforts all the more worthy.'

I readily agreed. Apart from my natural instinct to help someone in these circumstances, my many responsibilities as Director General of the UN Office in Vienna included the UN world-wide programme on disabled persons, so I was delighted to have the opportunity to put our policies into practice personally.

The man in question was very small and thin. He had lost most of one arm in a manner all too familiar in Bolivia: in the country's multitudinous fiestas it is the custom to celebrate by letting off sticks of dynamite, such as are used in the mines. It is a matter of machismo to hold onto the stick, once lighted, until the very last moment. In most Bolivian villages you will find someone who hung on too long, as well as those who lost limbs using rudimentary explosives in the mines.

In contrast to his size this particular victim rejoiced in a grandiloquent classical name, as is often the incongruous custom on the *altiplano*. His was Calixto, which immediately brought to my mind Cervantes' dreadfully stilted and boring pastoral novel *Calixto and Melibea* that I had had to toil through at university – so different from the witty and sparkling Don Quijote, that wickedly comic pastiche of the pastoral fashion. Naturally, this Calixto's wife had to be called Melibea, at least in my mind. Like her husband she was an unlikely classical replica, her not inconsiderable bulk amplified further by layers of none-too-clean petticoats, skirts and shawls, topped by a grubby bowler hat.

I had actually had the wild thought that this couple might eventually look after me and the property, once the house was finished and I moved in. Any illusions on that score were swiftly dispelled on this latest visit. For one thing Melibea had left Calixto and disappeared from Tiquina, for reasons undisclosed then but which I could more readily guess at in the light of subsequent events. For another, Calixto, who had originally lived in a temporary construction hut on the site, was now camping in the house, in slovenly bachelor style. There was food on the floor, rubbish lying around everywhere, and an unpleasant odour permeated the whole building. I resolved to build him a house with a bathroom, but recognised that Calixto was more suited for outside, rather than household, tasks. Calixto, for his part, was most anxious to please and earnestly answered me that he was going to find another Melibea *muy pronto* so that proper service could be assured. Quite what a young woman might see in poor Calixto to go and live with him and be his love, in true pastoral tradition, was not immediately evident.

Calixto and I were to have an up-and-down relationship for the next six or seven years. During that time several other Melibeas came and went, one with a small child. Sadly it all ended in tears, as will be recounted later.

I have never got to the bottom of the effective bush telegraph that operates on the *altiplano*. News travels fast, certainly faster than one would believe possible given the very rudimentary forms of transport – by foot or bicycle – and the almost total lack of modern forms of communication. At that time the cellular telephone had not yet reached the *altiplano*. True to form, our presence on this occasion did not go long unnoticed. Hardly had we settled down to our picnic when the new mayor of San Pedro (as he gravely introduced himself) appeared from nowhere to make sure there was no misunderstanding about the football pitch, since the work had not yet materialised. Reassured by Lucho that the problems had been resolved and the work would soon begin, he withdrew, to be succeeded by two little men who came scurrying down the hill behind the house to offer their services and lime for the construction. Lime would be useful, Lucho conceded, but what he really needed was stucco. Could they provide that? Apparently not, and they too withdrew, somewhat crestfallen, to wherever they had come from. Where that was, was unclear. Had they been lurking on the hill above, waiting for us to appear? Then, and ever since, I have been conscious of a myriad hidden eyes up on the hillside, charting my comings and goings and all my doings. Friendly eyes, I hasten to add, but eyes also firmly fixed on the main chance.

Once we had finished our interrupted picnic, my friends produced guitars and accordions, and the music that invariably accompanies any Bolivian party worthy of the name began to sound out across the lake. Lucho himself was no mean performer, and even a composer of folk music. The sun blazed down from a limpid sky, the mountains shimmered, and a small flotilla of boats, crammed with local revellers, sailed past to another fiesta further along the lakeshore. So the *Fiesta Patria* was very suitably celebrated. As our ferry boat came to take us back across the lake we broke into the national anthem, with its stirring chorus '*Morir antes que esclavos vivir*' – 'to die rather than live as slaves'.

In the market place in San Pablo de Tiquina the celebrations were still in full swing. All the *comparsas* from the surrounding villages had gathered in a cacophony of colours and competing bands. Each group had its own costumes, sometimes of fantastical complication and ingenuity, mingling indigenous and colonial themes and requiring an enormous investment of time and money in their fabrication. Great strength and stamina were also required to dance for hours and even days under their enormous weight, and it was questionable whether the beer and other less salubrious libations being liberally passed around, without any pause in the dancing, were working as a help or a hindrance in maintaining the relentless rhythm beaten out by the bands. By the time we arrived there were some faltering steps, and some grandly accoutred figures looked in great danger of toppling over.

Then, through this milling throng of swaying, gyrating figures, a pathway opened, and two men pushed through towards us, wearing ponchos and *lluchos* – the typical Andean woollen cap, with earflaps pulled well down over their ears.

'Good afternoon,' the pair chorused in unison, above the deafening noise of the music. 'We hear that you want stucco. We have stucco, and we would like to do business with you.' It was barely an hour or so since the word 'stucco' had been uttered on the other side of the lake. The Bolivian bush telegraph had worked again. So had the innate business sense of the Aymara, even on a feast day when many neighbours were given over to Bacchus and the spirit of the dance.

It seemed very appropriate that the next day President Jaime Paz, of his own initiative, signed a Supreme Resolution according me Bolivian citizenship, in recognition, he said, of my services to Bolivia over many years. So after a breathless whirl of fingerprinting, photographing, stamping and sealing, which involved offices all over La Paz, it was with a Bolivian passport in hand that I left for Europe two days later.

A year later, in August 1991, I returned for what, unbeknown to me, was to be my last official mission as the Secretary General's Special Representative for Bolivia. There was the usual round of meetings with the president, and the principal ministers, to review the situation and agree on further initiatives that the Secretary General should take in support of the government's efforts to conform to the requirements of the international community. The fact that I now made only one visit a year, compared to frequent visits every two or three weeks and then every two or three months as I had had to do when I started my functions nine years before, was a clear indication of how far the situation had improved. By 1991 Bolivia had not only managed to achieve, and maintain, a stable economy through two successive governments of different political persuasion, but had also attained the lowest inflation rate on the whole continent (having previously held the dismal record of the highest, at over 24,000%, in 1984), had re-launched economic growth to a remarkable 4% of GDP, and developed an accompanying programme in the social area that was being used as a model by many other countries in Latin America and elsewhere.

At the weekend I escaped to Villa Margarita. This time, I had the satisfaction to find the house and access road finished, only three years behind schedule, which is not bad by Bolivian standards. True, the house was still without electricity or water. My earlier plan to buy a generator had been superseded by the news that a rural electrification line would soon be installed on the road above, although negotiations were still underway about extending a branch cable to my house.

There was of course no furniture, but Lucho's wife had kindly provided one or two items on a temporary basis, as I was determined to spend a night in my new abode. I went there with a Bolivian friend, Elba, who had been my secretary many years before, and with my old driver Víctor. Calixto was there to greet us.

We had a big barrel of very cold lake water for washing and sanitary purposes, candles and a gas lamp, and logs to burn. It was a bitterly cold night, but a blazing fire and some whisky kept us all warm. Víctor and Calixto retired to sleep on the floor downstairs, while Elba and I had sleeping bags in my upstairs bedroom.

I woke to a chilly dawn to see the fiery red light of a new day seeping over the serrated contours of the long chain of the Andes, and the lake below my balcony flush to rose. I went for a long walk before breakfast, scrambling down to my little beach and jetty, and then climbing back up the steep and stony fields above. As I stood on the crest looking at my little whitewashed house with its red roof an indescribable feeling of mingled joy and pride surged through me. An endeavour that had initially seemed impossible had at last been realised, in spite of apparently insurmountable obstacles.

After a frugal breakfast Elba and I went down to the fishing village and port of San Pedro, where lumbering pontoons and smaller craft were moored alongside one another, and visited the colourful Sunday market.

At lunchtime friends came from La Paz for an al fresco and simple picnic of *salteñas* (spicy meat pies, a peculiarly Bolivian speciality) and drinks on my incipient terrace. The brilliant sun and translucent skies of late winter were still much in evidence, and at midday it was hot enough to sit outside in a summer dress. Then the temperature dropped rapidly and we repaired indoors to a log fire, before returning to La Paz in the late afternoon.

Two days later I was on my way to Peru, and from the aircraft, as we gained height over Lake Titicaca, I again spied my land, but this time unmistakeably identified by the little white house with its red roof. As I continued my Latin American tour from Lima to Santiago, and then to Bogota and so back to Vienna, I reflected that it would not be long before I left the United Nations and came to live in Villa Margarita. My tenure as Director General in Vienna was due to end on 31 March 1992, three months after the end of Javier Pérez de Cuéllar's second period as Secretary General.

Once again I was proved wrong. Early in 1992 the new Secretary General, Dr Boutros Boutros Ghali, asked me to go as his Special Representative to Angola, and to head the military peacekeeping mission there. This time it was to be two years before I set foot in Bolivia and Villa Margarita again, two turbulent years in which I was caught up in a whirlwind of terrible events, and witnessed much shedding of blood. In the midst of the maelstrom my thoughts often turned longingly to the tranquillity and beauty of far-off Lake Titicaca.

PART TWO

The Dream Begins

5

Return to Bolivia, 1993

I was sent to Angola for seven months, but in the end had to stay for seventeen, because of the resumption of the civil war. I left there at the end of June 1993 and a month later, after reporting to the Security Council and the Secretary General, I retired from the United Nations after 41 years of service, ready to take up a new life in Bolivia.

It was a moment of change there too. Elections in June that year had been won by Gonzalo Sánchez de Lozada (universally known as Goni) and the Nationalist Revolutionary Movement (MNR). This was the third successive peaceful and democratic transmission of power between different parties since the restoration of democracy in 1982 – a remarkable achievement given the very shaky foundation on which the process had originally started. All the governments had continued the strict economic policies adopted in 1985 that had ensured a degree of stability and been a *sine qua non* for aid from the International Monetary Fund (IMF), the World Bank, and the international donor community generally.

The election of Bolivian presidents takes place at the same time as the elections for the two houses of Congress and in order to win outright the successful candidate had then to obtain over 50% of the vote. The fragmentation of Bolivian politics and the plethora of parties made this virtually impossible. Unlike other countries with a similar system, Bolivia had no second run-off round of voting between the top two contenders of the first vote. Instead, it was the Congress that made the final choice. Predictably this was arrived at only after much political manoeuvring and horse-trading, and usually on the very eve of 6 August, the traditional date for the new president and his government to take office.

To me that second phase always seemed a profoundly un-democratic process. Indeed, in 1989 Gonzalo Sánchez de Lozada

45

had won 36% of the popular vote but, in the end, he was pipped at the post by the machinations of other parties and it had been Jaime Paz Zamora, with a lesser share of popular support, who was voted into presidential office. This time Sánchez de Lozada played his cards better in the subsequent wheeling and dealing, thus winning the support of Congress. This was done through a coalition of several parties, an arrangement that made coherent government more difficult since favours had to be repaid and key government posts allocated by quota. These negotiations were invariably long drawn out and impeded the effective rule of government for many months.

The new president had sent me a personal invitation to attend his inauguration on 6 August, but then UN Secretary General Boutros Boutros Ghali asked me to represent him. So, only a few days after leaving the organisation, I found myself once more in an official position, albeit briefly. The inauguration was an occasion full of hope, and a great antidote to the Angolan experience. The president asked me to act as an adviser, particularly with regard to the innovative social development policies which the government was planning to introduce, and I agreed to do so, on a part-time and strictly *ad honorem* basis. Here too the contrast with Angola was appealing – to try to help people to live better, rather than ineffectually trying to stop them killing one another.

This short visit enabled me to drive out to Lake Titicaca and inspect progress on Villa Margarita. My impressions were not encouraging. Perhaps predictably, everyone had sat on their hands while I was far away in Africa and the house was far from ready for occupancy. I warned all concerned that I was returning in six weeks' time and expected to be able to move in immediately.

In the interim I had other business in the United Kingdom and the United States, including receiving the Emery Reves Peace Prize awarded to me by the College of William and Mary in a rather grand ceremony in Williamsburg, Virginia.

In New York, in July, I had packed up and shipped furniture and other household goods, in the hope that they would arrive in La Paz before me. All these items had been hastily sent to New York from Vienna in early 1992 when I received the sudden summons to Angola, and had languished in my apartment there for the succeeding eighteen months, making it look more like a warehouse than a dwelling.

On 6 October Sissy and I arrived in La Paz. Sissy, a remarkable but highly-strung Austrian lady, had been my housekeeper since 1988, first in Vienna, and then in Angola, where she gallantly accompanied me, braving many hardships and dangers. She longed to come to Bolivia, but we both knew that she could not stay permanently in my employ there, given the remoteness of Villa Margarita, her lack of Spanish, and the fact that I would probably be travelling a good deal. So a compromise was struck whereby I would take her to Bolivia for my first two months, a combination of holiday and helping me to settle in.

Our arrival was not auspicious. Thick fog shrouded the airport and almost prevented our landing. October is one of the best months on the *altiplano*, sunny and dry, with the temperature beginning to warm up, but that year the rains arrived early and for the whole of our two-month stay there were torrential storms, dramatically accompanied by thunder, lightning, and strong winds.

Nor were other problems lacking. My New York bank had transferred money to the wrong bank in Bolivia, something that took several anxious days to elucidate, while the ship carrying my furniture had been delayed and had only just arrived in the Chilean port of Arica; in the best of circumstances it could not clear customs in La Paz for another couple of weeks. When the lift van eventually arrived from the coast there was a strike in the customs, and a host of bureaucratic inefficiencies that could only be resolved by greasing a few palms. I hated doing this but it was the only way to speed things up.

The delays were also increasing our expenses so, after a couple of days, we left the hotel and installed ourselves in an 'Aparthotel' in Sopocachi. I had no transport until I could buy a vehicle and here my old UN driver, Víctor Vera, with whom I had travelled the length and breadth of Bolivia and survived many dramatic adventures in the 1960s, came to my aid. Now retired, he had his own station-wagon, and I hired them both until December. So, on 7 October, the day after our arrival, we drove out to the lake. Here I will let my sporadic diary take up the tale.

Thursday 7 October

Víctor arrived at 9, as agreed, but smartly attired for the city, and without his Toyota or my boots and field clothes which I left with him in August. He explained that I had said only that I wanted to 'charlar' (to chat). True, but I had meant 'charlar' about going to the lake with his Toyota.

We took a taxi to where the Toyota was garaged in Avenida Perú and then proceeded to the lake, V. and I very unsuitably shod.

For that reason, and to spare Sissy's lungs, we took the car across the straits on the ferry, instead of crossing by small passenger boat and walking up the hill. A stowaway on the ferry revealed herself as 'Primitiva' a neighbour, vociferously complaining that she had owned part of the land on which Villa Margarita now stood but had received not a cent. I suspect a visit. In San Pedro, the Navy was banging out martial music, and marching up and down in celebration of the anniversary of the 'Distrito Naval'. As V. said, they don't have much else to do. We stopped in the plaza and bought rudimentary provisions for a picnic lunch.

Great activity at the house, where we were met by Lucho's foreman, Jorge. But things are not nearly as advanced as they should be. Electricity has only just been connected. Originally I was to have had a generator, but then the rural electrification programme reached Tiquina, the line to the next village, Camacachi, passing two hundred metres above my house. I had had to buy a very expensive transformer, and link it to the house. Water from the lake will not be available until next Thursday (?) – well still being dug, pipes up from the shore not yet laid. The floors were being polished by a chap with earplugs and a plastic bag over his head, wielding a fearsomely large and noisy machine, and the carpenter was working on the stairs. The new dining set is there, but out on the veranda, and the workmen seem to be using the chairs ... !

Calixto, my one-armed guardian, presented his new 'Melibea'. I fear Lucho and his wife are right and that they are not suitable to take on the new responsibilities that will arise now I come to live here permanently. Their cleanliness and hygiene are sadly wanting. The new little house for my main staff is almost ready, with all mod cons but I fear would lapse quickly into a slum with them. But I don't want to abandon Calixto, who has done his best according to his lights. I have hit on a solution – to retain him for the garden, which he does well, let him live in his house in the village, and interview the couple Marcos (a UN driver of my confidence) has recommended for the main work. In due course I plan to see about getting him an artificial arm.

Rain on the way to the lake, but then the skies partially cleared, there was no wind and we picnicked on the rocks by the veranda. I can't wait to get into the house, and over all this uncertainty. I feel – perhaps mistakenly – that I will feel happier and more settled once it is all resolved. A fine drive back, with the Cordillera Real and the Illimani actually showing themselves. But when we reached La Paz a terrible storm broke – lashing rain, thunder, and lightning. It continued all evening.

Took Sissy to the hotel restaurant for a good dinner, but she had one of her 'turns' and left most of it. Curious headache and earache during night. Can't make out whether it's altitude or because I banged my head on the shower tap this morning. Since everyone knows I *never* suffer from the altitude, have adopted the second theory as a matter of pride!

Friday 8 October

We moved after breakfast to the Aparthotel, in Sopocachi. Rather frugally furnished and appointed, but we have much more space, a beautiful view of the city and the Illimani, and it is a quarter the price. Also we can cook, and stay as long as we like. Sissy is in her element again and went immediately to the market with Víctor, dictionary in one hand, calculator in the other.

I to the office to try to sort out all the pending matters – visit to Portugal (where I am to lecture on Angola), visit to the hospital in Otavi that bears my name (since we can do nothing on the house for the next few days) and above all, chasing the missing money from New York. Success on the first two, none on the third, except that, after an expensive call to New York, I found out Chemical Bank had sent the US$ 5000 to Banco *Nacional*. And they promised it in 24 hours. Did, however, successfully withdraw my remaining US$ 500 from Banco Mercantil. Hope this will be enough for weekend.

This took all day, as the centre of La Paz was virtually paralysed by a 'paro general' (general strike) and 'manifestación' (demonstration) of the COB (the Bolivian Workers' Federation) in protest against the many dismissals of personnel as a prelude to the 'capitalización' of the state industries (a form of privatisation). Almost like old times in the sixties, with bursts of dynamite, a huge mass of people near San Francisco, and marching 'gremios' (guilds) chanting and waving banners.

This social unrest, combined with the precipitate change this week of the top military command, amid rumours of implications in arms traffic to Yugoslavia, and the sluggish start of the new government all add up to a disturbing picture. I was to see Minister Fernando Romero, the Minister for Human Resources Development on Monday, but have now asked for this to be postponed to Wednesday, as Ing. Jorge Córdoba this afternoon confirmed arrangements for me to visit Otavi.

Saturday 9 October

At last a quiet day. Woke early, after a much better night, earache in retreat, though much tossing and turning at 3 am. Birds were singing, a lovely pale yellow light flooded the circle of hills opposite.

Alejandro, the husband in the couple recommended by Marcos as caretakers for Villa Margarita came to see me at 9:30. I liked him. He promised to return at 2:30 with his wife.

A bit later in the morning, Víctor appeared, with my boots and sweaters. He had been my first choice to work at Villa Margarita, if his wife agreed to act as cook and housekeeper, but he had declined. Now I mentioned Alejandro and his wife (who had worked with the Salamancas, a Bolivian diplomat whom I had first met as an undergraduate at Cambridge, and his Scottish wife, until their death). Víctor made warning noises, especially about the wife, saying cagily he would neither recommend nor 'disrecommend'. During lunch, Alejandro reappeared, very apologetic, saying his wife 'se había desanimado' ('had lost heart'): San Pedro was too far away (in the morning he had said this was no problem). Coincidence? Anyway I'm back to square one on domestic help.

After lunch, when the inevitable rain stopped, I went for a walk on the Montículo. At the top young couples walked arm in arm, a little girl in pink satin and covered with confetti was being photographed, with proud family (mamma in bowler hat, and turquoise satin *pollera*) after being christened (or confirmed?). The little church is delightful – sienna coloured, with curly colonial roof tiles to match, and a miniature turret. At the door a very smart group was assembling, though for what occasion was not clear. The women were all in black, but everyone was in such high spirits it could hardly be a funeral. Inside the church a demoniacal-looking priest, with flowing locks and robes was haranguing a group of children. In his catechisms he did not wait for their replies but bellowed fiercely 'Qué es la misa? la misa es un *sacrificio*!' ('What is the mass? It is a *sacrifice*!).

The weather had cleared again and the view from the top was spectacular. Illimani was in full view. I love to look at the tiny houses scrambling up the hills around the city, clinging on for dear life, as well they might. There is always present in La Paz a sense of the transience of things material – the landslide about to occur, the fragile eroded silhouettes of the land against the sky. No wonder everyone crosses themselves as they start on a journey or even just pass a church. Below our windows is further evidence of this phenomenon. Elegant, solid-looking houses are roofed incongruously in corrugated iron, often held in place by the odd brick. Others have parts of the walls unplastered, raw bricks roughly cemented together, even with holes in places. There is a pervading sense of incompleteness, uncertainty, change. But this is part of the inexhaustible charm of Bolivia for me.

At last light there was a lovely view from our window of the fading rays of the sun, mottled by cloud, moving up the gaunt face of the Illimani, gilding first the black rocks at the lower levels, then the snow, and then at length, when the golden glow faded, leaving the great mountain in deepening, mysterious shadow.

Sunday 10 October

Woke at 6 after a good night, ready to travel to Otavi to visit 'my' hospital in Linares province in the Department of Potosí:
Head OK
Sinus OK
Earache gone
Bliss!

Enter Sissy:
I: Morgen
S: Morgen – pause – Ich habe angst (I am nervous)
I: ???
S: I don't think I should go on the trip I think I should stay here.
I: Is your cold worse?
S: No
I: Did you not sleep well?
S: I slept perfectly
I: So???
S: Ich habe angst.

It was a foregone conclusion of course that she would go in the end. I refused to be drawn into her decisions, or to persuade her either way. But my morning mood was spoiled.

We left at 8 am, in Víctor's Toyota, with his son Edgar also coming along for the ride and to help if necessary (he seems to be only intermittently in work). We arrived in Potosi, between 4:30 and 5. 8½ hours from La Paz is pretty good timing, especially considering we had a picnic lunch by the reservoir lake just after Challapata. As usual, Sissy had made enough sandwiches for a small army, so I think Víctor and Edgar did not need to buy dinner that evening.

Thunder was rumbling ominously through the mountains during our brief picnic and heavy black clouds overhung the scene. There were many birds on the water – black ducks (patos negros) Edgar called them but they looked more like Andean coots to me. White wings flashed like brilliant lightning against the coal-black sky as a trio of Andean gulls swooped and dived in a series of aerobatic manoeuvres.

We were lucky that on our onward journey only a few drops of rain spattered our windshield, though local downpours could be clearly seen everywhere around us. But the lowering weather, and forbidding light accentuated the wild desolation and stern beauty of the landscape between the lake and our destination. The blues and greys of those endless ranges of mountains, and seemingly infinite vistas, dimmed to a sombre monotone. Even the reds and ochres, apricots and pinks of some of the escarpments, rich in minerals, were subdued and stripped of their warmth. The melancholy effect overall was in keeping with the searing poverty seen along the way – tiny huts of stone or adobe huddled in a barren landscape into which people seem to merge indiscernibly, ragged children begging by the wayside. The road, though still unpaved, has been greatly improved since I first bumped along it over thirty years ago, but the desolate lives of those people who have remained here – many have migrated to the drug-producing area of Chapare and other lower and more kindly regions – have not changed at all. Nor can one see much hope that they will, when one contemplates this stark, stony land, cracked and dry from long drought.

Only the llamas and the (much less numerous) alpacas seem to survive well, on the tufted 'paja brava' (literally 'wild straw', the spiky, coarse grass that covers the 'altiplano'): In the UK Powys is supposed to be a county where there are more sheep than people. Here there are thousands of llamas scattered over the enormous expanses of countryside, but only a very sparse human population.

Potosí has spruced up considerably since I was last here. We found our way with difficulty through the narrow streets to the Hostal Colonial, our arrival there coinciding with a very slow moving procession of the Virgin being carried through the streets to the church of Santo Domingo. A band and a large crowd of dignitaries (male) and devout black-clad women followed, and from the overhanging balconies, draped with lace, and coloured shawls, the inhabitants threw down artificial flowers on to the huge, swaying statue of the Virgin. The music was almost funereal, as was the pace – three steps forward, two back – which must have made the journey seem interminable to the sweating bearers.

The Hostal Colonial has been extensively and beautifully expanded since my last visit several years ago. I was given a 'suite' (really a slightly extended bedroom overwhelmed by two huge beds) and told proudly that Queen Sofía of Spain had slept in the exactly similar one next door. I can only hope she had more luck than I with the bath plugs – missing as usual, and when I requested one, I was given two, both too big...

The Mesón – the best restaurant – being closed on Sunday, we went to a small, very crowded 'boliche' about two streets away. It was full of foreigners and we had to share a table with a man who informed us, in a strong German accent 'soy Cochabambino' ('I am from Cochabama'). Needless to say, S and he chattered away happily all evening in German.

53

Monday 11 October

While we were having breakfast, at 8 am, Ing. Jorge Córdoba appeared. We were shortly on the road, and arrived in Otavi just before 10 am.

Although we were later than announced, the reception was still under frantic preparation. One arch draped in leaves and 'aguayos' had been erected at the entrance to the village, and another was in process of going up about 200 metres along the road. So we waited respectfully until the 'Corregidor' and other dignitaries arrived to greet us, as well as the women who showered us with the ritual confetti, rubbing it well into my hair for good measure. I was touched that a large delegation had come from Kepallo, carrying the plaque commemorating my parents at the health post which I donated in 1974. They were headed by a Corregidor with an irrepressibly twinkling eye, and a face constantly creased in a smile that suggested some secret, slightly ironic joke. Kepallo had also brought its band, with zampoñas and a huge drum, which played lustily the while.

While we were exchanging courtesies the reception had been put into place with miraculous speed. Children in white uniforms were lined along the route between the arches, boys on one side, and girls on the other. A deafening explosion of dynamite, perilously close on the other side of a wall near where we stood, was the sign for Sissy to jump out of her skin and for me to be hoisted on to the shoulders of two young men and carried, feeling distinctly wobbly and insecure, between the clapping children, while the women rushed alongside hurling confetti at me, sometimes even into my mouth, rashly opened in a smile.

The ordeal, which seemed endless, did not conclude until we had reached the hospital entrance. I suspect the two bearers were as relieved as I was when it was over. At least this time my safety had been entrusted to two young men. On one earlier occasion, years before, in the mistaken belief that by then I must be a frail little old lady, the honour had been bestowed on two frail little old men, which nearly shortened all three of our lives; and, on another, to a nineteen-year-old girl, admittedly sturdy, but encumbered by a bowler hat, and voluminous skirts and petticoats. This time, in addition to the customary 'angst' that assails me on these occasions, I was in pain, having slipped and hurt my leg that morning in the shower (a further penalty of no bath plug). It was precisely on this injured part of my anatomy that one of my bearers kept grasping a strong purchase in his efforts not to drop me. It did, indeed seem the lesser of two evils!

During the ensuing ceremony of speeches, dances and massed Andean bands of various kinds (increasingly inebriated as time wore on and the beer and pisco 'coctelitos' flowed but still indefatigably blowing away at their pipes and banging their drums) gifts of a somewhat embarrassing kind were liberally bestowed on me. There was no problem about the hat placed on my confetti-clogged hair, but then a large vegetable marrow was hung round my neck, followed by a smaller but still significantly weighty gourd, about a pound of potatoes, strings of onions and carrots, and then five chains, each made up of three or four corncobs. Thus apparelled I was expected to dance and make a speech! Apart from not having yet acquired my 'altitude legs', being recently arrived, my head was bowed down to my chest by the sheer weight of these various offerings, and I was nearly throttled by the innumerable strings and asphyxiated by the pungent smell of the onions. It was almost the kiss of death!

In Bolivia it is essential to have contacts if you want to get anything done and they don't necessarily have to be at a high level. My long acquaintance with Víctor was proving highly advantageous in that regard and Marcos, another UN driver was equally useful. It was he who had produced Alejandro as a possible majordomo and on our return from Potosí he informed me that he had managed to persuade Alejandro's recalcitrant wife to change her mind.

They came together to see me that week – Alejandro a stocky man in his late fifties, with a ruddy complexion and an open, smiling face; Aida, a year or two older, with a much more severe expression on her deeply lined countenance and a mouth that did not seem very ready to smile. We came to an agreement quite quickly as to the terms of their employment. They were to install themselves in Villa Margarita as soon as possible, once my furniture had arrived. I assured them, with more hope than faith, that there would be a new house awaiting them and gave them money with which to buy beds, chairs and tables and other necessary accessories.

My own furniture was released from the customs a day or two later, after some complicated negotiations and some cash transactions, and so, on Saturday 16 October, we set out for the lake. Our rendezvous with the truck carrying the lift van took place at the little ferry port in San Pablo de Tiquina and then we embarked on separate pontoons. There was a sharp wind, the lake was choppy, and the lorry with the lift van tilted at disturbing angles on the ferry ahead of us, rocking from side to side. We dared hardly breathe until we reached San Pedro on the other side. When we got to the house and unpacked we found that the furniture was miraculously undamaged. Not so the china and glass I had had packed by self-proclaimed 'professionals' in Angola...

By nightfall we had beds set up, a fire lit, and ate a simple supper by candlelight. And so at last we spent our first night in Villa Margarita.

The next days were fully occupied, trying to put everything in order and sort out a myriad problems. A week later I had to leave Sissy and Víctor to work without me, as I had been officially invited to Portugal to speak at a conference on Angola and give other lectures. I took the opportunity to pass through England to assure myself that all was well with my aunt Christina, and so was away ten days.

6

A New Life and New Work

On my return there was still much to do to put the house in working order and I was plunged into my new functions with the government. My diary again tells the tale:

Wednesday 3 November

Arrived back in La Paz. The BA flight left Heathrow two hours late, packed even to the jump seats. Fortunately it picked up an hour on the way, as the Varig flight from Sao Paulo to La Paz decided to leave an hour earlier than scheduled.

Even first class, thanks to an upgrade thoughtfully provided by BA, was cramped and hardly luxurious. I had a voluptuous Brazilian blonde next to me, with an equally voluptuous 2-month-old baby, who behaved quite well – better than his three-year-old sister who screamed hysterically until – thankfully – dragged away to Club Class by a minion. Sleep was hard to come by and I was grateful to the purser who organised a visit to the cockpit in the middle of the night. It was the first time that I visited the cockpit of a 747–400, just two pilots and a mass of computers, the glittering constellation in the roof, as they told me, having replaced the Engineer Officer. A far cry from the cockpit of the Beechcraft on which I left Angola on 29 June – also with two pilots, in a tiny aircraft. And this time I was not invited to fly the plane!

In La Paz Victor and Sissy were waiting and we proceeded to San Pedro de Tiquina, arriving at 3:30 pm local time – 27 hours' journey from door to door.

According to the calendar, the celebration of Hallowe'en and All Saints should have been over but in Bolivia the festivities continued, with the strange mix of pagan myths, overlaid by a thin layer of Catholic religious teaching, during three centuries of Spanish rule, that characterise all such rites in the Andes. Along the way the cemeteries were still full of people, bands, and dancers, all a little tired by now and swaying irresolutely to music that was also flagging by the third day of celebrations. Both Aymara and Quechua believe that the spirits of their dear departed descend at 12 noon on 1 November to greet them, to see how they are, and ensure they themselves are not forgotten. Their families receive them in the cemeteries, with meals of their favourite food laid out, accompanied by generous provision of liquid refreshment and music.

From San Pedro I phoned Fernando Romero's secretary, to learn that I was expected to attend a meeting at 8:30 am the next day. Fortunately I slept well, and seemed not to have lost my 'altitude legs' during my 10-day absence.

I was now beginning my work with the new government, mainly with Fernando Romero, the Minister for Human Development, and was also made a member of the Social Council and of the National Commission for Popular Participation.

The government had interesting and ambitious plans. Their strategy was to carry the economic reforms introduced in 1985 one stage further by intensifying activity on the social front, which had not benefited from the reforms – indeed in some aspects there had been a regressive effect. Their electoral campaign had been based on their *Plan de Todos* – a plan for everyone. Improved social expenditure figured high among their objectives, especially on educational reform and health and social services. Another main priority of the government was to divest itself of unwieldy and inefficient state industries. This was in accordance with the current trend towards privatisation and reduction of the public sector, made almost an article of faith – and condition for assistance – by the international financial institutions as part and parcel of the so-called Washington Consensus. Bolivia, however, under the leadership of

Gonzalo Sánchez de Lozada, had given the process a novel twist, opting for 'capitalisation', under which some of the assets of former state enterprises would be distributed to all Bolivian citizens.

Another big change was the drastic reduction of the number of ministries, all economic ministries being placed under a Minister of Economic Development, Fernando Illanes, and the social ministries under a Minister of Human Development, Fernando Romero. While a reduced cabinet had many advantages, the two main areas were very large empires for one minister to straddle, and the dichotomy between 'economic' and 'social' was still not resolved. The government had also got off to an unfortunate start, with a badly handled dismissal of public employees prior to privatisation, and a slow start on the imaginative programme of capitalisation. Social conflict was brewing and there had already been a number of strikes.

It was in this context that I attended my first meeting with Minister Romero and the members of his ministry heading the different social sectors under his command.

Thursday 4 November

Left home well before 7. Usual contretemps over ferry. Reached Ministry about 8:45 to find discussions of educational reform in full spate. Competently presented, competently handled by Minister Romero but I worry about a reform which will not be completed for ten years or so, during which there will be elections, and the usual Bolivian pitfall of lack of continuity. I caught Horst Grebe's eye across the table and sensed he was thinking the same. [Horst was then in charge of social development.] We are to lunch next Wednesday.

The government faces a terrible dilemma, needing at one and the same time to bring about fundamental structural changes which need careful thought and execution, but also to take immediate and effective action, particularly in the social field, to offset the alarming growth in civil unrest and disenchantment of the population at large.

Bought, with some difficulty, a desk. But it is beautiful – white and black, and an unusual design. Next problem – how to get it to Villa Margarita. It had to be taken apart to fit in and on the station wagon (i.e. the roof). This process, which I left to Sissy and Víctor to supervise, reduced Sissy to tears and a mass of quivering hysteria. Return journey to Tiquina not congenial, but otherwise uneventful.

Friday 5 November

The nights since my return have been gloriously clear, with a nearly full moon streaming across the lake into my (still uncurtained) bedroom windows. The shadow of the leaves of the eucalyptus nearest the house trace an entrancing pattern on the ceiling, but it is a dangerous tree. Two equally sumptuous dawns followed, and today's I was able to enjoy from my bed, watching the sun rise over the Cordillera, serene in the knowledge that I had several days of less hectic activity before me. Or so I thought. With Sissy and the morning tea came more tears. She flung herself down by the bed, clasped my hand, said she had only me, she had no teddy bear (a huge one had accompanied her to Luanda) no dog (we have three!) and no cat. Calm was eventually restored but not the wonderful tranquillity of my waking mood.

Most of the day taken up in arranging things about the house, where every day I find more glaring structural faults. The 'front' door, for example, is at the back, on the lake side, and opens directly into the living room. Things are moving, albeit slowly. The door has now been moved to the corridor leading to the study – a big improvement. But the curtains and furniture promised to be ready by my return are still awaited. Water was eventually made to function only 2 days before my arrival – larger pipes were installed in the lower part. The little house, which Jorge promised for my return, is far from ready – Juanito (one of two workmen, the other being Paulino) says *at least* two more weeks.

Sissy and Calixto have planted one or two native species in the garden – including an unprepossessing cactus, which redeemed itself by putting forth two huge lily-like blooms this morning, highly perfumed.

Saturday 6 November

Spent whole morning with Víctor and Paulino hanging pictures. But we couldn't finish the job because the curtains aren't up. Sent Víctor off for the weekend to La Paz as there is little he can do just now.

Calixto, after lunch, brought in some splendid wild flowers, which Sissy arranged beautifully. One, a bulb with daffodil-like leaves, has the most exquisite long flute-like flowers in a beautiful apricot colour, shaded with green, and with yellow stamens. Calixto took me to see where it grows in the rocks – quite a scramble. He assures me we have it in the garden but it looks a long way off flowering.

Collect one or two tiny plants from the verges of the fields on the hill above and observe I am being watched by a man in a trilby hat. Hastily inform him of what I am doing (i.e. not stealing bean, pea or potato plants) and so make the acquaintance of Tomás.

Sunday 7 November

Tomás is at the gate at 7:30 bearing 6 small red kantuta bushes (the kantuta is the national flower of Bolivia) plus daisy and dahlia plants and sunflower seeds which I am not so keen on. I pay him 10 Bolivianos. Calixto and I spend most of the morning planting them, which does little to improve the appearance of my new white jeans, donned in anticipation of visitors for lunch, including Lucho and his wife.

In similar anticipation, Sissy has been on the hunt for fish since Friday, when we had some tasty but very bony, small fish (perhaps 'boga', my favourite fish when here thirty years before but now reputed to be extinct). A bowler-hatted, bell-skirted lady duly appears at our gate with an offering long before breakfast time, but they are small. Another toils up the hill from a sail-boat moored at the jetty, but again has only one small fish to offer. S. eventually trudges to the village and gets good 'pejerrey', after a long search, surprisingly from a man carrying them in a paper bag on his bicycle.

Alas none of our guests turned up. Luckily the freezer compartment of the fridge could accommodate the goodies prepared by S.

Monday 8 November

At 9 I visit the Naval Commander, Captain Gutierrez, a wiry little man, initially not disposed to be forthcoming to this strange lady, but who unbends rapidly when I tell him about Angola and of having had troops including a General (but no naval personnel!) under my command. Is helpful about ensuring a ferry pontoon is available when I have to leave early for La Paz, and about my becoming a 'socia' of the archaic single telephone in the village. Even offers security when I am away from Villa Margarita. I rashly ask him to dinner, tomorrow night, with another officer. Sissy immediately begins planning an ambitious meal which they will no doubt find full of surprises.

Really get down to my desk and write lots of letters, long outstanding. This task facilitated by really awful weather, cold, grey, and some torrential rain. In the afternoon, terrific lightning and thunder. The wind changed to the south, and the waters of the lake changed with it. The surface was striated with thin, diagonal lines of angry-looking foam, like blue grey granite veined with chalk. In the distance a great wall of cloud, mist and rain advanced inexorably down the lake towards us. The Cordillera was blotted out, non-existent.

My balcony door leaks, another item for the list I prepared for Lucho on Sunday and had no chance to deliver.

Tuesday 9 November

Walked to village and had frustrating time trying to telephone La Paz. There is only one telephone, which also serves the Navy and is run by them. It is always besieged by a queue of bowler-hatted 'cholitas' and other local folk and the imagination boggles as to what would happen if the President wanted to give the Navy an emergency order or if there was an invasion . . . Today the Commandant was using the line and continued to do so until 12 noon – closing time! The little naval chap who runs this rather desultory service was peacefully copying out a piece of music the while. He has been fifteen years in the Navy.

Suddenly, after lunch, Rodolfo the 'cortinero' (curtain-maker) appears unannounced with brother and small son. They work all afternoon putting up rails and some curtains. In the process they knock over Sissy's flowers and break a precious vase. Tomás also appears after lunch with lots of flowering cactus which Víctor and Calixto plant.

Wednesday 10 November

Last night's dinner with the Comandante Naval, Capitán Gutiérrez and his Ayudante, went off very well. All very jovial and they brought a gift of a bottle of red wine. Much talk of politics and the present difficult situation. Interesting to hear rather caustic comments by the Comandante, reflecting general military discontent with the conduct of government (all governments, that is).

Left at 7 this morning for La Paz. The Comandante was almost as good as his word – there was a pontoon available to take us across, albeit 15 minutes later than the agreed time.

Dismal rainy journey, not enlivened by the news on the car radio of events in Potosí – general strike, and a disagreeable reception being prepared for the President who visits today for the town's anniversary. Got to the Ministry by 9:30 when the Consejo Social was supposed to start work. Because of the crisis Minister Romero did not turn up until 10:15, and then announced that, because the President had asked him to join him in Potosí on the morrow, the meeting of the Comisión Nacional de Participación Popular would have to be postponed from Thursday to Friday. This meant that I had to spend two nights in La Paz instead of one. Luckily, the naval connection worked like a charm and I was able to get a message to Sissy not to expect me until Friday.

The meeting continued to discuss Education Reform, notably how to overcome opposition by offering a salary rise to teachers, without increasing the cost to the Treasury, by dint of getting rid of the 'fantasmas' ('ghosts' – i.e. people who are on the payroll, but do nothing). No one knows how many of these there are, but the figure of 10,000 is repeatedly mooted.

I had to leave the meeting before it was over to go to Miraflores to look into the question of buying a car. Virtually settled on a Mitsubishi Montero (small) but may have to wait till December for it.

My lunch with Horst Grebe expanded to include the Minister, and Fernando Ruiz. The Minister had been bidden by the President to take part in the church's mediation efforts between the government and the COB (the Bolivian Workers' Federation), a role he clearly did not relish. We encouraged him *not* to go to these meetings – there are other ministers whose job this is; he should not be 'burnt' and is needed to do things that may help resolve the crisis in the long run. He seemed cheered by this (but still went to Potosí next day). It is clear that the government is caught in a vicious circle (according to Horst, deliberately created by the opposition), prevented by the immediate demands of the deepening crisis from devoting time to implementing the promised programmes that would, in the longer run, help to alleviate the problems underlying the crisis.

Some conversation also about preparations for the World Bank Consultative Group in Washington in December. (This is the regular meeting at which the government presents its programmes and requirements for external aid, and donor governments pledge support.) I have the disturbing impression that the documents are far from advanced.

Rather a dim evening in hotel, gloomily watching on TV the dreadful treatment given to Goni in Potosí, including a virtual boycott by the media. Fernando Illanes retorted by virtually boycotting questions by the press, saying he had to have a pee, and could he please be allowed to go to the bathroom! TV had fun and games, of course expressing indignation, but repeatedly showed the episode with undisguised glee.

Thursday 11 November

Saw Alan Court of UNICEF in Obrajes early, about my hospital, then battled against traffic back up to the centre (where the daily 'manifestación' and 'paro' were in full obstructive swing) to meet Lucho and Jorge to discuss my long list of things still unfinished at Villa Margarita. Extracted some promises, but am still worried things won't be properly in hand by the time I leave in December.

Friday 12 November

The meeting of the Comisión Nacional de Participación Popular was hardly worth staying over for: the Minister came for only ten minutes, having to go to a mediation meeting with COB (so much for our lunch time conversation!); Chacho Justiniano, Minister for Sustainable Development, had to leave for an emergency Cabinet Meeting; the Vice-President (along with some others) didn't show up at all. Those of us who did plodded through the draft of the 'Proyecto de Ley Marco de Distritación' (draft framework Law on Districtisation).

I had to leave before the meeting finished, having agreed with Víctor that we would leave for Tiquina at 11:30 as Rodolfo, the 'cortinero', had promised faithfully to come on Friday to finish hanging the curtains. Of course, he was not there. Sissy was, with a face full of woe, complaining bitterly of terrible weather, and of no water or electricity (on the last two counts, her report was certainly exaggerated). My bathroom was still as left at 7 am on Wednesday. S. apparently spent that day in bed.

Saturday 13 November

Rodolfo the cortinero came about midday. Victor, Calixto and I planted a number of plants and shrubs C. had brought from the hills. In the afternoon he announced that he was again going to the 'selva' (jungle) for more plants, though nothing could be less 'selvático' than the virtually tree-less *altiplano*. He came back laden, as it was growing dark.

The garden is really beginning to take shape, especially the natural rockery near the house. The early rains also help, but do not lift the spirits. We have had almost a week of grey, cold days, with heavy intermittent downpours, including some hail and snow. The Cordillera and the Illimani have been invisible for days.

I spent much of the day composing notes for the Minister ('Negro' Romero) on strategies for handling the Grupo Consultivo, about which I am increasingly worried.

Sunday 14 November

When we had just given up, Lucho and his wife and daughter turned up for lunch. Sissy produced a gargantuan meal, to which no one could do justice: vegetable soup, a 'contundente' fish dish of 'pejerrey' with roast potatoes, spicy goulash with noodles and cauliflower, apricot parfait. Calixto and family, and the three dogs, did well, though what the dogs made of the hot goulash I can't imagine.

We looked over the things remaining to be done. To my horror, they include a septic tank that I thought was installed, and that I suspect everyone hoped I would forget.

After a rainy morning, the afternoon turned out marvellously sunny, although windy and cool. The wind was not from the usual direction, hence Sissy and I sat by a very smoky fire in the evening (normally the chimney draws very well). Lucho's daughter could not get over the fact that we have no TV; but we are quite content – at least I am, to sit by the fire reading our books. I am now into Anthony Powell's Memoirs.

Monday 15 November

After a cloudy, watery start, the day brightened up. Went to the village in the morning to phone La Paz – long, tedious process. No meeting until, theoretically, Wednesday.

No sign of the foreman, Jorge, who'd promised 'sin falta' (without fail) to be here early this morning with labour reinforcements and additional building materials. Five men were working today, but spent the whole day marching up and down in single file to the beach to collect black sand, which the poor things lugged back uphill in sacks on their shoulders.

After lunch, misled by the warmth of the sheltered side of the house, I took the plunge – literally – and went for a swim in the lake. The water was *freezing* and I only did about 120 metres before coming out, for fear of cramp. There was a stiff breeze on the beach too. All made good by a hot bath.

Tuesday 16 November

The weather seems to have taken a turn for the better. Woke at 5:30 to a rosy dawn over the Cordillera Real, and wondered whether this caused misgivings to Bolivian shepherds, of whom there are many hereabouts. The colour quickly faded to a lovely amber light and then bright sunshine in a cloudless blue sky over the blue lake, dotted here and there with the coloured sails – blue white, violet, pink – of fishing boats. Last night we witnessed an equally breathtaking sunset. The Cordillera was suffused in a soft apricot light, misty snow peaks seeming to float dreamily on ephemeral banks of cloud. For a few minutes it was a decidedly Turneresque spectacle. How I wish I could paint!

Before 9 this morning one of the former owners of this land called on me with a very official missive addressed to 'Srta. Margaret Hansty' by the Comité Cívico Regional, (Regional Civic Committee) Tiquina and duly stamped and signed by all its members, with their official titles – not a woman among them! They want to call on me on Thursday. An appointment was fixed for 2:30. I sense large demands for money in the offing! The letter is beautifully written in the most florid official Spanish.

Jorge (expected yesterday) turned up by boat at our jetty in the afternoon, bringing some of the items needed to finish the 'small house' (but not the tiles for the floor) and once again I went round the main house with him (as I had done with Lucho on Sunday), to review the things needing to be done. These included getting the shower in my bathroom to produce water at a constant rate rather than leaving one shivering at intervals, with nothing emerging. Dealing with this involved another hilarious display of mime with one lot of people waist-deep in the well, 80 metres below, gesticulating and bellowing at others stationed on my balcony and continually ordered to rush in and turn the water on and off. Each time the cry would come up from below, 'Hay agua?' (Is there any water?) and each time back the forlorn response, 'No hay!' (There's none). Eventually, as I was able to prove to my own satisfaction when I took a shower subsequently, the problem *seems* to have been solved.

I am *promised* that the 'little house' will be finished *inside* and ready for occupation, by next Tuesday. We shall see...

Wednesday 17 November

At the meeting of the Consejo Social today the Minister read out my 'Strategy Paper' on the Consultative Group, rather to my embarrassment. I hope that my 'devil's advocate' approach, meant only for him, will not arouse susceptibilities among his senior collaborators. Invited to further meeting on preparations for the Group on Friday.

Our departure from La Paz at 5 pm was greatly delayed by half a dozen 'cholitas' who had sat down, in some protest or other, in the Avenida Montes. Traffic snarled, but police took no action (the major general strike has been put off for two weeks, but streets were also blocked at midday by striking employees of the 'Alcaldía', the Mayor's office). The result was we arrived after dark at the Tiquina ferry, having enjoyed a spectacular if menacing sunset en route. Our crossing was decidedly dicey, with very strong winds, and the barge rocked by strong waves. The electricity had been cut in both San Pablo and San Pedro, so we made the crossing in total darkness, except for a flickering candle in the stern of the pontoon, by the engine. It was impossible to see where we were going and how the man steering the craft eventually found the other shore, I shall never know. It was an alarming experience and I reflected how stupid it would be to have survived the more tangible perils of Angola, only to drown in Lake Titicaca. I resolved never to make the crossing again after dark. When we reached the other side we learned that, after we had left in the morning, all crossings were suspended because the wave conditions were too dangerous – in daylight!

Thursday 18 November

Another sunny day, but with high winds. My fears that the eucalyptus near the house may fall upon it, increase. Calixto promises to find the man with the electric saw to cut it down.

All the materials have now arrived for the small house and Juanito and company are hard at work. I had agreed to different colours for the bedroom, as the originals would not be available for some time, but had not bargained on two colours for one room – a pleasant blue and white (of which there was apparently not enough) round a square of a rather garish red!

The main reason for being here today was that Sixto, the carpenter, long overdue, was finally going to deliver the furniture he made. No sign all day. Then at 6 pm a truck laden precariously with large items of furniture came lumbering gingerly along the rough track down the hill towards the house. A lot of banging and drilling went on until 10:30 pm.

Friday 19 November

Reached the car place in La Paz about 10 and paid for new Mitsubishi but it won't be ready before I leave. I requested the loan of a vehicle meanwhile and a jeep or car was promised for tomorrow at 1 pm 'sin falta'.

Later I attended a lunch meeting with Ministers Illanes (Economic Development) Romero and Justiniano (Sustainable Development) to coordinate documents for IBRD Consultative Group, now only two and a half weeks away. There was the usual delay and disarray but Illanes and Romero, who have very different views and personalities, seemed to hit it off better than I'd expected. My suggestions for the political strategy were presented by Romero and there seems hope that some of my ideas will find their way into Illanes' umbrella speech. Jeffrey Sachs had been advising them the day before, and had suggested the best line was to say that Bolivia was nearly over the hump, and just needed a further push, after which an end to aid could be foreseen. I objected to this as dangerous, since there will inevitably be a long haul to full recovery, and reiterated my own line – Bolivia is one of the few success stories for its economic and political policies to which the international community can point, and it could quickly crumble if aid is not only sustained, but increased, and continued. I believe/hope my line will prevail. This is not the first time I have disagreed with Jeffrey Sachs, going back to Bolivia in 1985, and later in Poland and the Soviet Union, after the collapse of the Berlin Wall. Then he was an ardent advocate of strict adherent to IMF policies and 'shock' tactics. Now his views are beginning to change dramatically.

Meeting went on till 4, when I went to Lucho (to be told the estimate for a swimming pool 12 × 6 m, *without* filter or heating, came already to US$ 28,000!)

Saturday 20 November

9:30 meeting on 'Participación Popular' with the President, comprising also Fernando Romero and his technical group, and some members of the 'National Commission on Popular Participation' did not get underway until after 10 (Goni, characteristically, was late) and went on to 1:30. It mainly consisted of a very long but reasonably competent presentation of the various technical and legal proposals.

The last hour of discussion was by far the most important. Goni, relatively silent until then, pounced on the technical and bureaucratic trend of the proposal, presenting strong arguments for a more radical approach. He pointed out that popular participation was the only point on which, in opinion polls, the Government's policies still had support and it was therefore imperative to act quickly and decisively. I could not attend the second meeting on the other 'bomb', as Fernando Romero calls it, the Educational Reform, to be discussed with the President, and (I think) the Cabinet from 4–8 pm this afternoon, as I must get back to Tiquina.

Ironic thought indeed. V. and I were to have left by 1:30 pm in the loaned vehicle but the promised jeep was not road worthy and the driver bringing the other car simply disappeared, and all efforts failed to locate him. In the end, the salesman took V. and me up to the Avenida Perú, and we came back in V's station wagon, which, fortunately, the garage had not yet begun to service. In the meantime I had sat for *three* hours in the hotel lobby, unable to do anything. We finally left only in the nick of time, arriving in San Pablo as night was falling.

Sissy full of woe, after a terrible thunderstorm at 3 am on Thursday night. A transformer had been struck by lightning in San Pedro. Hence there was already no light or water when I left on Friday morning. It had not been restored until 10:30 on Saturday! Tea and later a whisky by a blazing fire were a wonderful antidote to a very frustrating day.

Sunday 21 November

A marvellous red, dawn, unblemished blue sky, the Cordillera Real and the Illimani limned in silhouette against it, a lone fisherman and his boat the only sign of life on the vast expanse of water between. This idyllic calm was broken very early by an unaccustomed roar of high-powered engines coming from the hill leading up from San Pedro – a car race between La Paz and Copacabana was out in full throttle. Later dark clouds moved in and the hills opposite rumbled with thunder.

It was clearly not going to be warm enough to sit outside, but it was less clear (once again!) whether there would be any guests to sit out with. Roberto Jordán Pando has always been notoriously unpunctual, but when he and Willma eventually turned up at two o'clock (they'd been expected at noon) in a state of exhaustion, the delay had not been their fault: they and a queue of some 50–100 vehicles, seeking Sunday release from La Paz had been held up at Huarina for over one hour because of the car race!

By then the sun had returned, we sat outside for drinks and Sissy gave us a marvellous lunch. Roberto is now totally at odds with his old party, the MNR. He is (as in his editorials in the newspaper 'Hoy' where he now works) vituperative about the government and its empresarial bias. He alleges also that it is absolutely in the hands of the Americans, describing the comparative experience we had with Ben Stephansky in the early 60s as child's play. [Stephansky was then Kennedy's Ambassador in Bolivia.] Both loved the house and the view, but I think R. privately considers it a mad undertaking. Nor does he think I'll get very far in advising the government, but that may well be a reflection of his own disillusionment.

Monday 22 November

A fractured and fractious day: those who *should* have come – the local carpenter from San Pedro, the tree-cutter to cut down the dangerous eucalyptus tree, and the Regional Civic Committee of Tiquina (a visit postponed three times already) failed to turn up. Others, totally unexpected, did so: Alejandro and Aida to inspect their new home; Sixto, the carpenter from La Paz because the bank wouldn't honour my cheque on account of an ink smudge (a five hour journey for him!); and a boat offering 8 quintals of wood, which had to be lugged uphill from our jetty.

To cap it all, the electricity suddenly went off at 9 pm. By candle light to bed.

Tuesday 23 November

The night was to get worse. A cacophony of dogs raged and barked around the house until well into the small hours. Calixto has three dogs, which I am rapidly inheriting: Perla, a lovely golden-coloured bitch of uncertain but indubitably superior ancestry, and her two sons, Pedro, a slight darker colour, and his younger brother Bandido (so named because of his mischievous antics) whose black coat, with white flashes, testifies to Perla's catholic taste in mates. Perla is again on heat, which delights Calixto, who says he can sell the puppies, but not me. Very hard to sleep – impossible to read (no light). Moonlight on the lake in the early part of the night then very dark. Dawn seemed a long while coming. When it did, it was overcast and grey, and raining a little. Still no electricity – it is out right along the lake shore, as far as Huarina. This means no water either. And I worry about all the food poor Sissy has prepared for the big Sunday lunch party for UNDP, which is now in the freezer.

In the evening I washed my hair and, as there was still no electricity, buckets of water had to be carried up the hill, from the lake, and heated on the gas part of the stove. When I had finished the laborious task of pouring jugfuls of water over my hair and had towelled it dry, hey presto! the light at last came on at 7 pm, just in time to save the food in the freezer!

Wednesday 24 November

To La Paz at 7:15 am. Arrived at the Ministry at 9:30 am – no one there. The meeting didn't begin until 10:15. The subjects were the 1994 budget, and the Consultative Group meeting. Discussion on the former was dominated by the colourful Secretary for Sports, Rolando Aguilera, who dilated on sports as a political factor – the origin of this eloquence being the elimination from this year's budget of Bs 100,000 including money for the prizes to be awarded to the footballers who will defend Bolivia's honour in the World Cup next year.

Thursday 25 November

Left Villa Margarita at 9, for La Paz. We now have the loaned car, an ancient Honda, with poor tyres and wobbly steering, which fills me with dread. Víctor drives it with great assurance, however.

Virtually all the time until lunch was spent in talking to Ambassador Lichem (the Austrian Ambassador in Ottawa, with whom Sissy is to work when she leaves me), as the line kept getting cut. She is to report there about mid-January.

2 pm interview with Juan Cristóbal Soruco, Deputy Editor of Presencia, very wide-ranging over all my experiences and perceptions of Bolivia from the 1950s on.

3 pm Meeting in Illanes' office, with Romero, Justiniano and others, on the Consultative Group. The main subject was the so-called 'zero option' for coca cultivation and Jeffrey Sachs' fax on this – whether or not to propose such a strategy, openly, or privately at the Consultative Group. Opinions rather divided. All Government Ministers deeply concerned by recent contacts with US Ambassador and revelations that coca production is increasing. This would seem to demonstrate the ineffectiveness of the 'Alternative Development' approach, widely publicised by the US as their 'star project'. But apparently they won't hear of the 'zero option' alternative, no doubt because it would imply a considerable financial commitment for the overall social and economic development of Bolivia (no one, except me and the newspapers, ever mentions the need to reduce demand!) I suggested a direct approach to President Clinton by Goni.

Romero was surprisingly vehement about the US Embassy. He said, à propos of some arguments I put forward, that he had used the same in a meeting with them but had desisted when he saw the expression in the eyes of the DEA (US Drug Enforcement Administration) man: 'If you make enemies of them, they can destroy you' he said – 'accuse you of corruption, make charges that you can't overcome, throw your reputation to the winds.' I, reflecting from my own experience of thirty years ago that this was not a new phenomenon, suggested that this was all the more reason for Goni to go straight to his US counterpart.

Discussion of the documents themselves and of the strategy of presentation was disjointed and disorganised. One hoped it will be 'all right on the night'. Meeting broke, rather inconclusively, about 5 pm, Victor, Sissy, and I just managed to cross the straits of Tiquina before nightfall.

Friday 26 November

Lolled in bed on awakening to a bright fresh morning, but was rudely shaken from this torpor by the arrival of the Bolivian Navy in the small cove between Villa Margarita and San Pedro. After an initial desultory interlude during which their main occupation seemed to be skating pebbles on the lake, they got down to business with a vengeance and conducted a series of manoeuvres which, with a great deal of banging, reverberating through the Cordillera, caused great anxiety to Angola survivors, dogs and wild life generally and went on inexorably until 1:30 pm. It all seemed rather futile, boatloads of men being launched on the beach, and then running to and fro between the rocks firing madly and it seemed indiscriminately. I hoped they were blanks, for once or twice I heard things falling on the roof. Sissy, who went to San Pedro, said they were firing at 'dolls'! What is the purpose? To stage a beach landing for an invasion of Chile from rowing boats?

Alejandro and Aida arrived at midday in a dangerously tilting truck piled with the furniture I had agreed they should buy. Aida is away in the kitchen helping Sissy for Sunday. Suspect Víctor's nose is slightly out of joint – he went off to lunch in the village without helping to unload the furniture. Calixto, on the other hand – bless him – delayed his lunch in order to help them.

In the evening, as we settled down by the fire, a terrible storm blew up – lightning, thunder and a vicious gusty wind, coming, unusually, from the south. Calixto shook his head gloomily and said, 'Wind from this quarter is no good for the potatoes.' Be that as it may it was certainly no good for the chimney, which usually draws beautifully. Huge clouds of smoke blew into the room, choking and blinding us. When we opened the door, the dogs tried to get in (Perla already traumatised by the noisy naval antics of the morning). When we opened the window, the flowers were nearly blown over, and hail came rushing in. In the end there was nothing for it but to retire to bed, and pray that electricity and water would not be cut.

Saturday 27 November

Late last evening Víctor brought confirmation of a meeting with the President this morning, at 9:30, on 'Popular Participation'. So it was off to La Paz at 7:15 am. We arrived at the palace in Plaza Murillo at 9:20, the President at 10:30! An interesting meeting but it is clear that even the greatly improved draft of the 'Decreto

Supremo' will not come out until well into December. The constitutional complications of making any changes are far reaching and the political pitfalls innumerable. Yet decentralisation is a cornerstone of the new government's policy, and the only part that seems to appeal to the public.

Back to Villa Margarita by 3:30 pm to find the tree-feller had *not* come (or rather had come but had forgotten to bring his tackle) and wants to come tomorrow, which is clearly *out* with 20 people coming to lunch; but that Sixto the carpenter (due on Monday) *had* come, reduced my bathroom to chaos, and is now painting the kitchen cupboards around poor Sissy who is trying to cook for tomorrow but typically producing far too much food, of a much too complicated kind.

Fury, fury, fury this evening. When I left at 7:15 am I had told all the men outside about the tree-felling that was to take place today. Calixto's story that the man had come without his tackle must be a figment of his imagination. The man himself turned up tonight. It appears that in the village he encountered only Sissy who told him (correctly but unfortunately) that I would not be back until 4 pm. Sissy was the one person whom I had not told about the trees, because it was not her affair and the men were briefed. The man was insisting on coming tomorrow but we finally agreed on next Saturday. I just have to hope that the big tree doesn't fall on the house meanwhile.

Sunday 28 November

This is the day of our first party for the UNDP visitors, including many friends from UNDP New York. We have no idea of whether 6 or 20 people will turn up, but Sissy has made food for about 40, exaggerating as usual. What we are sadly short of is plates and glasses thanks to the disastrous breakages en route from Angola.

Alejandro and Víctor have rigged up trestle tables, using the sides of the movers' crates as tops, and the builder's trestles and bricks as supports. With table cloths they look almost presentable. Thank God the day dawned crystal clear, clouding over as the morning wore on, but still showing Villa Margarita at its best.

In the end only 7 people turned up – bad organisation by the UNDP office. There was too much food, but the drivers and all the helpers benefited. As coffee and maté were served, a thunderous cloud appeared over the Cordillera and the reverberations of the distant storm echoed all around us. Rain drove us indoors and I had a fire lit. Sissy announced that both electricity and water were cut. The visitors left, the sun came out again, and in the unusual circumstance of no wind from that quarter I sat on the north side of the house reading until the sun disappeared behind the hill.

Monday 29 November

To La Paz early for the UNDP Regional Workshop on 'Participative Development'. The three main panellists at the Workshop were all good, but the main problem is *how to do all these things in practice?*

Lunch at Hotel Sucre with Flavio Machicado, who worked with me here in the sixties, and in Chile during the Pinochet coup, and has since been a Minister here several times. He was critical of government policy, on the lines to be expected.

All of this paled into insignificance when he told me of the grave illness of a close Chilean friend of both of us, Gonzalo Martner, Allende's former Planning Minister who had earlier worked with me here, and in Ethiopia. Gonzalo, who loved Bolivia, had told me of plans to come on an extended visit and asked me to accompany him to the Oruro carnival. Later I telephoned Gonzalo in Santiago, and his weak, almost unrecognisable voice made it tragically plain that that visit will never take place.

Tuesday 30 November

The tree-feller was again awaited this morning but again failed to appear. The village carpenter, Señor Márquez, *not* expected, did materialise. I have indented for a wardrobe for the 'small house' as well as for tables and benches for the terrace. The small house was to have been *completely* ready by this afternoon. Now I am told, with ominous vagueness – 'perhaps some time next week'. A worse shock was to find that Aida and Alejandro can't use their toilet – there are no pipes outside, nor will there be until 'next week'. And this was handed over *last* week, as having all the *inside* fit for living...

76

The tree-feller arrived, conveniently, in the middle of lunch. He came with an 'ayudante' in whose support Víctor, Calixto and Alejandro were quickly called, as well as Juanito and a couple of others from the construction team. With a great deal of shouting and mirth, and in very precarious conditions, the really dangerous tree overhanging the house was lopped at about 20 feet up, the huge crest of the tree falling with a crash in the garden. Great hilarity because Víctor, in the mêlée, fell over a steep bank, but appeared unhurt. The other tree to be lopped got a reprieve, because the tree-feller had again forgotten to bring the right equipment. I *hate* cutting down trees, but these were really a peril to the house in the constant high winds. Moreover, being eucalyptus, they will sprout again. We should have firewood and kindling for some time to come...

Rather against my better judgement, I left for a UNDP reception in La Paz at 4:30 pm. The party was small but 'simpatico' though, as I'd feared, not really worth the long drive from the lake.

The UNDP group went on to a folklore 'peña' but I thought it more civil to return to Willma Jordán Pando, my hostess for the night, whom I found (rather characteristically) doing something complicated to her hair. We had a most enjoyable chat over a whisky (me, of course!) and tea (Willma). She really is a most sensible and down to earth woman. While loyally supporting Roberto through forty years of marriage and enduring great sacrifices (frequent political exile, bombs in the front garden, constant upheavals) she has maintained a mind and firm opinions of her own. Some of these are openly disapproving of her husband (whom she calls a 'Quijote') because of his inflexibility, while at the same time she admires him as a man of principle.

We waited up for Roberto to come home from his newspaper but after two telephone calls when he said he was 'just leaving', but subsequently didn't appear, we gave up the ghost and went to bed at midnight. Very late in comparison with Tiquina early 'lights-out'!

Wednesday 1 December

In the office by 8:30, I rang Fernando Ruíz in the Ministry for Human Development to say that, as on Monday, I was available to help with papers and the Minister's speech for the Washington meeting. The papers had not been ready on Monday. Today Fernando was not there but I left a message. Nothing further transpired, so at 1 pm I set off back to Tiquina.

There was a parallel call from 'Betty' of the Human Development Ministry, inviting me to yet another meeting between the President and the National Commission on Popular Participation: 'at 10 am tomorrow, but we are asking everyone to be there at 9:45 am so the President doesn't have to wait'. Since on the last two occasions we had to wait for him for at least an hour, this produced a hollow laugh from me! I also decided to refuse because it would mean coming to La Paz every single day this week, which is really too much.

Got home to a terrible scene of despair and agitation from Sissy, Aida, Alejandro and Calixto. Pedro (the larger of Perla's two puppies) had been found near death that morning, having apparently been poisoned by some malevolent person (another dog, not ours, had been found dead nearby). Calixto had given oil to Pedro, and he seemed better though very weak. No vet nearer than La Paz, of course.

Thursday 2 December

Sissy, Víctor and I set off for Copacabana at about 9 am. We had hesitated, because the day dawned very gloomy, after a sharp storm during the night, but then the sky resolved itself in a pattern of snowy clouds separated by blue patches.

The drive along the road, high above the shore, with expansive views of the lake on both sides and the Cordillera beyond, was magnificent. We encountered several small herds of llamas being driven along the road, including some adorable small ones, and Víctor indented with one of the herdsmen to buy one (or two) for Villa Margarita when I come back. That is a 1994 project, however.

The plan had been simply to do some shopping, lunch, and return early. We went to the little port first, and I, thinking that Sissy was unlikely to come here again, allowed myself to be lured into hiring a launch to the Isla del Sol (Island of the Sun). 'Three to three and a half hours – back by 1:30,' said the personable young contractor, whom I would place in his early twenties. We set off with him, a much younger boy and a small child. At the 'Naval Base', the contractor jumped off to deliver our navigation plan, but didn't return, and, to our dismay, we found ourselves speeding on with the young boy at the helm. He said he was *13*, and the contractor's 'pilot', while his 'assistant' admitted to *five* years of life!

The journey to Isla del Sol took two hours. Once there, the 'piloto' insisted that we climb not only the 150 steps of the Inca waterworks, but then up a rough track winding up an almost perpendicular hill to a 'museum', only to find, when we got there, in a state of collapse under the hot sun, and with the steepness of the climb at 4000 metres, that it was hermetically closed!

When we had staggered down again and begun the return voyage the 'piloto' urged us to see Inca ruins further down the coast. By then we were so exhausted, and it was so late, that we refused. (We also glimpsed another daunting set of steep steps...) We did not get back to Copacabana until after 3 pm. That in itself was a miracle for we ran out of gasoline, and I had to take a major part in two refills from a meagre spare tank, on one occasion doing the steering, and on the next the actual filling. On arrival we lodged a complaint. The contractor, no longer so personable, tried to claim that the boy was 17 (patently untrue). But his most masterful defence related to the museum. 'But it's almost *always* closed,' he said, and remained impervious to our queries as to why, then, we had been dragged up there. Presumably we ought to have known!

The boat was liberally decked with encouraging messages – 'Servicio de Lujo' (!) (Luxury Service), 'Bienvenido al Crucero del Amor' ('Welcome to the Love Cruiser'), 'Cristo es Amor' ('Christ is Love') and 'Bienvenidos a la Nave del Recuerdo' ('Welcome to the Memory Boat'). Each of those had a special ring in relation to our experiences. Certainly we would never forget that particular boat!

Very late but pleasant lunch in the flower-decked patio of a restaurant. Sissy went to the church and later insisted that I visit it also, including the Camarín de la Vírgen where the glittering white figure of the Virgin Mary looks out over Lake Titicaca, with her back to the body of the church.

Since yesterday, we kept bumping into the same group of men – first on the Tiquina crossing, then on the Isla del Sol, and again at the restaurant. The group is from Dan Church Aid, and included a Bolivian doctor and nurse, and two foreigners, one English (who knew me through a Financial Times article) one Danish, who are evaluating the organisation's hospitals and health posts. They ended up coming to Villa Margarita for tea and coffee on the way back to La Paz. One of their main conclusions is that more reliance must be placed on Andean traditional medicine in these regions.

I should have consulted them about Pedro. Only after they had gone did Sissy tell me she didn't expect him to last the night.

Friday 3 December

Pedro survived the night, though very frail, and hanging on to life by only a thread. Just after 2 pm Sissy, Víctor and I left for La Paz.

In the evening Sissy and I went to the UN Christmas party in Obrajes: choir, play (two hours) – 'Prohibido Suicidarse en Primavera' ('Suicide is prohibited in Spring') and then dancing and supper (not served until 1 am). I enjoyed the Bolivian dances best – huayños, cuecas, etc. partnered by someone I don't recall meeting before and who described himself as Lucho's elder brother. It seems he was the Director of the 'internado' in Cochabamba where Lucho was put as a small boy because he was so obstreperous.

Saturday 4 December

We arrived back in Tiquina at 11. The electricity promptly went off for the rest of the day. Víctor left immediately back to la Paz, Aida and Alejandro this afternoon, all to vote in the municipal elections tomorrow. Fingers crossed that they can all get back early on Monday, when I have to leave for New York.

Pedro was alive, thank goodness, looking better, and eating a little.

Of course, the tree-feller, expected to come back on Monday, arrived this lunchtime instead. He had great fun and games until tea-time, cutting down the tree by the front of the house in sections, perched high up there, hacking away with an axe. I did not see how he got up or down that great height. A large section of the trunk had to come down in one. Calixto, his 'wife', Alejandro, and a young helper of the tree-feller all had a great time yanking on cables until the thing came down with an almighty crash.

80

Calixto's 'wife' comes at the weekends, with her (not his) little girl. Neither seems very bright, but the woman has a cheery smile, and weighed in with a will, sawing up felled branches. She crouched beside me before lunch and said how she enjoyed this. She has 'chacras' (plots of land), sheep and donkeys about an hour's walk away across the hills. The little girl is seven, but doesn't go to school, allegedly because the teacher threw her out as too naughty. I am trying to insist that she *does* go to school. Far from naughty, she seems very timid to me. According to Victor, village gossips in San Pedro say Calixto hates the child and beats her. He is also said to have beaten his first 'wife' and even his mother, which scandalised Aida. 'In Aymaran lore one doesn't lay even a little finger on one's mother,' she said... Am having second thoughts about the wisdom of arranging for Calixto to have an artificial arm fitted, if it only means that he will then have *two* hands to beat his women folk with. One of them of wood and metal, to boot!

Sunday 5 December

Light returned last night at 11 pm but by that time we had given up the ghost and gone to bed.

Great joy this morning – Pedro was waiting at the kitchen door when Sissy got up to make morning tea and he also ate something. His condition has been up-and-down during the day, but on the whole he seems better. After breakfast, packed (Sissy's packing, and proposed amount of baggage is, as usual, causing major crisis).

I took Sissy for a walk, which I discovered last Sunday evening, The track leads off from the unpaved rural road that runs across the top of our approach track, and leads up, up over the hill, to a high point where one has a panoramic view of another bay of the 'small' lake, dotted with islands and then winds precipitously down to a village in a sheltered fertile valley by the shore called Chicharro. Locals make the walk from San Pedro in 45 minutes. Our ascent was somewhat slower, under a broiling sun, and we did not go further than the viewing point where we sat on rocks to catch our breath. Even at the highest, steepest and most barren parts of the hills there are rough stone terraces, first hewn in Inca times and tiny plots of cultivation. The people, especially the women, work terribly hard. Returning the other evening, with night not far off, I met a young

81

woman with a bulging 'aguayo' on her back containing a huge load of potatoes, on top of which she was trying to pile an even larger sack of bread. I helped her heave it on to her already laden back, and settle her bowler hat somewhere in the middle, but could hardly lift the sack from the ground. And she had this long hill to climb, and a perilous descent to Chicharro to negotiate with darkness fast approaching. Today we met only people returning from voting in the municipal elections, proudly demonstrating their indigoed thumbs.

The beauty of this walk is that it takes you high over the lake, with dazzling vistas of the Cordillera Real and the Illimani, when weather permits. Today was a mixture of cloud and sun, the temperature on the way back extremely pleasant. There are many different species of plants and flowers. This time I had my trowel and a plastic bag and we brought back quite a collection, which Calixto and I planted in the late afternoon. Huge black clouds were rolling over the Cordillera and thunder was roaring through the mountains as we returned. Now, after the storm, there is a lovely clear sunny evening, with the magnificent frieze of the Andes stenciled clearly on the horizon.

I reflect again on the tremendous stamina of the people here. Whenever I comment on it to Víctor, he deflates my wonderment by saying, 'Oh, they get used to it.' Somehow, I don't think I ever would.

The day after tomorrow I shall be far from this magical but often infuriating place. Recently a Minister asked me how I was getting on. I replied, 'Well, it's rather like Angola – no water and only intermittent electricity, but at least there is no shooting.' That rash remark was uttered the evening before I was rudely awakened by the naval manoeuvres on the beach below and target practice on the hill above, and immediately groped for my non-existent radio to call my Force Commander ... But that was a single occurrence and I shall miss the peace and tranquility and even the irritations that lend spice and variety to every day, since the expected never happens. And, in spite of all the setbacks, my house and garden are rapidly becoming home.

We left on 6 December. Sissy's mound of suitcases, bags and sundry packages was so huge there was no way we could all fit into the small loaned car, so she had to travel to La Paz by minibus and take a separate taxi to the airport next morning. When we reached New York, I discovered that, in addition to the many purchases she had made in Bolivia, one suitcase was filled to capacity with her skates, which she had brought all the way from Austria because she wanted to fulfil her dream of skating on the rink at Rockerfeller Plaza. This I gather she did with a skill and elegance that brought everyone else to a standstill – a star again (as a child she had been an international skating champion).

While she enjoyed a ten-day holiday in the Big Apple, I went to Washington as a member of the Bolivian delegation to the World Bank Consultative Group. After all our concerns, the meeting went well. The donors, both multilateral and bilateral, declared themselves very impressed with the new government's policies, especially the much-needed emphasis on social development, and pledged a satisfying level of financial support.

The meeting ended at midday, on Saturday 11 December and snow was falling lightly as I took the shuttle back to New York. We had taken our seats in the plane before being informed that a freak blizzard had hit New York and totally blanketed both La Guardia and John F. Kennedy airports. After two hours of fruitless waiting I gave up the unequal struggle, carried my luggage back into town, and caught the train. Consequently I did not arrive until late in the evening to find a distraught Sissy who, unaccustomed to the vagaries of New York weather and the New York shuttle, had practically given me up for dead.

On 15 December we flew to London, with the intention of driving straight to my Aunt Christina's house on the borders of Wales, where we were all to spend Christmas together. But on the way to the airport Sissy complained of feeling ill and asked to fly direct to Vienna. That was complicated to arrange late at night when we arrived in London, but was eventually accomplished. She recovered from her afflictions which were diagnosed as a severe bout of flu and bronchitis brought on by her hectic round of activities in New York in inclement weather. But it was an anti-climactic end to our Bolivian adventure, and to the six years she had worked for me.

7

Widening Horizons

When I planned my retirement I had assumed that no one would remember me in the United Kingdom, since I had lived most of the previous four decades in other parts of the world. I had also lost all my close family, my one remaining tie being my aunt Christina, with whom I expected to spend some time every year in the Welsh Marches. Otherwise I thought to pass most of the rest of the year in Bolivia, particularly in view of my advisory role with the government. But events in the early months of 1994 obliged me to modify these plans.

In the New Year's Honours List I was made a 'Dame Commander of the Most Distinguished Order of St Michael and St George' in recognition for 'services to the United Nations'. As one of my friends said, it was good to know that Her Majesty's Government regarded work for the UN as also being of value to the UK. It also demonstrated that I was not quite forgotten in the country of my birth.

Further evidence of that came in the form of numerous requests for my services in various fields, such as peacekeeping training and as a member of the Board of Help Age International. My help was also sought by international organisations. The UN Conference on Trade and Development (UNCTAD), based in Geneva, invited me to undertake a study of UNCTAD's technical cooperation activities, and this involved considerable travel, keeping me busy until the summer.

In late January I attended a conference on South Africa organised by the Carnegie Corporation and the Ford Foundation on 'Peacekeeping and Peacemaking in Southern Africa'. That took place in Harare, Zimbabwe, and it was from there that I left, on 30 January, on the long round-about journey back to Bolivia, via Johannesburg and São Paulo in Brazil. From São Paulo I took the 'milk run' up into the Andes. When I arrived, exhausted and breathless, at El Alto airport Alejandro was waiting with my new Mitsubishi jeep and a face as long as a wet week. This was to become par for the course for nearly all my subsequent arrivals, so much so that I began to dread descending from the plane to grapple simultaneously with a dearth of oxygen and a surfeit of bad news.

'How are things, Alejandro?'

'Everything is well, very well,' said Alejandro, in a forcedly cheerful tone at variance with the expression on his face ... There was an ominous pause, after which he hurriedly adjusted this assessment. 'Well, there is one small problem...'

Predictably, the problem was anything but small: someone had nicked my newly installed water pump, down by the lake shore. So, when I arrived at last at Villa Margarita, longing for a bath after this gruelling trip, it was to find that, once again, there was no water available in a house located close to one of the largest lakes in the world. Worse still, when we installed the new pump it did not have sufficient power to feed the bathroom upstairs. So the pantomime of semaphore communications between gesticulating men on the balcony and their colleagues down below began all over again. None of this was helped by frequent electricity cuts.

We never did discover who stole the pump, although it must have been someone with inside knowledge. Suspicion inevitably fell on Calixto, the only person with local contacts. Alejandro had immediately informed the local *carabineros*, but all that emerged from this was a pile of documents with seals, signatures and fingerprints, and a record of inconclusive dialogue consisting of 'he said that' and 'I said that' variety. No proof could be found, however, although everyone was agog when a *carabinero* was one day seen striding down the garden in search of Calixto. As later transpired, however, this was in connection with mistreatment of his mother, or his *compañera*, or quite possibly both.

On top of all this, the insurance company claimed that my policy did not cover pumps and refused to pay up. One of the problems was that Calixto's small house down by the beach, which would give a constant view, day and night, of the lower part of my precipitous garden, was inexplicably still unfinished and Calixto was housed, to my shame and concern, in a ramshackle shack at the side of Aida and Alejandro's house. All I could do was install a guardlight down by the shore, and harangue Lucho once again. Nor was Calixto's house my only complaint: I now had a spanking new vehicle, but no garage in which to keep it and the *parrilla*, or barbecue, of whose design Lucho was inordinately proud, was still not finished. To descend to the lake you had to scramble down a vertiginous and rocky path, at great risk to life and limb. Lucho had agreed that stone steps would be laid down the whole hillside but remarkably little progress had been made. What did progress, with great regularity, was the presentation of ever increasing bills, and requests for money 'up front'.

Even more depressing was to find that jobs purported to be complete were clearly defective. The vaunted 'colonial' tiles from Lucho's old 'hacienda' in Cochabamba, no doubt exhausted by old age, were no match for tempestuous *altiplano* winds and slipped, fell off, or cracked and otherwise let in the rain and other elements. These also entered through the ill-fitting window frames, and the attractive, open plan of the ground floor rooms linked by arches, Mediterranean style, allowed cold draughts to waft throughout the house. Lake Titicaca is a Mediterranean body of water, but at nearly 14,000 feet above sea level there are some important differences from its European counterpart that we had overlooked in our enthusiasm for stylish design.

Other deficiencies that had gone insufficiently remarked in the euphoria of my first two months of residence now impinged with a vengeance. Every time I walked across my bedroom the floorboards oscillated as if on a ship in a storm and the brass handles on my chests of drawers tinkled madly. It was clear that too few joists underpinned the structure.

Getting up and down the stairs was another disagreeable experience, as the steps were fitted at an angle with the outer edge an inch or two higher, and sloped backwards. Lucho's foreman, Jorge, injudiciously came on an inspection visit. He was not sympathetic about the stairs, cajoling me blandly, 'But you will get used to it, señora!'

I was not about to be blandished. 'I most certainly will not! And how did such a ridiculous thing happen anyway?'

After some further tart exchanges he grudgingly conceded that the carpenter had made a mistake in his calculations and, to fit the steps into the stairwell, had had to tilt them at an angle. When

I insisted that this must be rectified, it turned out that the stairs had not been built by Sixto, the excellent man who had made furniture and cupboards to my entire satisfaction. Sixto was summoned but, when asked to take the staircase out and start again, proved obdurate, claiming that professional pride would not allow him even to contemplate such an indignity.

'I am a good carpenter and would never do such shoddy work. The man who did should set it right.'

I painstakingly persuaded him that his stance was not logical, since the other chap was patently not up to the task and this argument, with the addition of a modicum of flattery, eventually produced the desired result.

During my next absence the stairs were duly rebuilt, but there is still one step deeper than the rest that trips up the unwary. The floor of my bedroom was also lifted, and additional joists put in place. Every time I went away it became a sad routine to take apart various parts of the construction and rebuild them.

The reader who has got this far will surely be wondering why on earth I didn't give up the whole project there and then. I was sorely tempted to do so, but stubbornness has always been a strong trait of my character and by that time I had invested so much time, money and energy that there was no going back. What I did not realise at that time was that the same experience was to repeat itself over and over again during succeeding years.

Fortunately, there were many compensations. Just waking every morning to see, from the comfort of my bed, the sun rising over the Royal Cordillera and the lake made me forget that the floor was probably unsafe, and that there was a pool of water inside the balcony door from rain in the night.

Alejandro and Aida were working out well. Alejandro turned out to be a born gardener, as well as a good driver and mechanic. He loved all his plants, especially his roses, and was blessed with a green thumb. With Calixto's help – surprisingly agile, despite his single arm – he had begun to tackle the massive task of taming the rebelliously rocky terrain of my property. Small, Inca-type terraces were gradually being developed down the steep hillside and sown with grass and plants.

Aida was a good plain cook, knowledgeable of Bolivian dishes but also a dab hand at making pastry, and an able bargainer in the markets of La Paz, where we went weekly for household shopping (locally one could purchase only the most basic goods). She was scrupulously honest, but also an inveterate bossy-boots. Aida was one of those people endowed with the happy faculty of believing that they are always in the right, a conviction she visited upon Alejandro, Calixto and anyone else who ventured into the precincts of Villa Margarita, with predictably disastrous results. She was, for instance, convinced that Calixto was responsible for the theft of the pump and made no bones about saying so.

With me she was respectful while at the same time wordlessly conveying her despair at my (in her view) soft attitude to Calixto and all locals, whom she considered to be unredeemed crooks and villains. Every now and again silence became too hard to bear and she would relieve her feelings with a long drawn-out and melancholy 'Ay-y-y ... señorita.' She was a good soul, but her innate gloom and pessimistic view of human nature in general, and certain individuals in particular, proved perversely resistant to blandishments.

I was trying to write a book about Angola, but with all the domestic problems besetting me, progress was slow. Moreover, I was continuing my advisory activities with the government and on that front there were difficulties too. It was a critical moment as the budget was being finalised – rather tardily – and it was painfully clear that financial constraints, and particularly the limitation of the fiscal deficit to three per cent of gross domestic product (GDP), demanded by the International Monetary Fund, would make it extremely difficult for the government to keep its commitment to increase spending on social programmes without some hard economic and political decisions.

Fernando Romero, the Minister for Human Development, was deeply worried: everything we had worked and planned for was in the balance. The issue brought him into confrontation with the other 'Super Minister' for Economic Development, Fernando Illanes, whose programmes would have to be cut if the social sector was given priority. He begged me to intercede with the president. I was not very sanguine about the extent of my influence but Fernando insisted, and so I asked for an appointment.

Despite Fernando's own intervention, no answer came, and my short visit was coming to an end. Other commitments in New York and Europe meant that I had to leave on the Monday of Carnival Week, when nothing else would be happening. But in Bolivia the unexpected is always the norm. Late on the Friday afternoon an urgent message was received at Villa Margarita. Would I accompany the president and his family to Oruro the following day, for the Entrada del Sábado (The Saturday Entry), the main event of Oruro's famed carnival, and then spend the rest of the holiday weekend with them in Cochabamba? If so, I should be at the airport by 8 am on Saturday to join them on the presidential plane.

This posed an enormous logistical problem, difficult to resolve when the only telephone was a kilometre away, functioned only sporadically, and was usually occupied by other people. I had to change my travel arrangements so that I would take the Miami flight from Santa Cruz, rather than from La Paz and get the Navy Commander to provide a pontoon to take me across the lake before dawn. I also had to pack in great haste, not just for Cochabamba but also for my whole trip back to Europe.

Somehow it was all accomplished and I duly arrived at El Alto airport at 8 am. The president and his family, predictably, did not. The amount of my luggage also caused a problem in a small plane and had to be transported by road. Eventually we took off and flew across the bleak *altiplano* to the even bleaker town of Oruro, where a euphoric welcome awaited the President.

I described the Oruro carnival earlier as 'famed', but for many years few people outside Bolivia had heard of it. Now it is one of UNESCO's World Heritage sites. But its deserved renown has wrought significant changes in the essence of the occasion. I had not been to an Oruro Carnival for a long time, but during the five years I was UN Head of Mission in Bolivia in the early 1960s I was captivated by it, and never missed a year. So I was delighted to relive the experience.

In the book I wrote about Bolivia at that earlier time, *Gate of the Sun*, I described the complex origins of the Oruro Carnival, and its principal characteristic, the *diablada* (the devil dance), a mixture of pagan myth, unbroken since before the Conquest, and of Catholic religious observance then imposed by the Spaniards. The two threads are so closely interwoven that it is virtually impossible to disengage them, a prime example of the duality that runs through almost every aspect of Bolivian life.

The curiously hybrid phenomenon of the devil dance was originally developed by the miners who, at carnival time, renew their allegiance to *La Vírgen del Socavón* – the Virgin of the Mine – and ask for her protection. Yet it also has close links with the age-old cult of the *supay*, a spirit living in the centre of the earth. I quote some passages from my earlier book:

> The Virgin's devotees pay homage to her by dancing for days on end in the guise of devils. This seeming anachronism has several explanations. The most plausible is the miners' own superstition, relating to rites practised in this hills long before the Catholic religion spread the cult of the Virgin. In pre-Spanish Andean mythology, a spirit known as Supay lived in the centre of the earth; it was a spirit of evil, but could also bestow blessings and protection on people if suitably appeased. This ambivalent image of the supay became further confused, according to some writers, when the Spanish missionaries arrived and decried all the old Inca idols – whether representing good or evil spirits. Since the Indians received only suffering at the hands of the earthly followers of the new Christian God whom they were asked to serve, and since the exponents of this new religion insisted that their former cult had been devil-worship, the supay or devil came to seem a kindly spirit in contrast to what had come after.
>
> The miner, who is very superstitious, has developed this concept into the cult of the *tío*, a spirit who lives in the centre of the mine and is the owner and donor of all the rich veins of ore. His goodwill has to be assured if the miner is to be successful and is to escape harm from the myriad hazards which lie in wait for him inside the mine.
>
> At the entrance to most mines you will find a small clay or stone figure, with horns, standing sentinel over the adit. This represents the *tío*, and every miner, each time he goes underground, presents the image with his well-chewed wad of coca leaves as a votive offering. The *tío* is a very jealous god, and the name of Jesus must never be pronounced in any mine lest the *tío* cause the ore to disappear. Priests are not welcome in most mines either, though it is not clear whether this is an extension of the superstition that there will be a death if a woman enters the mine (and indeed, women are not allowed in most mines), by virtue of the priest's long skirts, or whether it arises from fear of displeasing the *tío*.

Thus, although there is also an altar to the Vírgen del Socavón at the entrance to the Oruro mine, throughout the year the miner's daily devotion is directed mainly towards the *tío*, who is supposed to watch over him while underground. The duality is given a new twist when, at Carnival time, the miner reaffirms his devotion to the Virgin by identifying himself with the diabolical personage whom he reveres throughout the year. This ambivalence is not exceptional but a striking expression of the Andean-Indian's syncretic approach to religion. The new faith does not supersede the old one. Nothing is discarded, but the new dogmas are absorbed into the existing framework of beliefs, and the two become so closely intertwined that it is no longer possible to unravel them. No one finds it in the least strange that, after three days of fervent veneration of the Virgin, Carnival Tuesday is traditionally – as elsewhere in Bolivia – the *Dia de la ch'alla*, the day when obations are poured to the Pachamama, the Earth Goddess, who, in some scarcely defined way, also represents the Virgin. Everything which is *ch'alla'd* on that particular day will be blessed with the protection of the Pachamama and of the *achachila*s, the spirits that inhabit the mountains, the rivers and the lakes.

The *diablada*, as the devil dance is called, is not a celebration lasting only a few days. It is a highly organised affair and preparations for it occupy almost the whole year. That it is an exceedingly vigorous popular tradition is beyond doubt: nearly every family in Oruro is represented, irrespective of professional or social standing, and over the years new features have gradually developed. By no stretch of the imagination can it be called a static or moribund phenomenon of a fast disappearing folklore.

At the same time there is something curiously mediaeval about it. The different *comparsas*, or dancing groups, are often composed of guilds or *gremios* representing a certain occupation. The two most famous are those of the miners and the railway men. The full version of the dance – the *relato* as it is called – is obviously a close cousin of the mystery and morality plays of the Middle Ages. Similarities have been traced with Catalan *entremeses* of the twelfth century and with an ancient Catalan dance called 'The Seven Capital Sins', in which the Vices argue with a lady who represents Virtue, apparently a

91

forerunner of the present-day *Bal des Diables* of Tarragona. It has much in common, too, with the *autos sacramentales* that so enriched Spanish religious drama in the sixteenth and seventeenth centuries, and were preoccupied with the temptations of the flesh, except that it is simpler in conception and does not have the Eucharistic significance of the *auto sacramental*, which was customarily performed at Corpus Christi. Again, there is something of the Quixotic concept of chivalry in the vigil that is observed on the first night and this, combined with the cruder aspects, such as the buffoonery of the bears and condors, produces an almost Cervantine polarity of the romantic and the picaresque.

Though much of the *diablada* is Creole-inspired – from ideas and forms transplanted from Spain's Golden Age by the eager conquerors of the New World and preserved through the centuries – there are also indigenous aspects going back to pre-Colombian times. As they execute their flying leaps and curvets at the apogee of the dance the masked performers, with their short flaring skirts and flowing capes, might be the personification of the winged figures decorating the frieze on the Gate of the Sun at Tihuanacu, or of the dancers depicted on ceramic plates found at Nazca and Mochica in the coastal areas of Peru.

The *diablada* is a religious dance, and all the roles are performed by men, including that of the *China Supay*, the wife of the devil, who is pictured as a lascivious woman. It demands rigorous training and exceptional physical stamina, for it is a wild leaping affair and the performers dance practically without ceasing for four days at an altitude of 13,000 feet, borne up only by their religious fervour and, be it said, by large quantities of the beer and *chicha* that accompany all festivals on the *altiplano*. It is a mimed representation of the submission of the Devil to the Queen of Heaven, atonement, as it were, for the superstitious cult of the *tío* which the miner observes for the rest of the year. The dancers are in the service of the devil until the Monday afternoon when they remove their masks and transfer their allegiance to the angels.

The public part of the ceremony begins on the Saturday afternoon with the *Entrada del Sábado*. The *comparsas* dance in procession through the main streets of Oruro and so up the hill to the church of the *Vírgen del Socavón*, which dominates the whole town. Each group is accompanied by its *pasantes*, or sponsors, usually two or three devout, portly ladies, who carry the group's standard, ornately embroidered with their name and an image of the Virgin. At the head goes the *cargamento*, a fabulous display of silver, hand-beaten salvers, plates, spoons and ornaments of all kinds, of great antiquity and value, arrayed on *aguayos*, the brightly-hued Indian shawls, which are draped over the roofs and bonnets of a whole line of cars. Sometimes, as a relic of an older and more picturesque tradition, the *cargamento* is carried on the backs of donkeys or oxen, and occasionally even of a llama, or a small calf or lamb. Some of the guilds are immensely rich and on the Saturday of Carnival a breathtaking amount of wealth is solemnly paraded through this town, which normally wears such a down-at-heel air.

Behind, to the traditional strains of the *diablada*, come the dancers, headed by the diabolical and richly dressed trio of Lucifer, Satan and the China Supay. The costumes of all the devils are ornate and extravagant in the extreme. They consist of a breastplate thickly embroidered with silver thread and stones, and fringed with silver, a short skirt divided into five leaves and worn over white tights, white boots laced in red and a small shoulder cape, usually also embroidered. The boots are spurred and each devil carries in his right hand a viper, or, more often nowadays a brightly coloured kerchief. The costume is rich in colour, bright blues and reds and greens overworked with silver and glittering stones, but it is quite outshone by the monstrous, baroque magnificence of the mask that each devil carries on his head. Bulging, billiard-ball eyes studded with bright artificial stones and huge grinning silver teeth, hideously pointed, leer grotesquely out of an exuberant tangle of horns and ears and tusks, painted in a wild cacophony of colours, and crowned by a three-headed viper or other misshapen reptile. The whole contraption is fashioned from plaster of Paris and weighs several pounds, so that it is no mean feat to dance for hours on end encased within it.

Lucifer and Satan are distinguished by their even more luxurious dress, long embroidered capes reaching down to their knees, flowing manes of blond hair and even larger and more magnificent masks. Lucifer wears a crown on top of his mask and carries a gilded sceptre. Between them pirouettes the *China Supay*, decked out in the typical *chola* dress of about 1930 – a richly embroidered blouse with a peplum, over a brightly-coloured velvet skirt puffed out by layers of other skirts and starched white petticoats, white stockings and high-heeled white boots laced up over the ankle. Her mask is pink and white with the same bulbous eyes, conveying an impression of pop-eyed innocence rather than the lust and temptation of the flesh which she is supposed to represent, and is topped by a pair of horns, a crown, and a female wig with long braids hanging down her back.

The Archangel Michael follows the main contingent of devils, a celestial figure in pale blue and white, glittering with sequins and silver embroidery, with long feminine locks cascading down his back to tangle with his gold and silver wings, and bearing in his right hand a curving silver sword and, in his left, a shield aflash with mirrors. His mask, too, is pink and white, and dominated by the same protuberant eyes, this time in a seraphic blue. The overall effect is somehow pallid and emasculated compared with the lusty vigour of all these Mephistophelian figures prancing ahead. A brass band brings up the rear, blowing away at the traditional, diabolically martial music. In the larger troupes there may be as many as a hundred devils, besides two or three clowns, traditionally disguised as bears or condors and sometimes accompanied by children, who provide comic relief and perform the useful function of clearing enough space for the dancers.

When the more celebrated *comparsas* are about to arrive an almost religious expectancy enthrals the crowd that throngs the streets, leans over grossly overloaded balconies or perches insecurely in the rickety trees round the *plaza*. Suddenly around the corner they come, caracoling and curvetting, a hundred pairs of feet or more dancing as one with marvellously formal precision, and the workaday street explodes in a blinding galaxy of light and colour, like some immense pyrotechnic display. One is caught up as if mesmerized by the movement, the pattern of interweaving colours, the compulsive rhythm of the music. The onlooker loses his identity and is at one with the dancers, tapping out the irresistible beat with his feet, as the head of the column turns to weave its way back unerringly through the forest of flaming cloaks and kerchiefs in a series of gyrating caprioles executed as to a metronome. Not a murmur is to be heard from the crowd which watches utterly absorbed, in pent-up exhilaration that finds relief in applause only when the dancers have completed their intricate movement and the cavalcade has moved on. It is a cathartic experience shared by performers and audience.

Not all of the procession attains this high point of emotion. Some *comparsas* are acknowledged veterans who can evoke such a response from their audience; others are more ragged in performance. Other types of representation also traditionally take part in the Oruro Carnival: the Morenada, a grotesquely-dressed group with black masks and enormous skirts laden with sequins and tinselly decorations, who personify the Negro slaves brought to the Indies by the Spaniards, and shuffle round sedately – for their cumbersome skirts preclude anything more boisterous – whirling *quirquinchos*, rattles made of the carapace of the armadillo; the Incas, who represent their pre-Colombian ancestors, and hilariously burlesque their Spanish conquerors with a buffoon-like Conquistador staggering about in helmet and chain mail; and the Tobas, equipped with enormous feather headdresses and spears, who perform the acrobatic war dance of a tribe once numerous in the lowlands which, in the words of Alcides d'Orbigny, 'made the Spaniards and the neighbouring nations tremble'.

At the church the mood changes. The contained passion and virility of the dance humble into devotion. As they enter the temple, the devils remove their masks and spurs, and, preceded by the *pasantes* with their banners, advance to the High Altar. The dehumanizing effect of the masked headgear and bizarre dress has been so complete that it is disconcerting to see the faintly mongoloid features and coffee-coloured skin of an Oruro miner or railwayman emerge from his gaudy finery. Each *comparsa* sings its own special *copla de llegada* to the Virgin, a ballad of arrival. They are simple songs, unpretentious in both music and words, usually sung by the man playing the Archangel Michael, while the chorus of devils joins in the refrain. Once the priest has blessed them, the groups retire, without turning their backs to the altar.

* * *

Thirty years later, the *Entrada del Sábado* was still a magnificent spectacle, but its nature had subtly changed. Then it had been largely a local affair. Now it was much larger and longer, the *entrada* lasting from lunchtime until almost midnight, with many more groups participating, some from La Paz composed of people from the middle and professional classes including a few women, in contrast to the old days when it was exclusively male and the miners and the railwaymen competed fiercely to see who could cut the finest caper in honour of the Virgin of The Socavón. Sadly, both the mines and the railways have suffered a severe decline, but at least the tradition has been maintained, though now more stylised, and less of a spontaneous outburst of exuberant popular culture. New more modern dances have been introduced, usually performed by sylph-like young ladies looking more like American-style 'majorettes', although the music remains unmistakably Bolivian. Yet there is still nothing that can stir the senses more, or make the pulse beat faster, than to see serried ranks of devil dancers, magnificently accoutred, come prancing and swirling down the street, in a kaleidoscope of brilliant colour, to the music of a brass band fairly bursting their lungs. For a brief spell every year Oruro is no longer a drab mining town that has lost its *raison d'être*.

In the evening we flew on to Cochabamba where in a hotel on the outskirts of that most pleasant town of eternal spring, the president and his wife had gathered relatives and friends for a relaxing weekend. Relaxation, I may say, included long, very hot walks up to the lower slopes of the Tunari, the mountain that dominates the verdant valley of Cochabamba, during which the hyperactive president held discussions on the hoof with local authorities. Some of them, panting visibly, did not look as if they did this often, or enjoyed this particular mixture of business and idiosyncratic pleasure. Their discomfiture was increased by their attire: they had come wearing their best dark suits, complete with waistcoat and ties, as befitted a presidential audience, but not an energetic hike, and were most unsuitably shod. Cochabamba is considerably lower than La Paz but the going was still hard.

With all this activity and the family reunions, I still had not had the ten minutes' conversation with the president that was the sole object of my coming here. I was leaving at crack of dawn on Monday and so, as Sunday afternoon passed without a sign, I exerted a little pressure.

At dusk we at last sat down in the darkening garden. I had asked for ten minutes but the conversation lasted two hours. The main point that I tried to convey was that, while everyone would understand that financial difficulties made it difficult to do everything the government had promised, it was essential to transfer at least a marginal amount of funds to the social area, by giving lower priority to other sectors. If the overall 'cake' had not become bigger, as had been hoped, then it would just have to be divided up differently.

The president listened attentively, and I felt that my message had got through. He confided to me his frustration that his super-ministers, the two Fernandos, in charge of the economic and social spheres, were at loggerheads. He was fed up with the clashes between them, which led to much of his time being taken up in resolving their differences and were obstructing the implementation of the government's programme. I remarked that there was always a tension between the economic and social sectors, exacerbated in this case by strong personalities. It was also an inevitable consequence of a government structure that made such sharp distinctions between the two, by grouping several ministries under super-ministers. It was clearly inappropriate for me to proffer advice on such a sensitive matter but privately I sensed that a cabinet reshuffle might be in the offing.

The next morning I was away before dawn to catch the first plane to Santa Cruz, and thence to New York. From there I telephoned Fernando Romero to tell him that I was reasonably sanguine that our message had had some impact.

Commitments elsewhere made it impossible for me to return until 10 April, to find that at Villa Margarita the garage, the *parrilla* and Calixto's little house were still not finished.

There had been problems in the government, too. The budgetary exercise had ended in tears, with strict fiscal discipline and adherence to IMF dictates outweighing the government's policies of increased emphasis on the social sectors. In fact, social expenditure in the 1994 budget showed a decline over 1993. My conversation with the president in Cochabamba had evidently had no effect. The charismatic and exceedingly able Minister for Human Development, Fernando Romero, had resigned. His successor, Enrique Ipiña (previously Secretary for Education under Fernando), asked me to continue to advise him, which I was glad to do.

97

With the budget decisions, however, and the disappearance of the dominating personality of Fernando Romero, the centre of political gravity swung away from the Ministry of Human Development, which had previously been envisaged as the spearhead of the government's frontal attack on widespread poverty – poverty that persisted in stark contrast to the great successes in stabilising the economy and reducing hyperinflation (around 24,000% in 1985) to single digits.

Moreover, action on the social front was constrained not only by lack of funds but by the Herculean efforts required of the president and his cabinet to get through Congress an ambitious programme of legislation aimed at bringing about another peaceful revolution, comparable to that of 1952. It rested on three main pillars: the capitalisation programme, a unique form of privatisation of state enterprises where investors would buy shares, obtain ownership of 50% of the assets and bring in their own management, while the other 50% would be distributed to all Bolivian citizens over 18 in the form of pension funds; the law of popular participation, which aimed to decentralise government to the municipalities and local organisations; and the educational reform, which, *inter alia*, envisaged early schooling in their own languages for the many Bolivians who do not speak Spanish. While it was a considerable achievement to get most of this through in the government's first year of office, there was not much to show in practical benefits for an impatient electorate.

One person anxious to see me on my return was the new commandant of the Bolivian naval base in Tiquina. Having lost its sea coast, although still actively campaigning to reclaim it, Bolivia's navy operates on Lake Titicaca, and on the many large rivers in the tropical part of the country. He had met the president at a naval parade organised for US Vice President Al Gore, and had been instructed to 'look after me', a command from his head of state which he took very seriously.

After a dinner for him and his entourage at my house, he in turn invited me to lunch in a mysterious British 'pub' somewhere on the lakeshore between Tiquina and La Paz. On the appointed day, 22 April, he duly turned up, driving his own jeep and resplendent in gold braid, which made me, in sweater and jeans, feel rather under-dressed. First we had to cross the straits of Tiquina. The naval base has its own ferry, an imposing metal boat with a high bridge in front, and a proper engine, all vastly superior to the rickety wooden barges with temperamental outboard motors to which I normally entrust my person and my Mitsubishi. Or so it seemed. But it wasn't ready, and, while that was being remedied, the commandant, a dynamic chap, with a spirited manner of talking, swept me off to visit the base, insisting that we weave our way, at great risk to life and limb, through the lines of some hapless recruits who were practising the gentle art of goose-stepping to the strains of a deafening brass band. We survived but left them in considerable disarray. Boats, docks, offices, even tailor's and barber's shops, as well as a store full of diving equipment that looked so perished I wouldn't care to use it, were all visited in very short order.

At last our jeep was waved on board the ferry, with a great deal of saluting and shouted commands, the commandant driving, with me beside him. The engines roared into life and the commandant launched into a new monologue which I had to interrupt after a few minutes to point out that one of his officers was trying to attract his attention, judging by frantic gesticulations from the bridge. The engines stuttered and stopped and soon we were wallowing helplessly in the middle of the lake, which a brisk wind had churned up into quite a swell. It transpired that our ferry had been under repair, hence the delayed but clearly too precipitate start. It further transpired that the only means of communication with the base was bellowing 'Ahoy!' – or rather *'Hola!'* and *'Socorro!'* (help!) – in the general direction of the shore. This eventually attracted notice and the despatch of a small boat with another officer and a mechanic, who needed a great deal of help to scramble aboard, as both vessels were rocking up and down but not in unison.

We were all so engrossed in that exercise that no one noticed our craft had drifted back to another part of the shore and was about to be dashed against some rocks. I was beginning to feel acutely embarrassed for the Bolivian Navy at this generally rather inept display of seamanship, and especially for my would-be luncheon host. I need not have worried. He was totally unfazed, happily nattering on in light social vein. He even said *'No hay problema!'* (There's no problem) – the dreaded phrase that in Bolivia banishes hope from even the most optimistic heart – 'This will only take a few minutes to repair.' At this point one of his young officers, patience exhausted, was goaded into crying, '*Señor Comandante*, this will take DAYS!' Even the comandante's ebullience was dented by this onslaught and we ended up scrambling ignominiously onto the rocks and walking back up the hill to Villa Margarita (his jeep marooned on the hapless ferry, mine up at the house with no means of summoning it). There was no lunch waiting, of course, since I had been invited out, so we drank gin and tonic on my terrace overlooking the lake and the distant chain of the Andes. I never saw or heard from him again, so I suppose he must have been embarrassed by the incident after all. But I cannot say I ever felt deprived of the 'protection' which had proved so precarious.

This time I stayed a month, spending as much time as possible writing my book on Angola. There were many interruptions, however. Tiquina and Camacachi – the two villages between which Villa Margarita is located – were already competing for my favours, convinced that I was a millionairess. Various delegations beat a path to my door.

From Tiquina came a delegation of teachers and parents. They asked me to help the school, and of course I agreed but was taken aback by the nature of the request: to equip a school band, by paying for all the instruments and the uniforms for a large number of boys and girls! Apart from the astronomical cost this did not provide the kind of educational support I had envisaged. Moreover, an American-style high school band, with girl cheerleaders flaunting very short skirts, would hardly advance the cause of Bolivian culture. As tactfully as possible I made the counter-suggestion of books or other school equipment. Their faces fell and it was only after months of negotiation that we arrived at a compromise: a set of living room furniture for the school director's office so that, as they put it, he could receive the parents and visiting dignitaries in proper style. It was far from my ideal, but in the end I acceded.

The delegation from Camacachi was headed by Don Gonzalo, a tall, impressive chap. He had been a teacher, trained at Warisata, which gave him special credentials in my eyes. Warisata is the progressive normal school for training teachers that had been set up in the 1930s, another instance in which Bolivia had taken the lead over other Latin American countries. However, Gonzalo had given up teaching, and was now a small farmer and village leader.

This was not our first encounter. During my initial visit with Sissy he had appeared with another delegation. On that occasion they wanted payment for the installation of the rural electricity line that served both Villa Margarita and Camacachi, claiming that the community had provided the labour, and that all beneficiaries were contributing. The sum involved was not inconsiderable, and the request unexpected, since Lucho's foreman, Jorge, had already received a large sum from me for the same purpose. When I consulted the latter, he was adamant that no further payment was required. Someone was obviously making some money but in the end I opted to pay up, in the interest of developing good relations with my neighbours. As usual the deal was sealed with a lot of official-looking documents, stamps, signatures and fingerprints for those who could not write.

Perhaps this was a bad precedent, giving the impression that I was a 'soft touch'. This time, the Camacachi men wanted me to pay for the corrugated iron (*calamina*) needed to roof two new classrooms for the village school and two dwellings for teachers. I approved of the general purpose but was cautious about the modalities, on the basis of earlier unfortunate experiences. I would not give money, I told them, but would purchase the material, and this only when the adobe walls of the building, which were to be constructed by the community, were already in place. This was clearly not what they wanted to hear, but in the end they accepted, inevitably demanding yet another written agreement, another example of how bureaucracy is rampant throughout Bolivia, in even its remotest corners.

My caution proved justified. This was to be another saga of many months, stretching into years. Whenever I enquired about progress, new obstacles appeared. Doubts arose about the ownership of the land where the building was to be constructed and it took a long time to obtain legal title. Meanwhile the community's priorities changed. They abandoned the idea of schoolrooms and teachers' houses in favour of a large community hall for village gatherings that would need even more corrugated iron. Visions of rowdy groups imbibing beer and *chicha* immediately assailed me, and I only grudgingly agreed after extracting the promise that it would also be used for schoolchildren's activities.

When at long last the walls of the edifice went up, I bought the *calamina* in La Paz, and had it transported to Camacachi for installation. By this time Don Ezequiel, a small man of uncertain age, with a roguish twinkle in his eyes, was in charge of the

101

project, and a frequent visitor to Villa Margarita. In return I was invited to drink beer and *chicha* with him and his wife in the patio of his tumbledown adobe cottage, among the chickens, rabbits and guinea pigs scrounging for scraps at our feet.

The new village hall was eventually inaugurated, and *challa'ed* with a splendid fiesta of music, dancing and injudicious imbibing of beer, *yungueños* and other *coctelitos*. That was not the end of the story. Sometime later, when the Popular Participation Law came into force, development funds from the central budget were distributed to rural municipalities to use according to their local priorities. One day, inspecting our joint achievements with Don Ezequiel, I came across a spanking new building just behind our hall, a much more sophisticated structure clearly built with more expensive material brought in from the city and by labour imported from the same source.

'What is this?' I asked Don Ezequiel incredulously.

'Oh,' he replied, not a whit abashed, 'it's a new village office and community centre.'

I could not help exclaiming, 'But you've got one already!' Then I recovered some equanimity and ventured, 'Surely your first priority should be water?'

The village had no general water supply but an itinerant Venezuelan water diviner had detected water at the top of the hill above and now money was needed to pipe it down to the houses.

Don Ezequiel was unrepentant. This attitude was typical of preference for prestigious projects all over rural Bolivia, rather than down-to-earth practical ones that would improve living conditions. In San Pedro de Tiquina the Popular Participation money was used to smarten up the plaza, and quite a lot allegedly went into the mayor's pocket, according to local gossip. And Camacachi remained without water until 2006.

Even when I was far away Bolivia impinged. In October 1994, Help Age International, of which I was a trustee held their Annual General Council in Harare, Zimbabwe. For the first time delegates came from the Bolivian affiliated organisation, Pro Vida. They were two sprightly middle-aged ladies from Cochabamba, eminently respectable, each the epitome of the popular image of Lady Bountiful – in short, pillars of society. They had not been often abroad, if

The entrance to Villa Margarita.

Villa Margarita seen from the hill above.

The author taking possession of her land on the shores of Lake Titicaca in 1988, in accordance with Aymara custom.

Making totora reed balsas on the shores of Lake Titicaca
© Tony Morrison, South American Pictures.

Lake Titicaca and part of the Cordillera Real © Tony Morrison, South American Pictures.

The Straits of Tiquina as seen by the French explorer, Alcides d'Orbigny c. 1830
© Tony Morrison, South American Pictures.

Crossing the Straits of Tiquina today.

Embarking the jeep on the pontoon to cross the Straits of Tiquina © Peter Johnson.

View from Villa Margarita across the Straits of Tiquina.

The author and Johnny, at the Cumbre, en route to the Yungas in August 2008 © Peter Johnson.

Llamas on the road to Potosí, March 2009.

Aida and Alejandro with
Pedro and Bandido.

Aymara women by the church in San Pedro de Tiquina © Peter Johnson.

An Aymara homestead on the altiplano © Tony Morrison, South American Pictures.

A roadside market © Tony Morrison, South American Pictures.

at all, certainly not to Africa, and spoke only Spanish. They were bursting with enthusiasm and a spirit of adventure. On the Saturday morning there was no general meeting, and the pair of them came tripping down the stairs, full of beans, and announced that they were going shopping.

That evening we were invited in different groups to have supper with our Zimbabwean hosts in their homes. I was invited to the modest house of the president of the Zimbabwean organisation, a former minister. It was a most agreeable affair, reminiscent of Bolivian hospitality; we sat outside for our meal, with chickens pecking away between our feet and other domestic animals wandering around, the difference being that the night air was delightfully warm, and scented with flowers. The two Bolivian ladies should have been with us, but did not appear.

When we got back to the hotel enquiries were made, but no one had seen them. Hospitals were rung, to no avail, and after many hours we discovered that they had been arrested for shoplifting and were in a prison cell! This was unbelievable, but it was not until Sunday that someone was allowed to see them and hear their story. After making purchases in several stores they had ended up in a large supermarket just before lunch. Suddenly a loud siren sounded. Thinking it meant a fire or a bomb they dived for the nearest exit where they were promptly apprehended, the siren having signalled merely that the shop was about to close. Having no English, they were unable to explain the misunderstanding, and although they had plenty of money to pay for the goods they were holding, and had receipted bills to show they had religiously paid for everything at other stores, they were carted off to the police station. They had no means of communication and so had languished for hours in what must have been a desperately frightening situation, and in less than salubrious conditions.

There was no Bolivian ambassador or consul in Harare and so, as their compatriot, a Spanish speaker, and someone who (probably wrongly) was considered to have some clout with the Zimbabwean government, I was asked to negotiate their release. This proved difficult. The foreign minister was about to leave on a mission and I was rushed out to the airport to ask him to intercede, since a prolongation of this incident involving international delegates at an international conference would cast Zimbabwe in a poor light. I also warned him that if the problem was not resolved quickly, I would have to telephone my friend, the president of Bolivia, and ask him to speak to President Mugabe. These tactics worked. By good fortune, the home affairs minister, responsible for the police, was also there. They were both most sympathetic and promised to give orders right away for the ladies' immediate release.

I returned, as I thought, with my mission accomplished. But the hours ticked by and nothing happened, so I had to contact the home affairs minister again. He was embarrassed and apologetic: incredibly, the Harare chief of police was refusing to obey his orders! Later I discovered that this had nothing to do with the two ladies but was an internal problem of politics and personalities: the chief of police had been suspended some time previously for accepting incorrect orders from ministers and clearly wanted to get his own back at the expense of these unfortunate women.

In the face of this impasse I had to take the matter up with President Mugabe personally, when he came to close the conference. I also informed President Sánchez de Lozada by telephone. Even so, the two ladies were not released until Monday afternoon, and that only after having to make, at the police chief's insistence, an appearance in court which, though perfunctory, must have been deeply humiliating for two such upright citizens.

After three wretched days in an African gaol, I fear these ladies returned to Bolivia determined never to visit that continent again.

8

The Vicious Circle of Wealth that Impoverishes

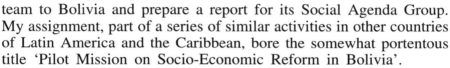

Early in 1994 the Inter-American Development
ment Bank (IADB) asked me to lead a
team to Bolivia and prepare a report for its Social Agenda Group.
My assignment, part of a series of similar activities in other countries
of Latin America and the Caribbean, bore the somewhat portentous
title 'Pilot Mission on Socio-Economic Reform in Bolivia'.

Quite whom we were piloting, and whither, was never very clear
to me. What was evident, however, was the bank's wish to give
more prominence to social issues in its policies and lending criteria.
It was an early realisation of the negative impact of the orthodox
economic policies of the so-called Washington consensus being
plugged by the international financial institutions and by the major
donors who provide a high proportion of their funds.

The new programme was the brainchild of a brilliant Dutch
thinker and writer on social issues, Louis Emmerij, whom my old
friend Enrique Iglesias (President of the IADB) had engaged as
his special adviser. Louis was a perfect choice for making a
breakthrough in an area then considered by most pundits as secondary
to economics: his personality was as large and dominant as his
huge frame and spectacular height. He, too, was a friend of long
standing. We had first met at a conference in Santiago, Chile in
1974 and after an initial public crossing of swords, had found that
we shared many common goals.

Over several months we mapped out the composition of the
mission, and its terms of reference, through correspondence and in
Washington. Enrique Iglesias and I had first met 37 years earlier
in Montevideo, when he was a brilliant young economics lecturer
in his home country, and I was the head of the United Nations

office there. Later, in the early seventies, we worked closely together in Chile as the two senior UN officials, he the Executive Secretary of the UN Economic Commission for Latin America and the Caribbean, I the Resident Representative of the UN Development Programme (UNDP). During the Pinochet coup in September 1973, and the horrific blood-letting and torture that followed, all our efforts and energies were united in trying to save the lives of the many thousands under threat, including exiles from military dictatorships in other South American countries, who had found a haven in President Salvador Allende's democracy. Such experiences make for friendships that neither time nor distance can sunder.

In all, the mission numbered seventeen persons, covering a wide gamut of specialities: macro-economics and finance, social development, education and health, agriculture and land matters, urban and rural development, small and medium enterprises, credit, decentralisation and popular participation, government structure and functioning, poverty, and women's issues. Ten nationalities were represented, mostly from Latin America, the rest from Europe and the United States, but all with good local knowledge. Four were from Bolivia itself, including Fernando Romero. A more controversial Bolivian member was Roberto Jordán Pando. I had been warned in La Paz that his inclusion would not be welcomed by some elements in the government because of his outspoken criticisms of their neo-liberal economic policies. I decided, nonetheless, that such views should be represented if the mission was to achieve objectivity. Moreover Roberto had vast experience, going back to the 1952 MNR revolution, when he had been involved in the agrarian reform promulgated in 1953 and from 1960 to 1964 had been a young Minister of Rural Affairs and of Planning. He had unrivalled knowledge of the country, its ethnic complexity and the problems of its poorest and most remote regions.

The bank raised queries about my choice of the Colombian, Gabriel Betancur Mejía, on account of age (he was 76). For over half a century Gabriel had been an extraordinary innovator in the field of education, both in Colombia and the whole of Latin America. I had worked closely with him, too, in Colombia in 1956–7 when he was Minister of Education. I knew that I ran no risk in appointing him and he proved one of the most energetic members of the group, brimming with innovative ideas and imaginative proposals. Another, Sergio Molina, whom I knew well from my time in Chile, and who was advising on finance and budget, was called back to Santiago halfway through the mission to become Minister of Education. Altogether I had an impressively distinguished and experienced team.

A key characteristic of the mission was its total independence. I had to submit the draft of our report for comments both to the bank and the government before publication but was not obliged to incorporate them in the final version. A notable advantage, it also presented dangers.

Our task was to propose conclusions and recommendations that would help the government to strengthen its economic and social policies in order to accelerate social progress and the bank to orient its future lending policies. The main objective was to support national efforts to reduce the grinding poverty suffered by large segments of the population and improve living conditions that are among the most dramatically deprived in the whole continent.

The mission was to last from 29 August to 24 September, but I needed to finalise the preparations and so flew to New York, en route to La Paz on Monday 15 August.

A sad drama in my personal life prevented me from proceeding. Early that year my best friend, Mary Gibson, had been diagnosed with cancer. More than a best friend, she had become the sister I had never had. We had met on our first day at Newnham College, Cambridge University, when she was Mary Beveridge, and an instant bond had been formed that had lasted half a century, despite long separations and very different styles of life. As the months passed I had watched the relentless progression of the dread disease. Now I would be away for six weeks, on a mission I could not interrupt. Two days before my departure, I telephoned to find out whether I should postpone my departure but Jimmy, her husband, said the consultant had been vague and there was no need to change my plans.

As I opened the door of my apartment in New York on Monday evening, the phone was ringing. It was Jimmy, 'If you want to see Mary alive you must come back at once,' he said starkly. I hurriedly made arrangements and flew back to London. Mary was in hospital but it seemed nothing more could be done and we took her back home for the last time. Over the next two and a half days I spent as many hours with her as her frail health would allow. We reminisced and talked of many things, and laughed and cried as two friends do who love one another and know they will never meet again. The final parting was heartbreaking and I wept most of the way back to New York.

I was physically and emotionally exhausted when I arrived in Bolivia on 23 August. A low pall of ground fog lay over El Alto airport above La Paz when we flew in as dawn was breaking. We spent an hour circling between the Royal Cordillera, the magnificent ramparts of the Illimani, towering like a snowy colossus over the town huddled in the shadowy canyon below, and the shores of Lake Titicaca. It was a rare sight, the sun rising behind the mountains and gradually suffusing the myriad peaks that stretch from the Illampu to the Illimani in an aureole of golden amber light. Even that palled after a while, and nerves were not improved when the pilot aborted an attempted landing at the very last moment when the runway was leaping up to meet us through tendrils of drifting mist. We flew on to Santa Cruz, away in the eastern lowlands, and only when the sun finally elbowed his way over the Andes and put the fog to flight were we able to return and land, hours late, at our destination.

It was just as well that I had to throw myself into a hectic race against time to prepare for the mission. Our first days were spent in La Paz in intensive meetings and research, with ministers and government bodies; international and bilateral programmes of co-operation; non-governmental organisations; the church; the private sector; labour organisations; political parties and so on. The mission then split up to visit various regions of the country. Afterwards the members of the team compiled their contributions and presented them to me before departure. Despite the heterogeneous nature of our group and cramped and difficult conditions, the team worked exceedingly well together. I nonetheless found my job as Chief of Mission quite taxing: it was not easy to integrate the different sectoral analyses that had to be brought to bear on an essentially multi-sectoral issue. The worst part was the logistics. For some days, when we had no secretary, I felt more like a Cook's tour operator than anything else.

Villa Margarita proved splendid for receiving guests and the *parrilla*, at last completed after many reminders to Lucho, was well and truly inaugurated with two large Sunday barbecues for the mission, one combined with a working visit to the nearby village of Camacachi, the other complete with guitars, singing and dancing. During the week I stayed at a hotel in La Paz. Gabriel

108

Betancur was at the same hotel, and also came out to the lake for two weekends, so there were agreeable occasions for reminiscing about the old days in Bogotá.

For the field trip I accompanied the *altiplano* group which spent five gruelling days travelling southwards by road to Oruro, then through the northern parts of the Department of Potosí, to the Imperial City itself, and on to Otavi, before returning to La Paz. Just as we were about to leave La Paz at six o'clock in the morning of 7 September my aunt Christina rang to tell me that Mary had died a few hours earlier.

Every time I traverse the *altiplano* between La Paz and Oruro I am reminded of Victor Hugo's opening lines in his poem 'Waterloo': 'Waterloo, morne plaine...' That stretch of *altiplano* is indeed a dreary, dismal plain, despite a few scattered villages en route – memorably Patacamaya where in the old days, returning cold and dusty from project visits (we usually travelled in the winter months, when river beds were dried out – there were no bridges then) we would stop and warm ourselves with *té con té* (literally 'tea with tea' but the second tea meant a good slug of *pisco*). The road is now paved, so there is less dust and the journey is smoother, but there is still scant habitation or sign of life, except for scattered flocks tended by lone shepherds, or most likely shepherdesses, sometimes very small girls. So flat and featureless is the land that as one nears Oruro the eye is bewitched by shimmering mirages of imaginary lakes. The reality is bone dry and saline.

Even these barren landscapes bear a benevolent air compared to the north of Potosí. This is a desperately deprived area, one of the poorest in Bolivia, high, cold and barren, an inclement place, long neglected, where people live in the most frugal conditions imaginable, often whole families in tiny huts of adobe or rough stone shelters, indistinguishable from the earth and the rocks around them. We were bound for the province of Bolívar, and the town of that name. It was somehow symptomatic that, when we stopped to ask a smart police officer in Oruro which of the many dusty roads leading off into the seemingly limitless flat vistas ahead would take us to our destination, he looked as if we were asking the way to the moon and exclaimed, 'There's no such place!' It was only two and a half hours away, although what passed for a road was a bone breaking abomination and those parched uplands did indeed resemble a lunar landscape.

We stopped at a small hamlet lost in arid hills where UNICEF was inaugurating a mini water project which the *campesinos* had built with their help. Water is desperately short, and even a modest supply can transform life. The community was jubilant, everyone in their best finery typical of this region: the men in round felt hats, homespun trousers, and the most brilliantly coloured and marvellously embroidered jackets, waistcoats and cummerbunds, red and shocking pink the dominant colours; the women more sombre, in dark hand-woven skirts with fewer flashes of colour. The band played tirelessly the haunting Andean pipe music of the *zampoña* and *quena* and different groups danced in the dust, symbolic dances, each telling a story. The authorities made solemn speeches which became less solemn as *chicha* (maize beer) and *pisco* (grape brandy) circulated ever more freely. There were several more such ceremonies before we ended up at dusk in Sacaca, another little town forgotten by time and the world but which must have been important in the colonial era, for it is still dominated by a magnificent, crumbling church, now being restored. The men stayed with the priests while I and three women from the UNICEF group were the guests of the nuns. The senior one, from Spain, had been in this isolated and desolate place for many years.

Next morning we set off across country to join up with the 'main' road (still unpaved) from Oruro to Potosí, the Imperial City. The journey, over some of the wildest country imaginable, took from eight in the morning until eight at night. The atrociousness of the roads over which we bumped hour after hour was counterpoised by the savage beauty of the landscape that unfolded endlessly before us: vista upon vista of rolling, barren uplands, riven with yawning gullies, or sudden, huge outcrops of rock, worn into weird shapes by wind and weather, and sweeping away to the distant circle of mountains which we would struggle to ascend only to drop again into another high valley yielding yet another mirage of the horizons of eternity. For the luminosity at these high altitudes is such, and the air so thin, that one really does have the illusion of being able to see for ever.

Man has made little impact here. Small settlements cower in the lee of towering crags; flocks of scrawny sheep and herds of llamas and alpacas could occasionally be discerned, tiny specks lost in

110

the immensity of space; and once we came upon a small, solitary figure waiting for a rare vehicle to pass. He told us it had taken him three hours to walk from his village to the road (if such it could be called). He was decked out in all his colourful finery, on his way to a 'fiesta' in Llallagua – a grim decaying town presiding over the decline of Catavi, the huge mine that once produced great wealth for the tin barons of Bolivia. Only a few years before it still provided much of the country's foreign earnings but now, with the collapse of the price of tin, it lay crumbling and virtually idle. We dropped him off in Uncia, another grim mining town, where we had lunch. There were still several hours of hard pounding to go, and even snow and hailstorms to endure at one particularly high pass in the mountains before we at last came to the 'main road' to Potosí. Somewhere along the way we lost our second vehicle, which took an even less benevolent track, and there were anxious hours before we were all reunited in Potosí that night.

There we visited some remarkable micro-irrigation projects, which demonstrated the enormous potential to be exploited if only water can be provided. We went on to Otavi, the village to the south of Potosí where my hospital miraculously still stands. It was in good physical condition following its remodelling two or three years before, but not functioning properly for lack of continuity in doctors and nurses, no funds for drugs and running expenses, and abysmal administration by the Ministry of Health. Yet in this area there were 25,000 people requiring medical attention. I could only hope that decentralisation, and 'popular participation' would make a difference.

We nearly didn't make it back from Potosí to La Paz on Sunday 11 September. On a sharp curve the jeep station wagon skidded on the loose shale of the dust road and fell into a deep ditch, the vehicle landing almost on its side. We were all thrown about, but fortunately there was a wall of rock, rather than a precipice, on the side on which we fell. Miraculously neither the vehicle nor any of us (we were five) received so much as a scratch. The only casualty was a huge bag of popcorn which one of our members had bought to demonstrate the wonders of small-scale Bolivian industry. It flew all over the place, and we spent the rest of the journey crunching through oceans of popcorn – with our feet!

The team members left by 23 September, leaving me a plethora of embryonic chapters to mould into a comprehensible and consistent report. During what can only be described as a week of forced labour I wrote 50,000 words in Spanish. Our findings and recommendations were rather radical but they took into account the very real constraints confronting the government and were aimed at supporting the latter's declared aim of bringing in dramatic new social policies. We had tried out some of the more controversial proposals in a long meeting with President Sánchez de Lozada on 22 September, and he had urged us to be imaginative and hard hitting (always a rash challenge to take up).

The thrust of our report was epitomised in its title: *Desarrollo Diferente para un País de Cambios: Salir del Círculo Vicioso de la Riqueza Empobrecedora* (A Different Development for a Country in Process of Change: Breaking the Vicious Circle of Wealth that Impoverishes).

The report analysed the results of the market-oriented policies of economic liberalisation religiously followed since 1985, recognising that there had been no alternative since otherwise access to international finance would have been denied. Yet, although Bolivia had become a model of orthodoxy and the favourite child of the International Monetary Fund (IMF), the expected scale of inward investment and of economic growth had not materialised and the social situation had deteriorated. The policies had benefited only the better-off segments of the population. In spite of the improvement of a few social indicators, poverty remained endemic. Stabilisation had become stagnation. Bolivia was falling further and further behind its neighbours, leading to a haemorrhaging of its best human resources, driven to seek work in neighbouring countries and further afield, and, within the country, to increasing migration from abandoned rural areas to urban centres.

The essence of our message was that, while the economic and financial stability achieved must not be jeopardised, ways must be found to improve the abysmal social and living conditions of most of the people, without which long-term political stability could not be assured. We recognised that this was the declared policy of the government, but that stringent financial constraints were preventing its full expression.

Bolivia, we stressed, was at a critical and most dangerous crossroads. A cynic might argue that Bolivia has been constantly at such a crossroads ever since its hard-won independence in 1825. Indeed, several of our interlocutors posed anew the question that had echoed sporadically down these 169 years: 'Is Bolivia viable?' Our reply was 'It *must* be viable.' We praised the innovative policies of the three pillars of Popular Participation, Educational Reform, and Capitalisation, and made suggestions for improving their practical implementation. But our report deplored the fact that social expenditure had actually declined in the 1994 budget (the story told in the last chapter). While recognising that this had been imposed by the limitation of the fiscal deficit, imposed by the IMF as a condition of future lending, we argued that cuts should be made elsewhere and that social programmes must and could be given priority, given sufficient political will.

The mission did not recommend any fundamental departure from current economic policies, since these remained the quid pro quo for international aid, but rather the adoption of a more flexible approach to permit the improvement of social conditions. Otherwise, it warned, the mass of the population, which had been waiting for the realisation of promises made by successive governments ever since the seminal revolution of 1952, would at last lose patience and take matters into its own hands.

Our subsidiary title, 'the vicious circle of wealth that impoverishes', derived from our historical examination of Bolivia's economy, going back to the famous silver mountain of Potosí, which financed the astronomic growth of the Spanish empire in the sixteenth and seventeenth centuries and eventually led to its decline by bringing about the first galloping inflation that economic historians record. None of this vast wealth benefited the Indians who had discovered it. It is hard to believe now, when Potosí is the capital of the most poverty-stricken department of Bolivia, that this decaying town was once the largest in the whole of the Americas. All that is left of former grandeur are the crumbling turrets and bell towers of over 200 churches.

Tin, which launched the next boom in the nineteenth century, did no better for Bolivia. The tin baron, Simón Patiño, became the fourth biggest multi-millionaire in the world and married into the French royal family, but his home country remained mired in misery. Now the tin mines are mostly defunct and Bolivia's new wealth lies in hydrocarbons, and especially natural gas.

The phenomenon of wealth that impoverishes has its roots in Bolivia's traditional reliance on the export of raw materials, without any value added. Wealth extracted from the country's mineral-rich

113

earth is sent abroad to fill the coffers of others. The mission echoed the call of many before for the diversification of the economy, faster development of industry and higher employment. In its concrete proposals it emphasised that the main thrust should be on promoting small and medium industries and the informal sector, all areas in which Bolivians excel, but whose development remains stunted because of lack of accessible credit and effective marketing.

To provide the financial impetus now lacking we recommended that parts of the assets obtained from the capitalisation of state industries should be invested in a 'Capitalisation Fund for Small and Medium Producers', instead of the government's policy to distribute these funds as *bonos* or bonds, for elderly people over 65 years of age. The mission pointed out that this *Bono Sol* was unlikely to have much effect, given that average life expectancy was only 60; moreover, it was the better-off citizens who had the best chance of reaching the age of 65, and the *Bono Sol* was to be paid indiscriminately to all over that age, irrespective of income.

Most poverty in Bolivia is concentrated in the western part of the country, on the high, cold *altiplano* at the foot of the Andes, and in the high valleys on the other side. Another question posed to us was 'Is the *altiplano* viable?' In Inca times this inhospitable region sustained a considerable population who suffered no hunger and were protected from the perennial droughts by large granaries of food. Today's situation is sadly different. Yet we concluded that it was still possible to develop a viable economy in carefully selected areas, provided a sound programme of investment and technical cooperation was put in place.

We proposed a study of the whole *altiplano* to determine which areas had the potential for development (water being the key factor) and which were practically upland desert. For the first category integral development plans should be instigated encompassing infrastructure, roads, irrigation, agricultural extension and marketing sources, credit at reasonable rates, and, where possible, technical assistance to set up small agro-industries. The *altiplano* also offers great possibilities for tourism, but has been deprived of investment for many decades in favour of better-endowed regions. Now that situation should be reversed wherever possibilities for development existed.

For non-viable areas of the *altiplano* the mission suggested a programme of incentives to encourage migration to lower regions.

114

This should not be directed colonisation as in the 1950s and 1960s, nor would it be the kind of spontaneous colonisation of later decades, which had only one destination – the Chapare, to cultivate coca. Our recommendation was for such investment to concentrate on other departments not conducive to growing coca such as Pando and the Chaco.

We had, perforce, to deal with the almost intractable problem of drug cultivation. The coca plant has been central to Bolivian culture since time immemorial, chewed to offset the cold, hunger, and physical strain of living in the high and hostile altitudes inhabited by the Andean Indians, and used for traditional religious rites. It was grown in the warm valleys of the Yungas where, under international treaties that I helped to negotiate when Director-General of the UN office in Vienna and in charge of UN narcotic drug-related programmes, limited amounts of coca can still be grown for traditional purposes.

The explosion of illegal coca production for export and fabrication of cocaine was a relatively recent phenomenon, brought about by corrupt military governments before the return of democracy in 1982, and by the escalating demand for narcotic drugs in North America and Europe. The blame is always placed on producing countries although, as I once pointed out in Washington, during the Reagan era, drug traffic was no more than Reaganomics in action: where there is demand there will be supply. The Bolivian coca grower may not be well educated but he is not a fool: if there is a market he will produce for it. This argument had not gone down well!

The large gains to be obtained from coca growing tempt ever-growing numbers of impoverished peasant farmers to migrate from the *altiplano* to the Chapare. Thus, the mission concluded, the coca problem cannot be resolved in isolation, but only as an integral part of an overall development strategy. The coca problem is rooted in the problem of poverty.

In our opinion there were only three solutions: a massive reduction in demand for drugs in the consumer countries; reduction in the price of coca through the international legalisation of cocaine; or broad-based development of viable zones of the *altiplano* and other regions of the country so that they offered better incomes and living standards to potential coca farmers. We affirmed our conviction that the acclaimed 'alternative development', which pours millions into the Chapare to entice farmers away from coca growing, can never provide a lasting solution but only a palliative, or worse still an incentive for more people to move down from the *altiplano* to replace those coca growers who have opted for alternative development, in order to enjoy the same benefits as previous migrants.

As very little progress was being made on the first of the three solutions (reduction of demand) while the second (legalisation) seemed likely to be politically unacceptable in consumer countries for the foreseeable future, the only viable option was the launch of a massive programme of integrated development of selected zones of the *altiplano* and high valleys as well as in lower regions unsuitable for coca production. This would require a significant level of initial investment but we added (possibly with a little tongue in cheek!) that, since most of the consumer countries were wealthy, support to this effort should prove more acceptable than the phenomenal economic and social cost caused by drug addiction and drug trafficking.

We also pointed out that Bolivia's strategic geographic location at the heart of South America, and the ongoing negotiations to make it a transit corridor between the Atlantic and Pacific oceans, offered a splendid opportunity that should not be missed. The aim should be to convert Bolivia into not only a transit country but also one that would provide services. This would require investment in infrastructure and personnel training in order to provide the necessary services, including support to tourists. We favoured special attention to eco-tourism, since Bolivia boasts many remote and remarkable habitats, thousands of different species of birds, and many rare plants and animals. Eco-tourism also has the advantage of not requiring enormous capital investment.

The new infrastructure would also widen the agricultural, livestock and forestry frontiers, but care must be taken to ensure that they did not fall into the hands of wealthy national and foreign owners, but were used to settle people from the 'zones of expulsion' in the *altiplano* and high valleys.

The 'different development' proposed by the mission entailed a radical re-orientation of investment policy. A main objective was to take urgent measures to diminish the growing, and dangerous, divisions in the country, evidenced in the duality between the poor *altiplano* and the rich tropical lowlands, between prosperous commercial and struggling subsistence agriculture, and between rich and poor, to name only three examples. In our view it would be impossible to achieve social integration and eliminate the marginalisation of the majority of the Bolivian population without urgent measures to reduce this inherent duality. We also made proposals on government structures and administration, as well as for financing the proposed strategy.

On 30 September I presented the report to the government and the Inter-American Development Bank who were to give their comments within a month. One good omen was that, immediately on receiving the report, President Sánchez de Lozada invited me to dinner with several members of his cabinet on Sunday 1 October. Gabriel Betancur, who had stayed to finish his work on education, was also there. I presented our main findings which, to my relief, seemed to be well received. There was a lively but very positive discussion that went on until 1 am. At 5 am I was at the airport en route for New York, very tired but well satisfied.

I received the bank's comments within the month, but the government remained silent. This was ominous and I heard on the grapevine that our proposals had really put the cat among the pigeons within the cabinet, which was perhaps to be anticipated. A more encouraging development was that the president had already acted on one of our main recommendations (removing the economic development ministries from the tutelage of the over-burdened 'Super Ministry' of Finance).

The government's comments were still not available when I arrived in La Paz on 9 February 1995 and I had to engage in another gruelling round of individual meetings before revising the report. The most important of these, a working lunch, was chaired by President Sánchez de Lozada on 17 February, and proved a marathon session of nearly five hours. It was attended by all the ministers responsible for the sectors covered by the report, with the conspicuous exception of the finance minister (the main opponent of our findings) who, although invited by the president, neither went nor sent a representative. Without his dissenting voice, the reactions of the rest to the report's main proposals were encouragingly favourable.

The main opposition to the report came from the more orthodox officials of both the bank and the government who resisted any modification of the economic stabilisation policies applied in Bolivia since 1985, despite our warnings that failure to make adjustments to improve the social situation would adversely affect long-term stability.

I was able to accept the majority of the suggestions made by the bank and the government. There were, however, two points of concern to both parties on which I could not and would not give way, on grounds of principle. One was a statement to the effect that the Bolivian people had lost faith in 'government' – not just the current government but any government. The other comment mooted the alarming prospect that, if social conditions were not improved, a situation similar to that in Chiapas (the region of continuous indigenous uprising in Mexico), could arise in Bolivia.

I finished the revision in early March and on 13 and 14 March spent two days renewing the final text with the Inter-American Development Bank in Washington. I was struck by the concern evident in some parts of the bank, including my old friend Enrique Iglesias, that nothing at all sensitive, however well founded, should be said that might raise hackles in Bolivia (for example the two comments mentioned above). This was not my idea of an 'independent' report, for which I and the rest of the team, not the bank, had to take responsibility. Fortunately Louis Emmerij staunchly supported me.

I had written the report in Spanish to facilitate its prompt publication, a grave tactical error: the bank never had it translated into English, so a wider audience was deprived of access. Had I written it in English, then it would have had to be translated into Spanish. I could not help thinking that the bank's decision not to translate the document was not inadvertent. They did not want the report to be circulated widely among donors.

It came as no surprise that, two months after it had been officially released in Washington and presented to the government, the report was still unknown to the Bolivian public at large. In this age of leaks and media predominance it must have been almost the world's best-kept secret! This was the frustrating situation I found when I came back to Bolivia at the end of April, with the express purpose of helping with the report's public presentation. Instead, I spent several weeks hanging around, waiting for the government to authorise its release. More puzzling still, the ministers, with the expected exception of the minister of finance, all professed to like it as, I was informed on reliable grounds, did the president. I was told an amusing story about a visit, in the meantime, by an official mission from the Inter-American Development Bank, headed by its female vice-president. Apparently she bounced into Goni's office and, after the most cursory of greetings, proclaimed, 'Don't worry, Mr President, about the Anstee report, the bank intends to ignore it!'

Presumably meant as reassurance, this had the opposite effect, for the president retorted, to the discomfiture of the lady, 'I find it most interesting and useful and certainly do *not* intend to ignore it.'

Unfortunately, the difficult political situation prevailing at that time meant that I was unable to see the president until nearly four weeks after my arrival, on 22 May, and only a few days before my departure to New York and Europe. The president quickly saw that more was to be gained by a balanced public presentation than by pretending the report did not exist – a subterfuge that could not long be sustained – and gave orders for its release. A forum was hurriedly arranged by the Bolivian think-tank Fundación Milenio, for Friday 26 May where I presented the report. The Minister of the Presidency, José Guillermo Justiniano, and other government authorities spoke, and there was full and animated discussion with an audience composed of representatives of political parties, academe, the private sectors and the media. It was a highly successful occasion and, contrary to the fears of some in the government, the opposition did not use the report as a stick with which to beat the government. The debate centred rather on the validity, or otherwise, of the report's ideas in helping to solve Bolivia's development dilemmas, which would remain the same for any government. But since all this crystallised on the eve of my departure, I was unable to discuss with the authorities which of the recommendations might be translated into action, and how.

The report did receive prominent and lively comment in the media, most of it extremely favourable. I was flattered to find myself variously described as 'the distinguished English Dame'; '*la bolivianísima* [very *very* Bolivian] Margaret Anstee'; and as someone having immense knowledge of Bolivia 'on account of her vast professional experience over nearly forty years'.

Several newspapers published editorials and the specialist weekly *Nueva Economia* devoted many pages to an in-depth analysis. The most notable editorial appeared in the respected daily newspaper *La Razón*. It made a gratifying comparison with the Bohan and Keenleyside reports of the 1940s and 50s, which had had an enormous and positive impact on the course of Bolivia's development, expressing the view that our report was just as important at the present critical juncture of the country's history. It urged the government to take immediate action to translate its recommendations into action, especially our proposal for a follow-up mechanism under the ministry of the presidency.

In that, the writer had unerringly hit the nail on the head: the perennial problem in Bolivia has been the failure to follow up and implement recommendations. Our report had put it bluntly 'Bolivia does not lack ideas ... what it does need is management capacity to translate them into practice in an effective form.'

Looking back, over a decade later, the mission's findings remain tragically relevant and the concerns of the editorial writer of *La Razon* have proved all too well-founded.

When I came back in mid-September the report was still exciting public interest. More gratifying still was a request from the president and Minister Justiniano to help the government prepare a presentation on sustainable rural development for the next World Bank Consultative Group meeting due to take place in Paris in March 1996, based on the policies enunciated in the report. Perhaps it was no coincidence that there had recently been a cabinet re-shuffle, and the recalcitrant minister of finance had now been appointed ambassador in Washington. I said that I would be glad to help but that such a document would carry little weight if it did not reflect policy shifts in domestic investment priorities already included in the national budget. This was agreed, but once again only right at the end of my stay.

My commitments elsewhere were multiplying and I was unable to come back until 26 November, to work with a national team. During that visit I discovered quite accidentally that the president's brother, Senator Antonio Sánchez de Lozada, was launching a parallel initiative more narrowly based on intensified agricultural research. I met him and suggested that we merge our efforts rather than risk developing two different sets of overlapping policies. In typical Bolivian fashion I heard nothing further until I received an urgent call in Knill, in late January 1996, begging me to go to

Bolivia for an important meeting two days later! I arrived in La Paz at 6 am on Sunday 28 January, travel-stained and weary, only three hours before the meeting.

The rush was caused by the fact that an American professor from Minnesota, Antonio's guru on the agricultural research side, was in Bolivia that weekend. A group had produced a preliminary paper on which we worked all day with the ministers of the presidency and finance, and over a working lunch with the president. The American professor departed but I stayed working with my Bolivian colleagues on what was now known as the Strategy for Sustainable Rural Development.

On 28 February I embarked on a gruelling trip round Europe as a kind of roving Bolivian Ambassador to 'sell' the strategy to the principal European donor governments who would be at the Consultative Group meeting in Paris on 14–15 March 1996. This mission was the brainchild of Finance Minister Fernando Candia, who felt it was important to get the strategy accepted at ministerial levels in the donor countries before the meeting. My 'Grand Tour', arranged at the last moment, was a jigsaw puzzle involving one-night stands in seven capitals: The Hague, Copenhagen, Stockholm, Bonn, Berne, London and Paris. The effort paid off because all the governments were enchanted with the strategy, greeting it as the kind of overall, comprehensive approach they had long awaited.

I arrived in Paris fairly pleased with myself and with the prospects for launching an integrated rural development programme, an unfulfilled dream of mine of forty years. On the eve of the official start of the consultative group meeting I was immersed in contented ruminations of this kind as the ministers of the presidency and finance rehearsed their presentations. Suddenly I was jolted out of this reverie by the realisation that something was different: the title of our proposal had been changed to 'Strategy for the Transformation of Agricultural Productivity'.

The ministers looked embarrassed: the change in title had been forced upon them by the president's brother as they were boarding the plane in La Paz. The rest was the same but, as I pointed out to them, not only had I been selling the product under another brand name, but the new one gave it a decidedly sectoral flavour completely at odds with the integrated concept at the heart of our proposal.

The last-minute change did not go down well with the donors

who, publicly and privately, expressed their surprise and dismay, and caused me some embarrassment. Nonetheless they pledged over $700 million which, in those parsimonious times, was not bad going. They also warned, however, that they would be watching implementation closely, as this is Bolivia's Achilles' heel.

Unfortunately it continued to prove so. The ministers and I agreed on follow-up action before we went our separate ways but when I next went to La Paz on 4 May I found that little had been done. During that visit we worked on the institutional framework for the strategy and searched for the right person to become technical director. On my last day, Saturday 18 May, I had a *tête-à-tête* lunch with the president at which I impressed on him the key importance of the strategy and the urgency of putting it into effect.

To my dismay, when I got back to La Paz on 11 August, and despite many telephone calls and faxes in the interim, there was still little progress to show. The Minister of Economic Development had been put in charge of the programme (I had recommended overall direction should be located in the Ministry of the Presidency, a central and non-sectoral position close to the president) but the Supreme Decree had not been issued nor had a technical director been appointed. When he was, just before I left on 3 September, he was soon dismissed because almost immediately after his appointment he had departed on a trip to Europe. A replacement was appointed, but as I pointed out to the president during meeting with him on my next visit in November, time was running out as electoral fever was already gripping the country (the presidential elections were due in June 1997).

In April 1997 the World Bank Consultative Group met again on Bolivia. This time the emphasis was on debt relief, under the programme then just introduced by the World Bank and the International Monetary Fund for reduction of the multilateral debt of 'highly indebted poor countries', known as HIPC. Most of the countries eligible were in Africa, but Bolivia had been included, as the poorest country in South America, and became one of the very first to benefit from the scheme.

I spent most of February working with the ministers of the presidency and of finance to draw up the debt relief strategy, which was agreed with the president at a working lunch. I was also asked once again to undertake a mission round Europe to persuade donor governments to support Bolivia's bid to be among the first developing countries to benefit from the HIPC initiative and on favourable terms.

I undertook this mission in March, with considerable misgivings. The government had not been efficient in implementing the strategy for integrated rural development that I had successfully sold to the donor community a year earlier. That could not only affect Bolivia's international credibility but was also a political error back home, where the longstanding programme of economic stabilisation and the more recent 'capitalisation' of state enterprises cried out for complementary action in the social field. The mission was another series of one-night stands: The Hague, Brussels (for both the European Union and the Belgian government), Vienna, Berne, Copenhagen and London. The Consultative Group, meeting in Paris, on 10–11 April, once again enthusiastically supported both the government's programmes, to which some US$650 million were committed for the coming year, and its HIPC initiative. The main concern of the international community was the continuity of these programmes, given the approaching elections and the probability of a new government.

Their concern was all too prescient. The ill-fated 'Strategy for the Transformation of Agricultural Productivity', which I still tried to push as a vital programme of integrated rural development, became totally swamped by electoral fervour. I was in Bolivia for the British elections at the beginning of May and in the UK for the Bolivian elections a month later. In both cases the incumbent government party had been upset but in Bolivia there was no overwhelming majority for one party. General Banzer, the former dictator of the 1970s, won most votes but only just over 23% of the total poll and had to join forces with a number of other parties in a 'mega-coalition'.

A major impediment to effective government in Bolivia is that a change of administration results not only in a totally new cabinet, but also in a complete replacement of personnel at all levels. In the case of a 'mega-coalition' this means a lengthy process of horse-trading, with posts all too often assigned according to political affiliations rather than ability and experience. Naively perhaps, I hoped that I might serve as a rare element of continuity for the ill-fated rural development strategy, especially as it is well known that I have never belonged to any party, my only party being Bolivia and its people.

At first the omens seemed promising. At the inaugural ceremonies on 6 August the new Minister of the Presidency asked me to see him next day. At that meeting he said the government wanted me to continue advising them on development matters and I explained to him the genesis and importance of the rural development programme. A date was set for me to give a briefing to key ministers at the end of August. That occasion never took place, however, because the government became embroiled in the political problems of holding its coalition together and satisfying the demands of the numerous parties composing it.

At the end of 1997 I wrote ruefully:

> I spent August in Bolivia and most of November, but the government is still getting its act together. They have, naturally, denounced the programmes of the previous government but their own 'plan' (more a long wish-list), just published, is, almost inevitably, a continuation of the same. The most crying need for Bolivia remains effective social development programmes to reduce widespread poverty... These are precisely the things that I have been working on for the past four years. I have again been told that my help is needed but what form it will take remains to be seen.

That call never came. Over the five years of the Banzer government various overtures were made to me, by the president and Vice President Jorge Quiroga, but they never came to anything. The government was embroiled in a series of political and other problems. General Banzer became seriously ill and had to resign in favour of the vice president. Our carefully elaborated plan for rural development sank without trace and no similar programme was put in its place.

The World Bank and the IMF imposed their 'Poverty Reduction Strategy Paper' as a pre-condition for financing. This policy was being applied worldwide. Being still connected with Angola I noted with astonishment that both countries, though vastly different, were being required to jump over the same series of bureaucratic hurdles at the expense of action. An interminable 'national dialogue' was instituted to determine the priorities of the population, but endless debate proved no substitute for effective social action and the seeds of discontent were disseminated ever more widely.

There was, however, an epilogue. In 2000, when Gonzalo Sánchez de Lozada was planning his electoral campaign for the next presidential election in 2002, he remembered the Inter-American Development Bank report of 1995 that had caused such a furore and had provided the basis for the integrated rural development strategy. He asked me for a copy, declaring that its ideas would enjoy a prominent role in his electoral proposals, and I took part in several discussions with him and his immediate advisers as to how they might be used.

It was all too little, too late. Sánchez de Lozada and the MNR were returned to government in August 2002 with a dangerously small majority, amid increasing social unrest and conflict. The government lasted barely a year, ousted by a massive popular uprising in October 2003. The people had, in effect, lost faith in government, and I later learned that persons from Chiapas had come to advise some of the more radical elements of the insurrection.

It gave me no pleasure that the major warnings in our report of eight years earlier had been vindicated by history, or that our two most contentious comments at the time had been borne out by later events. These events are food for a subsequent chapter.

PART THREE

Living the Dream

9

The Best Laid Plans of Mice and Men...

In this case the plans of a woman went sadly 'agley'. As the months and years went by more defects in the structure of Villa Margarita appeared and my personal life came to mirror the complications and frustrations besetting the government's programmes.

The electricity was now functioning, provided by the rural electricity grid running along the top of the hill where my transformer had been installed, but was distributed down at the house through a box of tangled cables nailed to a eucalyptus tree. The precariousness of this arrangement was soon manifested by the frequency of short circuits. General electricity cuts occurred often but were nothing like as frequent or as dramatic as the ones in my house, where they announced themselves with flashes and bangs. Nearly every night Alejandro had to sally forth and, in wavering torch light, twiddle the wires until the system worked again. One cold Saturday night when I was entertaining friends, I misguidedly plugged in heaters in two bedrooms at once, with spectacular and immediate results.

In due course I learned that Lucho and his men had omitted to install the stronger cable required to supply power points and heavier equipment. It was a miracle that no one got electrocuted.

Water continued to turn up where one didn't want it and not when one did. Whenever it rained, it poured in under the balcony door into my bedroom, and seeped through the roof in various parts of the house. A nightly ritual was performed with Calixto; I would stand shivering on the balcony and shout to him, down on the beach, that my ablutions were completed and he could turn the water off. There were endless problems with the various pumps.

129

Inside the house, while the stairs and my bedroom floor had been reconstructed, the wardrobes were just two inches too narrow in depth to accommodate a coat hanger and also had to be torn apart and rebuilt. The winds rattled through the windows and the chimney smoked. Construction of the outside buildings dragged on endlessly. When I returned at the beginning of 1994 I had the impression that little had been done during my two-month absence. This pattern was to repeat itself during my subsequent travels. Whenever I was there two delightful workmen, Juan and Paulino, who became like members of the family, were on the job, but as soon as I left they were whisked away to Lucho's other building projects. Lucho remained characteristically debonair and unruffled by my increasingly anguished pleas for rapid and more effective action.

During the ensuing months of 1994 the chimney was raised and the barbecue completed. After its successful inauguration during the Inter-American Development Bank Mission in September, I made it a custom to invite friends from La Paz for Sunday barbecues and engaged a carpenter from San Pedro to make two long, folding trestle tables, with accompanying benches. The tables lived up to their description all too readily, especially if the meat was tough, tending to buckle under any undue pressure.

Worse still, I became aware of an unpleasant odour, just in the place where guests drank pisco sours before lunch. This clearly had something to do with the septic tank or, more aptly, with the lack of same. Lucho's right-hand man, Jorge, dismissed my concern in the cavalier manner that he had presumably acquired from his boss. Pointing his nose in the air he said, 'It's not too bad, surely? *I* [with emphasis] can hardly smell it.'

I was, not for the first time, irked by his patronising, 'macho' manner, and his habit of planting a kiss on my cheek on arrival, which I considered over-familiar. He perhaps thought that he was ingratiating himself with me, when in truth he was producing quite the opposite effect.

So I stood my ground and, in time (everything seemed to take very long) connections were made to a septic tank perched on a rock some way below the house. I could not avoid the suspicion that the waste merely got decanted into the lake. The smell decreased but there were repeated problems both in the main house and that of Alejandro and Aida.

Locals asked me anxiously 'Were the proper rites performed

when the house was built? Was a llama foetus buried in the foundations and proper tribute paid to the Pachamama and the resident spirits?' In their eyes these are crucial questions, and the main explanation for the many misadventures that have befallen Villa Margarita. They are questions to which I do not know the answer, for I was far away when the foundations were laid. Lucho, ever obliging, constantly reassured me that all proper steps to appease the gods and the spirits of the sacred lake had been taken, but in the light of the flimsy basis on which his reassurances on other key matters proved to rest, I cannot be sure.

Perhaps more to the point, I had not been there to oversee vital stages of the construction. Every time I went away I left a list of agreed matters still not accomplished, and of the innumerable new problems that had arisen. This gave me some spurious assurance that I was on top of the situation, quite unjustified in fact, and provided me with a check-list on my return. Disappointingly the list changed very little from one visit to the next.

One particular bone of contention was the building of the stone steps leading down to the beach from the house. These progressed at tortoise pace. Admittedly the work was hard because of the rocky nature of my promontory, and dynamite often had to be used to carve the steps out of the boulders strewing the steep drop down to the lake. The real problem, however, was that work was suspended during my absences.

As if all this were not enough, the rains decreased in the first years of my occupancy and the level of the lake dropped dramatically. My old friend Julio Sanjines, whom I had first known in the 1960s when he was a military officer, and who is now the national expert on Lake Titicaca, began to proclaim, from every platform available, that we were in danger of ending up with a catastrophe similar to that of Lake Aral.

My stone jetty was left marooned high and dry above the water. New stone gabions had to be built out into the water, so that small launches could land goods and passengers. Later even that was not enough and a much less elegant contraption of rickety boards was harnessed to the end of the jetty.

Looking back it seems positively reckless that, despite all these delays and dissatisfactions, I decided to add a swimming pool to my list of requirements. I signed the contract with Lucho in August 1994. The swimming pool was to measure fifteen metres by six, and was to be initially in the open air, with the possibility of covering it and heating it by some form of solar energy at a later date. The work was to start on 5 September and, amazing as it seems now, Lucho committed himself to having it finished in 90 days, by 30 December 1994. The cost was estimated at US$29,600, a substantial amount of which Lucho, always more prompt in collecting his dues than in meeting deadlines, wanted to have up-front.

Simultaneously, Lucho was urging me to buy an apartment in a building he was planning to erect on land he had acquired in Obrajes, an old residential area slightly lower than the centre of La Paz, hitherto mainly of traditional family homes. The cost would be US$35,000. Lucho was positively bubbling with plans. He was finishing substantial contracts to build water and sewage systems in a small town on the *altiplano* as well as building housing and a Palace of Justice in Cochabamba, and had acquired the concession for developing the new port of Ilo that Peru had just made available to Bolivia and for which he was seeking financing.

I had always intended to acquire a pied-à-terre in La Paz, and divide my time between there and the lake, My preference, however, was for something in the centre of the city, from which I could see the astounding view of the Illimani. Moreover, I wished to *see* what I was buying and not merely commit myself to a plan on paper. Again Lucho wanted the US$35,000 in advance and it seemed evident that he hoped to finance the actual building with prior sales of the finished product, sight unseen. Fortunately, for the first time, some elements of prudence and common sense informed my calculations and I refused the bait. The work on the house was proving much longer, more complicated and more expensive than I had bargained for and I decided to put any La Paz apartment on hold. There it still remains today.

Work did begin on the swimming pool virtually straightaway. A very large hole began to appear in the south-western corner of the garden. Even the digging went very slowly however. During the early months of 1995 my frustration, as I cooled my heels waiting for the government to take a position on my report for the Inter-American Development Bank, was compounded three-fold every time I contemplated that yawning hole which now filled with stagnant water every time it rained and proved fertile ground for breeding large rank weeds. Nor was this the only thing behind schedule: apart from Calixto's house, still incomplete, and the odorous septic tank, the perimeter walls had still not been coated with cement and painted, while the elevated water tank remained a castle in the air and the earth oven had not even been started.

It gradually became clear that Lucho was having problems. The government, he said, was not paying him for the projects he had executed on their behalf, a well-known hazard in Bolivia where cash is always in chronically short supply. Later I gleaned from third sources that it was not only government dilatoriness and penury that had caused the problem: the quality of some of the work, it was alleged, had not passed muster. Given my own experiences, this was not hard to believe. In addition, Lucho told me, the foreign investors he had been trying to interest in financing the port project had cheated him out of a large sum of money.

Whatever the rights and wrongs of all this, Lucho was desperately short of cash. On 18 May 1995 he presented me with an updated statement of accounts, showing a balance of US$21,611.25 to be paid, although this presupposed the full completion of the swimming pool which was far from the case. My concern, however, was that if I did not provide him with cash, the work would never be done. So I paid up, more promises were made, and I hoped against hope that we might at last have turned the corner.

In the midst of all this professional and domestic turmoil it was a relief to get away for a few days. Having time to spare, since the Bolivian government was still procrastinating about the public presentation of my Inter-American Development Bank report, I travelled to Tarija (12–15 May 1995) to visit my old friends Víctor and Chichina Paz Estenssoro. Don Víctor was the main architect of the seminal 1952 revolution that transformed the political, social and economic framework of Bolivia. He has been president four times and was a great statesman, not merely in Bolivian terms, but in Latin America as a whole. He was head of state for much of the five and a half years I spent there as UN Resident Representative in the early 1960s, and in 1985, when I was advising the government as Special Representative of the Secretary General, he took the courageous steps that halted the galloping inflation and stabilised the economy. I wanted to give him my report personally, since most of its recommendations sought to introduce far-reaching social measures that I knew would be very near to his heart, since they represented the very essence of the aspirations of the 1952 revolution that he had spearheaded.

I had not seen him since he retired to Tarija in the far south of Bolivia, on completion of his last presidential term in 1989, and he was now well into his eighties. When the plane landed at the small airfield, I was greatly touched to find him waiting to greet me, a frail figure leaning on a stick, with his wife Chichina. Apart from some physical disability, I found him in fine fettle, as intellectually brilliant as ever. The three of us met every day, and he and Chichina took me to see all the sights of Tarija, and out to the home of 'Moto' Méndez, the local guerrilla and liberation hero renowned in Chapaco music and song. Don Víctor displayed his great sense of history, regaling me with tales of Bolivia's struggle for independence, and of the controversy with Argentina in the early nineteenth century as to which side of the new frontier Tarija should be placed. Today, when the uproar over the export of natural gas has reawakened threats of secession in some quarters that story has an alarmingly contemporary ring.

Tarlija brought back memories of my ill-fated journey from Montevideo in January 1960 to take up my new post in La Paz. As a result of heavy rains, floods, and impending revolution in Bolivia, my five-day train journey turned into a two-week odyssey. Stranded in Villazón, on the Bolivian–Argentine border, I eventually made my way to Tarija on top of a lorry, with all my luggage. This proved to be a horrendous all-night journey over the mountains, as the lorry broke down at 14,000 feet in the midst of a torrential thunderstorm. So it was in a very muddy and bedraggled state that I staggered into Tarija next day, to the dubious 'comforts' of the run-down Social Club (there being then no hotel in Tarija). On this return thirty-five years later, I found the charming, typically Hispanic centre of the town virtually unchanged, the Social Club still standing (improved, I was assured, but did not feel disposed to explore). This time I stayed in a pleasant hotel, Los Ceibos, but I seem always to suffer some ill fortune in Tarija: in the early morning I imprudently plunged into the swimming pool, which proved intensely cold and I contracted an infection that was to dog me for two months.

As 1995 wore on and things worsened, I realised that Lucho was in even deeper trouble than I had thought. I decided to rescind my various contracts with him and again I sought the help of my trusted friend, Roberto Jordán Pando. Once he started investigating matters the reason why work at Villa Margarita had not progressed, despite my cash advances, became painfully evident: Lucho had used my money not to buy materials and pay workmen, but to pay off his debts to his many creditors. He was also in legal difficulties over the very piece of land in Obrajes where he had wished to sell me an apartment as yet not constructed. It seemed that he had bought the plot, allegedly at an unjustifiably low price, from an elderly lady. On her death her family and heirs accused him of exploiting her age and frailty and had initiated judicial proceedings. Lucho's young brother-in-law, who had been his partner in the business, had been put in prison.

After months of difficult negotiations, agreement on a 'clearing' of accounts was reached on 1 December 1995. This showed that Lucho's firm owed me US$27,376.83 plus a sum for the electrical installation calculated at US$482. On 4 December Lucho and his wife signed a private legal document rescinding our earlier contracts, since the work had not been completed, recognising their outstanding debt of US$27,858.83 and committing themselves to pay.

I obtained Lucho's signature in less than propitious circumstances for by now he was himself in gaol, having been arbitrarily seized in the street in one of the well-known vagaries of the Bolivian judicial system, although there was still no substantiated case against him. It was not the first time I had visited the old San Pedro prison in La Paz. In June 1965 I had gone there incognito, to say farewell to men with whom I had worked during the government of Paz Estenssoro and whom the military had thrown into prison when they seized power in November 1964. It had been an unnerving experience, on entering, to hear my name 'Margarita' being called in joyous welcome from almost every cell.

San Pedro has a nice sense of class distinction. Those who can afford it are kept in a superior part of the prison and allowed to bring in some home comforts. In 1964, having penetrated this sanctuary after a body search at the gate, I found the former minister of finance nicely installed in a small apartment with his own carpet and furniture, tapping away at a typewriter from which he scarcely had time to look up. In an arrangement that could surely take place nowhere else but Bolivia, he had been contracted by the same government that held him in prison to advise on tax reform.

'It pays my legal expenses,' he explained, adding with the tart irony for which he was well known, 'and besides, I'm doing a useful job in a field in which your UN financial experts never managed to produce what I wanted!'

Also in the prison was the minister's former Budget Director, who embarrassed me greatly by proclaiming in a loud voice his plans for imminent escape. His indiscretion evidently went unnoticed for, shortly afterwards, escape he did, jumping over the prison wall and onto a bus to Peru.

This time I did not enter but approached a large barred gate behind which, in an open patio, the privileged prisoners were strolling, smoking and chatting with one another, for all as if they were promenading in El Prado, the main social thoroughfare of La Paz. Lucho was among them, his customary debonair self, not a whit abashed to have the document curtailing his contract with me and recognising his debt shoved through the narrow grille, signed and then passed back.

This scene did affect me, however, for it emphasised the extent to which Lucho was down on his luck. That same day I gave Roberto a power of attorney, authorising him to seek a new contractor to complete the outstanding work but telling him that I did not want to treat Lucho harshly: no interest was to be charged on the debt and I was amenable to an arrangement whereby he might pay off all or part by further work on the unfinished items.

After a couple of months in gaol Lucho was released without charge and asked to be given a second chance at Villa Margarita. Roberto concurred and on 18 February 1996 signed a new legal document with Lucho, listing all the tasks to be completed. The work was to be finished by 17 June 1996 and for every day beyond that there would be a penalty of US$50. The work was to be funded by the debt of US$27,858.83, for which a *letra de cambio* was issued. An independent architect was appointed to supervise the fulfilment of the contract and the quality of the workmanship.

This additional tolerance was to no avail. On my return in April 1996 a note from Roberto awaited me, written with his usual pithy sense of humour: 'Welcome to Bolivia, country of the unexpected, in competition with Alice in Wonderland' – a comment as much on the political situation as on relations with Lucho. June came and went with no notable difference except that the hole in the garden had grown larger but still remained a gaping pit with none of the appurtenances one associates with a swimming pool. Lucho's excuses became ever more outlandish. One was that the sand he had collected from the cove below the house to make cement was 'the wrong kind of sand'. This struck me as the Bolivian counterpart of the celebrated British Rail explanation for the late arrival of its trains: 'the wrong kind of leaves on the line'! Worse still, irate people claiming to be the owners of the sand kept coming to the house to complain they had not been paid.

On 2 September 1996, acting on Roberto's advice, I wrote to Lucho rescinding the new contract, reiterating that this had been a last chance for him to fulfil his commitments. We were generous in estimating what further work had been done, the cost of which could be deducted from the total debt. Again the negotiations went on for months. At last, in March 1997, agreement was reached between Roberto and Lucho that the debt had been reduced to US$10,338, which Roberto suggested should be rounded to US$10,000. Lucho, however, wanted another *letra de cambio* for that amount, which was not agreeable to me. But, since he apparently had no funds, there was little alternative.

Lucho was profuse in his promises to pay off the debt within a reasonable period. Some hope! Another characteristic note from Roberto later in 1997, summed up the position perfectly: 'Lucho, as always, talked, promised and failed to deliver, having assured me he was able to give me the ten thousand. In the end I spoke with his wife ... I hope that this time they will fulfil their commitment.'

But they didn't, and every fresh arrival of mine produced new promises or held out hopes that some payment for one of Lucho's big projects was going to be made. Whether they were or not I shall never know but, if they were, none of the money ever came in my direction.

In 1998 Roberto was appointed as Bolivia's Ambassador and Permanent Representative to the United Nations in New York. By another curious twist unique to Bolivia, he was personally asked to take up the post by none other than President General Hugo Banzer, democratically elected in 1997, but who, during his long military dictatorship in the 1970s, had repeatedly chased Roberto into exile.

Roberto transferred my problems to another lawyer, equally punctilious in pursuing Lucho for payment. The pattern of promises unfulfilled and expectations was by now deeply ingrained. Lucho seemed to be the epitome of a Bolivian Mr Micawber. On one occasion a year or two later a cheque was actually produced for US$3,000, but Lucho had had it signed by one of his sons, and when I tried to deposit it, it turned out to have no funds. What he wished to achieve by this crass move is hard to fathom, particularly since to sign a cheque without funds is punishable by prison in Bolivian law.

Now, twenty years since I first engaged Lucho in the construction of Villa Margarita, the balance of that debt still remains outstanding and I am resigned to the fact that it will never be paid. It is more difficult to accept that a friendship of thirty years has been irrevocably broken.

On 30 September 1996 Roberto signed a contract on my behalf with a new building firm. This new contract foresaw the completion of the swimming pool, but this time as a covered pool heated by solar energy and with all the appurtenances: pumps, machines, two dressing rooms, showers and toilets. The pool itself was to be slightly smaller – twelve metres by six, instead of fifteen by six – but would be surrounded by ceramics and stonework.

The new contractor was also to complete all the tasks Lucho had left unfinished. The roof was to be taken off and replaced with Spanish tiles; gutters were to be installed; all the windows were to be replaced with double glazing; a skylight was to be built into the roof above my study; and the electrical installation was to be ripped out of the walls and replaced with safer cabling. You could say that the house was being completely rebuilt.

There was a lot of work to be done outside: the front courtyard, which became a sea of mud when it rained, was to be paved with stones from Comanche; stone steps were to be constructed from the house down to the pool and to the beach, to match the ones on the other side that Lucho had at last finished; a reserve water tank holding 10,000 litres was to be constructed, pumps were to be installed and a distribution system connected, including the elevated reserve tank that Lucho had built. The perimeter wall was to be provided with sound foundations, proper drainage, and a tiled roof to match the tiles on the house and prevent rain from soaking into the adobe walls. These were to be coated in a lime and cement mixture and rendered white.

All this work was to be done in 120 days, between 1 October 1996 and 31 January 1997. This looked exceedingly ambitious and,

138

indeed, so it proved. The contract recognised that it had not been possible to cost some items, and that the price was likely to rise. It most certainly did!

Thus began a very exciting period in the history of Villa Margarita. Fortunately I was in and out sufficiently often to inspect progress and prevent irretrievable errors. My land is very rocky and a particular outcrop intruded into the rectangular form proposed for the pool. It did not affect the pool itself but only the surrounding area. The builder wanted to dynamite it away, but I persuaded him to leave it as an interior feature. Later we developed a tiny internal garden, including cacti and bougainvillea, as well as a small cascade that falls over the rock.

By Christmas work was well advanced but there were delays in the arrival of equipment needed by the specialised firm sub-contracted for the technical aspects of the swimming pool. By the end of January the work was still a good way off completion. Taking advantage of the presence of the builders and their equipment – a major consideration given the remoteness of Villa Margarita and the difficulties of transport from La Paz, not least the crossing of the lake for heavy items – I added other jobs to the contract.

I had long been unhappy with my front door on the wrong side of the house, because visitors tended to enter through a kitchen not always as presentable as I would wish. We decided to modify the dining room, alongside the kitchen, taking out the window and adding a glass porch and entrance hall. Roberto wanted me to change the whole layout of the downstairs rooms to build a large circular extension, with panoramic views overlooking the lake and the *cordillera* but I decided that this was altogether too grand a design. The new entrance comprised several arches faced in rustic stone, and, to match these, I had similar arches constructed along one side of the front courtyard, looking on to the sloping lawn and garden on the northern side of the property.

I also had improvements done to Alejandro and Aida's house, including a new parquet floor and the complete overhaul of the defective sewage system. The sewage system for the main house had to be completely rebuilt and directed into an altogether different direction, with a soakaway system. Calixto's house also needed much more work while another of Lucho's truncated projects, the traditional earth oven, had to be completed.

On 25 May 1997 a new contract was signed with the builder,

modifying the completion dates for the work and reducing the fines for late delivery. This contract also listed the work to be done, by 30 May 1997, after which fines of US$50 per day would be levied.

On 18 June the supervising architect informed Roberto that he had provisionally accepted the work as satisfactorily completed. On 28 July he reported the definitive acceptance of fulfilment of the contract. The final settlement of the accounts with the builder took place on 31 July 1997. Later that year, in a separate contract with the supervising architect only, I had another small house built on the northern end of the property, to house a third employee and also provide a deposit area for tools and equipment.

Thus, by the end of 1997 I had at last completed my building programme (or so I thought!), three years later than I had been confidently assured by Lucho that I would have an operating swimming pool. The struggle had been long and hard, but I was pleased with the result. I now had a very presentable-looking property and a weatherproof house where most things worked properly.

The *pièce de résistance* was the swimming pool, a veritable palace of gleaming glass dominating one end of the garden, in comparison with which my whitewashed adobe house remains very modest. Its cantilevered roof is supported by fretted girders painted the same colonial blue-green as the woodwork on the main house. Half the roof is glass, the rest is covered with rows and rows of tiny black pipes through which the water from the pool is pumped, heated and circulated back, whenever the sun shines (which fortunately is often). It is the least attractive part of the structure from outside but very effective. In theory the pool can also be heated by cylinders of natural gas when the sun fails to shine but this proved not to be practical, as the gas is quickly depleted, and twelve heavy cylinders have to be transported to San Pablo for replacement.

The lakeside wall is made of huge sheets of plate glass, with doors that can be swung open if the heat becomes too much. Inside, one could be in the Caribbean surrounded by bougainvillea and other tropical plants. As you swim, lapped in this delicious warmth, you can look out on the lake and beyond to the chilly snows of the Andes.

The pool was such a signal of conspicuous consumption that I felt a pang of shame. It was not meant to be thus, but somehow had just developed to meet the demands of the climate, for everyone

140

advised that an open pool would be virtually useless on the intemperate *altiplano*. I had another concern too – that small boys passing along the hillside above might be tempted to take a pot shot with stones. Fortunately there has been no such incident up to now. I enjoy my daily one-kilometre swim and countless friends have luxuriated in the waters of this very special pool. One of them rather aptly remarked, 'Some people have houses with a swimming pool. Margaret has a swimming pool with a house!'

Despite being on the shores of this immense inland sea, water was a constant problem. The lake continued to fall, which complicated pumping for irrigation, and obliged us to extend the perimeter wall at both ends of the property with a high, close-meshed wire fence to deter intruders. There was also doubt about the capacity of the well, supposedly fed by an underground flow from the top of the hill, whose water we used for drinking (after boiling and filtering) and domestic purposes.

The constant intrusion of unexpected and often unlikely events into Bolivian life is well illustrated by the following anecdote taken from my annual newsletter in 1996:

When I arrived early on 4 November ... I found a representative of the national syndicate of *campesinos* awaiting me on the dock as we disembarked in San Pedro. Tall, well-built and with a mass of long curly hair and a beard to match, he seemed an unlikely *campesino* from the *altiplano*. As we talked on the way up to the house I deduced from his accent that he wasn't Bolivian either. He introduced himself simply – '*Soy idealista*' ('I am an idealist') – as if announcing his name or profession. He turned out to be a Venezuelan who had come to Bolivia to study the '*yatiri*' or witch-doctors, but had then found he could help the peasants with other skills that he was providing voluntarily. '*Soy radioestesista*,' he explained, which rhymed nicely with '*idealista*' but left me completely in the dark. 'A dowser,' he added in English. He had studied water-divining in Surrey, England and was now passing on these techniques to Bolivian *campesinos*. Around San Pedro he said he had discovered several promising underground sources of water which would solve a long-standing problem for the community. One of them is near Villa Margarita and could help me also.

My new acquaintance's idealism did not translate itself into practical results. As so often in Bolivia all the potential projects fizzled out. When I next saw the dowser, some months later, the talk was not of water. This time he was enthusiastically seeking my support (financial and other) for the creation of an indigenous university on the *altiplano* that would teach only Aymara history and Aymara lore, astronomy and so forth. Sadly, that idea did not prosper either.

During all this time I remained very busy, not only advising the Bolivian government but also undertaking many international commitments. Living out on the lake lent a certain spice to travel to La Paz and further afield, as another excerpt from my 1996 letter shows:

I have excellent relations with the Naval Commander, who is more reliable than his predecessor with whom I was shipwrecked in the middle of the lake. Things don't always work out, however. One Friday in August there was a terrible tempest and the ferry was suspended all day so that we found a long queue of buses and lorries on our return from La Paz and still no crossing. The prospect of a night in the jeep was distinctly unappealing (I also had a visitor with me) and so I tried to enlist the help of the Commander to send a naval pontoon over to me as he had so often bidden me to do. To no avail – the battery of the naval radio was flat and they couldn't communicate across the straits! (On occasion the Commander has to resort to the single public telephone in San Pedro, above which there is a touching appeal in block letters: 'CONSULT YOUR POCKET BEFORE YOU MAKE A CALL!' I often wonder how the Navy would manage if there ever were an invasion. At the very least they would need a lot of small change.) In the end we managed to scramble aboard one of the regular pontoons when the wind had abated – a very bumpy crossing.

There were other travel adventures in November. On one perfectly calm morning a boatman neglected to secure the mooring chain of the barge and as Alejandro reversed the Mitsubishi on to the dock, its back wheels were suspended above a widening gap of water. There was no risk to life or limb as the water is shallow at the shoreline but I feared for my jeep. In any other country rescue would have entailed waiting for a breakdown truck with a hoist but here a small crowd of men assembled from nowhere, a handy plank of wood was used as a lever and in no time we were on our way to La Paz, the jeep undamaged. Large sections of the road to La Paz are being repaved. The work was started early in the dry season, in May, but then inexplicably abandoned until the rains had well and truly set in, at which point work began in earnest (there is a distinct predilection in Bolivia to do things the hard way). The result – miles of rutted, muddy detours in which you could all too easily get bogged down, even in a four-wheel drive, as we did on our next journey to the capital. Chivalry is not what it was. In the old days every vehicle would stop to help someone in difficulty, aware that they might be the next. Not now. Lorry drivers sailed impassively past the sight of two mud-bespattered women (Aida and myself, and me in ministerial-meeting garb to boot) as we fruitlessly pushed and Alejandro struggled with the controls. In the end two *campesinos* dug us out for a consideration. A shovel is being added to the jeep's standard equipment.

A happier local occasion was the celebration of 7 November 1996 of the thirtieth anniversary of the 4th Naval District of Titicaca ... Boatloads of dignitaries from La Paz, including an Admiral and sundry Argentine naval officers who train their Bolivian counterparts, were ferried across the straits and all the local worthies from San Pedro were present. A grandstand had been erected and serried ranks of ratings and their officers, complete with band were drawn up on the parade ground. I was the only one to arrive in a vehicle and Alejandro was told to park the jeep at the side of the parade ground. The final marching display had been ingeniously contrived to wind among the surrounding buildings in different columns which were then to re-converge in a final splendid march-past with the obligatory show of goosestepping which is truly a feat of endurance at 14,000 feet. As they moved smartly off to the rousing strains of the band I saw, to my horror, that my jeep was blocking the entrance to a narrow passage and the column that had to pass through it was beginning to falter at the sight of this unprogrammed obstacle. My fevered imagination saw them all going down like ninepins and that it would all be my fault. But luckily Alejandro was near at hand and moved the jeep in the nick of time. At the end there was a 'sail-past' of naval ships, three or four tiny vessels decked out in flags and bunting – hardly a convincing show of force but then, as the Commander told us during his address, the Bolivian Navy does much more than defend the country's non-existent shores. It undertakes a lot of community work, such as building and mending roads, and taking medicines and supplies to remote islands and lakeshore villages. The culminating act was a so-called *vin d'honneur*, which turned out to be a huge lunch with salmon trout, whole roast suckling pig, *sajta de pollo*, and other spicy national culinary delights, washed down, naturally, with lashings of excellent local beer as well as some wines and spirits. Before long no one was feeling much pain or very observant and I was able to slip away unnoticed.

In November 1996 both Roberto and I were invited to speak at a conference organised by the University of New Mexico in Albuquerque. The subject was a plan to improve education in science and technology throughout Latin America by better use of modern systems of communication, computers and distance learning, by pooling resources and harnessing the assistance of specialised firms in the private sector. I was delighted to go as this innovative idea was the brainchild of Roberto's son, Ramiro, now a professor at the university, whom I had known since he was a small boy. Getting to the conference became a nightmare, as my Christmas letter recounted.

The journey from La Paz to Albuquerque was hideously long and complicated, involving changes in Miami, my least favourite airport, especially if you are coming from the south, and Dallas. This time Miami exceeded even its own reputation in my book … Roberto has a multiple-entry visa of indefinite duration issued by the US Embassy in La Paz and he and I travelled on the same flight. He was two persons behind me in the immigration queue in Miami and we had an hour before our flight to Dallas. You can imagine my alarm when he did not appear in the Customs Hall below where I was waiting for him. There were only two explanations; either he had been taken suddenly and violently ill, which seemed unlikely, or he had been detained by US Immigration. The worst of it was that I was denied all information. I was not allowed to go back upstairs to immigration or talk to an immigration officer to find out what had happened. American Airlines looked visibly alarmed by my story and resolutely declined to do anything.

It was hard to know what to do. I felt a heel to abandon an old friend to an uncertain fate but I knew no one in authority to whom I could turn in Miami and the airport is so vast it would be difficult to find one another again. I decided that the only thing was to continue on to Albuquerque and get the university to intervene. It was a nightmare journey because, in addition to the worry, bad weather caused several flights to be cancelled and it was midnight (or 3 am Bolivian time and I had been up since 4 am) before I reached my destination. I had not known quite how I could break the news to Ramiro that I had lost his father on the way but by that time Roberto had telephoned his son. He had been held for five hours and initially treated in a very high-handed manner. The problem was not a new one. In the early 1960s Roberto had been Minister of Planning and had attended the US-sponsored Alliance for Progress meeting in Punta Del Este in 1961 (I was also there, assisting the Bolivian delegation) and the first UNCTAD meeting in Geneva in 1964. At both he had contact with Che Guevara who was heading the Cuban delegation. A black mark seems to have been entered against his name in the computer and although he has been assured by responsible US officials that it has been erased, has been, in a later ministerial incarnation, an official guest of the US Administration, has been given the aforesaid multiple-entry visa and has three of his children in the United States (two of them American citizens), it still keeps appearing from time to time (yet in May this year he and his wife went to visit their children without difficulty). When this happens Washington has to be contacted and gives the green light, a procedure complicated in this instance by the fact that the first immigration officer refused to talk to him at all for the first hour, treating him as guilty of some crime that was never defined, and that it was

145

Saturday afternoon. When he was eventually released, without apology or explanation, he had missed the last onward flight and had to spend the night in Miami, rejoining us in Albuquerque only on Sunday afternoon. It seems incredible that this outdated witch-hunt should still be going on after 35 years and even more so that there should be no redress or way of getting the reference deleted from the computer memory.

Rather to my embarrassment, Roberto used that extract from my letter to complain to the US Embassy. The Bolivian Foreign Ministry also delivered a protest, and in the end the embassy apologised, with the rather lame excuse that there had been a mix-up with 'another Roberto Jordán'. This clearly did not hold water, since similar incidents had occurred on several occasions, to the extent that it had become the custom for the US Consul in La Paz to insert a special comment to avoid it happening. Unfortunately on that occasion the Consul had insisted that it was no longer necessary.

Two years later Roberto became Bolivia's Ambassador to the United Nations. At last his diplomatic status assured him hassle-free passage through Miami.

10

The Human Factor

My original intention to employ mostly local people from Tiquina and hereabouts was frustrated by a series of bad experiences. Calixto lasted the longest, entering my service while the house was being built and staying on until February 1997. A likeable rogue; small and wiry, Calixto performed amazing feats with his one arm. The extent of his involvement in the theft of the pump in January 1994 was never cleared up, but there were no further incidents. There were, however, frequent unauthorised absences on high days and holidays, and bouts of drunkenness, all too frequent occurrences with the local employees who followed him.

Calixto had several endearing qualities. He was assiduous in bringing Andean plants for the garden, often from land away over the hill that belonged either to him or his latest female companion. Calixto also provided the dogs to guard the property, initially Perla and her sons Pedro and Bandido, although of course I fed them. But then Perla became pregnant and produced a huge litter; at one point we had no fewer than eleven dogs. This evidently could not go on but, there being no veterinary service nearer than La Paz, there was little that could be done. Calixto took Perla and her pups away to his property. I think he sold the pups but I never found out what happened to Perla and felt guilty about her fate.

I felt equally guilty that, owing to Lucho's dilatoriness, for a long time Calixto did not have a decent place to live, sleeping in an adobe shack alongside the house of Aida and Alejandro. He was never very clean but I felt I had no right to criticise that so long as he did not have a proper home. At long last the little house down on the beach became habitable but, as I discovered when Calixto left, the availability of water did not promote cleanliness and the new dwelling deteriorated into a slum.

I lost count of the successive Melibeas who accompanied Calixto.

As mentioned earlier, the second had a little girl of about seven years old, though she may have been older, as children here are small. She too was rather grimy, but her pride and joy was a floppy sunhat, too large for her small head, evidently fairly new and of a pristine cleanliness much at odds with the rest of her attire. She was a silent, timid child but she had a disconcerting habit, as dusk was falling and I was settling down to an evening by the fireside, of pressing her face on the sitting room window and fixing me with an enigmatic stare. There was something almost reproachful about that smudged little face, half obscured by her hat, peering in at me.

My repeated insistence that she should go to school fell on deaf ears. Calixto, as usual, was never lost for a reply: 'The teacher says she causes too many problems.'

It was hard to believe that this withdrawn little person could be disruptive in class, but perhaps she had learning difficulties. I offered to intervene with the teacher and that worked for a while but in the end proved of no avail. I fear that poor little girl was the victim of the general indifference to the education of girls on the *altiplano*. I never knew what happened, though, because her mother, after having another baby for whom I knitted a jacket, left and was replaced. It was hard to imagine what fascination Calixto – small, wizened, and disabled – exerted over these ladies but there could be no doubt that he must have had a special something.

The new Melibea settled in and also produced a baby. The succession of female occupants did not seem to improve the upkeep of the little house, but ample, brightly hued skirts and petticoats, as well as other items of washing, became a regular feature, left out to dry on the boulders strewn on the shore.

Calixto had entrepreneurial aspirations and came to me one day in late 1996, with the following request:

'Señorita,' he said, adopting the irritating wheedling tone that the Aymara uses when requesting money or other material favours. 'Please can you lend me one thousand bolivianus?'

'What for?'

His reply flabbergasted me. 'To buy a part share in a fishing boat.'

Searching for the most tactful way of voicing my concern, I enquired how he could manage a boat with only one arm.

Easily, it appeared. 'My señora will do the rowing,' he said, adding entreatingly, 'Please Señorita; *No seas mala* [don't be bad!].'

148

I had no intention of being bad and rather warily forked out the money. Calixto asked for mooring rights and the boat was brought round to our cove. For some time after it became a common sight to see him struggling off shore with his fishing nets, while the current Melibea strained at the oars. They never seemed to catch any fish.

Despite my pandering to this whim, Calixto's behaviour continued to be erratic. His culminating misdemeanour occurred early in 1997, as I recounted to my aunt Christina in a letter dated 12 February:

> Calixto, the one-armed chap who helps Alejandro in the garden, is not very reliable. Aida, who has a sharp tongue, can't abide him. On Friday Alejandro, Aida and I went to La Paz (Aida won't let Alejandro out of her sight in case he goes off the rails). I warned Calixto that we might spend the night there if my Ministerial meeting went on late and enjoined him to be responsible. Unluckily for him we got back just as night was falling to find the house in total darkness, the dogs escaped and Calixto barely able to stand because he had invited the workmen to 'ch'allar' the swimming pool i.e. pour libations of beer into it as well as themselves. We later found that he had thrown all his keys in too for good measure but luckily there is no water in it yet. Worse still, during the night a truck of expensive plate glass for the pool house was delivered and encountered Calixto's lady, also rather the worse for wear, on her way back from San Pedro with liquid replenishments, and incapable of ringing the bell to apprise us of the delivery (we were all asleep) or of opening the gate to let in the truck which stayed in the field outside until morning, fortunately without mishap.

The driver and his assistant had walked back to San Pedro, leaving their precious cargo untended. One could, of course, wonder why anyone in their right senses would deliver a valuable consignment, worth several thousand dollars, to a remote place at two o'clock in the morning, not least given the perils of the pontoon crossing of the lake in total darkness. But such oddities become the norm in Bolivia.

This was not the end of the matter for Calixto, as my letter went on:

C. did not dare show his face for a couple of days and then said he wanted to leave my employ. Aida could scarcely contain her glee at what she considered to be an offer one couldn't refuse. But I felt sorry for him as he has two children and only one arm, and he obviously didn't really want to leave. He clearly couldn't go on being a watchman but I've managed to find a compromise solution. A man we know well – trained as a teacher but without a job – will take his place. Calixto will no longer live on the premises (he has a house in the village) but will come in daily to help with gardening. When we got to this point, C. who had kept telling me how ashamed he was, perked up noticeably and asked: a) could he anchor his fishing boat on my beach and b) could he have a *raise*! No prizes for guessing my answer to both though I had a hard time suppressing a smile.

But the matter didn't end there either. Calixto eventually refused the offer of a non-live-in day job and insisted on resigning, a decision he confirmed in writing. I was sorry to see him go, for he had worked for me for six years and I was pretty well acquainted with his foibles. At the same time I had begun to think that, now that the swimming pool would soon be functioning, I needed someone more mechanically qualified to assist Alejandro.

The social and labour laws in Bolivia weigh heavily on the side of the employee, which is fair enough considering how labour was exploited here during many centuries. I paid Calixto his one-month salary for each of his six years, as the law required for someone voluntarily leaving his job; he signed the receipt and went away seeming happy enough. I was therefore greatly surprised when, six months later, I received a request from an inspector to present myself at the Ministry of Labour to respond to a demand from Calixto. The note ended by reminding me amiably that 'failure to comply with this request constitutes an offence penalised by law'.

Roberto Jordán went in to bat on my behalf. The ensuing meeting gave rise to two portentous legal documents, one giving a blow-by-blow account of the proceedings, the other sealing the eventual agreement. Calixto first wanted social benefits that he claimed were owed to him by Lucho, who had employed him during the construction. Calixto also wanted a payment from me known as *deshaucio*, an extra three months' pay not applicable in this instance

150

since Calixto had resigned of his own accord. Roberto reminded him that he had been guilty of bad conduct on account of his continual drinking binges and of abandoning the work place and leaving the house unguarded. Surprisingly, Calixto had the grace to recognise these shortcomings but added, as if in self-justification, the tardy revelation, certainly no longer relevant to the case in hand, that he had now given up the demon drink! Roberto then pointed out that, despite the drinking bouts, I had offered to let him continue working at Villa Margarita as a day employee, but he had refused this arrangement and resigned. His departure had been his own decision.

Calixto then demanded *aguinaldos* (the one month's extra pay due at Christmas under Bolivian law), but it was pointed out that this did not apply either, having been paid regularly every December. Since Calixto was determined to have something, the inspector worked out a compromise whereby I would pay extra vacation time over the six years, plus the two-month fragment of the 1997 *aguinaldos*. This was more than the law required but, in the interest of solving the matter, Roberto agreed. The money was paid and Calixto signed, declaring his complete satisfaction for a second time.

This time the agreement stuck but a similar convoluted process remained par for the course whenever an employee left. I began to dread such events and once remarked wearily that I had spent more on social benefits for departing personnel, whatever the reasons for their separation, than I ever had on actual wages!

This tardy demand by Calixto may well have come about because his fishing venture had not proved a success. I fear he had been duped by unscrupulous partners in the ownership of the boat, taking advantage of his disability and his lack of business acumen. Nowadays we sometimes glimpse Calixto tending the new plaza in San Pedro (refurbished with popular participation funds) as a municipal employee.

Other revelations later painted a darker side of the whole affair when we learned that Calixto, when drunk, had been wont to beat his female companions and even his mother. One of the Melibeas had reached such a state of despair that she had waded into the lake one night and threatened to drown herself. I was away at the time, and it was Aida and Alejandro who successfully dissuaded her. That was a drama I was glad to have been spared.

151

Calixto left my employ officially on 28 February 1997 and Gonzalo, the 'man we know well' as I rashly said in my letter to my aunt, joined our little team. He has already figured in these pages: he was the community leader from Camacachi who negotiated the double payment for the electricity power line, as well as my gift of corrugated iron roofing sheets intended for new classrooms and housing for teachers at the school, which after long delay, ended up on a community hall.

The twists and turns of those negotiations should have warned me that I really did not know him at all. But Gonzalo was a smooth talker, as befitted a man who had been trained as a teacher at the prestigious Warisata Normal School, which had been started in 1935 and acclaimed as the very first attempt in Latin America at integrated rural education. Gonzalo's wife wore the *pollera* (bell-skirt on layers of petticoats) and bowler hat of the *cholita*, and like so many of her peers was an astute business woman, running a butcher's shop in San Pedro and regularly buying cattle in Peru and driving them over the nearby frontier. They lived in a two-storey house near the lakeshore in Camacachi, an impressive residence by local standards where, years before, Sissy and I had been invited to drink tea when walking in the vicinity. They now took up residence in the tiny house on the beach.

Aida knew the pair and seemed to hold them in high esteem, and so I looked forward to a more harmonious domestic atmosphere. I had not yet fully realised that anyone who came to work alongside Alejandro was doomed to be the object of Aida's intense disapproval and suspicion, no matter how qualified they might be or how cordial the relationship prior to their entry into my employ. Aida was an excellent housekeeper, devotedly loyal and honest, but also incurably bossy, constantly interfering with the men who worked with Alejandro, much to the latter's annoyance. I endlessly remonstrated with her, insisting that the bounds of her 'empire' (as she obviously considered it to be) were restricted to the house, and that everything outside was Alejandro's domain. It was to no avail: clearly she had ruled Alejandro with a rod of iron for many years and was determined to go on doing so.

War broke out almost immediately between her and Gonzalo, and in my absence Roberto was the first to get caught in the middle. In one of the cryptic little notes that greeted me on each return to Villa Margarita he quipped: 'I leave you to act as referee between Aida and Gonzalo. Her happiness faded when I told her that only you, and not she, could take decisions about the fate of her intimate enemy, Gonzalo.'

Aida made it clear that she would not rest until Gonzalo left my employ. Admittedly he did little to help his cause. The person who I had fondly thought would demonstrate a sense of discipline acquired through learning proved as feckless as the rest. Every time there was a high day or holiday – and the Bolivian calendar is scattered with 'fiestas' – Gonzalo and his good lady, granted leave for the specific day or weekend, would disappear for days on end, returning dishevelled and slightly sheepish. Remorse did not figure in their vocabulary. Upbraided by me for dereliction to duty, Gonzalo would mutter, peevishly, that it was 'a matter of culture'. Tradition, according to him, demanded observance to excess, overriding any other minor obligations one might have, such as paid employment. He was not amused when, exasperated at last, I docked him of pay for days spent absent without leave, or subtracted them from his annual holiday.

No amount of talking to, or material penalties, had any effect on his behaviour. Matters reached crisis point in the small hours of one particular night when Gonzalo and his bell-skirted spouse rolled down the hill to Villa Margarita after many hours of carousing in San Pedro. In their advanced state of inebriation, which took the form of raucous rendering of some unidentifiable Bolivian folk song, they had either lost their key to the entrance portal, or were incapable of making it work. The quiet night was shattered by an ear-splitting caterwauling, interspersed with frantic banging on the metal gates. We were all woken by the hullabaloo, and Alejandro was soon on the scene, closely followed by Aida, never one to miss a dramatic scene, particularly one likely to bring down the fortunes of her arch enemy. The dogs went mad. A dreadful altercation followed, almost coming to blows, until I ordered everyone to go to bed and report in the morning.

It was a mystery how the unsteady pair negotiated the nearly 100 steep steps down to their abode and managed to avoid falling into the icy waters of the lake once they got there. But survive they did, in a purely physical sense, favoured perhaps by the proverbial luck of the very drunk.

They did not survive in my employ. Gonzalo, whom I had thought such a likely lad, left in October 1997 and the usual complicated procedures ensued regarding his right to compensation despite the reasons for his dismissal. He had lasted just eight turbulent months and left the little house down by the water dirtier that ever. So much for the values imparted by Warisata, I thought.

As mentioned earlier, I had decided that with the swimming pool becoming operational I needed three men in the garden. Roberto Nina joined us in August 1997. He had been a bricklayer and plasterer engaged by the architect who rebuilt the house and completed the swimming pool. He was young, good-looking and intelligent, and I had always liked the look of him. So, when he expressed interest in working permanently at Villa Margarita, I jumped at the idea.

This time I was not disappointed. Roberto proved to be reliable and hardworking and had a pleasant disposition. He had mechanical ability and experience, soon mastering the complications of the system of pumps, pipes and thermostats of the swimming pool. He and Alejandro made an excellent team, completely interchangeable. The only fly in the ointment was Aida who, true to form, never missed an opportunity of criticising Roberto or questioning his honesty. Notwithstanding, for some time it was relatively plain sailing but, with the departure of Gonzalo, I was once again down to two outside staff.

In November 1997 Roberto Jordán recommended that I employ Enrique, who was well known to him and his family, for whom Enrique's elder brother and sister had worked for some years. The Jordán family had also helped them to pursue their studies. Enrique was only 18, and I was assured that he came from a family belonging to some evangelical sect that strictly forbade alcohol consumption of any kind. The third house, at the northern end of the garden, was now ready for occupancy and so Enrique was duly installed there.

At first, all went very well. Even Aida, perhaps moved by Enrique's youth and some unaccustomed maternal stirrings – she had no children of her own – warmed to the new recruit and took him under her formidable wing. I suppose he did not constitute any threat to her or Alejandro.

The first warning signs, had we detected them, were that Enrique used his earnings not to save for the education to which he claimed to aspire, but to spend on articles of conspicuous consumption: a television set, despite poor reception; compact discs and tape recorders; and a streamlined, ultra-modern bicycle equipped with more gears that one could think it possible to cope with. On this gleaming machine Enrique would speed off up the hill into San Pedro for lunch, and sometimes in the evening. I did not actually see his performance there but, by all accounts, he would play the young beau, swaggering round the plaza, parading his bicycle and chatting up the local girls. Soon there was news of a liaison with a particular girl, the daughter of a man who sometimes did casual work at Villa Margarita, and it was at her parents' home that he spent the innumerable fiestas when he did not go back to his own family in La Paz.

Aida began to mutter darkly that the local girl's family and the young men with whom he consorted in the village were leading our young innocent astray. Alcohol, she implied, was no longer forbidden fruit. A number of untoward incidents came to light. A group of local boys got him drunk and the prized bicycle was stolen. Worse still, over the 1998 New Year holiday Enrique disappeared for two days. When he eventually turned up Aida opened the metal gates to a sorry sight: Enrique had been badly beaten up. He had two black eyes, a bruised and swollen face and was still suffering from a monumental hangover.

In the face of this incontrovertible evidence, as opposed to local gossip, action had to be taken. Through Roberto Jordán, Enrique's parents were informed, and his father Mateo came out to read the riot act. At least, that is what I hoped had happened, but it had little effect.

As if all this were not enough, frictions had arisen between Roberto Nina and Enrique. In one of his 'welcome' letters, this one dated 24 April 1998, Roberto Jordán alerted me to the situation, explaining it in the context of historical and cultural factors: 'There is no news of Lucho,' he wrote. 'Nor are there any new developments except that your so-and-so Roberto has dedicated himself to harassing Enrique and making his life impossible. Aida will tell you all. This must be stopped. He even threatened to hit him. Enrique is timid, he doesn't lie, smoke or drink, but Roberto accuses him of everything. Enrique has 500 years of colonisation within him, as you can prove. The other one (Roberto) is more "citadino" [a street-wise city boy] and I believe he was once a policeman, which explains everything. He is trying to bully Enrique into resigning so that he can bring his brother to replace him. You must talk to Aida, Enrique and

Roberto. But have a meeting with both of them so that the lies and contradictions become clear. Have we got to make Enrique a protester and a revolutionary? What do you think! You will resolve the matter. It's not as complicated as Angola.'

I was not at all sure about this last point. Moreover, ready as I was to bow to my friend's superior, and undoubtedly deep-rooted knowledge of the culture and peoples of the Bolivian *altiplano*, I found it difficult, in the light of objective events, to think of Enrique as timid and retiring, and Roberto Jordán was certainly wrong about his supposed aversion to drink. I wasn't convinced that he didn't lie sometimes, either. But he was Roberto's protégé and he clearly considered him to be the underdog, deserving more lenience. To me it seemed to be Enrique who, possibly envious, wanted to assert himself above Roberto Nina, especially in the matter of pool maintenance, although it was patently evident, to me and Alejandro, that he was much less technically capable than Roberto, and less quick in learning skills.

To my chagrin, it was Roberto Nina who threw in the towel, tired of the constant bickering. He resigned in January 2000 and no amount of persuasion either from me or Alejandro could induce him to change his mind. He was a real loss.

Roberto's place was taken briefly by Julio, a *tiquinense* who had worked earlier on the construction, and who now sold gasoline down by the ferry landing stage. He was also the father of Enrique's girlfriend. This arrangement did not work out either, lasting only a few months.

Once again we were looking for a new recruit; it was never easy to find anyone suitable who was ready to work in such a remote place. At length Alejandro proposed his nephew, Ricardo. Ricardo, a solemn, stoutish man of about forty, peered at the world myopically through very thick pebble glasses. They made him look serious, if perhaps not well adapted to the kind of work required. He had good references from various organisations in La Paz for which he had worked, including none other than the International Monetary Fund. So he was engaged.

Caught in my abysmally slow learning curve like a fly in a spider's web, I naively congratulated myself that this time Aida would be pleased since, apart from Enrique whom she had virtually adopted, it was all being kept in the family. Not a bit of it.

'*Ese Ricardo* – that Ricardo,' she fumed, 'is a wretched good-for-nothing. It is he who drags Alejandro off to bars in La Paz and brings him back drunk, not till the next day,' adding truculently, 'and sometimes not till later still.'

At Villa Margarita, and with me generally, Alejandro was always a model of abstemiousness and I found this image hard to believe. But Aida, in rare moments of confidence sharing, would burst into tears, saying that when Alejandro was led astray by his city friends, and returned drunk, he would beat her up. This was behaviour incomprehensible on the part of such a mild-mannered man, but, even allowing for Aida's predilection to exaggerate the dark side of things, domestic violence is so rampant in Bolivia that it could very well have been true.

So the atmosphere at Villa Margarita continued tense. Sometimes it was an uneasy truce, but more often a subterranean war between Aida and Ricardo, with Alejandro caught awkwardly in between. Not that Ricardo was a very active belligerent. He was terrified of Aida, as well he might be, and complained to me that she had hammered on his door in the middle of the night, on what pretext of his wrongdoing was never very clear to me.

Meanwhile Enrique had educational aspirations. 'Señorita,' he said to me one day. 'There are classes in Janckoamaya that I can go to three afternoons a week. If you'll give me the time off, I could finish my secondary education.'

I discussed this with Alejandro, who wasn't too keen. Enrique's work had not been satisfactory, and there had been more instances of falling into bad company in Tiquina, for which I had had to reprimand him in writing, warning that if there was one more incident I would have to dispense with his services. Nevertheless, I urged Alejandro to agree.

'This may be the opportunity he needs. It will keep him busy and, hopefully, out of mischief.'

Initially the new arrangement worked well, despite some jealousy among the others on account of Enrique's special privilege. But, as I pointed out, he was the youngest and deserved this chance to better himself.

Janckoamaya is the first lakeside village you encounter on the other side of the straits of Tiquina, on the way to La Paz. Enrique had to travel to the school first by launch and then by mini-bus, about an hour in each direction. At first he came home punctually after his classes but then his arrival became later and later in the evening. Confronted with this, Enrique admitted sheepishly that he sometimes went out with friends he had made in Janckoamaya.

He remained deaf to further warnings and one night, if Aida was to be believed, staggered in drunk, not through the main gate but along the lake shore, a perilous path over rocks even in daylight, and potentially lethal in the dark. Then, after a festival, he turned up once again bloodied and bruised. This was the last straw, and I told Enrique he must leave. Apart from other considerations, I felt I could no longer be responsible for someone so young and feckless.

Enrique did not go quietly. He whined and wailed constantly: '*Señorita, no seas mala* – don't be bad' (a common form of appeal in Bolivia that always irks me because it cavalierly assumes that the fault is on my side). 'Let me have one more chance! I swear by God that nothing like this will ever happen again.'

With difficulty I hardened my heart: 'Enrique you have promised this so many times, and sworn by God on each occasion. But each time it has happened again and again. So how can I believe you?'

Enrique's father, summoned from La Paz, also pleaded his son's cause, aghast that he should throw away a well-paid job when unemployment was exceedingly high. I remained adamant. Eventually it was agreed that Enrique should join the armed forces, to serve his one-year conscription and, we hoped, learn some discipline. Mateo offered to work in his place at Villa Margarita, to keep the job warm for his son when he emerged from the army. He seemed a serious man, who also claimed teetotal status by virtue of his religion, but I declined to make any commitment regarding Enrique's future.

That was in December 2000. Nine years later Mateo is still with me. Enrique was rejected by the armed forces because of some abnormality in his spine. He did not get another job but went to Santa Cruz, the boom oil-town in the eastern lowlands, and lived it up there on his indemnity pay from me. For some time his parents did not know whether he was alive or dead. Now, I am told, he is back in La Paz, married, with a baby and I hope gainfully employed.

So, at the beginning of 2001 I thought my garden team was at last settled, with Alejandro, Ricardo and Mateo. I had not bargained for a cataclysmic development that turned everything topsy-turvy again less than six months later. But that comes later.

11

Halcyon Days – Andean Days

Dawn over the Andes is a daily spectacular, dizzying the spirit, except during those few days and weeks when the rains come to drench the parched *altiplano* briefly in green.

It is my favourite time of day. Every morning I get up at the first glimmer of light and draw back the curtains. The surface of the lake is still grey and cold as steel, and through the clumps of eucalyptus down by the beach I can make out the shadowy outlines of small fishing boats, their solitary occupants pulling in the nets laid the night before, huddled against the biting chill of every dawn throughout the year, the silence broken only by the creak of straining oars.

The sun – the ancient god of the Aymaras and the Incas – announces his presence long before his actual appearance. First he illuminates the lesser deities, the *achachila* who live in the mountains, as a broad band of pale light across the eastern sky etches the jagged graph of the Cordillera in sharp relief on the far horizon. Each day the colours are subtly different, sometimes pale saffron, sometimes a warm apricot, sometimes the most delicate intermingled pink and turquoise hues. As the light gathers the lake too gains in luminosity, reflecting the rainbow colours that now suffuse the heavens.

Then, at last, this crescendo of colour reaches its zenith. The sun breasts its way over the mountain tops, flooding my bedroom with a river of gold, and climbs swiftly up the sky, eclipsing all its minor harbingers. The other colours fade, both sky and lake reassume their intense, cobalt blue, and the mountains become again a shimmering silver palisade, an idyllic scene that, for me, is incomparable to any other place on earth.

Only the bleakest soul could fail to be happy and exhilarated on such mornings. Out on the balcony the air is crisp and cool, there is a tang of eucalyptus on the faint breeze off the water, and the incipient warmth of the sunshine gives a lift to the spirits. It is as if the secret world of the Sacred Lake, cradled within its encircling hills and mountains, is born anew with every sunrise and Viracocha daily celebrates his ancient creation. It needs no great stretch of the imagination to understand how the Aymara, both in ancient and more recent times, have peopled this landscape with gods and demons, spirits and ancestral ghosts, or conjured up fables of miraculous happenings and magical adventures such as those of Manco Kapac and Mama Ojllo, children of the all-powerful sun-god, setting out at their father's command to establish the Inca Empire at Cuzco. According to local lore, the Sacred Lake has dark, telluric powers, and on mornings such as these it is surely not fanciful to feel the forces of life revived and strengthened within one by the mere contemplation of this almost surreal landscape.

Everything is still and tranquil. There is scarcely a sound to be heard except the braying of a donkey, heard distantly over the water from San Pablo, or the crowing of a disoriented cockerel who constantly proclaims false dawns, whatever the time of day.

The real world is stirring, however. The men are diligently watering the garden. From my windows I can see that, down in San Pedro, the *barcazas* are already plying their somewhat desultory way across the straits, ferrying buses and trucks on their way to Copacabana and the Peruvian frontier, or travelling back to La Paz. A few *campesinos* are quietly working on their plots on the hills around, or taking their animals down to the lakeshore for watering. It is a sparsely populated landscape, where no one is in a hurry. On the lake the odd motor launch is chugging up and down between the lakeshore villages, one or two small boats with brightly coloured sails have appeared, and to the south, beyond what we now call Smugglers' Cove (since the furtive nocturnal manoeuvres that we have witnessed from a safe distance), a whole string of rainbow sails is stretched out like a line of distant washing, as the fisherman of Camacachi join forces to net the ever scarcer, ever smaller fish of Lake Titicaca.

Because one can cross the lake on the better of the only two roads from Bolivia into Peru, San Pablo and San Pedro have acquired somewhat more importance than mere fishing villages, although they make little effort to live up to their status as tourist staging posts. Seen from the lake they are both picturesque huddles of small houses crouched round their plazas between the encroaching hills and the water's edge, some of plain, untreated adobe, others whitewashed or even painted in delicate blues and pinks. On a sunny day you could almost believe them to be quaint Mediterranean towns were it not for the unmistakeable nip in the air, the whiff from what is euphemistically proclaimed, in large letters, to be the *Baño Público* (public bath) and the garbage blowing around the streets. These buildings fronting on the plaza and the waterfront are plastered with disfiguring advertisements for Coca Cola and other such products in a jarring note of modernity.

Round the two squares of the twin villages on either side of the straits, and along the dusty street that is San Pedro's main thoroughfare, there are rows of identical little shops. All consisting of one small, dark and cluttered room, they seem to contain exactly the same commodities for sale – shelf on shelf of tins of fish and meat, sugar, powdered milk, sacks of bulging flour and rice encumbering the floor, piles of slightly stale *maraquetas* (the traditional bread), the product of yesterday's baking in La Paz, packets of unappealing beige-coloured biscuits, large bottles of the inevitable Coca Cola, as well as cans of local beer. In each doorway presides a lady of formidable proportions, enhanced by her billowing petticoats and skirts and endowed with an intimidating air of authority by a bowler hat perfectly poised on black hair, rigorously scraped back into a bun. There are seldom any fruits or vegetables, except occasionally potatoes, which originated on the *altiplano* anyway.

The little shops are so indistinguishable from one another, both in appearance and contents, that they remind me of an artificial opera or stage set, and it has always been a wonder to me how any of them ever make a living. In an effort to be scrupulously fair, I purchase from each of them in turn. The ladies are always friendly and invariably greet me as if I were a long-lost member of their family. So do the men lounging at the corner, or waiting hopefully for passengers by their pontoons, moored at the quayside and connected to the shore by uneven and dilapidated planks of wood that test the skill and nerve of every intrepid driver who dares to board them. The *tiquinense* may appear dour of mien on first encounter, but these faces, chiselled and wrinkled by the harsh winds and strong sun of these uplands, readily break into a smile of recognition. They now consider me, too, as one of them, a local inhabitant, and greet my jeep with friendly waves.

161

As you come down the hill from Villa Margarita towards the port, the modest bay that opens up below is crowded with small white launches. These take passengers from buses and trucks across the straits, a custom imposed by the naval authorities after one or two tragic accidents when vehicles full of people sank during the crossing on the pontoon. In an excess of zeal in the immediate aftermath everyone in the launches was provided with bright orange lifejackets, but zeal is not in great demand hereabouts and the habit has lapsed – at least until the next accident. Along the shore rows and rows of the big black flat-bottomed pontoons are lined up, usually with small boys ineffectually baling out water from the leaking timbers in their wells, with ridiculously small tin cans.

Like the launches, the pontoons all have names, often of saints or some other unremarkable origin. But just occasionally there is evidence of some more quirky imagination at work. One bright spark, whether inspired by a sense of black humour or – more likely – bereft both of historical memory or any inkling of irony, has dubbed his craft 'Titanic'. Because of the strict rota of the syndicates, superstitious users have no choice but to trust themselves and their vehicles to this ill-named craft, but may be consoled by glimpsing others called 'Titanic I', 'II' and 'III'! Some nautical tradition persists though it is not always well understood. For some time I was acquainted with a likeable young rascal called Nelson, who was amazed to learn the heroic exploits of his illustrious namesake.

There are far too many pontoons – competition among them seems as unknown as it is between the identi-shops on shore – and so they operate as syndicates, with strict rotas for their turns at ferrying vehicles. It is a maddening system for the regular traveller like me, often forced to wait while another barge is leisurely poled from far along the shore although a perfectly viable one has just moored at the quayside after crossing from the other side.

It is all spectacularly uneconomic, but part of the enduring charm of the place. Every so often the idea of constructing a bridge across the one kilometre of water separating the two villages crops up but is swiftly quashed by the locals. A complicated, but not impossible, engineering challenge, it would bring enormous advantages for the tourist trade and for commercial traffic with Peru, but even the imaginative scheme of a former finance minister to use local labour in the construction and then establish a toll system, of which the proceeds would be used exclusively for the benefit of San Pablo and San Pedro, has failed to win any local hearts. While embracing some of the brasher aspects of modernity, such as plastic bags and garish Coca Cola billboards, the *tiquinense* remains firmly wedded to tradition, regarding it already as a major concession to have abandoned the sails and poles that were the only form of locomotion when I first visited these shores, in favour of outboard motors, often ill maintained and even known sometimes – just to add to the spirit of adventure – to run out of petrol in the midst of choppy waters.

For the lake is unpredictable, a veritable inland sea, which a wayward wind can whip up into wild and dangerous storms, causing crossings to be suspended for hours and even days on end. It is fitting, therefore, that the landlocked and shoreless Bolivian navy should have one of its main bases in Tiquina, dominating San Pedro from a high white building on a hilltop, once a hotel greatly favoured by foot-weary pilgrims breaking their journey from La Paz to the miraculous Black Virgin of Copacabana, herself the patron saint of fishermen. The navy has few boats, all small, except for a hospital ship which serves remote lakeside villages inaccessible by land, whenever a forgetful and cash-strapped treasury remembers to provide it with fuel and medical staff. Every year, however, several hundred young conscripts pass through the base and are taught not only to goosestep in time to martial music, but also to read and write and master a basic skill, such as carpentry or mechanics, that may serve them well in later life.

The presence of the navy brings with it many ceremonies, parades and frequent band practice whose echoes reverberate back and forth between the surrounding hills. Perhaps it is because of this prevalence of formal, military and patriotic music that San Pedro does not go in for more homely fiestas as much as San Pablo across the water. Considering that their inhabitants spring from the same Aymara stock, and probably even from the same families, the difference in spirit between the two communities is extraordinary. There is always some jollity going on in San Pablo, music wafting across the water, fantastically costumed figures cavorting around the plaza or, when nothing else is happening, the plaintive, slightly out-of-tune notes of a *corneta* being practised by a would-be aficionado.

In short, apart from a few superficial trappings of modernity, the underlying currents of life go on much as they always have. True, many inhabitants of Tiquina own a minibus, as well as a *barcaza*, a *boliche* or small shop and some sparse plots of land scattered over the surrounding hillsides. They may also have a son or other close relative working in La Paz and are among the most privileged inhabitants of the *altiplano*. But underneath they cling to the old ways of life, their traditional feast days (when everyone gets drunk and does no work for several days), a general insouciance that insidiously takes over, even during sporadic spurts of energy and striving for economic gain. It is an attitude and way of life that can goad the wanderer from the outside world into paroxysms of frustration, a useless expense of effort. As the days pass you learn to go with the flow, you come to accept that time, after all, is not that important, and you allow yourself to be absorbed, at least for a short spell, by the calm and leisurely pace of *tiquinense* life.

Once a week we drive to La Paz for shopping, since little other than staples is available in Tiquina. The drive, including the odyssey of the pontoon crossing, takes two and a half hours each way. The hills above and behind San Pablo are barren and devoid of dwellings, the one immediately behind the village bizarrely crowned along its long, curving ridge by a string of sparse and stunted eucalyptus – the brainchild of an earlier naval commander bent on social works and reforestation – which from a distance look for all the world like the spines on a dinosaur's back. The road winds round this hill and then, from high above, follows the contours of the lake shore, sometimes along narrow necks of land dividing the Lago Mayor and the Lago Menor, with tantalising glimpses of both sparkling far below, and sometimes also of the immense hydra-headed bulk of the Illampu, and the long chain of snow peaks leading south to culminate in its twin giant, the Illimani, standing guard over the invisible city of La Paz.

Though no dwellings are to be seen, tracks lead into the hills and at the roadside a few people who have walked from afar are waiting for transport to La Paz, women with *aguayos* bulging with goods for sale, men with sacks of potatoes. Soon we come to the first village – Janckoamaya – and others follow in quick succession, a litany of almost exclusively Aymara names: Compi, long the site of a famed annual festival of folklore music and dance from all over the country; the two Chias – Vissalaya and Cocani – where

164

the navy has a base for the marines; Huatajata, home of the Yacht Club; Sancjkahawira; Huarina, the junction for the road to dreaded Achacachi, capital of the 'Empire' of the indigenous leader 'El Mallku', a road that then branches off round the lower slopes of the Illampu and down to the high, sub-tropical valleys on the eastern side of the Andes, to the more benign climate of sleepy Sorata; Huancane, where we once came on a fiesta of llama drivers, dancing the age-old traditional dance that symbolises their pastoral and herding life; then Batallas, a less sonorous name, commemorating a decisive battle in the War of Liberation; Khara Khota; Chirapaca; Pascana or Palcoco; Patamacita; and, finally, San Roque, the toll gate leading to El Alto and so, eventually, down to the city.

The first half of the journey hugs the shores of the lake, which abound in signs of burgeoning prosperity in this more humid and less hostile part of the *altiplano*. Houses are often of two storeys or more, the upper floor of brick, on top of a lower one of the traditional adobe. There are numerous small restaurants, all sporting fading notices announcing '*¡Trucha hoy!*' ('Trout today!') that have obviously been displayed for some time, because there is rarely anything other than trout on the menu. Indeed the monotony of the delicacies on offer raises the perennial question once again: whatever happened to the spirit of competition?

Along the road well-nourished-looking children are scurrying along to school, carrying books and backpacks and wearing astonishingly white uniforms, considering the inadequacies of clean running water. Their elders are on their way to the fields and here the signs of progress are more muted. The women are almost invariably still attired in the traditional ample, brightly coloured skirts, mounted on tiers of petticoats, dark shawls or brilliantly hued *aguayos*, all set off by the regulation bowler hat. Nearly always they are bent under heavy burdens of tools or produce or, on the homeward journey, of firewood gleaned from the scant pickings to be found on the largely treeless *altiplano*. At the same time they are herding their few animals out to graze on the *paja brava* or the *totora* reeds in the shallows off the lake. These animals mostly spend the nights in the safe shelter of corrals attached to their owners' houses.

One of the curiously endearing features of the *altiplano* is that almost all the animals are taken around on long rope halters. All animals, that is, except the very ones you would expect to be on a lead, namely the dogs. Bullocks, cows, donkeys, the occasional llama or alpaca and even pigs and sheep, are chivvied along by the owners desperately hanging on to the end of a straining rope and more often than not pulled into the ditch or into the path of oncoming traffic. The road between Tiquina and La Paz may now be asphalted but it is the livestock who command the right of way.

Meanwhile the dogs run wherever they will, a danger to themselves and everyone else. Some are splendid specimens, mongrels with undoubtedly noble forebears. According to local lore, maids from the countryside who went to work with wealthy families in the city were often given the unwanted pups of pampered pets which they brought back to their homes. Tiquina boasts a positively Cruft's-like dog show of different breeds and half-breeds, ranging from Alsatians and Dalmatians, to bulldogs, dachsunds and Pekinese, with some strange mixtures resulting from the most unlikely pairings. The dogs along the route have developed the habit of sitting by the roadside, begging for food from passing motorists, so it has become the custom to buy rolls in the market and throw them out whenever a supplicant appears. It is tragic but not surprising that on each journey there are usually more than a few mangled canine carcasses along the highway. Dogs are clearly of lesser value to the *campesino* than their more productive livestock.

The land near the lake is dark and fertile and crops are taller and sturdier than elsewhere. There are areas of semi-swamp where egrets and varieties of duck abound, and elegant skeins of black Andean ibis fly up to form a delicate fretwork of sculpted wings against the pellucid sky. The fields are flat and it is not unusual, at sowing time, to see a tractor turning up the black soil into neat furrows.

Beyond Huarina the landscape changes. Just before you reach that very frugal town, the road breasts a rise and you come suddenly on a majestic panorama of the whole Cordillera, its crenellated peaks piercing the blue vault of the sky and proclaiming the magnificence of nature in contrast to the puny, crumbling works of man far below. Now the beneficial influence of the lake fades, and the arid plain stretching endlessly to the sere and distant hills seems scarcely changed from when I first saw it nearly half a century ago. Gone are the ugly brick houses, unsightly perhaps but still denoting some degree of greater affluence and comfort. Instead this landscape at first sight appears devoid of both colour and habitation until, as your eye gets used to the shifting shades, you descry, widely scattered and far away, the brown huddle of isolated adobe homesteads, made of earth and cowering close to the ground as if seeking protection against the wild elements that roam untrammelled across these upland wastes. In true traditional Aymara style they have only one or two tiny windows because windows are thought to let in not only the cold but also alien and evil spirits. Here you seldom see a tractor. At sowing time it is still yoked oxen which pull a primitive wooden plough little changed since biblical times. The fields are stone-pocked, even though great cairns piled along their sides show that a diligent, if hopeless, effort has been made to remove them.

It seems a colourless countryside compared to the vivid blues and greens around the lake but during the long miles you discover it to be painted so skilfully from a palette of muted reds and browns and greys that the sepias merge into the buffs, grey rocks flush imperceptibly to soft pink and so to madder, and the distance becomes infused with warm apricot light. The strange luminosity of the *altiplano* weaves its own enchantment over land and sky and the traveller's eye, looking westward, is tricked into imagining that it can see almost to eternity. To the east, the Cordillera circumscribes the horizon and, below its peaks, the foothills are furrowed by the traces of terraces dating back to Inca times and earlier, testimony to a more prosperous and productive agriculture in bygone centuries. Some of these ancient terraces are still tilled today, but many lie fallow, for the land here is so barren that it has to be left seven years without cultivation to recover its strength.

These uplands are unobtrusive in the modulation of their moods and the subtle shifting of their tints. Only when the grain is young after the yearly rains is the earth spiked with unambiguous green, interspersed with the pale mauve of potato flowers, while at harvest time nature allows herself a brief festival of colour when the millet-like grains of the indigenous *quinua* and *cañahua* glow vermilion and orange against the yellow stalks of the barley. Harvest itself is often a collective affair, when whole communities gather together to help their neighbours bring in the crops.

Music and dancing are as much part of these poorer communities as among the more prosperous lakeside dwellers, and national and traditional fiestas are observed with enthusiasm. Once a week also, in places of any size, there is a market in the plaza where every conceivable object is sold: coca leaves, magic charms and potions, hot peppers and vegetables, local cloth, earthenware pots, reins, slings and ropes made from llama hide, wool for spinning and spindles to spin it on, and even a wide selection of musical instruments. In some places, barter is still the preferred system of exchange, and time no object, so that many hours are whiled away while the contenders, squatting on the ground, add and subtract from their minute piles of merchandise, against a chorus of vociferous argument.

At the San Roque toll one is precipitated into the urban sprawl of El Alto, the township that did not exist when I came originally to the country but which has mushroomed into a huge and scattered conurbation, containing nearly 800,000 inhabitants, almost as many as in the main city of La Paz down in the ravine, over which it looms almost menacingly. El Alto is feared as a ghetto of poor people, mostly exiles from poverty – stricken rural areas or unemployed miners, now that the main mining industry has collapsed – and as a focus of much social and political unrest.

Yet although there is much poverty and a dearth of basic services, such as water and sewage and electricity in its outer reaches, the main thoroughfares show evidence of a certain prosperity. It is a little-known fact that El Alto is now the largest exporter of manufactured goods in the whole country. The principal route into the city is fringed for a number of miles by an imposing array of brick buildings, some several storeys high. Imposing, that is, until you look closely, for none of them is finished. The ground floor may already function as a shop, and a grubby curtain or two flutter from an upstairs window, but most of the windows are just gaping holes, the brickwork left rough, and sometimes the topmost storey is just a mass of aspiring pillars and girders. There seems to be no evidence of any overall design, bits just being added as means become available. I used to think that this was the mark of a particularly engaging Bolivian trait – the triumph of hope over experience, denoting a persistent national optimism undeterred by the ineluctable realism of mere facts. Someone recently destroyed this fanciful and romantic notion, however, suggesting that the phenomenon had more to do with something much more mundane: so long as the building is not finished, then property tax does not have to be paid!

Small and medium entrepreneurs flourish in Bolivia much better than large companies, and El Alto is no exception. Little shops throng the sides of the road: tyre repair (strategically located near the largest potholes, road maintenance not penetrating the outer confines of the city), batteries, electrical repairs and a host of small-scale metal industries, as well as food shops and bakeries. Once again, like establishments are situated cheek by jowl with one another, apparently indistinguishable, leading to the conclusion that, though initiative is abundant, competition is not.

El Alto, fuelled by a constant influx of migrants from the interior desperately looking for a better life, is not only expanding to skeletal brick buildings beyond the San Roque toll towards the lake but also spilling over the rim of the crater-like ravine in which La Paz lies several hundred feet below. All the crumbling, eroded cliffs that loom over the city are covered with layer upon layer of jumbled red brick houses, like some gigantic collection of half-finished dolls' houses defying the laws of gravity and risking doom (and every year when heavy rains fall some of them slip into the abyss).

La Paz itself, once so relaxed, has become an overcrowded city where both driving and walking are a challenge for the intrepid. Unregulated buses and mini-buses and collective taxis stop with a shrieking of brakes whenever a possible passenger is glimpsed, bringing whole lines of traffic to a shuddering halt. The narrow cobbled streets of the old town, impossibly steep, constantly echo with the grinding of gears from ancient, ill-maintained vehicles struggling to reach the top. All the buses and mini-buses sport names, some fanciful and even witty. My favourite, blazoned on the back of a bus, proclaimed belligerently: '*Soy rebelde. Y qué?*' 'I am a rebel. So what?' It seemed to sum up, very neatly, a key trait of the national character.

That same strand of individualism, of the determination to survive against all the odds, is everywhere apparent in the crowded streets of La Paz. The pavements pullulate with people struggling to pass the hundreds of makeshift stalls occupying half the space and plying passers-by with everything from sunglasses to kitchen equipment. With the collapse of traditional industries such as mining, and high unemployment, it is the informal economy that keeps many Bolivians going and it is an art in which they demonstrate great natural ingenuity. You cannot help being struck by the large numbers of young people on the streets. Bolivia is a young nation, and many of them are high school or university students, for many private universities, albeit of varying quality, have sprung up in the city besides the public university of San Andres – often another hotbed of social unrest – where tuition is free. Education remains an abiding national passion among all classes with aspirations for self-improvement, but one fears for the future of these eager young students unless the country's prospects improve.

Amidst much brash modernity the traditional sights of the city still survive. In its upper reaches passers-by pick their way between *cholitas* squatting in long lines, almost clinging to the steep surface of the street, their bowler hats tilted at equally impossible angles, as if in counter-equilibrium, as they offer their wares of vegetables and fruits – a few eggs or tomatoes precariously balanced on top of one another – trinkets and protective charms tumbled together on the ground around them.

Then there are the more formal markets where you can get everything from huge cuts of meat to coca leaves and herbal remedies. The *cholitas* are the empresses of these cavernous, echoing halls, almost literally enthroned upon gigantic pyramids of fruits and vegetables, many of them trucked up from the sub-tropical valleys of the Yungas, just over the snow-capped mountains that gird the eastern approaches to the city. These ladies drive formidable bargains and many of them are reputed to be wealthy, but they still sturdily and proudly cling to the old ways of life and traditional forms of dress, their ample and colourful skirts artistically draped above their multi-hued produce like the panniers of an enormous embroidered crinoline.

The Calle Zagárnaga, though nowadays teeming with tourists and backpackers, still plies its ancient trade of witchcraft and magic potions designed to ward off evil spirits, including the dried foetus of llama that according to local superstition must be buried for luck in the foundations of every new dwelling. There is nothing one cannot buy in Calle Zagárnaga. Bright skirts and *aguayos* swing like banners on poles jutting out from the doorways, bowler hats nodding in serried ranks above. Inside the counters are piled with silverware of all kinds, old and new, and the walls are hung with the brightly beaded blouses and hats worn by the Indian women on ceremonial occasions, and even with flamboyant devil costumes and macabre masks in the tradition of the Oruro carnival.

Inevitably there are modern supermarkets too, but these are

mainly in the southern suburbs of the city. Situated in the comparative shelter of a river gorge, gouged out from the bleak expanses of the surrounding *altiplano*, La Paz was originally built in Spanish colonial times as a staging post to break the long overland journey by llama trains carrying the fabled wealth of Potosí to the Pacific coast for shipment in galleons to Spain. But the very geography which favoured its creation became a severe constriction to its further expansion in modern times. In recent years, however, it has extended further and further down the valley of the Choqueyapu and up into the surrounding hills. These are now the affluent suburbs to which most of the better-off families have migrated, as well as many offices and institutions formerly located in the centre of the city. The result is a sharpening of the class distinctions between its various levels, a phenomenon that has assumed troubling dimensions during the social upheavals of recent years.

La Paz has always been a rebellious town. It was here on 16 July 1809 that Pedro Domingo Murillo launched one of the very first cries to be heard on the continent for outright secession from the rule of the Spanish monarchy. His 'Defensive Junta' was short-lived and he was put to death. The precursors of liberty in Alto Perú were almost the last to achieve their liberty, for it was not until 1825 that the new Republic of Bolivia was established and named after the Liberator, who became its first president. But La Paz is a resilient city, despite all the buffeting of political upheavals during the 180 years since independence. It is not just its rarefied air, and the fact that it is the highest seat of government in the world that gives it its unique atmosphere but also the sturdy independence of its inhabitants and their gritty resolution to withstand all the challenges that an adverse nature and the world can throw at them.

Even so, at the end of a crowded day, it is a relief to take to the road again, towards the westering sun and the lake. The *campesinos* are gathering in their animals for the cold night ahead, flocks of under-sized sheep hurried along by women and small girls skilfully wielding slings armed with pebbles, llamas with coloured tassels in their elegant ears surveying both the landscape and their handlers with expressions of withering disdain, wayward cows and donkeys creating new hazards on the darkening road.

If dawn is my favourite time of day on the lake, sunset comes a close second. At Villa Margarita I take tea in my bedroom, the balcony windows thrown open on mountains, sky and lake throughout the day now closed, for as the sun sinks lower, so does the temperature. Lit by a pale golden light from the west, the mountains play out their last dramatic performance of the day. As the western sky deepens into gold and then fiery red, silhouetting the dark shapes of far hills on the distant fringes of the Lago Mayor that are far away in Peru, so the reflected and shifting colours of the sunset play on the peaks and gullies of the Royal Cordillera. The show does not last long for we are in the zone of the tropics here and night falls fast. First the distant Illimani fades into the gathering dark and then, one by one, the jagged peaks that stretch a hundred miles or so to the tumbled mass of the Illampu merge into the penumbra in their turn. Alone, the imposing cone of Huayno Potosí (literally the young man from Potosí), flaunts the last rays of the dying sun, flushes deep rose and then pink and is finally consumed as if by its own fires in an all-enveloping opalescent haze.

Down below the waters of the lake that a few moments before had been a mirror image of the pyrotechnics in the sky have also lapsed into darkness, swallowing up the small fishing boats that are once more laying their nets for the night in the bay below. Just before the light finally fails it is the far edge of the lake that seems to define the eastern horizon, as if marking the end of the known world.

There is still one more intense pleasure to savour before the day finally comes to an end. Every night, before retiring to bed, I stand for a while under the wide glass roof of the entrance porch of Villa Margarita. From there I have an untrammelled and sheltered view of the Andean sky, a huge dark vault studded with a myriad brilliant stars and galaxies, precious gems sparkling in the clear and frosty air. And on those nights blessed with a full moon the Sacred Lake comes alive again with all its ineffable magic.

The Aymaras for long ages past have had their own cosmography, reading the stars not only in order to predict the weather for their crops and their sowing and harvesting seasons, but also for portents of forthcoming cataclysmic events; natural and man made. It is at moments like these that one feels oneself caught up in the unfathomable mysteries of this most beautiful and magical place, adrift from the cares of the rest of the world.

172

12

Paradise Gained?

One of the most rewarding moments during the seesaw emotions of those years was sparked by an encounter with a fellow *tiquinense* in the pot-holed street that is the main thoroughfare of San Pedro. After we had exchanged the customary courtesies of tender enquiry about each other's health and those of all our family members, near and far, this man, whom I did not recall ever having met before, exclaimed enthusiastically, 'Señorita, when you came, you found a desert in Wila-Wila. Now you have transformed it into a paradise!'

True, the original land had been a rough, rocky promontory, inhospitably dry, but it had also possessed a wild beauty, its rugged contours muted by the softer contours and colours of wild flowers and shrubs native to the hostile ambiance of the *altiplano*. My little kingdom, though arid, was by no means barren. Apart from the peerless view, one of the main attractions for me initially was the grove of eucalyptus, the only large tree to flourish on the treeless *altiplano*. It is of course an interloper, some rather fancifully say the product of seeds brought under birds' wings from Chile. When I first moved in and had not yet hung curtains in my bedroom window, I loved to lie in bed and watch the leaves of the tree nearest the house weave delicate shadows in constant motion against a moonlit sky, reminiscent of the filigree pattern of bamboo foliage that had enchanted me in warmer climes. Alas, eucalyptus proves frail against blustery *altiplano* winds and the danger of large branches falling on the house obliged us to fell that tree and lop others nearby. But the eucalyptus irrepressibly springs back into life, lovely, fragrant silvery green leaves emerging from the severed trunk. Eucalyptuses grow very fast and soon the grove down by the shore had to be culled because they were obscuring the view. At first I had great difficulties in buying wood to fuel my log fire, scouring the villages all along the lakeshore. With this and subsequent harvests I enjoyed an ever plentiful supply of logs.

The *altiplano* does have a few native trees but they are more stunted in growth, though none the less graceful. The *kiswara* has beautiful clusters of creamy orange flowers, set off by almost clover-shaped leaves of a grey-green colour, silver-edged. Then there is the *kena* which has not dissimilar leaves but whose main distinction is its bright, reddish-brown bark, which peels off like the papery bark of birch. There was already one old *kiswara* when I acquired my land and I have added many more, as well as a number of *kenas*.

The most eye-catching of all the plants growing wild in Wila-Wila was the *kantuta*, a large spreading shrub bearing elegant, elongated bell-shaped flowers, most commonly a striking carmine red. Huge clumps of these flourished among the boulders and we left them where they were. There were also two or three specimens of the rarer, and more fragile yellow-flowered version. The *kantuta* is Bolivia's national flower, and it is not hard to see why. One of its varieties is bi-coloured with yellow at the base of the bell and red above. Thus, with the green of its sepals, it combines the three colours of the Bolivian flag. I have planted several of these but they are the weakest of all and do not do well.

There were many smaller flowering plants on the hillside that I found difficult to identify and efforts to obtain advice from someone with local botanical knowledge drew a blank. Cascades of bright yellow daisy-like flowers gilded my promontory, growing happily among the rocks, as did a pale mauve version of what appeared to be a malva, and a delicate apricot-hued flower closely resembling an evening primrose. There were also flowering cacti, some hugging the ground and, in their season, dazzling the eye with masses of starry blossoms in vivid colours. Others stood pillar-like, thorny and unprepossessing, until the ugly excrescences at their tip suddenly burst into huge white, lily-like flowers. They lasted little more than a day but filled the air with almost overwhelming fragrance. Then there is the *tarwi*, a species of wild lupin, with small blooms of a heavenly blue, set off by silvery-grey leaves. The seeds are harvested and eaten by local folk. All of these I increased in number.

I had less success with a tiny alpine-like plant that carpets the ground in some parts of the *altiplano*, starred with minute mauve flowers that give off perfume of a strength disproportionate to its

174

diminutive size. The most exciting discovery of all was of a bulb with daffodil-shaped leaves that, around December and January, produces the most exquisite blooms of a deep apricot shade fading into yellow and green. Clumps of it were growing in the lee of rocks that had to be dynamited to excavate the swimming pool and so had to be transferred to other parts of the garden, where they still flower, but less exuberantly. I had more luck in identifying this plant as I spotted a photograph in an article about the Cambridge Botanical Gardens, which described it as the Andean lily.

On all of my walks in the surrounding countryside, I kept a sharp lookout for new plants that were not already in the garden. I am almost ashamed to say that I carried a trowel and a plastic bag during those early days. My justification was that most of them were growing in profusion and that the locals often had scant consideration for them, destroying them at will in their cultivation or burning them off with surplus foliage at the end of the harvest.

My walks also led to some pleasant encounters. Once a wrinkled old lady, with a kindly face, instructed me in the virtues of the various species, obviously prized more for their utilitarian medicinal virtues than for the beauty which attracted me.

'This one is good for the stomach,' she explained. 'This one for headaches,' and so on.

On another occasion, driving round the old coast road to the Peruvian frontier, Alejandro, Aida and I spied a hillside rosy with a low-growing, wild form of cosmos, of a delightfully deep pink colour. We clambered up the hill and found that the patch of earth where they grew was lying fallow (land on the *altiplano*, being poor in quality, lies fallow for several years, and the rural farmers practise rotation of crops on a number of tiny parcels of land). A bowler-hatted lady tilling another patch nearby turned out to be the owner. She agreed readily that, for a consideration, we might dig up some of the cosmos plants. This, however, turned out to be a harder task that we had bargained for: the ground was rocky and we did not have the proper tools.

The lady obligingly said that her husband would dig some up and bring them to us – 'the white house, just before San Pedro' we explained. The hillside where these flowers grew was ten to fifteen kilometres away from Villa Margarita and I didn't think any more would come of this. But next morning at 7 am, a wizened little man in ragged jacket and ancient battered felt hat presented

175

himself at the gate of Villa Margarita, with a donkey laden with wild pink cosmos. The cost: 20 bolivanos. Those plants have seeded themselves all over the garden and are a delight to see in their due season.

It had been my aim to create a purely Bolivian garden, composed only of plants native to the *altiplano*, or at least to have one part of the garden devoted to this purpose. That proved yet another unrealisable dream, partly because it was difficult to achieve in any circumstances. An added problem in this instance was the number of people who enthusiastically and indiscriminately planted during my absences, and, above all, Alejandro's unsuspected passion for gardening and his extraordinarily gifted green fingers.

Alejandro adored roses. I had no quarrel with that, for I too love them and in my garden at Knill I have well over a hundred varieties. But the richer soils and damp conditions of the Welsh Marches, only five hundred feet above sea level, are a far cry from dusty, stony terrain at an altitude of fourteen thousand feet.

Alejandro was undeterred. At his insistence we bought roses to border the stone steps bordering the lawn below the *parrilla*. 'Yellow,' I specified, yellow roses being my favourite.

Alejandro duly went and purchased the rose bushes, all guaranteed by the vendor to be yellow. I had appreciated that it would probably be impossible to acquire named varieties of roses in La Paz but was unprepared to find that differentiation of colour was equally unattainable, unless you bought them when in bloom. Our first rose planting went well but every bush sported blooms of a different hue: yellow, white, pink, multicoloured – this last one possibly Masquerade. It was not the effect I intended but it evokes admiration from my visitors.

And so it went. Alejandro continued to buy and propagate roses and after two or three years we had rose bushes on all the high terraces of the garden as well as climbing up the white boundary walls with their picturesque tiled copings. At the last count we had nearly two hundred. Left to themselves they flower all year round, most richly from October to March, but even in the cold Andean winter, when there is almost permanent sunshine during the day; then we do cut them back, to stop them exhausting themselves.

Other 'imported' species also flourished: gazanias; pelargoniums; climbing geraniums; red-hot pokers, much beloved by humming birds and flower-piercers; gladioli; iris; dahlias; marguerites of various colours (which no self-respecting Villa Margarita could be without); crocosmia; fragrant honeysuckle so rampant it constantly threatens to block the gutters and bring the roof tiles off once again; passion flowers which bear huge fruits; and periwinkle, blue vinca, trailing over rocks and walls. Alejandro planted several mimosa trees, which have grown and flowered rapidly, but are no match for violent *altiplano* winds which tear out their tops or break large branches, leaving them sorely disfigured. Apple, peaches and cherry flower but seldom produce more than two or three fruits which are devoured by the birds before they are ripe.

In planting grass on the terraces and around the house, I applied the lessons I learned from Ethiopia, namely that local grass, though coarser, is much more resistant to climate vagaries than grass grown from fine, imported seed. In one corner we have a small plot where we grow potatoes and broad beans as is customary on the *altiplano* and sometimes lettuce, carrots, onions etc. A solar plastic tunnel has been on the agenda for some years so that we can grow more vegetables, but still has not materialised.

On the *altiplano*, virtually an upland desert except for the unpredictable rains that all come in one or two seasons of the year, irrigation is the indispensable key. In the early days when our water supply was scant, and as unpredictable as the rains, the competition between Alejandro's watering and my bath or shower was intense. They could not go on at the same time and Alejandro made it abundantly clear that his plants had a vastly higher priority than my cleanliness. In the fullness of time these problems were overcome. Water piped from the lake waters the garden, the only drawback being that it is slightly salty. Water from the well, probably infiltrated by lake water since it is down by the shore, is reserved for domestic purposes – baths, showers, washing and, boiled and filtered, for drinking. A network of pipes and taps covers the whole promontory to ease the task of watering, but it inevitably takes up several hours daily for the men working in the garden. A large underground tank constructed near the house stores thousands of litres. Needless to say, all this intricate system becomes useless when the electricity is cut and the pumps cannot work. Then we have to rely on the tiny tank in the water tower, which operates by gravity, for our most minimal needs.

In the corner of the swimming pool, where I had persuaded the second builder not to blow up the natural rock, I asked them to leave space for a tiny garden. There Alejandro planted three bougainvillea, one the common purple variety, the others carmine and pale yellow. They were trained up to the roof and fall over the rustic canopy of totora reed – the reed from the lake used to build the famous *balsas* which provided the inspiration for Thor Heyerdahl's Kontiki expedition – that protects the bar from excessive sunlight. The bougainvilleas thrived, but we made the mistake of planting the more prolific purple in front and so the more delicate colours struggle to be seen.

Plants in large ceramic pots arranged around the inner walls and the huge glass windows on the lakeside have found it hard to thrive in the hot sunlight. Two common bougainvilleas, thus planted, soon wilted, unlike those planted by the rocks and were also chanced outside. One promptly expired but the other, in a sheltered angle between the swimming pool and the perimeter wall, has flourished amazingly, and is constantly smothered in blooms, although it does not dare raise its head above the protecting wall. I wonder whether bougainvillea flowering outside at 14,000 feet is not a candidate for the Guinness Book of Records!

My 'hanging garden of Babylon', as I like to call it, has its fair share of wild life. Of the four-footed kind there are occasional sightings of *vizcacha*, a fox-like Andean creature. We have also had small resident colonies of the *conejo de las Indias*, literally 'rabbit of the Indies' but in fact a guinea pig. *Conejo de las Indias* is a favourite dish on the Bolivian menu. The ones in my garden did not suffer that fate but had the misfortune to catch the gimlet eye of a passing owl or eagle, and so were snapped up as a tasty morsel. The guinea pigs seemed only to eat the grass of the terraced lawns we had developed despite fierce climatic odds but the numerous mice nibbled even more precious plants. Sometimes the dogs would catch one, but during the brief period I had a cat she, alas, preferred a diet of birds. Luckily she was not very adept at catching them.

The proliferation and variety of birds is one of the greatest charms of Villa Margarita. One accomplished bird-watcher estimated that there were probably around fifty different species over a year. I described some of them in a letter sent in November 2001 to entertain an ailing friend in England:

You would be fascinated by the birds here. There are an astonishing number, considering the lack of vegetation, altitude and rather harsh climate. I like to think that there are many more in my garden now because we have given them trees, shrubs and flowers. Sadly, on Sunday, we found a dead bird in the swimming pool. Goodness knows how it got in, or how it met its end – perhaps crashing against the glass roof to get out. It was a lovely little dove, of which the proper name (according to my 'Birds of the High Andes') is bare-faced ground dove, altogether too brazen a name for such a gentle little creature. The bare skin round its eye which gives it its name is bright orange, so I prefer to call it the orange-eyed ground dove. They travel in small coveys, and, when disturbed, fly off with a delightful whirring sound.

At present we have a visitation of yellow-billed pintail duck down at the lake, a happy little flotilla splashing about in the shallows. Puna teal often come too. They have bright UN blue beaks.

There are also ruddy ducks, aptly named for their colouring, but you may think also for the problems they cause by inter-breeding with other species, and eventually eliminating them. I expect you've seen all the concerns in Europe about this, since they've taken to migrating from Spain. Well, the South American variety is equally promiscuous. The other day I saw one down by the lake consorting with a Puna teal. When I commented to one of my neighbours, who was tending his tiny plot of potatoes on the beach, that the pair consisted of two different species he looked at me pityingly and said: 'Oh no, Señorita, they're simply wearing different clothes!'

Andean coot are numerous, and look exactly like ours but bigger. Alas, all hunted by the locals. There are two sorts of gulls, the neat little Andean gull similar to our black-capped gull, and a larger gull, that I think flies up from the distant Pacific coast. A rarer sight is that of the flightless Titicaca grebe, found only here, but its haunts are further along the lakeshore.

Round the house we have a sparrow – the russet-cheeked sparrow. In the garden there are gaudy, noisy flocks of Andean (or black – difficult to distinguish) siskin, small, glossy black, splashed with bright yellow. A gloomier denizen is the morning sierra finch – aptly named, as it is all black and grey, and constantly emits a dreary, rasping cry. The male at least has

179

a cheerful yellow beak but the female is unrelievedly drab. In contrast the Peruvian sierra finch is altogether gayer (if you permit the word) in shades of green and yellow.

Several kinds of tiny, shimmering green humming birds, that I also find hard to distinguish, visit us at various times of the year. My favourite, though, is the giant humming bird, who also comes at certain seasons. He looks so sad and alone, poor thing, and very plain, with dull brown plumage. As large as a thrush, he makes an awful fist of hovering and the effort must absorb all his energy: he often sits exhausted on a bough or electric cable. I had an idea it was always the same one, and was sad when we didn't see him for the last couple of years. His favourite haunt was the big kantuta bush that was on this hillside before I came (the kantuta is the Bolivian national flower – lovely elongated crimson bells) but the other day I thought I saw him, or a relative, high up in a eucalyptus tree. Much more canny than the humming birds are the flower-piercers. No endless wing bashing for them! They simply perch on the base of the blossom, pierce a hole with their sharp beak, and get straight to the nectar. There's a beautiful one here, black, with dark red and white beneath – the rusty flower-piercer.

The main bird of prey is the Andean kestrel but one sometimes sees larger eagles, especially on the hills above the house. There, too, and occasionally in the garden, there is a woodpecker, which, there being practically no trees, has adapted by jabbing its beak into the ground for insects and larvae. It has the lovely name of Andean Flicker, but is rather a muted green/grey, with a pale yellow rump. Once, walking up the hill, I actually saw three or four large green parrots, but they must have had severe navigational problems and were right off course. On the other side of the hill there is a deeply cleft valley, sheltered between two lines of hills, where there is a micro-climate, and I've often seen huge flocks of tiny, chattering green parakeets and a few times they have found their way over the hill and flitted past the house like a flurry of spring leaves.

Some small birds have ridiculously long names. A neat little grey and white number, that I sometimes see among the flowers outside my study window, labours under 'cinereous ground-tyrant', though anything less tyrannical can scarcely be imagined.

There are many Puna mynahs in the garden, as well as members of the thrush and blackbird family. Owls have reputedly eaten my one little wild *conejo de las Indias* (literally 'rabbit of the Indies', but 'guinea pig' to you!), a recent arrival who used to enjoy nibbling the lawn outside the swimming pool.

I shall post this letter in La Paz, where I go tomorrow for a meeting with the ex (and I hope future) President Gonzalo Sánchez de Lozada and one of his chief lieutenants, to discuss a long overdue programme of social rural development (my hobby-horse for over 40 years here). Social unrest and violence is increasing every day down in the Chapare and the Cochabamba valley with the *cocaleros* (coca growers) and is having repercussions on the *altiplano*. Rumour had it that 'El Mallku' (the local Aymara leader) would block the road between here and La Paz tomorrow. I rang Capt Angel Corrales, the local Naval Commander, this morning to enquire. Grave mistake! He wants my lawn mower again tomorrow. Fancy having all these naval vessels but no lawn mower! He says they are making one! He also says the road will be open tomorrow. I hope it will be on Saurday when I go to La Paz again to start my journey back to UK, via New York.

The rather throwaway reference at the end of this letter to troubles in Cochabamba and potential roadblocks masked a critical point in the crescendo of civil unrest that was to have unpredictable consequences for the country and, in microcosm, for Villa Margarita.

PART FOUR

Things Begin to Fall Apart

13

Alarums and Excursions

The social problems ever simmering in Bolivia had come to the boil in 2000, halfway through General Banzer's presidency. Two parallel grievances in the valley of Cochabamba lay at the heart of the matter.

One was related to the supply of water to the city, a conflict that reached such heights of violence as to be nicknamed *la Guerra del Agua* – the water war. The other arose in the nearby countryside, where the *cocaleros*, or coca growers, were literally up in arms on account of President Banzer's proclaimed intent to eliminate all cultivation of the coca plant in Bolivia by 2002 (the last year of his presidency) except for that grown in the higher valleys of the Yungas. The latter was supposed to be produced exclusively for traditional use among the indigenous dwellers of the *altiplano* and was, exceptionally, permitted by the UN Convention on the Illicit Trafficking of Illicit Drugs and Pschotropic Substances that I had helped to negotiate in Vienna in 1988.

Banzer's ambitious policy – some might say over-ambitious, even rash – had been launched in response to the demands of the United States government. Compliance was deemed necessary if Bolivia was to remain in the good books of its huge neighbour to the north, on whom it was almost totally dependent. It was not merely a question affecting direct bilateral aid; the United States also called the shots in international financial institutions such as the International Monetary Fund, the World Bank and the Inter-American Development Bank, all of whom provided invaluable support to Bolivia's fragile economy.

The *cocaleros* were led by a charismatic Aymara, Evo Morales, a master of inflammatory language, one of the many thousands who had come down from the poverty-stricken *altiplano* to seek a better – but still hard – life growing coca in the lowland area of the Chapare.

185

On the *altiplano* there was another dissident movement, led by an equally fiery *caudillo*, Fernando Quispe, also known as *El Mallku*. He too was an Aymara but his was an indigenous movement, aiming to reassert Aymara ascendancy. Some years earlier he had adopted terrorist tactics, attempting to blow up an electrical installation, and had spent some time in gaol. His base was in Achacachi, a notoriously violent small town a little way off the main road from La Paz to the lake, and thus to my house.

El Mallku's demands were nothing less than apocalyptic. He wanted a return to Aymara traditions and values, in particular to the age-old Aymara form of government, based on the *ayllu*, or village community, dating back to the pre-Inca Kingdom of Kollasuyu. He went so far as to declare the independent republic of Kollasuyu, with Achacachi as its capital. Along with this went other well-founded and long unrequited demands for a better life for the *campesinos*. Bizarrely, these included the provision of one thousand tractors. Sceptics, of whom there were many, pointed out that there is no record that either the Aymaras or the Incas, whose famed agricultural techniques sustained a large population on the inhospitable *altiplano*, discovered such mechanical marvels. But consistency was the least of El Mallku's concerns.

In September all these disaffected groups came together and brought the country to a standstill by blocking all the main roads. In a country like Bolivia, tortuous geography and poverty of means conspire to make this all too easy. Only a few major roads thread their way through the mountains and even across the flat plains of the *altiplano*. They form the backbone of the country's communications. Simultaneously the trunk roads between La Paz and other major towns, such as Oruro and Cochabamba, as well as between Cochabamba and the major oil centre of Santa Cruz in the eastern lowlands, and between La Paz and Lake Titicaca, all came to a full stop. Hordes of angry *campesinos* and *cocaleros* thronged all these highways, building barriers of rocks and broken glass, cutting down trees to block the passage of any vehicles and throwing rocks and stones at any imprudent driver who tried to make his way through. The threats were reinforced by sticks and machetes and in some cases even by ancient muskets.

In short order the whole country was reduced to total chaos. On the road between Santa Cruz and Cochabamba busloads of tourists, numbering thousands in all, many of them foreign, were stranded

186

without food or water. After some days of this intolerable situation the government was obliged to send military contingents from Santa Cruz to liberate them.

The impasse lasted nearly three weeks and was resolved only after difficult negotiation. It was not a lasting solution but rather a temporary truce, in what was to become a long-running battle between the large mass of the poorer population and a government regarded as alien to their needs. The gravest of all the lessons to be learned was that the concerted power of these disaffected groups could, at the drop of a hat, bring the country to a standstill and the brink of economic disaster. It was a lesson no one was likely to forget, least of all the leaders of the popular protest. My warnings in 1995 of the danger of an imitation of the Chiapas revolt in Mexico taking root in Bolivia, and of a population that had lost faith in any form of established government, were beginning to look all too prescient.

I had not been present in Bolivia during those days but, as everyone had feared, the truce was proved fleeting, and in July 2001 I experienced some of the consequences at first hand.

In June I had been in Ecuador, working with US Southern Command on one of the simulated peacekeeping training exercises for US and Latin American military personnel for which I volunteered my services every year. These had begun to include dramatically realistic staged incidents, all filmed. In Honduras, the previous year, acting as the Secretary General's Special Representative heading a UN mission in a fictitious, conflict-ridden country, I had been taken hostage, amid red smoke and simulated bombs, by masked guerrillas who abseiled down from the roof. I was thrown into a jeep and driven, blindfolded, into the bush. When I was eventually released I was flung over the shoulders of one of the masked guerrillas (in actuality a young Honduran Special Services officer, who proved agreeably handsome when he removed his disguise) and dumped into the midst of the morning assembly of some six hundred officers from all over the Americas, among more red smoke and loud explosions.

In Ecuador I was once again the object of a 'hostage incident', this time being dragged from my vehicle on a remote road in the bush. My security guards were 'killed' and I was tied blindfold to a tree. On this occasion the military were canny enough to seek a political solution first before resorting to military crash tactics of

187

search and rescue (in Honduras they had got it wrong, and I was nearly 'killed'). I was delivered back, blindfold, on a distinctly rickety stretcher, an experience almost as unnerving as being thrown over someone's shoulder.

Ecuador was also in a high state of tension. During our earlier planning meeting for the exercise in February 2001, there had been marches on the capital, Quito, by the indigenous population, similar to those in Bolivia. There was also grave concern about the Plan Colombia, recently introduced by the United States in Ecuador's strife-torn neighbour to the north, which had led to incursions into Ecuador by Colombian guerrillas and civilian refugees fleeing the conflict. The Ecuadorean generals feared that our routine exercise could be interpreted as the training ground for a UN peacekeeping force patrolling the border between the two countries, which was certainly not the case.

In the next few weeks some real-life adventures followed. The first is described in my annual letter:

Between the end of the exercise in Ecuador and my return to Bolivia I decided to give myself a holiday in the Galapagos Islands. It was hardly an unmitigated success. First my rucksack was stolen from beside my feet at the airport as I was checking in – from me, the experienced world traveller! It was a daring act for we were a small group in a special area, with wide spaces around, but although I detected the loss in seconds the culprit could not be found and police were conspicuously absent. I lost my best camera and binoculars, all my toiletries and make-up and, worst of all, my address book and telephone numbers. After this inauspicious start, on board the plane my eye fell on my horoscope in the local newspaper. 'Your love life will continue complicated for some time yet' it warned (interesting, since it was non-existent) but went on consolingly: 'You will have agreeable surprises in other spheres.' Since a stolen rucksack did not fall into this category, I awaited great things from my trip.

We were 14 passengers on a small boat on which we embarked on the main island of Santa Cruz, where I bought what toiletries I could find (hairbrushes are unobtainable on the Galapagos!). We sailed all night and spent the next morning scrambling round the island of Santa Isabela, on a very rocky path, watching blue-footed boobies and other natural life at close quarters. Just as we approached the Zodiacs to go back to the boat for lunch a huge American just a pace ahead of me (250 pounds by his own later admission), slipped and fell backwards onto me crashing me onto the rocks, with him on top. Second agreeable surprise? He was nicely cushioned by me and unharmed. By some miracle I did not damage my ever dicey back, nor break a bone, but I took the skin off the back of my right leg and bruised it badly so that I could barely walk for several days. The whole leg went bright blue, so I felt I could well qualify to join the ranks of the blue-footed boobies.

I was thus not in the pink of condition when I travelled on to La Paz and my mood was not cheered by advance telephone warnings from Aida that countrywide protests, mass demonstrations and road blockages had broken out again. Villa Margarita was isolated, food was running short, electricity cut and other essentials such as cooking gas and petrol could not be obtained.

Against her advice I proceeded with my plans. Being an obstinate soul I refused to be daunted and told myself I had weathered worse situations in Bolivia over the previous forty years. I also felt a strong responsibility to see how my employees were faring. From the Hotel Plaza in La Paz I spoke again to Aida. By this time cellular phones had reached Tiquina but reception was garbled and intermittent in communications with La Paz, although perversely very good with the outside world. Nevertheless, her message came through loud and clear:

'Don't risk yourself, Señorita. The road is completely blocked, even between here and Tiquina. *Las barcazas* [the pontoons] are not crossing the lake. The *campesinos* are very angry. Many are drunk. Some are armed. El Mallku threatens to go on indefinitely, *hasta las últimas consecuencias*' (literally 'until the ultimate consequences' a bloodcurdling threat beloved of all Bolivian strikers and protesters but of uncertain meaning in reality as it is seldom pursued to its logical conclusions). 'Por favor, Señorita, please listen to me,' and she ended with the long drawn-out 'ay-ay...' of despair that so aptly reflected her doom-laden outlook on life.

The same counsel came from less emotional sources, but I persisted and I telephoned a former naval commander at Tiquina,

Captain Torrico. I always had good relations with the naval commanders of the Tiquina base but Captain Torrico was my favourite. He had carried out first-class social and environmental projects in the surrounding area, and together we had launched an unsuccessful attempt to deal with the garbage problem in San Pedro. Through him I had been able to negotiate a contract with the navy for the paving of my entrance drive, previously a quagmire when the rains came. Captain Torrico was now stationed in La Paz.

'Well,' he said, after some consideration, 'there may be a way. You see, by chance, our admiral's wife's sister is the wife of the owner of Crillón Tours.' Crillón Tours is one of the two largest tourist companies in Bolivia and operates *aliscafas* or hydrofoils, across the lake to Peru. It also has the best hotel on the lakeshore, some way before Tiquina, at Huatajata.

'They are very worried about the damage to the tourist trade,' the Captain went on, 'and so we have arranged occasional escort by a *caiman* [literally a crocodile, the slang name for a lorryload of armed men] as far as Guaqui [a port at the southern end of the lake]. The road to Guaqui is also blocked but not so severely. At Guaqui they board an *aliscafa* and go by water to the hotel or to the Islands of the Sun and the Moon, to Copacabana and Peru. We could perhaps arrange for you to be dropped off at your landing stage at Villa Margarita. There is one leaving tomorrow but you'll have to be up at the crack of dawn.'

At 4.30 am next morning a four-wheel-drive vehicle drew up outside the hotel and I clambered in, with the rather large amount of luggage I had needed in New York and Ecuador. We drove to the Crillón office and sat there until nearly six o'clock. At length a Japanese gentleman got in, accompanied by a Bolivian girl from the company. She looked vaguely Japanese, perhaps from one of the colonisation settlements in the eastern lowlands, and spoke Japanese as well as Spanish, a rare combination but very necessary in that instance since the traveller spoke no word of Spanish. It transpired that he was a lone mountaineer who had come to scale Andean peaks and had first to acclimatise himself to the altitude ... and to a lot of other things, I thought to myself. Another four-by-four joined us, filled with a Paraguayan family of tourists.

But the promised *caiman* did not turn up, and with the passage of time the whole purpose of travelling under cover of darkness, before the barricades were mounted, was becoming meaningless.

190

Eventually a very decrepit lorry lumbered into sight, swaying over the cobbles. The open back part bristled with soldiers brandishing rifles, more like a ponderous porcupine than a crocodile. Our hearts lifted, but not for long. An even more essential element than weapons was missing – petrol. Some protracted pecuniary negotiations – par for the course in Bolivia – ensued, followed by a lengthy visit to a petrol station, until at last we were on our way, up the hill to El Alto and then across the *altiplano*, just as a cold dawn was breaking.

The road to Guaqui passes by Tihuanacu, the ancient pre-Inca ruins. In places rocks and stones were scattered over the road but they were easily removed or circumvented, and no living person came out to bar our passage. Guaqui was also deserted, a decaying little town now that it is no longer the railhead connecting the ancient Scottish-built ferries that used to plough the lake between Puno in Peru and Guaqui, to the train to La Paz. Both they and the railway are long since gone.

The local agent and the boatman who were to arrange our transfer to the *aliscafa* were not visible either, nor could the key be found for the company shed. After circling round the crumbling town's rough earthen streets several times and banging on doors in apparently random fashion the two men were located, and an elderly lady, clad in black, was roused, protesting and still putting the finishing touches to her dress as she stumbled out of the door, to produce the missing key.

Soon we were all huddled aboard the hydrofoil. It was bitterly cold. Our vessel reared itself up and, scattering wildfowl in every direction, rocketed out of the tiny harbour, spewing spray and a trail of creamy white foam. It is not my preferred mode of travel, especially not in these surroundings. We abruptly shattered the serenity of the lake and of the morning and must have woken even the most deeply slumbering of the still sleeping inhabitants of Guaqui.

The boat was small. The Paraguayans sat grouped at the front, the Japanese man, his interpreter and I behind them. Before we set off, and the vessel was still steady, our silent Japanese friend carefully set up a camera tripod in front of us. I was secretly rather touched that he was going to photograph this doughty little group embarking on an intrepid and historic venture. How wrong I was. It soon became abundantly clear that the only subject he was interested in recording for posterity was himself. This he did most assiduously, from every angle and in a variety of poses, for the rest of the voyage.

As we sped across the lake a lively discussion sprang up between the two-man crew as to who should be dropped off first and where, and whether the hydrofoil could navigate the shallower waters round my landing stage. They eventually decided a smaller model was needed and, by radio with Huatajata, arranged a rendezvous in the middle of the lake just in front of Villa Margarita. I could see my small staff gathered at the landing stage, anxiously witnessing the delicate manoeuvre as I and my copious luggage were gingerly decanted into the smaller boat. I could just imagine the expression on Aida's face. Amazingly, however, this potentially accident-laden operation passed off without mishap. I was soon standing on shore, embraced and congratulated by my incredulous employees.

I confess that I was more than a little chuffed by their reaction and later by that of the friends in La Paz who had all declared it to be impossible to get to the lake. Ironically, however, hardly had I arrived and been able to deal with all the problems of my household – we could get locally killed meat but no vegetables, apart from potatoes, or fruit and even bread was scarce – than I had to start thinking about how I could get back to the airport. I had to fulfil commitments in Europe and there was no sign of any let-up in the protesters' adamant determination to maintain their blockade.

As I walked on the hill and chatted to my *campesino* neighbours, I could not help asking the obvious question: 'Why are you continuing to block the roads? This is hurting you as much as the government: you can't get food in or produce to market, your boatmen are losing trade because no one is crossing the lake, the tourists are not coming and your little shops in San Pedro have nothing to sell.'

'It is so,' they would all sigh in unison. 'We are suffering much and we are not in agreement with the blockade.'

'Then why...?'

'You do not understand, Señorita. We are afraid of El Mallku. If we don't cooperate we are fined much money. And he may even seize our plots of land.'

The old order of repression and intimidation that has bedevilled Bolivia for centuries is giving way to another no less and potentially even more severe, I reflected to myself.

Meanwhile the conflict was worsening. A couple of busloads of tourists had got through as well as a truck bearing much-needed gas canisters for Tiquina but then things got very nasty. A number of people were hurt, some tourists were wounded from flying glass when their bus was attacked and the government ordered that no one should attempt to cross the barricades.

For my get-away, the Bolivian Navy was now the only hope. How useful it is, even in a landlocked country! I conferred with Capitán Ángel Corrales, the current commander. He too was dubious but later brightened. The stand-off was lasting too long, the economy was badly affected by it and the government was losing patience. They had moved two battalions of soldiers up from Santa Cruz and these were now being bivouacked along the road to La Paz, awaiting orders.

'They have to be fed,' explained Captain Ángel, 'and so I have soon to send an armed convoy to La Paz to collect provisions. I may be able to send you to the city in that convoy. But,' he added with a disarming smile, 'I will only arrange that if you agree to give a lecture on peacekeeping to my naval officers.'

That seemed a small price to pay. The lecture was scheduled for the day before the convoy was due to depart. It took place in a huge barracks of a room, with serried rows of seats arising in a circle from the middle. There sat the captain, presiding over the proceedings, and I stood shivering. Outside the winter sun was bright but here it was bitterly cold and my teeth were so nearly chattering that I wondered how I could be intelligible.

That was not the least of my problems in keeping my audience engaged. I had not long begun when a soldier burst into the room bearing a message written on a scrap of paper for the captain and whispering noisily to him. This charade was repeated several times and eventually the commander went out, came in again and went out. Communications with the naval base were still fairly embryonic and as I chuntered on about peacekeeping in the context of modern warfare, I could not resist feeling that I was witnessing in this intrusive sideshow something akin to the ancient art of despatching messages by runners armed with a cleft stick.

When the session ended the captain apologised. 'You see, while you were speaking, I received orders that the Minister of Government has decided to take military action to break up the road blockages and disperse the protesters and I had to deploy my men.'

This, we both agreed, was a very grave step that could lead to

193

armed conflict. Once again I was struck by the many ironies of the occasion. While I was earnestly preaching peacekeeping, all around me war plans were being hatched.

The captain then gave me my marching orders: 'The food will leave tomorrow morning at 7.30 sharp. Please be at the dock at that time with your luggage.'

In a country with a chronically insouciant attitude towards time, the military alone are sticklers for punctuality and so I was there on the dot. Captain Ángel, who usually lives up to his name, was today looking less than angelic. In fact he was distinctly cross. Overnight the Minister of Government had had second thoughts and rescinded his stern order of the previous day. The military were to clear the blockages from the roads but not apply force.

'There is nothing worse,' grumbled the captain, 'than making threats and then withdrawing them.' I sympathised, remarking that such vacillation was anathema to military commanders all over the world.

'The *campesinos* have vowed to attack all civilians who try to get through. They will surely go for you, even in our convoy. The only solution is to disguise you as a Bolivian soldier.'

With this he produced a voluminous camouflage reefer and a cap which I pulled down as far as possible over my hair and disguised my face with dark glasses. The convoy was waiting on the other side of the straits and it was in this guise that I hauled myself up beside the driver in the cabin of the first truck. Armed soldiers were in the back and on all the other vehicles.

The journey to the city from San Pablo normally takes two hours. On that day it lasted over five. Hardly had we left the square of San Pablo when we encountered, every few yards, a daunting barrier of rocks, stones and broken glass. In some places there were even large tree trunks dragged from who knows where on this predominantly treeless plain. Each time we met these obstacles we had to stop while the soldiers leapt out to clear a way through the rubble.

At Chúa, the headquarters of the Bolivian Marines, we stopped for consultation with the commanding officer and news of what lay ahead. After Chúa we caught up with his men, heaving rocks and débris off the road, together with the battalions from Santa Cruz. I felt sorry for these young conscripts, shivering in tropical uniforms quite unsuited to the winds and bone-chilling cold of an Andean winter and housed only in flimsy tents.

With these reinforcements we made better progress but it was weary work and the afternoon was well advanced by the time we arrived at the upper reaches of the city. The route had been thronged all along by protesting *campesinos* but most of them merely looked on sullenly as their handiwork was undone, at least sufficiently for us to pass. Perhaps they were intimidated by the armed convoy. Everyone knew, however, that that night all our painstaking work would be undone when they erected the barricades anew. To the relief and the surprise of all of us, there was only one incident of violent aggression when, in a village, a drunken *campesino* brandished a stick and shouted threats. Fortunately, nothing serious happened, nor did anyone rumble my disguise.

I stayed the night at a hotel and next day managed to reach the airport and fly off to northern and calmer climes.

14

Death Bolivian Style

The years 2000 and 2001 were traumatic for me as well as for my adopted country. In October 2000 my beloved aunt Christina died six weeks before her ninetieth birthday, which everyone had confidently expected her to reach with the same ease and grace that had characterised her whole life. Her illness had come upon her suddenly and at first had not seemed life-threatening, so the shock of her passing had been all the greater. I was devastated, for she was more like an elder sister than an aunt, having lived with my parents until I was six years old, a story I have told in my autobiography, *Never Learn to Type*. In my childhood she had been my idol and my glamorous role model and she retained her rare beauty even into her older age, with her wit and humour and unquenchable joie de vivre quite unimpaired. Her voice on the telephone was as light and lilting as that of an eighteen-year-old and she always had something amusing to tell.

She was the last of my close living relatives, so her death left a yawning hole in my life and an overwhelming feeling of loneliness and isolation. I knew I could not spend Christmas at Knill without her, and fled to Bolivia.

There Gonzalo Sánchez de Lozada, the former president with whom I had worked, and his family were immensely kind to me, as were other Bolivian friends. Being a Latin and Catholic country, Bolivia celebrates Christmas Eve, the *Nochebuena*. Some close friends in La Paz invited me to share that special occasion with their family, in the intimacy of their home. The Sánchez de Lozadas held a more Anglo-Saxon celebration on Christmas Day, inviting a large group of friends to a traditional Christmas dinner at midday in their sun-drenched garden.

I stayed the night of Christmas Eve in La Paz and on Christmas morning wandered up to San Francisco, the beautiful baroque church that has survived since colonial times. There I found a continuous Mass in progress. The place was packed, mostly with people of obviously modest means: women in their *polleras* and bowler hats, children strapped to their backs in brilliantly hued *aguayos*, the men with felt trilbys, woollen scarves twined closely round their necks and shabby jackets. It was hard to find a bench to perch on. The music was an eclectic mixture of ecclesiastical themes, interspersed with infectiously joyous Andean folk dance tunes, *villancicos* (traditional carols) and some incongruous foreign interlopers, like 'I'm dreaming of a White Christmas'! People wandered in and out all the time, children scampered about and even dogs came to inspect the proceedings. The air was heavy with incense, overcoming the smell of many unwashed human bodies pressed tightly together. I was struck by the notable absence of anyone resembling the middle classes, save for a very few. It was an astonishing illustration of the devotional fervour of the ordinary people, most very poor and with few prospects of betterment in their lives.

It was an extraordinarily potent atmosphere and I sat for a long time, drinking it all in and deep in my own thoughts of my lost loved ones. Presently a young girl squeezed in beside me. In her arms she held a tiny baby. We started talking, for the church was abuzz with conversation as well as incantations, and she told me, weeping, that the baby had a congenital heart ailment but that she and her husband, also very young, could not afford the treatment that would save its life. They were both well educated by Bolivian standards, but like so many others here he had just lost his job and she had given hers up to look after the baby. The sum of money needed was pitifully small.

Bolivia is awash with such stories, not all of them genuine. Perhaps I was emotionally vulnerable on that day, but theirs rang true to me. I am neither very religious or superstitious but it seemed a fitting coincidence that the encounter should have happened at a moment when I was remembering my own lost family. After all, no one else had spoken to me although I was surrounded by many in desperate need. And Christina, I felt in a surge of certainty, would want me to help.

I gave them such money as I had with me and invited them to visit me in the hotel on my next visit to La Paz. They duly came and for a few moments I held the frail baby girl in my arms. I

197

gave them the rest of the money they needed and asked them to keep in touch, in case they needed more. But I never heard from them again and so never learned the baby's fate.

That year I also spent New Year's Eve with the Sánchez de Lozada family. At midnight we all embraced and drank the traditional toasts for mutual health, happiness and prosperity. Back at Villa Margarita my small staff and I did the same. But it was not to be a good year for Alejandro and Aida.

They had worked for me for over seven years and to my great satisfaction, despite Aida's incurably lugubrious outlook on life and her rooted distrust of human nature. Alejandro was a more placid character, seldom roused to ire but on the rare occasions on which this happened – usually because of Aida's nagging – prone to sulk for days on end. By his own admission he had never gardened before, but faced with the challenge of taming the rugged promontory at Villa Margarita his hidden gift had blossomed. He was also an excellent driver and mechanic and, together with Aida, a loyal and devoted caretaker.

Alejandro was from Sucre, the legal capital of Bolivia in the south, though I believe his family had roots in Tarija, even nearer the frontier with Argentina. Thus he had a rural background, albeit in gentler climes than the harsh rigours of the *altiplano*. As a young man he had joined the Bolivian Air Force, where he had learned his trade as driver and mechanic, and had dramatic tales to tell of his experiences at the air force base at El Alto, above La Paz, during the momentous and bloody revolution of 1952.

Alejandro suffered from a series of ailments, none of them apparently serious – rheumatic pains in his feet and legs, digestive problems. He went off to Sucre for a strange cure and came back saying he felt much better, but not long after, in March 2001, as he drove me to the airport, he asked for time off during my absence for more medical consultations. These, I was informed at long distance, had not produced conclusive results. Alejandro's doctor assured him that his constant stomach pain was not serious, but offered no diagnosis. A few weeks later Aida called me, weeping, to tell me that Alejandro had collapsed and was in a small clinic in the upper reaches of La Paz, where he had undergone an emergency operation on his gall bladder. That was unpleasant, but did not sound threatening.

I was anxious to ensure that he got the best medical treatment available and, since my commitments in Europe would not permit me to return to Bolivia immediately, I telephoned my own doctor in La Paz, Fely Hartmann, who had cared for me for over forty years, and asked him to visit Alejandro and advise what should be done. I also asked close friends to see Alejandro and liaise with the doctor. Aida and I were in constant contact and I urged her to move Alejandro to the best clinic available in La Paz at my expense.

That was exactly what Fely recommended to me when he had reviewed the situation. I hastened to tell Aida but, after consulting Alejandro, she told me that he was adamant that he wished to remain where he was, as he had great confidence in his doctor, who was also the surgeon.

But the news got steadily and alarmingly worse. The wound from the first operation refused to heal and Alejandro underwent a second operation and then a third. Fely went again to see him, this time with other colleagues to form a *junta de médicos*, to provide a joint second opinion and hold consultations with the operating surgeon. Once again, however, both the latter and Alejandro himself refused to contemplate a move to another clinic.

By now, Alejandro's life was hanging on a thread. Aida met me at the airport at 6 am on 10 May when I arrived bleary-eyed after the customarily dreadful all-night American Airlines flight from Miami. We drove straight to the clinic and hammered on the door. Bolivian health services can be of variable quality but there is always someone there and visiting hours are fluid. Even at that early hour the door was opened promptly by a small young man who told us he was a medical aide, and was looking after Alejandro. The clinic was small and modest, but it looked reasonably clean although, judging by the furnishings, I could not help wondering about the availability of modern equipment.

Alejandro was lying in a room of his own, inappropriately furnished with an overstuffed sofa and chairs of bright red pseudo-leather. A crumpled camp bed in a corner indicated where the young man had slept. He seemed touchingly devoted and assured us he watched over Alejandro day and night.

Alejandro's face was a terrible, yellowish colour, his usually ruddy cheeks deeply sunken. He was being fed by a drip, since he could not take normal food, and ominous-looking tubes seemed to sprout everywhere, the main one, we were told, to drain poison from his navel.

I had to suppress tears when Alejandro managed a pallid smile when he saw me and grasped my hand. I held it tightly and, mustering all the conviction I could into my voice, told him that he had now turned the corner, that we loved and needed him, and begged him to promise me that he would do his best to get better. He could not speak but smiled again, pressed my hand, and whispered '*Si*'. We, in turn, promised to come back soon.

As we rose to go the clinic's resident doctor came in. When we asked him for an opinion of Alejandro's prospects he was cautious but seemed confident that the worst was over. Nonetheless, it was in despondent mood that we drove out to the lake, Aida quietly weeping most of the way.

At Villa Margarita more bad news awaited me. My cousin John, the constant companion of my childhood, had died the day before. We had not seen one another much in recent years but had kept close through correspondence. Recognised as an accomplished archaeologist, though he had no formal university training, John was an eccentric genius, always bubbling with imaginative new ideas and living life to the full. He was still full of energy when, the previous Christmas, he had suddenly been diagnosed with cancer.

With another cousin I had driven up to Cumbria to see him, a difficult journey because the areas around both our homes were restricted for travel by the outbreak of foot-and-mouth disease in cattle that had blighted the countryside. We had spent two marvellous days together, recalling our childhood exploits. John was in excellent spirits, confident that he would live a few more years. Yet, when I kissed him goodbye he gave me a long look and I detected in his eyes the fear that we would never see one another again. In the succeeding weeks he had seemed to do well but then there was a sudden decline and now he was gone, much sooner than expected, barely five months after the diagnosis of his illness.

We had seen Alejandro on a Thursday and Aida and I had planned to return to La Paz at the weekend, though Aida had been reluctant, since Alejandro's daughter by his first marriage, with whom she had a difficult relationship, had assumed the dominant role of caring for her father. Aida felt she was being deliberately excluded.

Then, at 5 am on Saturday 12 May, my cell-phone rang. I leapt out of bed and onto the chilly balcony, the only place where there was half-decent reception. I grew colder still when the caller announced herself as Alejandro's daughter and told me her father had just died. I then had the awful task of breaking the news to Aida. Together we wept.

In Bolivia funerals take place within twenty-four hours or so. Alejandro's was to be on Sunday afternoon. In the morning Aida and I drove to La Paz with Marcus, the now retired UN driver who had first recommended Alejandro and Aida to me in 1993. He was in his best black suit, Aida in black trousers and a black coat. With her black hair she looked the epitome of dignified mourning.

The body had been taken to a community hall in one of the poorer areas of the city. There it lay in an open coffin, raised on a dais and surrounded by flaming candles and masses of flowers, huge wreaths and garlands, ostentatious in their vivid colours. I realised with a pang that Aida and I, having travelled in from the country on a Sunday, had come empty-handed.

There were a lot of mourners already there, arranged around the sides of the hall, clad in funereal black. The group on the right was the most numerous. There was a pall of silence and no one moved as Aida and I stood hesitantly in the doorway. Then a man detached himself from the left-hand side and, taking Aida by the hand, led us to his group where we sat on hard wooden chairs and contemplated the scene. The man who had helped us, Aida whispered, was her nephew, the group on the right led by Alejandro's daughter. She had pointedly ignored Aida's entrance. It was as if she had had no part of Alejandro's life, despite thirty-five years of living together.

After a while her nephew indicated that we should approach the coffin, and pay our last respects. I had observed that most people went up to the head of the coffin, crossed themselves and kissed the dead man's face. Aida simply stood silent, gazing on him. I could not bear even to look at him and remained at the foot of the dais, head bowed, bitterly regretting that I had not thought of bringing one of Alejandro's own roses to place in the coffin. That would have been a far more fitting tribute, I thought, than all these gaudy wreaths.

The vigil seemed to go on interminably. It was very cold. Whispers went round that the priest, who was to conduct religious rites before

201

the coffin, could not be found. Then a sort of female deaconess swathed in black appeared and began to intone prayers and chant interminable Ave Marias, in which some of the faithful joined. Then silence would fall and, after an interval in which everyone looked hopeful but the tardy priest had still not appeared, she would start all over again. I found myself wondering irreverently whether this was another instance of the chronic unpunctuality endemic here, or whether there was some valid reason for the delay. Even more irreverently, the constant dirge of Ave Marias and references to the virgin's womb were becoming exceedingly tedious.

At long last the priest appeared. There was no apology or explanation. He launched into a rapid gabble of prayers as if in a hurry to get the business over. More Ave Marias and eulogies of the virgin's womb and then the coffin was carried out, followed by the mounds of flowers, and we all filed out in search of our vehicles.

After that the whole event lapsed into something dangerously resembling farce. The main cemetery of La Paz is a vast sprawling complex covering a large area high above the city. A confusing network of steep roads wind their way up to it. Before long we had lost the hearse and funeral cortège. Luckily Marcus knew the area like the back of his hand but then, incongruously, we ran into a festival of folk dancers, all twirling skirts, brightly-hued costumes and gaily rhythmic music much at odds with our mood. We had to make another detour and at last arrived at the cemetery, anxious that we were too late.

Outside its high white walls *cholitas* were selling flowers for the dead, others cooking pungently smelling food for the hungry living. Inside there was a church and behind a bewildering maze of narrow, cobbled alleyways each flanked by three-storeyed rows of niches in which the dead are laid to rest, a practice common all over Latin America. There were no green spaces, tombstones or graves.

Surprisingly we had arrived first and had to wait for the coffin. This was just as well for the nave of the church was full of coffins and mourners jockeying for position in a macabre, disorderly queue. It was difficult to keep track of the funeral cortège to which one belonged. Aida and I seated ourselves in a pew near the front. The funeral rites for each dead person succeeded each other in rapid sequence. There were candles and incense and swaying censers. When poor Alejandro's turn came he was despatched with the same speed, a few cursory prayers and more Hail Marys.

The coffin was then borne swiftly out by the bearers on the opposite side of the church from where we were sitting, and Aida and I had difficulty in keeping up. As we hastened across the nave we were nearly mown down by the next coffin which was being rushed up to the altar. It seemed to me very much like a crowded checkout at a large supermarket.

An amazing sight greeted us as we emerged, worthy of a Fellini film in black and white. Before us the alleys of niches splayed out fan-like, each with a crocodile of black-clad mourners, silhouetted against the white walls. They all looked alike and, since we had been delayed in leaving the church, it was hard to know which one to follow. At first, indeed, we found ourselves following the wrong cortège and had hurriedly to retrace our steps. As a consequence, we found ourselves at the back of the mourners following the bearers carrying Alejandro's coffin, whereas by rights Aida should have been chief among them, at the front. Alejandro's daughter occupied that position.

Our sad little procession was led by some kind of friar, who sang along the way, accompanied by a violin, his repertoire interspersing yet more chanted Ave Marias with some other religious songs set to jingly folk rhythms. They at least somewhat lightened the generally dirge-like atmosphere of that cold grey winter's day.

At length we came to a halt by the niche allotted to Alejandro and the bearers thankfully laid down their burden on the cobblestones. More prayers were said and Ave Marias sung and then some ill-kempt and poorly clothed children sang some more, afterwards moving among us, grubby hands outstretched, asking for payment. This was an altogether new insight into Bolivia's well-known informal economy, adding a touch of banality.

All the mourners were small in stature and I felt very conspicuous, towering over them at the back. That meant, at least, that I could see what was going on, which most of them could not. Across the crowd my eyes met those of the only other tall person present, a thin, quixotic figure who had come to represent the Spanish Embassy where both Aida and Alejandro had worked for many years, as housekeeper and chauffeur, and where Alejandro's daughter was still working as a secretary.

203

The bearers' respite was not to last long. Alejandro's niche was on the third and top floor. On another incongruous note in the general solemnity a workman clad in torn jeans and a bright yellow tin hat appeared, clambered up a very rickety ladder and opened the niche to receive the coffin. This latter, crowned with some of the wreaths, was then laboriously lifted by the bearers, straining every muscle, for they had to raise it high above their heads.

At this critical point a shout rose from the few people in the tail of the cortege behind us: '*Un momento!*'

The cause of this interruption was not immediately clear. The coffin stopped mid-air in its wobbly ascent. Then a huge wreath of white Madonna lilies began to be passed from the back, over the heads of the closely packed mourners.

'*Qué se ponga!*' came the cry, conveying the demand that this wreath too should accompany the coffin into its last resting place.

The people in front were not in agreement, among them the yellow-helmeted workman who complained vociferously, 'All these flowers are very bad. They cause coffins to rot and all sorts of problems.'

A brisk altercation arose, the people at the back chanting '*Qué se ponga,*' while those in front retorted '*Qué no se ponga,*' and both coffin and wreath swayed precariously above everyone's heads.

Those in favour of incarcerating the lilies with the deceased won the day. The coffin was lowered and the unfortunate bearers began their arduous work all over again. Some wept as the coffin began to enter the niche. Aida remained stony-faced.

And then, as the coffin was about two-thirds of the way into the niche, it stuck. Alejandro, it seemed, was in no hurry to be buried. The bearers pushed and shoved, almost purple in the face with exertion, encouraged by exhortations to greater efforts from the crowd. It was no good. Those who had been against the inclusion of the lilies opined that that had caused the blockage. The bearers wearily lowered the coffin, removed the offending lilies, and started all over again.

But the coffin still would not go in. In the end the yellow-hatted workman had to be recalled to scale his makeshift ladder again. It then transpired that there was a lot of rubble at the back of the niche that was impeding the full entry of the coffin. This was probably because of his own inefficiency in not clearing the space properly beforehand, but he grumbled as he threw out the offending material, still muttering about the pernicious effect of too many flowers.

At the fourth try Alejandro's coffin at last slid into place and the workman sealed the niche. We all then straggled back to the church where Alejandro's daughter held court, greeting the mourners as they presented their condolences. Poor Aida was just one of the crowd, the woman who had shared so many years of the dead man's life totally ignored. The brief encounter between her and the daughter was icily formal. I could not help but admire the glacial composure that Aida had maintained during all these hours, when she must have been ravaged by deep emotion. Such restraint in expressing her feelings was completely alien to her normal behaviour and nature but she had been a model of dignity and silent sorrow.

Among the mourners was the doctor in whom Alejandro had had such confidence. Aida introduced me to him. He was a tall, heavily built man and he and his wife were finely dressed, in contrast to the shabby black of all the rest. I questioned him about what had gone wrong with Alejandro, asking why his condition had not been diagnosed in time to save his life and why he had not encouraged his transfer to a more sophisticated clinic when things went wrong. I got no satisfactory answer, only glib protestations that all possible had been done. His eyes never met mine. I did not like the man.

On the way back, about halfway down towards the centre of the city, Aida pointed out the man's surgery in a back street in a rundown quarter of the upper town. It had a most unprepossessing entrance, shabby and padlocked, much at odds with the doctor's own prosperous appearance, that reinforced all my earlier premonitions. I felt indignation rise in me at this new evidence of the exploitation of people like Alejandro, ingenuous and trusting, who paid for his ill-placed confidence with his life.

The trauma was not to end there. Hardly had Alejandro been buried when legal battles erupted between his daughter and Aida. It seemed that Aida and Alejandro had never been married. I suppose I had vaguely known this, but it had never seemed important until now. Under Bolivian law everything Alejandro had left, including the indemnity payment due to him for his more than seven years' faithful service to me, was supposed to go to his daughter, on whom I had never set eyes until his funeral. (His first

205

wife was apparently still alive, and in Spain, I learned, but it was not she but the daughter who was interested in the legacy.) It all seemed cruelly unfair.

Aida's defences now collapsed and she wept a good deal. She also vented her spleen on the daughter, whom she called *una ingrata* claiming that it was she who had obtained the job in the Spanish Embassy for her.

We consulted my lawyers and later, dissatisfied with them, Aida visited a group of women lawyers who specialised in cases like this affecting women of modest means. There are, I was told, provisions in Bolivian law for protecting the rights of people in common law relationships who have lived together for a long time but for reasons I never fully understood – the lack of some joint declaration or other by Alejandro and Aida, or some such objection – these were not applicable to Aida's case.

The arguments dragged on interminably and although, with the passage of time, I was able to meet my commitments to her on Alejandro's behalf, other aspects were never fully settled. Aida, who had always had a chip on her shoulder over the way life had treated her, became even more embittered. Her health suffered and she became more suspicious than ever of her fellow human beings. It was a sad end to the story.

15

Winds of Change

Apart from the emotional trauma caused to all of us, Alejandro's sudden death posed serious practical problems at Villa Margarita. Ricardo promptly scarpered, unwilling, perhaps understandably, to face Aida's implacable hostility without the moral support of his uncle. I was left with only Aida and Mateo, the latter not capable of managing the swimming pool.

Ideally, I needed a couple: a woman to run the house, and a man the garden and the jeep. Aida clearly wanted to stay and it would have been unthinkable to suggest otherwise. Equally unthinkable was any arrangement involving a second woman employee – a sure recipe for dissent and quite possibly outright war! Aida was occupying the only house suitable for a couple, or a majordomo, and I could not ask her to move, even though she was only using half of it, having firmly padlocked the bedroom, saying, 'That is Alejandro's room and I shall never enter it again.' This seemed to denote excessive regard for the dead man's memory, especially as relations between them had not always been sunny, but she refused to budge.

Marcos agreed to act as driver temporarily whenever I visited but neither he nor his wife wanted to live in such a remote place. In any case, the poor man suffered a brain tumour not long afterwards, fortunately benign, but the operation to remove it affected him greatly.

One of the porters at the office mentioned a possible candidate to succeed Alejandro. This was Johnny Vera, the son of Víctor Vera, who had been my driver for nearly six years in the 1960s and had helped me when I moved into Villa Margarita in 1993. I was fond of Víctor and had a high opinion of him, a view not universally shared by others who complained of alleged dodgy dealings.

I interviewed Johnny and liked what I saw. He was intelligent and personable, like his father, had driven all over Bolivia and had worked for several years on a project funded by UNDP. He was in his early forties and quite prepared to live most of the time at Villa Margarita. His wife would not accompany him, he explained, as she was not only crippled by rheumatoid arthritis but also – as if that in itself was not sufficient suffering for one human being – had an incurable macular eye disease which was rendering her blind. I explained about Aida, and Johnny said he did not mind living in the little house down by the beach.

We agreed that he would start immediately but when Marcos got to know of it he threw a fit. 'Johnny Vera was dismissed from a UN project for some irregularity,' he warned. 'If you ask me he is a chip off the old block.'

This was a major spanner in the works. I consulted various people who knew Johnny and got a mixed response. Then I had it out with Johnny himself. He was adamant that he had done nothing wrong: the charge was that he had changed the wheels of a project vehicle, after a double puncture, without authorisation. According to him, his boss had instructed him to do this but had not confirmed the order in writing. The accusation had not been levied until several years after the event, by which time the official concerned had long gone. In any event, it was hard to see what Johnny got out of this, even if it were true, other than the dubious value of four tyres. It looked as if the alleged sins of the father were being visited on Johnny.

I looked him straight in the eye and told him I was going to give him the benefit of the doubt but that if there was any devious business on his part, however slight, then that would be the end of it. Johnny looked straight back at me and gave me his word.

You might think that would be the end of it, but that would be failing to take Aida into account. However harsh her judgements had been against earlier male employees of mine, all her not-inconsiderable powers of denigration were brought into play to unseat Johnny. She must have picked up the buzz in the office about his antecedents and, having never liked his father Víctor, she exploited every scrap of would-be evidence she could find. Worse still, she recruited Mateo into this game. Johnny, to his credit, took this barrage of criticism with great equanimity and good humour. He produced detailed accounts and supporting invoices

208

for every purchase, entered in neat handwriting in a notebook. This was more than Aida ever did, although I always had complete faith in her probity.

What is more, Johnny has proved a first-class majordomo, hardworking and responsible, intelligent, a good problem-solver and always full of creative ideas. We have developed a relationship of trust and friendship on a par with that I enjoyed with his predecessor, Alejandro.

Far-reaching changes were also taking place at the heart of the Bolivian government. In the third year of his presidency, General Hugo Banzer was diagnosed with cancer. His condition visibly deteriorated and in August 2001, a year before his term was due to end, he resigned and his vice-president, Jorge (more usually known as 'Tuto') Quiroga, assumed his mantle. Quiroga is a brilliant technocrat, US-trained and very US-oriented, his wife being also American. A *cruceño*, tall, and fair-skinned, he even looks like a *gringo*.

In the 1960s I had worked with some brilliant and dedicated young ministers and senior politicians. They were mostly lawyers and economists who had been educated in Bolivia, spoke little or no English and had scant experience of dealing with international organisations or the outside world (though they were fast learners in that area). But whatever their social or class background, all had a deep understanding of Bolivia and its people, and particularly of the indigenous complexities of the country. Roberto Jordán Pando as Minister of Rural Affairs and then of Development Planning was a prime example.

Twenty years later, when I again began advising successive Bolivian governments, and during the following twenty years, I found myself dealing with a very different cast of characters. Most of them, too, were intelligent and dedicated young men (there were, alas, all too few women) but their education was very different. The majority had been trained abroad, or had completed their higher education there, usually in the United States, many of them because their families had been exiled during the long years of military dictatorship. They spoke fluent English (with an American accent), were accomplished technocrats, and very much at their ease in dealing with international conferences, and organisations and with

209

the host of donor countries by now involved in Bolivia (in the 1960s aid had come only from the US and from the UN). I often felt very proud of them as I watched them defend their country's interests when confronted by immensely more powerful players in the international field.

Among all these advantages over their predecessors I did, however, detect a drawback. All that exposure to the outside world, desirable in so many respects, had been at the expense of a deeper understanding of the great majority of their fellow countrymen. These, the poverty-stricken denizens of the *altiplano* and the high valleys, had remained largely excluded from all these processes. Their world was still the old one, and the fault line with which Bolivian society has always been riven was gouged still deeper.

Even before he was incapacitated by illness, Banzer had been a disappointment as president. The man who, as a military dictator, had ruled with a rod of iron in the 1970s had proved singularly inept in governing effectively the second time around. It was tempting to think that his only ambition had been to become president by democratic election and so perhaps overcome, in the history books, his reputation as a dictator. In any case, it is clearly more difficult to govern in a democracy – and an unruly one at that – than in a military state in which the president's power is paramount. Some said he was too old (though he was younger than Víctor Paz Estenssoro when he saved the country from economic chaos in 1985) and perhaps the illness that drove him from the presidency was already exacting its toll.

People took comfort from the fact that he had a young and dynamic vice-president to lighten the burden. As in many countries with presidential systems, the vice presidency in Bolivia is usually more for show than action. At the outset of his mandate, however, Banzer delegated most of the day-to-day running of government to Tuto Quiroga. Eventually the inevitable happened: the general perception that he was the president in all but name and was overshadowing the titular incumbent provoked a backlash, particularly on the part of the First Lady, Doña Yolanda. It was even rumoured that this redoubtable lady, reliably reputed to have a finger in every pie, had slapped Quiroga's face. For a while he had receded into the background but now he was once again the man at the helm.

It was unfortunate that all this happened during the first period for which the presidential mandate had been extended from four years to five, under the constitutional changes introduced by Banzer's predecessor, Sánchez de Lozada. Desirable as the change was, in this instance it left a lame duck government in power when an election might have cleared the air. Quiroga did well in the short twelve months at his disposal, but it was beyond the capability of any human being to resolve the country's deep-seated problems in one year.

Campaigning was already in full spate for the election now looming in June 2002. The person considered most likely to win was Gonzalo Sánchez de Lozada, as the leader of the MNR, still the largest political party. It was he who had pulled the party together when the dominant figure of Paz Estenssoro had departed the political scene after some four decades as leader and there was no other person of the same stature or charisma in its ranks.

In conversations with me Goni was ambivalent about putting his name forward. On the one hand he felt he should run in order to complete the ambitious programme of reform that he had initiated during his first period and deal with the unfinished business in the social sector. Moreover the lack of any other person in his own party who was likely to win made presenting his candidature, in some sense, a case of 'noblesse oblige'. On the other hand, he was keenly aware that the political landscape had changed dramatically, especially with the emergence of strong populist movements led by men like Evo Morales and 'El Mallku', that social unrest had become endemic, encouraged by a series of successes in holding the government to ransom, and that it would be a very difficult task to achieve progress and maintain law and order while still governing democratically.

In all of this he proved tragically prescient. Yet during these talks when he appeared to be vacillating, I sensed that in the end he would feel obliged to take up the challenge. Apart from everything else, his age – he was 72 – meant that this would probably be his last opportunity, even though Víctor Paz had surprised everyone by wielding a vigorous presidency at the age of eighty.

While he cogitated about all this, Goni continued to prepare his party's platform for the elections. He was determined that the MNR would concentrate on reducing the huge and widening gulf between rich and poor segments of the population. The Banzer government had launched a poverty reduction programme, in cooperation with the World Bank. In accordance with the latter's standard conditions, this

211

had led to a plethora of reports – notably the Poverty Reduction Strategy Paper (PRSP), demanded of all developing countries, which in turn had to be based on a 'national dialogue'. In Bolivia the National Dialogue, carried out all over the country, had dragged on interminably. More paper had been produced than practical programmes of action.

For the MNR's internal discussions the 1994 report of the Inter-American Development Bank mission that I had led was dusted off, at Goni's request, and I was invited to attend several meetings with him and his advisers. The aim was to see how some of the report's key ideas could at long last be translated into action. There was a new sense of urgency because the two passages in the report that had caused so much controversy at the time – the possibility of a *Chiapas* occurring in Bolivia and the population's loss of confidence in government – now seemed all too relevant.

But I did not derive much encouragement from the progress of our talks. Political complications were multiplying by the day and tended to predominate over everything else. There were dissensions within the MNR itself, between the old guard and those supporting Goni's reformist policies, rather similar to the rift between Old and New Labour in the United Kingdom. Even Goni's inner ring of advisers was riven by competing ambitions and policies: his two closest lieutenants, the Machiavellian Sánchez Barzaín, reputedly responsible for the suppression of a *campesino* protest in Amayapampa during Goni's first presidency that had ended in bloodshed, and 'Chacho' Justiniano, who had been Minister of the Presidency, and quasi Prime Minister, who followed a much more open and transparent course, were constantly at loggerheads. Their popular nicknames were the 'black prince' and the 'white prince'.

New political parties were springing up to compete with the three main traditional parties, the MNR, the ADN (Acción Democrática Nacional – Banzer and Quiroga's party) and the MIR (Movimiento Institucional Revolucionaro). Evo Morales and his *cocaleros* had formed the Movimiento al Socialismo (Movement Towards Socialism) the acronym for which – MAS – means 'more' in Spanish. For his part, Felipe Quispe – El Malku – led a party called Movimiento Indigenista Pachacuti or MIP (Pachacuti Indigenist Movement). These developments increased still further the fragmentation that had long characterised Bolivia's democracy.

Social unrest and daily popular protests had become a way of life in both town and country. Virtually every day there were long columns of people in the Alto and in the main thoroughfares of La Paz itself marching in serried ranks, chanting and waving banners. Each demonstration represented a particular sector of the economy and their grievances, which also led to prolonged strikes. The marches usually took place at midday, bringing the centre of the city and all traffic to a standstill for several hours. They were accompanied by fireworks and dynamite explosions, and sometimes erupted in violence. Ironically it was the teachers, protesting against the educational reform, who were often the most intemperate and aggressive.

In the countryside road blockages occurred all the time. We never knew whether we would be able to get to La Paz and whether, if we did arrive, we could get to the hotel or the UNDP office and conduct our business; or whether, having got there, we would be able to get back home again to Villa Margarita. We often had to make huge detours along minor roads and byways, which Johnny fortunately knew well, in order to avoid angry, stone-throwing groups of protesters with whom we had more than one close shave.

Surviving perils of this kind had been par for the course ever since I had first come to Bolivia forty years before but they now acquired new and alarming dimensions. There was a real danger that the social fabric was being torn apart.

As if in sympathy the fabric of Villa Margarita was also disintegrating. One day early in 2002 I suddenly noticed a large and widening crack in the ceiling of the dining room. This part of the house has no room above it, only roof space. Javier Neri, the engineer who built the swimming pool, was a frequent visitor, for there was always something needing to be done and I took advantage of his presence to ask his advice.

When he tapped the ceiling, dust showered down. He then sent one of his men to climb through the trapdoor in the corner of the room and inspect the roof space. He came down with a grave face and told all with one dread word.

'Termites,' he said. 'They've gnawed away all the wood structures supporting the roof. Everything is rotten. At any moment the roof can collapse and this ceiling fall down.'

I was flabbergasted. 'Termites?' I repeated incredulously. 'At 14,000 feet and in a cold climate? I thought they were only a danger in tropical climes.'

213

Javier soon disabused me. It seems this was a common problem in La Paz, because wood brought up from the tropical lowlands, unless treated properly, imported their resident population of termites which, amazingly, had learned to flourish in the high altitude also.

'It seems your first builder didn't bother to decontaminate the wood,' Javier went on.

This sounded all too reminiscent of the general insouciance with which Lucho had built my home, but I was surprised that neither the architect who had replaced the roof the second time, when the whole house had been practically rebuilt, nor the supervising architect who had monitored his work, had detected anything amiss. The rafters then had been open to the sky.

When Javier and his men examined the rest of the roof space their verdict was damning and dismaying: all the rafters were riddled with rot. So were the floor supports below my bedroom, in the ceiling of the living room.

'It's a wonder that you and your bed haven't fallen through,' he commented, with the schadenfreude that always seems to seize builders when they have catastrophic news to impart.

The inspection was extended to all the other buildings: the garage, and the three small houses where the staff live. The results were all disastrously the same. According to Javier the only solution was to remove all the roofs and replace wooden rafters with aluminium structures.

'How much will that cost?' I asked faintly, when I recovered the power of speech.

'A lot,' said Javier. He took measurements back to La Paz with him and a few days later sent me an estimate: thirty thousand dollars!

I then remembered I had expensive house insurance, for everything from revolution to acts of God, fire, flood and burglary. I was further encouraged when I examined the policy to find that I had paid extra for cover for 'collapse of roofs'.

For a brief while I harboured the illusion that I was home and dry but I had not reckoned with the adeptness of insurance companies the world over at wriggling out of commitments. Bolivia was no exception, though the negotiations followed a peculiarly Bolivian logic. The exchanges went something like this:

Me: 'I want to make a claim under the supplement to my policy that covers roof collapse.'

214

Agent: 'Señora, have your roofs collapsed?'
Me: 'No, but as you can see from the builder's report, they are about to do so, and are very dangerous.'
Agent: 'Your policy stipulates that your roof must collapse first before we can consider a claim.'
Me: 'But that will cost even more and someone could get killed or seriously hurt if we don't take preventive action.'
Agent (wearily as if addressing a not very bright child): 'Señora, I have already told you, we can't do anything until the roofs collapse!'
Me (with heavy irony): 'Would it help if we knocked them down, since they are about to fall anyway?'

Sarcasm of course gets one nowhere. This dead-end dialogue went on for some time until I finally had to admit defeat.

Johnny was also appalled by the high cost. Why not have the aluminium structures put only in the main house, he asked. He and Mateo could replace the roofs in all the other buildings with properly treated wood.

This was the compromise we eventually adopted. Once again Villa Margarita was open to the sky for several weeks. The workers told me that not only were the beams rotten but that in some places scrap pieces of wood left over from the construction had been cobbled together, to save money. Not for the first or the last time I silently cursed Lucho. The cost still amounted to nearly $US20,000 for the main house plus expenditure for new wood for the other buildings. Johnny and Mateo worked methodically over several months. All the old wood from them and the main house had to be burnt. The new structures had to be thoroughly fumigated, a process that is now repeated at regular intervals. That also means hermetically sealing the main house for some days when I am abroad. Even so, I have quite recently found telltale holes in a picture frame above my bed and in a table in my study, but we hope against hope that we have the problem under control.

When at last the work was completed I ruefully reflected that this was the third time in a dozen years that Villa Margarita had been re-roofed. I could only try to console myself that, as they say in Spanish, 'la tercera es la vencida,' roughly translatable as 'third time lucky'.

* * *

Election fever was rising while the endemic problems and resulting disruptions continued unabated. To all of these another bone of contention had been added and was seized on by the numerous perpetrators of political chaos.

In tune with the paradoxes that have so often marked critical junctures in Bolivia's history, this particular *casus belli* arose from a development that should be the keystone for Bolivia's future prosperity. Immense reserves of natural gas had been discovered in the southern department of Tarija in the south of the country. This reserve had been named 'Campo Margarita', not, I hasten to add, on account of any relationship with me or its namesake Villa Margarita. The gas possessed properties that made it especially suited for export and there were big markets clamouring for supplies in energy-starved regions in Mexico, and in California.

The lucrative prospects of exploiting Campo Margarita had attracted much foreign investment. A coalition of three international giants, led by the Spanish corporation Repsol, and composed of two British firms, British Petroleum and British Gas, was already financing exploration and studies for the development and export of the gas. Export raised yet again the perennial problem of Bolivia's land-locked status and it was this that fired incandescent political repercussions. There were two possible routes to the sea, one through Chile, the other, much longer, through Peru. Studies demonstrated that Chile was the best economic option but this raised a public outcry, the most vociferous opponents being the populist leaders, Evo Morales and Felipe Quispe. It was unthinkable, they proclaimed, that the gas should be exported through Bolivia's age-old enemy Chile, the country that robbed Bolivia of its sea coast and a large tract of its territory when it emerged victorious from the Pacific War of 1879, in which Bolivia and Peru had been allies. This had been the rallying call for mass demonstrations for several decades. A subsidiary, but at that time less vocal, theme was opposition to the export anywhere of a national resource that the protesters insisted should be used to benefit Bolivia, recalling that the wealth produced by earlier riches such as silver and tin had all been exported abroad along with the minerals. This was an echo of the historical context in which we had placed the findings of our Inter-American Development Bank report in 1994. In this instance it was not a logical stance, however: estimates of the reserves in Campo Margarita were so huge that they could not possibly be absorbed by Bolivia, but convincing assurances had to be provided that Bolivia's needs would be met first and foremost.

Sometime in July 2002, at one of my Sunday barbecues, the discussion centred around this political hot potato. The outgoing foreign minister, Gustavo Fernandez, an old friend and one of Bolivia's best foreign ministers, cheered us all by firmly asserting that the Quiroga government would resolve this question before leaving office the following month. In his mind there was no doubt that the gas should be exported through Chile, as by far the most economically favourable solution for Bolivia.

Sadly his confidence proved misplaced. 'Tuto' Quiroga did not bite the bullet on that issue: after all, he was hoping to come back as a presidential candidate at a later date. So this crucial decision was left hanging and, as we all gloomily forecast, was to have dire consequences for the next government.

The elections were hotly contested and acrimonious as my annual letter recorded:

> Gonzalo Sánchez de Lozada ('Goni') won the highest popular vote, but since no party can reach the 50% required for outright election (there are just too many of them) weeks of cliff hanging followed until at last an alliance was patched up between Goni's party, the MNR and the MIR, led by Jaime Paz Zamora. Traditionally the MNR and the MIR have been strongly opposed, so this was quite a feat, but one that requires very careful handling to preserve a united front. Bolivia very nearly had a 'coca President', since the leader of the beleaguered coca growers came second in the polls. He would not have achieved this result had he not been helped by a statement by the US Ambassador who, just days before the poll, warned that, if any candidate who opposed the total eradication of coca-growing were to win the election, all US aid to the country would be ended next day. That brought a huge influx of voters for the coca leader who would never otherwise have supported him but who were incensed by what they considered to be unwonted intrusion into the country's internal affairs.

Goni won the largest number of votes, but a much smaller majority than before. The great surprise was that Evo Morales and his MAS party were in second place, close on the heels of Goni and his MNR and elbowing out other traditionally big parties, such as the ADN and the MIR, and the newer party of the NFR (New Republican Force) which had been expected to do well.

Had the constitution permitted a second round of the two candidates with the most votes, Goni would almost certainly have won over Evo Morales: those who had voted tactically for him, or as a protest, in the first round would probably have balked at the prospect of a 'coca' president, with all the resulting international repercussions, and chosen the more traditional 'safe' candidate. As it was Goni had to submit to the customary horse-trading needed to ensure a positive vote by Congress on the eve of the inauguration of 6 August. I could not resist asking him whether he regretted not having accepted my advice to include a 'second round' among the constitutional changes he had introduced in his first term, but received no clear reply.

After much haggling, agreement was reached between the MNR and the MIR, and later with the smaller party of the NFR, whose maverick leader, Manfred Reyes Villa, more usually known as 'Bonbon', played an exceedingly equivocal role, changing from side to side. It was a shaky coalition. Apart from political differences, Goni and the MIR leader, Jaime Paz were personally antagonistic. The omens did not look good.

16

A False New Dawn?

I was invited as a special guest of the president to his inauguration on 6 August 2002. It was a more subdued affair than usual, because of the serious situation faced by the country – economic recession, unemployment, poverty and social deprivation. But there was hope that, with Goni back at the helm, the ship of state would sail more smoothly. The new president's speech also lacked the brío that I had heard from him in 1993 and that had caused such enormous euphoria. There was, however, a novel flash of brilliance among the new members of Congress – the bright colours of the traditional dress of the indigenous representatives who had greatly increased their numbers.

The following Sunday, 11 August, the president, First Lady Ximena and their family, drove out to Villa Margarita for a *parrillada* and a swim. The guests also included Vice President Carlos Mesa, and his wife Elvira.

The nomination of Carlos Mesa as Goni's running mate at a relatively late stage in the electoral campaign had come as a surprise to many and was something of a political coup. Carlos Mesa was a well-known and respected intellectual figure, a historian and a skilled television commentator on political matters. A few months before he had conducted an hour-long interview with me about my experiences in Bolivia over more than forty years and he had also appeared in the BBC documentary on my life, 'Nine Lives', in early 2002. He was a great communicator, articulate, handsome and charismatic, and he did not belong to any political party. The choice of someone from outside the MNR had been a bold move by Goni, but it had been difficult to find anyone of the right stature from among the squabbling ranks of his own party. There was, moreover, political advantage to be gained in selecting someone from outside politics in the current atmosphere of public disillusion with politicians and the main traditional parties. Many thought that Mesa's popularity, and his skill in conveying a message of hope for the future, had sealed Goni's win of the highest level of popular votes, narrow as that margin had been.

The whole party arrived together, in a flurry of vehicles and jeeps full of security guards. Once the pisco sours had been served everyone repaired down to the swimming pool. Everyone but Goni, that is. He wanted to go for a walk and to talk to me. I suggested that we take the hill track towards Chicharro, but that was impossible because the security jeeps could not follow. Instead we walked along the rough road to Camacachi.

There was a faint air of ridiculousness about this straggling procession. In front were two security guards with walkie-talkies and telltale earpieces. Behind us crawled two jeeps while two more guards brought up the rear. These seemed excessive precautions, for the way was practically deserted. One boy, cycling towards us from Camacachi, was so bemused that he continued gazing at our strange cavalcade over his shoulder, and very nearly came to grief. A little later a mini bus edged its way past us, the passengers' faces glued against the window. I doubt if any of these rare passers-by realised that here was their newly installed president.

As we walked, Goni spoke of the many challenges confronting his government. High among them was the thorny question of the gas, which could secure the future prosperity of the country but which could, equally, spell disaster for his administration. I commented that it was a pity that this matter had not been resolved by the outgoing government but Goni disagreed: he was glad that the matter had been left to him, to deal with in his own way. We both concurred that the only way to sweeten the bitter pill of export through Chile was to obtain some significant, political concession from that country, directly relevant to the sensitive matter of Bolivia's access to the sea.

Goni asked me to advise on the steps that his government should take internationally in order to ensure the political and financial support that was essential for its survival. There and then I suggested that we should plan for an early Consultative Group meeting on Bolivia under the aegis of the World Bank, but the president was firmly of the opinion that this would be premature.

We returned to find everyone in good spirits after their swim. It was a convivial group that sat down to an al fresco lunch on the

220

upper terrace. The lake was shimmering in bright sunlight, the mountains glistening against a cobalt sky. There was not a cloud to be seen on all the vast horizon but we were all aware that many political storms lay ahead.

The very next day I drafted a proposed international strategy and sent it to the president. My thesis was based on two premises which were at the same time dilemmas. The government, I wrote, was on a knife's edge: on the one hand it faced external pressures to maintain the neo-liberal economic model; on the other, growing internal pressures to abandon that model, or at least make it more flexible. These were in fact, two sides of the same coin, exacerbated by very severe economic recession and by social and ethnic pressures.

To escape from the impasse I proposed an international strategy compatible with the government's national strategy, the so-called Plan Bolivia, and also complementing it. Bolivia was facing a grave crisis but so was much of the rest of Latin America. The international community should be warned about the imminent dangers looming, since this continent was not receiving the priority attention it needed. Bolivia's case should not be presented as an isolated one but in the continental context.

One favourable factor to be exploited was the growing appreciation in a significant number of countries and organisations of defects in the neoliberal economic model and of the need to remedy its negative effects, especially in the social sphere, which were prejudicing political and social stability in many places. I emphasised that this should be done in a manner that would not weaken economic stability.

The strategy must be an integrated programme of action, consistently applied across all aspects of foreign policy, and coordinated with other governments in the hemisphere. It would need a cooperative effort right across the government, and especially between the foreign and finance ministries, which had not always worked in harmony.

I urged that the first step should be for the president to attend the General Assembly of the United Nations, due to meet in a few weeks' time. He should request the Secretary General's intervention with international financial institutions (especially the International Monetary Fund and the World Bank) to request more flexibility in financial conditions and negotiations, and to bear in mind not only economic but also the political factors – the dangers to democracy and stability.

The president's speech should accentuate these political themes and risks, and place them in the wider context of the hemisphere. To have maximum effect, the president should speak beforehand with some of his fellow Latin American colleagues with the object of orchestrating a unified continental appeal for more attention. The visit to New York should be combined with one to Washington for discussions, using the same arguments, with the US administration, the IMF, the World Bank, the Inter-American Development Bank and the Organisation of American States.

As a second stage I proposed presidential visits to the European Community in Brussels, to the most important European donors and to Japan. These should be preceded by an immediate meeting in La Paz with all the ambassadors accredited to Bolivia, to be chaired by the president. Preparations should also be put in hand for a meeting of the World Bank's Consultative Group.

Among the general arguments to be used I singled out the causes of the crisis in Latin America that was endangering democracy and political and social stability, as the high incidence of poverty, the growing gulf between rich and poor; and the ever more vocal rejection of this situation by important sectors of the population, especially ethnic and indigenous groups who felt excluded from the development process.

In the case of Bolivia I suggested that the approach might be that, while Bolivia was not the most disastrous case, it was in grave crisis and was one of the poorest Latin American countries. Its geopolitical situation at the heart of South America made it especially vulnerable to events in surrounding countries. By the same token, a collapse in Bolivia would entail grave implications elsewhere on the continent.

For seventeen years Bolivia had religiously followed the orthodox policies demanded by the IMF but the results anticipated from these policies had not yet materialised, causing serious social unrest, further exacerbated by the policy of eliminating coca cultivation destined for manufacturing drugs, which the new government had pledged to continue. In great measure coca cultivation was a problem of poverty. The *cocaleros* were not the main villains – where there is demand there will be supply. The much vaunted 'alternative development' was not producing the desired results, and was causing an imbalance in the distribution of investment to the detriment of the neediest regions of Bolivia, especially the *altiplano* and the high valleys, the main areas from which people emigrated to grow coca, because of abysmal living conditions. So far, consumer countries had done little to reduce coca consumption and there had been no quid pro quo from them for the immense effort made by Bolivia to eliminate coca growing, e.g. by offering free trade facilities for the country's other products.

On top of all its endemic problems, Bolivia had suffered several years of economic recession, by contagion from the outside world. It was important that, in presenting these arguments to the international community, the government should emphasise the firm measures it was taking, through the Plan Bolivia, to resolve the economic situation: job creation; social programmes; an aggressive anti-corruption campaign; priority attention to the poorest strata of the population; elimination of illegal coca cultivation; and, last but most important, the dedication of the export revenues eventually accruing from the export of natural gas to programmes benefiting the population as a whole.

Such a programme would need strong international support: more flexible conditions for aid, and a continuing flow of aid and debt relief. To avoid the rivalries that had arisen in 1993–1997 between the foreign and finance ministries over the mobilisation of external aid, I suggested the creation of a small interministerial commission, under the Ministry of Sustainable Development, which would not only mobilise external resources, but also establish priority areas for its use, consonant with the priorities in Plan Bolivia.

Finally, I emphasised the need to appoint able ambassadors to key posts and brief them to pursue the government's international strategy in a coherent manner in all donor countries. The strategy should be widely publicised within Bolivia and swift measures taken to implement Plan Bolivia, especially in the social field. I urged that the ill-fated 'Strategy for Integrated Rural Development', which had been ignored during the Banzer government, should be brought up to date and implemented as quickly as possible. If the proposed international strategy was to have any chance of success, it was imperative to show both the international community and the Bolivian people that the government meant business. Although nearly eight years had elapsed since the publication of the Inter-American Development Bank report that I and others had prepared, I was in essence trying to revive some of its policy recommendations, which seemed to me even more vitally relevant now.

My proposals were discussed at several meetings culminating in a session late at night in the Palacio Quemado, at which Minister of the Presidency Chacho Justiniano, and Finance Minister Javier Comboni, were present, as well as the president. This was on 21 August and next morning, very early, I was leaving for New York, where I could prepare the ground for the president's visit. There was general agreement on my proposals but Goni demurred at the idea of attending the General Assembly, which was the cornerstone. He had been persuaded by others that this was not a useful forum for conveying his message, as many heads of state would be giving speeches. I emphasised that this was the one place where Bolivia's needs and programmes could be given international prominence, particularly if the ground was carefully prepared beforehand with his fellow heads of state. A concerted message about the continent's problems, so often overlooked, could have political impact. Moreover, I added, the principal advantages of attendance at the General Assembly were the informal contacts with other world leaders.

But Goni argued that Washington and George Bush were much more important. In the event, the deteriorating situation within the country clinched the decision not to go to New York. He also maintained his view that it was too early to hold a Consultative Group meeting, another key point in my recommendations.

One particular incident during that meeting remains seared in my memory. At about 11 pm the door burst open and in dashed Sánchez Berzaín, now Minister of the Interior. Javier Comboni was speaking at the time but Sánchez Berzaín rudely interrupted, informing the president that he had an urgent message. It was probably news of some worrying incident of social unrest but he could surely have waited for his colleague to finish speaking. It seemed to me not only an indication of the scant respect in which he held his colleagues, but also of his overwhelming influence over the president.

In early November, in Chile to speak at an international conference on women in peacekeeping, I had breakfast with my old friend and former boss, Gabriel Valdés Subercaseaux. Gabriel had served as Foreign Minister in the Christian Democrat government of Eduardo Frei in the 1960s. Then he had gone to New York as Regional Director for Latin America of the UN Development

Programme, during part of which time I had served under him, first as Resident Representative in Chile, and then as his deputy in New York. On his return to Chile Gabriel had been elected as a senator and became President of the Senate. He was probably the most respected political figure in Chile, a wise elder statesman in every sense of the term. He had always been on the left wing of the Christian Democrat party and was now close to the current Socialist president, Ricardo Lagos.

Our talks inevitably focused on Bolivia and relations with Chile about the gas. I gave my opinion that Goni's only hope of diluting the opposition of the general population to its export through Chilean ports was if the Chilean government made a significant concession about more permanent outlets to the sea. Gabriel agreed with this view and told me that President Lagos had indicated to him his readiness to facilitate an agreement with Bolivia. Whether this flexibility could extend beyond its financial and economic aspects was not clear but Gabriel thought it worthwhile exploring.

While in Santiago I received an urgent message from Goni that he wished to see me as soon as I arrived in Bolivia early the next day, 6 November. I went straight from the airport to the palace. Goni wanted to talk about his forthcoming visit to Washington, now agreed, but we also discussed my conversation with Gabriel Valdés. I ventured to suggest that it might be a good idea to invite Gabriel to La Paz, since he had the ear of his president. Goni listened attentively but in the end did not pursue the idea. I think he thought it would be impossible to keep the visit of such a prominent personality secret and that, given the irresponsible gossip and scandal-mongering that is the daily fodder of the La Paz rumour merchants and the press, the political fall-out would be difficult to handle. I sensed that there were other irons in the fire: on the plane I had sat next to a well-connected Chilean who was also going to see the president but was reluctant to divulge the nature of his business.

Goni, of course, had a million other problems on his mind. Not least among them was his difficulty in pulling together a precarious coalition and forming a government that could act effectively. Both the MIR and the other major partner, the NFR, headed by its notoriously volatile leader Bonbon, were clamouring for ministerial posts in reward for their support. The problems were exacerbated by the personal animosity between him and Jaime Paz, the leader

225

of the MIR, and Goni complained to me that Jaime was presenting candidates for ministerial posts who lacked the requisite qualifications. All of this was taking an inordinate amount of his time at the expense of getting on with the government's programme of action.

On Sunday 10 November, I flew back to England, via Miami. The president and his wife and a retinue of ministers were on the same plane, en route for Washington for the important meeting with President George W. Bush. On the way Goni and I discussed the strategy that should inform his talk with the leader of the wealthiest and most powerful country in the world, and the other dignitaries he was to see. We knew that it would not be an easy meeting but we thought we had good arguments in hand, not least among them the dangers of Bolivia falling apart and the grave wider implications that this would have, given the country's geopolitical situation at the heart of South America. One of Bolivia's key problems was an acute fiscal deficit which was making it almost impossible to carry out the programmes desperately needed to resolve the crisis or even pay the very low salaries of its public service. Bolivia's request was for a bridging loan of $US150 million, an enormous sum for Bolivia, but less than peanuts for the United States.

The following week Goni gave me, by telephone, an account of what had occurred. He had been given the full red carpet treatment: a meeting and photographs with George Bush in the Oval Office at the White House and a public appearance with him afterwards in the famous Rose Garden. He had also been received warmly by many other high dignitaries of state. It had all been very encouraging and cordial, but the upshot was that President Bush had told him that there was no money for the immediate, desperately needed, bridging loan – 'all our resources are already committed elsewhere.' He did not specify, but the word 'Iraq' came to mind.

In the autumn of 2002 I went back and forth to the southern cone of Latin America no fewer than three times in six weeks: after Chile I had two missions to Buenos Aires to take part in simulated training exercises in peacekeeping techniques for military personnel drawn from all over the continent, the first organised by the British Armed Forces, the second by US Southern Command.

I spent a few days visiting old friends in Uruguay and flew on

226

to La Paz on 18 December, to spend Christmas in Bolivia, where the Sánchez de Lozada family invited me to spend the festive season with them in a small and remote country hotel outside Sucre, in the Department of Chuquisaca.

Sucre, the official capital of Bolivia, is the site of the Supreme Court and boasts an important university as well as a famed and miraculous virgin – the Virgin of Guadelupe – in its vast cathedral. Traditionally it was the home of the Bolivian aristocracy and the names of several well-known Sucre families figure on the admittedly long line of Bolivian presidents since independence in 1825.

Sucre was an elegant centre of fashion and culture from colonial times. As Chuquisaca and the seat of the rich and powerful Andiencia of Charcas, it ruled over virtually all the lands to the south in the name of the Spanish king. Its residents surrounded themselves with wealth and *objets d'art* brought from Europe on mule back over the Andes. Some of them had bought princely titles in the Old World and transported them to the surrounding countryside. Crumbling, moss-grown walls, and dilapidated mansions, once magnificent and now marooned in the midst of their ruined Italianate gardens and pleasances and their mildewed gazebos, still bear witness to the European aspirations and forgotten elegance of a lost age.

Although it was from Sucre that the first cry of freedom from the peninsular yoke of Spain rang out on 25 May 1809, independence was not obtained for Bolivia until 1825. The pre-eminence of the city, hidden in a fold of the Andean foothills, continued but, with the transfer of the seat of government to La Paz at the end of the nineteenth century, its influence waned. Sucre closed her gates and the new currents of nationalist fervour and revolutionary zeal of the mid-twentieth century flowed around her, leaving her as an island of tradition. When I first went there in 1960 I found an enchanting town that somehow fell short of reality, like a film set carefully designed in every detail yet failing to create the impression of life. Its low white houses and russet roofs, clustering around the towers and belfries of many churches, still retained a fading colonial grandeur. Behind their deceptively simple white walls you entered a world of colonnades, patios paved with worn flagstones and flower-shrouded balconies, a dim walled world fretted with the delicate tracery of ferns and threaded with the sound of water tinkling from small fountains. The smell of jasmine hung in the air. In these houses that had been lived in for three or four centuries

227

one could imagine oneself in Seville or Granada. Sucre seemed perennially bewildered at finding itself in the twentieth century. Stripped of the main trappings of government, once the centre of administrative power had migrated to La Paz, it had relapsed thankfully into a quiet backwater.

Much of the same atmosphere prevails in Sucre today, although one evening when the first lady Ximena and I went into the city we found a night life of sorts, an art exhibition, gaggles of young people in the streets and even an Internet café. Some of the old houses had become hotels or comfortable pensions. When I had taken my parents there in 1962 the two 'best' hotels, both long past their prime, were called nostalgically 'Paris' and 'Londres'. Contrary to the European connotations of these names we were advised to stay at the Hotel Paris, because the plumbing was better (although, as we soon found out, still signally deficient) but to eat at the Hotel Londres because it had the better cuisine.

Our hotel for Christmas 2002 was new, about forty-five minutes drive away. It was surrounded by bronzed and ochre hills unrelieved by green except where delicately-fronded acacias crowd alongside rock-strewn, often dried-up, water courses, or where on roadside banks the agaves stand like sentinels picketing the distant horizon. The climate is benign and sub-tropical, for Sucre is at an altitude of only 2600 metres, but rainfall is scant. That year there had been a drought and the sun-soaked landscape bore an even more barren aspect than usual. In my annual letter I described that Christmas break:

We took long walks every day usually, at the President's insistence, during the full midday heat, so I have returned with quite a tan. There was plenty of time to talk, and many lunches and barbecues in the houses of their friends and relatives living nearby, faded remnants of the grandeur that was Sucre in the heyday of the nineteenth century. We attended midnight mass on Christmas Eve at the local village church in Yotala. They usually have a full-scale, live nativity scene with real cows and donkeys and a Madonna discreetly 'giving birth' behind a curtain and then emerging with the newborn babe. That did not happen this year but it was a very colourful occasion, with scores of small nativity scenes and treasured dolls being blessed, some really beautiful singing, children and

228

dogs wandering everywhere and the whole population of Yotala, many very poor, filling the church. During these few days I was made to feel very much part of a warm, extended Latin American family.

Those walks took place at the worst possible time of day, when the sun was at its zenith, because the president was a notoriously late riser. They were usually along rocky, disused railway lines circling the tawny hills that bordered the valley. We were accompanied by the mandatory posse of security guards, usually two in front and two behind. Christmas is nearly always a quiet time in Bolivia, when political fervour dies down for a week or two and the ubiquitous protesters observe the festive season in a civilised manner. There were, however, occasional visitors bringing news from outside. The most ominous one was Interior Minister Sánchez Berzaín. That day I hung back with the guards while the president and the minister walked ahead, deep in conversation.

Despite the problems, the first five months of Goni's second presidency had gone as well as could be expected. But delays in establishing an effective and united cabinet had evoked criticism that the president was devoting too much time to political manoeuvring. Moreover even graver difficulties loomed. The economic situation and the need to reduce poverty and soaring unemployment, exacerbated by the government's financial incapacity, were among the main themes we discussed on those daily walks.

Talks with the International Monetary Fund were throwing up the usual dilemmas and hard decisions. I once again broached the need to organise an urgent Consultative Group meeting so that we could obtain desperately needed external finance. Only in this way, I argued, could the government be enabled to implement the programmes that were essential if the demands of protesting groups were to be met and any semblance of social order achieved. But the president remained adamant that the time was not ripe.

One comforting memory of those walks stays with me. Whenever we stumbled, hot and weary, into a village or hamlet, people swarmed out of their houses to embrace the president and offer refreshments.

Afterwards, reflecting on this time brought to mind the comment made by Simón Rodriguez, Bolívar's tutor, when he visited Chuquisaca in 1823, two years before independence, to try out his new system of education. He had to confess failure and close his school in the face of traditional opposition.

'Only you understand,' he wrote to Bolívar, 'because you see things as I do, that to make a new republic you must first make a new people.'

Those words still have resonance nearly two centuries later.

Another recollection of that Christmas was recorded in my annual letter:

The President kindly provided a jeep that enabled me to visit the rural hospital that bears my name in Otavi, in the department of Potost, a bone-shaking journey of seven hours over dreadful roads from the hotel. There I was able to solve some problems and take the whole staff out for lunch at the local *boliche*, presided over by a huge *cholita*, sporting a verdi-gris'd bowler on top of masses of grey hair cascading down her back in thick braids, her voluminous skirts covered by an apron that bore signs of much cooking. Warned barely an hour before of our impending invasion into her modest roadside café she had bemoaned, 'I have only enough food for five!' But she came up trumps with plates of *altiplano* soup, followed by a spicy chicken stew. All of this was washed down with local beer. As we finished, a local *campesino*, who had clearly been imbibing quantities of the brew elsewhere, arrived on the scene to partake of more. This inspired him to launch into a wandering, laudatory speech about yours truly, proclaiming my work for the hospital, and ending grandiosely, 'We owe our lives to you and your name is always in our hearts ... Margaret ... Margaret...' At this point his eyes rolled upwards as he desperately strove to find the name that meant so much. At length he exclaimed triumphantly, 'Thatcher!' So much for fame.

I flew back to La Paz on 29 December and celebrated New Year's Eve much more austerely at Villa Margarita with Aida and Johnny. At midnight we went out into the chilly garden and watched some rather desultory fireworks set off in San Pedro by the Bolivian navy, half obscured by the intervening hill, and in the other fishing village, San Pablo, across the dark waters of the straits of Tiquina.

It was a tranquil, beautiful scene as we drank a toast to the year about to begin and poured the mandatory libations on the ground to placate the Pachamama. But, with war looming in Iraq and the threat of terrorism ever greater, I was filled with foreboding as to what 2003 would bring for the world at large and, not least, for Bolivia where the gathering clouds looked dark indeed.

The reality was to prove tragically even more dire than my premonition.

PART FIVE

Nightmares

17

The Storm Brews

The Christmas lull was short-lived. Hardly was the celebration of Reyes (the Feast of the Kings) over on 6 January when the country was again in uproar with popular demands. The themes of the constant marches through El Alto and La Paz and sporadic road blockages throughout the country were the familiar ones, and the hordes of people trudging down the cobbled streets, waving their banners, shouting their slogans and firing sticks of dynamite were the same as before, as were those manning the barricades. There were the *cocaleros* who wanted their right to grow coca maintained; the indigenous folk with their mixed message of a return to ancient Aymara forms of government and access to modern technology; the teachers who wanted the educational reform repealed and their salaries raised; the health workers who also demanded salary rises; the miners, remnants of an industry that had once been the mainstay of the Bolivian economy, clamouring for compensation; the Bolivian Workers' Federation (COB); pensioners, public workers and a host of others.

These were all manifestations of the perennial problems eroding the very basis of Bolivian society: poverty, unemployment, marginalisation and exclusion. I had seen many such movements in Bolivia over the past forty years whenever there was a government in power that allowed freedom of expression; not, of course during the years of military dictatorship, when they could be quelled by repressive measures. The difference now was the tremendous increase in the protests – they followed one another in such rapid succession that the narrow streets in the centre of La Paz were almost constantly blocked – and in the frequency of violent incidents.

Threading through the traditional causes of discontent, broader issues began to emerge and become common to all the groups, whatever their individual concerns. Their antagonism was directed not only against the government but also against the influence of the United States, regarded as tantamount to interference; the neo-liberal economic policies dictated by the International Monetary Fund, considered to be the fount of all Bolivia's current ills; the capitalisation programme carried out in the president's first mandate, denounced as a sell-out of state enterprises to foreign interests; and globalisation, feared as a phenomenon that would deepen the country's poverty even more.

The country was out of control but the government was caught on the horns of a dilemma. The two possible ways of restoring authority were denied to it. To come down hard on the protesters by using measures of strength or declaring a state of siege would smack too much of the methods of earlier dictatorship and were anathema to the democratic instincts of President Sánchez de Lozada. They were all too likely to fuel the flames of conflict in the longer run, even if they stemmed its popular expression in the short term, and would bring down international opprobrium on the government.

The alternative, and better, solution of urgently introducing programmes of action to meet the protesters' demands was virtually impossible because of the desperate economic and financial situation of the country. The fiscal deficit was growing and there were problems even in paying the salaries of public servants. Even if such action had been possible, its practical results would have been long in coming, although – as I had suggested in my proposed strategy – the inception of a few highly visible, quick-impact projects might have gone some way to allay public discontent and scepticism.

Widespread perceptions of the government's incapacity to act were heightened by the fragility of the ruling coalition and the exorbitant amount of the president's time absorbed in trying to accommodate internal disputes and hold his administration together.

In the past Bolivia had been helped out of similar straits by external assistance but on this occasion the international community was firmly sitting on its hands, following a familiar 'wait and see' stance. This was a vicious circle; the government could not take the measures demanded as a precondition for help without having some advance money for that purpose, its coffers being empty. As usual, donor countries were looking to the international financial institutions to take the lead, and the International Monetary Fund had its own conditions to exert, prime among them the reduction of the fiscal deficit. A few more generous countries did provide cash to offset the deficit, so that the civil service and the military could be paid, but most adhered to their traditional policy of not providing direct budget support.

In February matters came to a tragic head. In response to demands from the IMF, the government announced a tax reform designed to increase the revenue received by the treasury. The prospect of additional income tax produced a public furore. On 12 and 13 February 2003 the police staged a strike that amounted to a revolt. The pretext was a demand for salary rises, but the real cause was the new tax law, seized on by certain dissident elements in the police force whose real intent was to bring down the government. Some units surrounded the Plaza Murillo where the Presidential Palace and the Congress are situated and there was bedlam in the centre of the city. The government called out the armed forces, hoping to restore order peacefully; but in Bolivia the military and the police have traditionally been rivals, enjoying varying fortunes in successive governments. Historically, the police had generally fared better since the 1952 revolution, when the MNR authorities had reduced the military to its minimal expression. Now the situation was different.

Inevitably, shots were fired. Civilians converging on the Plaza Murillo to join in the fray, including students, were caught in the crossfire, and there were casualties. Police sharpshooters were stationed on roofs all round the plaza and shots were fired at the Presidential Palace. The bullets, with alarming and suspicious accuracy, pierced the windows of the room in which the president worked, and of his private dining room. Although in the palace at the time he was fortunately not in either of these places but had to be smuggled out and taken to a safe hiding place.

Hordes of people went on the rampage, destroying ministries, the headquarters of various parties and public buildings of any description and stealing all portable contents. Some of the perpetrators were protesters infuriated by the deaths, others opportunistic looters. La Paz had seen nothing like this for many decades: such scenes of unbridled violence belonged to an earlier age and most citizens were appalled by their re-emergence.

After two days the military were able to restore order. The offending tax law was withdrawn and the IMF gave the funds it had previously withheld, but it was plain to see that this was a crucially defining moment: if the government did not take effective action to assuage popular demands, its days would be limited. The warning was crystal clear. What was not so clear was how the challenge might be met. In hindsight, perhaps the task was impossible and the government irretrievably doomed.

I was not in Bolivia and so did not witness these seismic events, though I followed them closely from afar. Then in early April I received an urgent summons to La Paz: the president wanted my help in organising an early World Bank Consultative Group meeting. My recommendation of eight months earlier had been accepted, albeit tardily.

I arrived post-haste on 9 April. Goni himself was leaving two days later for an official visit to Spain. He received me immediately and we plunged into business. He was now firmly convinced of the need to have the Consultative Group meeting and wanted it as soon as possible. May was the suggested date. I pointed out that this was too short a period in which to ready the government position and all the needed technical reports. But all the ministers were equally insistent that it must take place soon.

Goni was deeply concerned by the attitude of the international community, which he perceived to be reluctant to provide funds to help resolve the crisis, and even hostile. His view had been cemented by a recent meeting with ambassadors and other representatives of donor countries and international financial institutions. This had been a disastrous occasion. Others recounted to me what had happened and I could hardly believe my ears. The discussion had become heated and the IMF representative had told the president, in the presence of the assembled gathering, that he, Goni, was responsible for the deaths during the February uprising. The president, usually calm and full of bonhomie, had lost his temper and retorted that it was the IMF that should have the deaths on its conscience. The meeting had broken up in disarray.

Goni now wanted me to visit all the missions of donor countries in La Paz to do some diplomatic fence-building, test the water for the Consultative Group meeting and report to him on his return from Europe.

The Goni I found on this visit was very different from the one I thought I knew well. For the first time he seemed unsure of himself. The events of February had affected him deeply by their cataclysmic violence. More personally he was traumatised by what he considered to be a premeditated attempt on his own life. He showed me the bullet holes in the windows; one was directly behind his worktable and could well have killed him had he been sitting there.

Many people thought his reaction exaggerated and the trajectory of the bullets accidental. As I told him, I was perhaps one of the very few people who could empathise with his feelings since I, too, had been in danger of assassination when Jonas Savimbi had issued death threats against me ten years earlier in Angola. It is possible to understand that people dislike you, or your policies, but much harder to accept that they hate you so much as to want to eliminate you entirely.

Personally, I did not believe that there had been a deliberate attempt on Goni's life but nor, given the position of the bullet holes, did I think that the shots were accidental. It seemed much more likely that, in the frenzy of the combat, someone, knowing the whereabouts of the president's apartments, had taken a pot shot, carried away in the heat of the moment.

It will probably never be known what really happened. What is sure is that this incident had an enduring effect on the president and his future actions. One could hardly blame him. A lamp-post garlanded with flowers in the plaza below his window was a perpetual reminder of the fate of an earlier MNR president, Villaroel, who was hung from it by an enraged mob in 1946.

I undertook a hectic programme of visits to the embassies of all the countries that had aid programmes for Bolivia, as well as the offices of the World Bank, the International Monetary Fund and the many agencies of the United Nations System represented in the country.

It was a sobering experience. With one or two exceptions, everyone I talked to was profoundly pessimistic about the future of the government and the prospects for external aid. They were harshly critical of the way the authorities had handled the events of February. They blamed what they considered to be the president's inaction in launching programmes to satisfy the demands of the population as the root cause of the upheavals that had nearly toppled the government. The same depressing theme was echoed almost everywhere: unless he took urgent steps to redress the situation they believed the government would not survive long and conditions would not be favourable for a successful Consultative Group meeting, because donors would be unwilling to commit assistance. For many, a main bone of contention was the government's request for direct budgetary support to the treasury, to resolve the chronic problems caused by the budget deficit, though a minority among them had contributed some funds for that purpose.

While it was true that the government had been slow in tackling the underlying problems, I was appalled by the self-righteous certainty, and even arrogance, with which many of my interlocutors expressed these damning views, and particularly their outright rejection of any arguments about extenuating circumstances. The fact that the president had no money and a divided cabinet cut no ice. The most vociferous were young, and did not appear ever to have run anything other than a small unit in a functioning bureaucracy, certainly nothing like a large, unruly country, politically divided and virtually bankrupt, although some of them evidently thought they were running Bolivia. Nor did they seem to realise that their position was exacerbating the situation.

But whether I liked it or not, the message was unequivocal and I had no option but to take it to the president. Our meeting, when he returned from Spain, was uncharacteristically stormy. Characteristically, however, it took place late at night, only a few hours before my own dawn departure for Europe.

I had prepared a detailed report, which I summarised for him, along with my recommendations for redressing the situation. I had hardly expected him to be pleased, but perhaps resigned at confirmation of what he had already feared. Instead, I was startled by his infuriated reaction. He was obviously deeply affected by the lack of comprehension of his difficulties and I could well understand his frustration. He seemed to be angry with me, almost shouting and at one point banging the table. I begged him not to shoot the messenger, pointing out that I had done what he asked and that it was my duty to tell him the blunt truth, so that we could take stock of the situation and decide what to do. Goni was not easily appeased and there came a moment when I found myself banging the table at him. At this point an ADC entered the room, either with an urgent message or alerted by the raised voices, but the startled look on his face was truly memorable.

Things then calmed down and we discussed the issues with the thoroughness that was always Goni's hallmark. We agreed that the Consultative Group meeting should be held as soon as possible but also that it must be properly prepared, not only technically, but also politically and diplomatically, particularly given the present atmosphere of scepticism. It was already 21 April and the proposed date of May was, I said, out of the question. The representative of the World Bank had expressed the same opinion to me. Goni hoped for June or July but I had to warn that even this might be too soon. It was agreed that ministers and officials should start on technical preparations right away, and documents would be sent to me for comments.

We talked about the steps that might be taken to demonstrate that the government was pro-active and not just reacting desperately, and tardily, to events, as well as ways of regaining the confidence of the international community. I had perforce to mention one particularly delicate issue constantly raised during my meetings: the alleged prevalence of corruption at all levels of government. Goni was all too aware of this and of the need to take visible action against this corrosive evil. He had charged his Vice-President, Carlos Mesa, with specific responsibilities in this regard, and had appointed a special investigator to assist him. The general complaint had been that, even with these procedures in place, things had been moving too slowly. Goni confided, in some despair, that much of his time was spent in forestalling demands from members of his coalition for posts that would bring a lucrative reward.

We parted friends, as always, and I pledged my readiness to help whenever needed. But I left next morning with a less than joyful heart, painfully aware that unless things improved over the next six months, the prospects for Bolivia looked very bleak.

18

Of Gods and Demons

If national politics were not going well, the same could also be said of the domestic variety at Villa Margarita. During that April visit the war of words continued unabated between Aida and Johnny, though it was a one-sided battle for Johnny usually kept silent. I was, however, kept informed by each of them, blow by blow, of every skirmish. Mateo for his part, lost no opportunity of stoking the fire, usually with darts directed at Johnny, and usually urged on by Aida. All the peacekeeping and mediation skills that I try to impart to military forces all over the world were called into action.

One of Aida's more serious accusations was that, when she was away in La Paz, Johnny allowed children and residents of San Pedro to use the swimming pool at a charge of one boliviano (then about 25 US cents) a head and pocketed the proceeds. She also said that he had been found drunk and incapacitated in San Pedro. Johnny vehemently denied these allegations and the matter was not resolved at that time. I had certainly never seen him drunk. Eighteen months later I learned that the practice was still going on. That time we did get to the bottom of it. It transpired that it was Mateo who, with the entrepreneurial skill typical of the Aymaras, was letting out swimming rights at Villa Margarita whenever he was there alone. He was let off with a severe warning. It was also he who had been found worse for wear in San Pedro, but he had retained sufficient sense of self-preservation to mumble that his name was 'Johnny'!

There had also been a natural disaster. After years of drought the rainy season in 2003–4 was torrential. The lake, which had previously sunk so low that we had to extend the original jetty several times, now rose with a vengeance. By January 2003 it had risen two metres, and encroached some fifty metres on to my land.

242

One Sunday Johnny telephoned me in the UK in an unusual state of agitation.

'Señorita, the water has flooded my house and is now up to my knees.'

I told him to save what furniture there was and install himself in the guest room in the main house until I returned. I had not taken into account Aida's intense antipathy to Johnny. She had the keys of the main house and, as I learned later, made it quite clear to poor Johnny that no way would she allow him to sleep in the 'big house'. In an unusual show of magnanimity she at least conceded that he should have a bed in the dry: she moved into my guest room, leaving her house to Johnny!

A sorry sight awaited me when I returned in April. The house down by the beach was a ruin, gaping roofless to the sky, its adobe walls crumbling but still painted a cheerful blue. Johnny explained to me that the lake had been tossed by huge waves (it is after all an inland sea), which the adobe construction could not resist. He had saved the tiles from the roof, but little else was left.

The storm had also destroyed large sections of the perimeter wall, as well as the supposedly strong wire fence we had earlier erected out into the lake to keep intruders out and (vainly) the dogs in. The latter invariably managed to swim out and disappear for days on courting sprees in Camacachi and San Pedro.

Even more seriously our main pumping station for irrigation from the lake, and domestic water from the well, had been flooded. Machinery had to be replaced and the installations moved higher. Even the swimming pool had been inundated, not by the rising lake, but by a torrent of muddy water that rushed down the hillside from above and seeped in over the rock garden.

Once again I became locked in arguments with the insurance company. This time there could be no question about the validity of the claim. My policy included provision for acts of God (which this most certainly was) and even for damage caused by civil disturbance and revolution, all three wise precautions in a country prone to disasters, whether god-given or man-made. The point at issue was the amount of compensation due. The correspondence went on endlessly and it was not until the end of the year that I received a cheque, albeit for less than the cost of repairing the damage.

This additional misfortune brought to a head the feud between

Aida and Johnny. I found myself in an impossible situation. I needed both of them to keep Villa Margarita going. It would be hard to find another man combining Johnny's qualities of honesty and technical competence, but he was a relative newcomer and Aida had given me long and loyal service. Ever since Alejandro's death, however, the poor woman had become increasingly dour and crotchety and though the relations between the two of us were unchanged she was not a cheerful presence about the house. The bedroom that she and Alejandro had shared remained irrevocably locked, in observance of some obscure rite of respect to the dead, and continuing legal problems added to her general gloom. I tried to help but she lost confidence in the lawyer that I had engaged and went to others. It was hard to discuss logically with her what should be done.

Among her other woes Aida complained of rheumatic pains and other ills of advancing age. She suffered insomnia and constantly wailed '¡son mis nervios!' ('It's my nerves!'). She repeatedly visited my doctor, who prescribed potions and pills, but none of it did any good. She then went to another doctor who advised that she must not live in the humid atmosphere of the lake.

We hit on a compromise: Aida would leave my formal employ and I would pay her all the social benefits for her years of service, but she would continue to work for me whenever I was in residence and be paid on a daily basis. This had advantages for both of us: she would live in La Paz, but would receive a substantial lump sum, and continue to earn something from time to time. I would be there to hold the ring between her and Johnny when she came to Villa Margarita. Furthermore, her house would become permanently available for Johnny. Given the unpredictability of the weather and the levels of the lake, I had decided not to reconstruct another house anywhere in the lower part of the garden.

Problems of electricity as well as water plagued me throughout 2003. The first issue might be considered as being of a diplomatic nature. The long stretch of beach to the south west of my property is owned by several *campesinos*, who grow potatoes, quinoa and broad beans on small plots. Many of these were now flooded and their crops ruined. Suddenly a makeshift hut of adobe and corrugated iron appeared on one of these plots, followed by a large and equally unsightly shed of the same materials. Johnny informed me that the couple who owned this piece of land were starting a project to produce chickens and eggs. This seemed a worthy demonstration of entreprenurial initiative but there was a snag.

The pair had requested through Johnny that they be allowed to take electricity from my power line, which brings electricity to Villa Margarita from the rural grid running along the hill above, via a transformer that is also my property. This proposition raised several problems. There were obvious considerations about its technical viability and how much electricity would be used and how paid for, but our main concern was the identity of the pair concerned. In general I enjoy excellent relations with all my neighbours but this couple were an exception. Don Heliodoro (not his real name) was not very agreeable but the real virago was his wife, whom I shall call Doña Perpetua because she was a perpetual troublemaker, always banging on the gate with a claim that part of Wila Wila had belonged to her, or that the dogs had been among her potatoes.

She had also been the main suspect of the double poisoning of poor Pedro, a most docile and beautiful dog. The first time Sissy had saved him, but the second the desperate efforts of Alejandro and Aida had failed. Pedro's replacement was anything but docile. Aida had bought him in La Paz – a pretty dog, golden in colour with a handsome curling brush of a tail.

'What's his name?' I asked when I first encountered him on an earlier visit.

'Suni,' said Aida.

'Is Suni an Aymara word?' I enquired naively.

'No, no!' explained Aida obscurely, 'it's the name of a well-known toilet paper.'

I expostulated that this was an unfortunate name for a dog.

'But he answers to it now,' Aida said, stubbornly.

I had a brainwave and suggested we change it to 'Suri', which would sound the same to canine ears and had the more felicitous association of being the name of a group of traditional folk-dancers who wear headdresses of tall plumes, which I thought resembled the dog's plumed tail.

Even renamed, Suri had not won his way into my affections. He was aggressive with Bandy, a gentle dog, and more than once tried to bite me. He also swam well and wandered far afield. Still, I certainly did not want him poisoned and if we did not agree to provide the electrical connection I feared that Doña Perpetua, given

245

her proven vindictive tendencies, might wreak her revenge on my dogs.

Thus I found myself in a quandary. I certainly did not wish to give an outright negative and so we entered into cautious negotiations. Several hundred handsome black hens could already be seen, scurrying over the beach and scavenging, so electricity was clearly not an indispensable element in the enterprise. There was also a wonderful bombastic cockerel who greeted the sun enthusiastically every morning, a congenial wake-up call that reminded me of my rural childhood. He was a splendid fellow and he knew it. Every morning there was a comical scene when he appeared at the door of the hut together with Don Heliodoro and they would greet the new day together side by side, the cockerel spreading his wings, his master his arms.

I consulted the local electricity cooperative about the advisability of sharing my line with my neighbours. As with everything here, there were many meetings and consultations over several months until, in the end, the electricity pundits gave their view that it was not advisable, on technical grounds, to accede to the request. I held my breath for some time afterwards, awaiting an angry reaction from Doña Perpetua, but to my relief there was none. We had achieved a diplomatic solution apparently acceptable to all sides.

Don Heliodoro's project soon proved to be a non-starter. It was his Chilean son-in-law who brought the technical knowledge and special chicken food. When he went back to Chile it was downhill from there on. The flock of chickens declined visibly. Some were being sold in San Pedro, we learned, but there was no breeding programme to replace them. Then, one day, the splendid cockerel was no longer there: he too had been consigned to the pot. Eggs were sold, and I bought some to maintain good relations. Soon they were no longer available. The rapidly diminishing flock presented a sorry picture: as I observed through my binoculars, the majority had lost most of their feathers, bald pink patches encroaching on previously glossy black feathers. Johnny reported that Don Heliodoro was no longer giving supplementary food but leaving them to survive as best they could on the scant pickings of the beach. By the end of 2004 no electricity was needed, for there were no hens left, and two ugly buildings were all that remained of the project. It was all too typical of a normal sequence of events.

Animal welfare was not high on the agenda of Don Heliodoro and Doña Perpetua. They had a donkey normally tethered high on

246

the barren hillside, under a burnished sun, with little to graze on and no access to water. Aida, who loved all animals, wept at the sight, but would not countenance my suggestion that we carry water to the donkey.

'They will accuse us of trying to poison it,' she said, and for once her general pessimism about human nature seemed justified. But when Aida was not there Johnny and Mateo carried water to the donkey, fortunately unseen by the owners.

To guard the chickens during their prolonged absences Don Heliodoro and Doña Perpetua had two dogs chained on either side of the track leading down to the beach. These poor animals were tied with strands of wire round their necks. They were never unleashed, and fed only once a week, and so were very fierce. It became impossible for me to take one of my favourite walks down to the lakeside because they barred the way. One died and was replaced by a younger dog, who managed to escape and sensibly never showed his face again. The other was left there, even when all the hens had died, presumably to guard the empty buildings. Johnny smuggled food and water to him, and so the dog became a friend, pathetically grateful for every morsel.

We were inured to frequent breaks in the electricity supply. Whenever there was a storm or high wind cables came down and repairs took a long time, since the damage often occurred in inaccessible places. The San Pedro side of the Tiquina straits seemed to be more vulnerable and it was a constant source of frustration to see lights twinkling gaily on the opposite shore in San Pablo, and at various points along the road towards La Paz while we struggled with candles and a standard gas lamp, mounted on its own incredibly heavy canister, that I used for reading. Sometimes the cuts lasted several days and we feared for the precious foods in the freezer, while all the pumps would stop, irrigation was impossible, the swimming pool ceased to function and there was no water in the house. A ridiculously small reserve tank, perched on the water tower by the main gate that Lucho had erected, provided enough water only for a couple of showers. Otherwise water had to be carried up from the lake and heated by gas – with admirable forethought, the kitchen stove combined an electric oven with gas burners.

This time was different: the power was off not for days but for weeks. Johnny enquired at the house in San Pedro where we paid our monthly bills and was told that the electricity supply to the departmental cooperative from Electro Paz, the company that generates the power, had been indefinitely suspended because the cooperative was not paying its bills and now owed an immense amount of money.

A vast area was affected, for all the villages now had access to the rural grid, and there were one or two small hotels and salmon trout fisheries along the lake. Consternation was widespread. When I took my regular walks over the hill behind the house, towards Chicharro, this was the only topic of wayside conversation with passing *campesinos*.

'Señora, we have no electricity, but we pay our bills regularly,' they complained. They probably had only one or two lightbulbs in their houses but these had become a necessity of life.

'I don't have any electricity, either,' I sympathised, 'and I also pay my bills on time.'

It was from them I learned the reason. Management of the rural cooperative responsible for collecting payment from consumers all over the Department of La Paz had been entrusted to Felipe Quispe, El Mallku, in the general hand-out of posts undertaken in order to shore up the government's fragile coalition. Quispe's party, the MIP, had several seats in the Congress. My neighbours alleged that El Mallku (who was in fact their leader), and the cohorts he had appointed to run the cooperative, had used the money they collected for financing the party's electoral campaign, and lining their own pockets, instead of passing it on to Electro Paz.

They were incandescent with rage. The extent of their disillusion with their leader was extraordinary and not confined to private conversation. In the plaza of San Pedro a mass demonstration against El Mallku was held by the very people whose interests he claimed to represent.

I telephoned the president and urged him to intervene to restore the electricity supply. I realised that it was not the responsibility of the central government, since this had been delegated to local control, but warned that, in the nature of things, the government would be blamed, especially by those who would seize on every pretext to attack his administration. Moreover, the situation was gravely affecting the fragile economy of the *altiplano* and the tourist industry. There was, I pointed out, some crumb of comfort to be derived since the *campesinos* themselves now realised that their leader had betrayed them.

The situation was resolved, the money paid, and the electricity restored. But I was left with a feeling of premonition and sadness. I had always considered many of the *campesinos'* demands to be justified although I did not agree with some of the means adopted to obtain satisfaction. Now I was dismayed by this new evidence that they were being led by the nose by leaders whose main interests were their personal ambitions and political aspirations and who, in their pursuit of power, would stoop to any means of intimidation or venality. These were the very iniquities that these same leaders alleged were endemic in the existing governmental structures, and said they aimed to eliminate, but they were, in essence, no different themselves.

Johnny was proving an excellent majordomo. In the garden he did not have fingers as green as Alejandro's, but learned quickly, and his mother, who knew about pruning, came to prune the roses at the due season. He was a city boy, while Mateo, like his son Enrique, was a *campesino*, rooted in the land and Aymara tradition and deeply superstitious. Mateo also worked diligently but never mastered the art of managing the swimming pool and the pumping systems. This would not have mattered had he accepted his lack of knowledge and left well alone, but unfortunately he could not resist tampering with switches and levers when Johnny was not around, with predictably dire results. Nonetheless they got on reasonably well and I congratulated myself on having at last got a stable garden staff.

And then destiny swooped again. Some time in 2003 one of Johnny's legs swelled alarmingly, for no obvious reason. I sent him to my doctor in La Paz who prescribed various treatments and drugs but the swelling obstinately refused to subside. Johnny, in despair, tried another doctor, and spent some time in hospital. But even extended bed rest proved to be merely a temporary palliative. Alarming thoughts of deep-vein thrombosis (though Johnny had never been on a plane) and fatal blood clots kept chasing through my mind.

Mateo came up with an alternative solution. This happened when

I was abroad, and during Aida's absence, as she would never have countenanced such goings on.

'We must call in a *curandero* to help,' he advised Johnny. 'A *yatiri*.'

The *yatiri*, or *kallawayas* as they are also known, are the witch doctors of the Aymaras. They carry out religious rites and traditional forms of medicine and are still revered in rural society today. We had successfully used their services to persuade villagers to take part in rural development projects launched by the UN Andean Indian Programme (Acción Andina) when I was heading the UN mission in Bolivia in the early 1960s. Health was an important feature of that programme, particularly the reduction of the infant and maternal mortality rate, one of the highest in the world. That meant careful prenatal care for pregnant women. The snag was that women resisted the periodic examinations that this entailed until we discovered that the *yatiri* performed certain rites at various stages of a pregnancy. By combining the traditional practices with modern public health procedures we managed to achieve our objective without offending local sensibilities.

Johnny was sceptical about what a *yatiri* could do in his case but was so desperate that he reluctantly agreed. The first *yatiri* lived in San Pedro, and often passed the house on his way to water his donkey down at the lakeshore. His name was Saturnino, which had a sinister ring appropriate to someone who dabbled in black magic.

'I will come to Villa Margarita tonight,' he said, 'to read the coca leaves.' This was the favoured method of divination.

Such grave consultations have to take place at dead of night and it was after midnight when the *curandero*, squatting on the floor with Johnny and Mateo, spread out his coca leaves and began his incantations. His verdict was surprising.

'This house is constantly struck by lightning,' he said. 'This part of the land, which we call Wila-Wila, has always been used for a *pachete*.'

That word was unknown to me but, in recounting their tale, Johnny and Mateo explained that this was the term used to describe a ceremony when *mesas* (literally 'tables') are prepared as libations for the earth, and for the Pachamama or Earth Goddess. The offerings include sweets, *sebo de llama* (llama fat), llama fur, incense and *sullu de llama* (the aborted foetus of a llama).

'You see,' said the *yatiri*, 'this is a magical place,' a statement with which I could readily agree. 'But,' he then went on sternly, 'for a long time no one has put anything here. The earth is thirsty and its thirst must be slaked.'

Then came the diagnosis. 'Johnny,' he declared solemnly, 'has been attacked by *katja*,' the revenge of the angry earth because he had not *pagado* – literally because he had not paid due tribute to the earth, or the Pachamama. Only in this way could Johnny's leg be cured. Johnny and Mateo organised a *mesa* for the Pachamama, and poured generous libations of alcohol to assuage the thirst of the parched earth. The first ceremony took place at midnight on a Friday and, by their account, went on virtually until dawn. For good measure, they repeated the ritual on the following Tuesday night. Notwithstanding, Johnny's swollen leg showed no improvement.

Mateo decided that they must obtain a second opinion, this time from a female *yatiri*, called Elena, living in San Pablo, the twin village on the other side of the lake where she received them at her own home. She did a more thorough job in reading the signs, not only with coca leaves but also with cigarettes and alcohol.

She also gave as her opinion the need to '*pagar una mesa*' – roughly to 'celebrate a rite' – this time in another sacred and magical place on the other side of the lake. It is marked by three eucalyptus trees planted on the skyline of the promontory where the road to La Paz curves abruptly to the left. It is the point where I always have the last view of Villa Margarita, embraced by its encircling white walls, when I leave, and the first glimpse of home on my return. From my bed I can see these three trees silhouetted against the far horizon of the Andes. To my fanciful imagination they have always looked like a posse of horsemen led by an intrepid leader, plunging across the hills towards the lake but forever frozen in mid-motion. When I heard Johnny's story it confirmed the special significance of that place.

It was there that the San Pablo *curandero* wished to celebrate a rite. Elena's verdict was the same as Saturnino's: Johnny was the victim of *katja* and therefore the earth must be paid its due. For that purpose she requested that they provide wine and promised, 'By the eucalyptus trees I shall call for your spirit. It is a place where lightning often strikes and thunder rumbles.'

She advised Johnny that he must expose his leg to the wind.

But Johnny, to her immense consternation, bathed it, which she said nullified the whole procedure. Nevertheless, she demanded more sweets in order to continue the process, and asked Johnny to return next day. Johnny, however, did not go back for a week. Whether it was on account of these shortcomings or not, his swollen leg showed no improvement.

When I heard the tale I was struck that the diagnosis and the prescribed treatment offered by the two *yatiri* had been so similar. Their charges were very different. Our San Pedro neighbour's fee was one hundred and fifty bolivianos, while the lady across the lake requested only fifteen.

Then Johnny's mother came on a visit, took a hand in matters and prepared her own *mesa*. She had great faith in the curative powers of such rites after a bad fall in one of La Paz's steep cobbled streets. The *curandero's* verdict had also been that 'the earth had seized her' with *katja*. In her case libations of fermented urine (*orina podrida*) in the place of her fall had cured her.

At Villa Margarita elaborate arrangements were made. With Johnny's half-sister Nancy they circled his house, pouring libations and bearing the other objects being offered. As Johnny explained to me, to be effective the objects offered in the *mesa* then had to be burnt in the doorway until they were reduced to ash. Finally, just before sunrise, these were buried in the magical place in my garden, marked by a large rock perilously positioned on the steep hillside above the beach, looking as if it might fall into the lake below at any minute. He showed me the rock, where, according to local lore, lightning always strikes, although we had never seen it. Similar rites were carried out in other parts of the garden.

For good measure, the San Pedro *curandero* Saturnino prepared a concoction of herbs with which he instructed Johnny to bathe his swollen leg. He was also told that he must not drink a drop of water for three days. Johnny obediently followed all these instructions. But his leg continued swollen and, more alarmingly, turned a dark reddish-purple colour.

Johnny went back to conventional medicine, but the advice he got provided small consolation. If the condition did not improve, they said, his leg might even have to be amputated. Most frustratingly of all, no one seemed able to devise a proper diagnosis. Johnny had all sorts of tests, including for diabetes, but all proved negative.

He finally consulted a Chinese acupuncturist, who enjoyed a

reputation for achieving the impossible. Here at last were results: the swelling gradually became less, and the discolouration faded. But this was by no means the end of the story.

19

The Storm Breaks

In June 2003 I paid two visits to La Paz to assist with the preparation of the government's strategy for the Consultative Group meeting and the supporting documents.

By now it had become clear that the World Bank meeting could not possibly take place even on the later dates previously proposed. As I had anticipated, the documents were not sufficiently advanced and the bank's programme was very full. Because of the holiday season in July and August and the annual meetings of the World Bank and the IMF in September, the date selected was early October. While that timing was the best available, it was far from good from an internal viewpoint. The need for action and for outside help was more urgent than ever, and the country was caught in the familiar vicious circle. Decisive action was difficult because of lack of sufficient funds while the failure to act provoked more civil unrest, strikes and roadblocks. These, in turn, damaged the already fragile economy further and made the provision of finance ever more difficult, whether from domestic or donor sources. Some money was still coming in but, ironically, dispersal of those funds by implementing programmes and projects was hamstrung by the reigning instability. There was an impending sense of doom if something dramatic did not happen and much speculation as to how long the government could last which, of itself, bade fair to become a self-fulfilling prophecy.

During those two visits I spent little time at Villa Margarita (where there was no electricity anyway), my days being taken up with meetings in La Paz. In several tête-à-tête encounters with the president I found him more relaxed than in April, though still not the dynamic Goni of old. The continuing problems of his fractious coalition, apparently oblivious to the need to work together to save the government and the country, weighed heavily upon him.

I did my best to cheer him up, and encourage him to press ahead with his plan to consolidate the reforms of his first term with sound social programmes. This time he listened quietly and did not vent his frustration on me as he had in April. He had several close confidants in his cabinet, but I gained the impression, perhaps ill-founded, that he found himself more able to unburden himself to me, as someone on the periphery of the unfolding events, with more objective judgement and no axe to grind.

Since the bloody events of February the government was living on borrowed time. In April I had sent a report emphasising the gravity of the situation to Mark Malloch Brown, the administrator of UNDP in New York. Mark was an old friend of both Goni and myself – in an earlier, private capacity he had advised him on the conduct of his election campaigns in 1989 and 1993. He rallied to the call and in May paid a flying visit to La Paz to talk to the president. As perturbed as the rest of us by the ominous portents, he proposed a high-level brainstorming session in New York to try to find a viable way ahead. He invited ministers and other senior officials forming the economic team, as well as some well-known international economists, the UNDP Resident Representative and myself.

The meeting took place on 30 June and 1 July, and some very hard-hitting discussion papers were prepared for the event. Goni was not supposed to be there but, as usual, he wanted to be in the driver's seat and so he flew to New York to take part in the debate.

There was very frank discussion. One of the economists was Jeffrey Sachs, who had worked closely with Goni when, as Minister of Planning in 1985, he had been the prime mover, under President Víctor Paz Estenssoro, in introducing the IMF-inspired policies that had stopped the galloping inflation and set the economy on a more even keel, albeit at great social cost. Supreme Decree No. 21060 that had brought these measures into effect was now one of the main bones of contention among all the protesters opposing the government. It was intriguing to see that Sachs's opinion of the economic liberalisation that he formerly espoused had undergone a radical sea change. He had recently published an article in the *Financial Times* severely critical of the failure of the international community and its financial institutions to provide adequate support to Bolivia in its hour of greatest need.

The main achievement of this informal gathering was to reach agreement on the strategy to be adopted in preparing for the Consultative Group meeting, especially the need to convince sceptical donors that the government did mean business and to prepare the ground with them ahead of the session.

There was a lighter moment. July 1 was the president's birthday. That night he was flying back to his troubled country and I to the UK. So it was late on the previous evening that a small party was held with his wife and family, and some close friends. On the stroke of midnight we drank a champagne toast to his health and success. I think we must all have wished most fervently as we drank, for this was much more than an ordinary birthday toast. So much was at stake in the coming months and it was to be the last time I saw the president enjoying himself unreservedly.

In the last days of August I received an urgent call to return to La Paz. I arrived in the dawn of 1 September, and went straight into meetings, culminating in a large working dinner with the president. The Sunday before I had had a stupid fall in Knill on the stone terrace. I arrived in Bolivia with the remains of a black eye, both legs black and blue and one of them heavily bandaged. This gave the president the chance to make some speculative jokes as to the kind of people I consorted with in the UK.

That was an encouraging flash of his old, sometimes rather acerbic, sense of humour that endeared him to some but alienated others. We were a large group around the table – cabinet ministers, financial officials, the UNDP Resident Representative and myself. The Consultative Group meeting was to take place in Paris on 8 and 9 October and time was short. The draft documents, though technically sound, were very long and I put in a plea for a concise covering paper that would present Bolivia's plight in dramatic terms. This, I argued, was necessary in order to grasp the attention of ministers and policy-makers in the donor countries, who would not have time to wade through wads of technicalities, and my idea was accepted.

In order to engage a favourable response from donors ahead of the meeting, most of us felt that it was essential the president should call a meeting of their local representatives. Goni resisted the proposal; the memory of his bruising encounter with donors earlier in the year, when the IMF representative had accused him of being responsible for the February deaths, was still fresh in his mind.

He was much more amenable to the idea of a preparatory mission round the capitals of Europe, on which I would go as his personal envoy, accompanied by officials from the ministry of finance. Such missions had borne dividends during his first mandate but I had to point out that the situation was now very different. Then I had been personally acquainted with some of the relevant ministers in the countries we visited. Not only was that no longer the case but in several European countries elections had brought in governments significantly more to the right and less well disposed to development cooperation. I was, nonetheless, ready to go but reminded everyone that we had been talking of such a mission for several months and that, if it was to have any effect, urgent arrangements must be made. Equally important was the early despatch of the documents, particularly the proposed policy paper, as it would serve as an aide-mémoire for the ministers we would meet.

Things then moved fast. Next morning I wrote a first draft of the covering policy paper which was discussed that afternoon with the talented young officials in the finance ministry in charge of the documentation. Later I met Vice President Carlos Mesa, whom I always kept informed of what I was doing.

During that day I and others were able to persuade Goni to hold a meeting with donors and it was hastily convened for the morning of 4 September. On 3 September I worked all morning on the finalisation of the policy paper with Vice Minister of Finance Roberto Camacho, and George Gray Molina, a brilliant young economist who was coordinating all the documents. Immediately afterwards I lunched with Goni. Our talk turned mainly on the donors' meeting and as we were on our own I was able to speak frankly, begging him to keep his cool and not be irked by the provocative remarks that were all too likely to be made by some of the participants.

In the early evening there was another meeting in the ministry of finance on the policy paper. This was a tightly worded five page document entitled 'A Strengthened Partnership to achieve the Millenium Development Goals'. These goals, or MDGs, adopted by the United Nations and the international community in 2000, aimed to reduce poverty worldwide by the year 2015. At the present rhythm Bolivia would not achieve them until 2042, twenty-seven years after the deadline. Under the stark heading 'Two Decades of Democracy and Reforms at Risk' the document frankly analysed the grave political, economic and social crisis of the country, but pointed out that the longer-term perspective was much more promising, provided the crisis could be overcome. This relative optimism was based on the prospects of significant increases in revenues from gas exports which, it was calculated, could come on stream by 2008 if exploitation began immediately. The request to the international community was for bridging finance to support the economy in the interim.

None of this could be achieved, the paper concluded, nor could the MDGs be attained by 2015, without strong international support. If the realisation of the MDGs was long delayed, the consequences were likely to be extremely grave. Moreover a reversal of the Bolivian reforms would have wide repercussions beyond its frontiers, by raising doubts over the viability of the strict economic policy adopted over the previous eighteen years, with the support of the international community.

Although the document did not say so in so many words, that policy, followed faithfully by Bolivia for nearly two decades, had been imposed by the international community as a pre-condition for their assistance. The strategy adopted for the Consultative Group thus bore relevance to the interests of the traditional donor countries as well as those of Bolivia. In addition it offered donors the encouraging prospect that outside aid could begin to scale down after 2008 if the gas was by then producing the anticipated additional revenue.

At 10 o'clock that evening we presented the results of our work to the president and his ministers of the presidency and of finance, who would lead the delegation to Paris, and they approved the paper, subject to a few minor adjustments. At the same session, which went on until after midnight, we also briefed Goni on the points to be made to the donors' meeting the next day.

Next morning he was in splendid form, making a brilliant presentation based on our policy paper, spiced with humour and showing all his old qualities of a charismatic leader. The room was packed and I could not help reflecting how much more complicated development aid had become over the years, with the multiplication of donor countries and organisations. Nor could I help wondering whether it had become more, or less, effective as a result. The atmosphere was certainly more positive than in April, although some of the questions were quite barbed, but Goni fielded them all with aplomb, supported by his ministers and myself.

The one really tense moment came when the Chargé d'Affaires of the German Embassy, in a quite impertinent manner, criticised the government for having passed a law the previous December about the use of funds forthcoming from the debt relief HIPC programme without first consulting them! This, he said, had given rise to heated debate in the German parliament and he demanded an explanation. One could hardly imagine more gross interference in the internal affairs of a sovereign country, and I sensed the president bristle beside me. But he kept his cool admirably and put the speaker in his place diplomatically but firmly.

There was an amusing incident at the end of the meeting. As a prompter to his remarks Goni had on the table in front of him a copy of the policy paper, not yet ready for release. The Spanish ambassador sitting opposite had his eye on this and, as we all stood up, made a lunge across the table to grab it. Fortunately I had my eye on *him* and got there first. So much for the sophisticated methods of modern diplomacy, I thought!

Afterwards we all felt that good progress had been made and that things were on course for the Paris meeting. It was a tough two weeks' work. I only managed to snatch a long weekend in Villa Margarita but I had a sense of accomplishment when, on 10 September, I flew to the UK to prepare for the mission to European capitals.

But the government's future was still hanging on a thread. Popular pressure through strikes, marches and road blockages continued unabated. I got out just in time before the road from Villa Margarita to the capital was once again impassable. This latest uprising on the *altiplano* was to erupt into an immensely grave incident that, in hindsight, signalled the beginning of the end, only a few days after my departure. I described it in my annual letter:

About a thousand tourists, Bolivians and foreigners, who were attending a traditional 'fiesta' in Sorata, a sub-tropical valley tucked away in the lee of the Andes, were stranded. The only way out was through Achacachi, the headquarters of El Mallku, and notorious throughout history as a focus of violence and the convoy of buses, trucks and cars bringing them out was held up in nearby Warisata. In the end the government had to send in police and military. The tourists were brought out unharmed but there were two or three fatalities, both police

259

and civilian. All the area around Tiquina remained inaccessible for most of a month and during the rest of September I was in anxious telephone-contact with Johnny at Villa Margarita. My main concern was the immediate physical welfare of him and Mateo (food was scarce and Johnny had a swollen leg and could not get back to the doctor) but the possibility of an invasion of my property was not far from my mind either. The local people are not in favour of these mass protests, which damage their livelihoods, and I have good relations with them, but they are also subject to coercion and retribution from their leaders.

The debate about exactly what happened and who was responsible for the escalation into lethal violence still goes on. El Mallku's men had firearms as well as the customary sticks and stones and machetes. But many observers point the finger of blame at Sánchez Berzaín, widely seen as the president's hard-liner. After the events of February the president had removed him from the post of Interior Minister and made him Secretary General of the MNR party. Then, in August, there had been another ministerial reshuffle, in which Sánchez Berzaín had become Minister of Defence. In that capacity he had himself gone to the site of the incident and, it was said, fired a pistol into the air which provoked a violent response from the protesters.

The repercussions from this open clash signified another nail in the government's coffin, both within the country and in its international standing. The omens for the Paris meeting now looked very bad, and there was much discussion as to whether it should take place at all. All this delayed decisions about the mission to European capitals and in Knill I sat anxiously by the telephone waiting for news.

Then things abated somewhat and I set out on 29 September with George Gray. It was again a series of one-night stands fitted into the space of one week. We started in London and then went on to Brussels (to see both the European Commission and the Belgian government), Germany (both Berlin and Bonn), Stockholm and Rome. Roberto Camacho was able to join the team in Germany. The strategy paper was well received everywhere.

On 6 October we reached Paris where we joined the ministers of the presidency, finance and public works and the rest of the

Bolivian delegation. On the evening of 7 October the World Bank gave its customary dinner for delegation heads. A technical innovation that year was a live TV appearance by Goni. A little hesitant at first, he soon warmed to his theme and gave an excellent presentation of the situation and of his policies. The only problem, I reflected, was that he was preaching to the largely converted: his message about the use of the gas for the benefit of the Bolivian people, was even more urgently needed at home. Extracts from my annual letter from Bolivia relate what happened subsequently:

Donor countries and organisations were well represented, some at a very high level: the United States by Otto Reich, the Presidential Adviser on Latin America, as well as the US Ambassador to Bolivia, David Greenlee. The ministers brought depressing news of a deteriorating situation at home, with violent clashes in El Alto, the sprawling urban community above La Paz, of some 800,000 people ... most of them having migrated ... from the countryside. Miners were also marching on the capital, as well as the other groups.

So it was with a real sense of urgency that our meeting took place on 8–9th October. The main problem was the yawning fiscal gap. Government strategy envisaged covering this over the longer term with receipts from the export of the vast resources of liquid gas found in Campo Margarita(!) ... after domestic needs had been met. The gas receipts would go into a special fund dedicated to increasing education, health and social programmes ... as part of the anti-poverty programme. This would also have the advantage of reducing dependence on foreign aid once the gas came on stream, which was expected to be in 2008, if agreement with the foreign companies could be reached. In the interim donors were requested not only to maintain their assistance, but also to modify its modalities, by providing budgetary support, accepting a programme approach responding to government priorities (instead of their own preferred projects) and generally being more flexible so as to make better use of the existing international resources. All the donors expressed support of this approach, except our hosts, the World Bank, which made an extraordinarily bureaucratic quibble about releasing funds urgently needed before the end of the year. (They are now being made available, which prompts the cynical reflection that governments have to fall before money can be provided!)

The meeting closed with a Joint Declaration that gave all the political and financial support the government needed. Sadly, it was to prove a case of a successful operation, but the patient died. The three ministers and I made a conference call to the President late on Thursday 9th October, to give him the good news and express the hope that the declaration could be given prominence in the media and help assuage public opinion. It was too late. La Paz was completely cut off by the blockade in El Alto, food and fuel supplies were running out – unruly mobs, a mixture of protesters and criminals, were running amok in the centre of the city, smashing and looting shops. Although some radical elements had been purged from their ranks, the police, still smarting from the events of February, did not come out to control the situation. On Saturday, 11th October, the government took the crucial decision to send in the military to escort a convoy of fuel bound for the beleaguered city ... There was armed confrontation and deaths resulted among both soldiers and protesters. Our success in Paris went unnoticed.

Ironically, the three protesting groups – coca-growers, indigenous people and miners – joined together under the common banner of opposing the export of gas, the main resource from which Bolivia's future may be salvaged and their own demands met. A main bone of contention had always been that the most economic method of export would be through Chile, the traditional arch enemy since the nineteenth-century Pacific war which robbed Bolivia of its seacoast. But the demand now was that the gas should not be exported at all ... Since Bolivia's relatively small population could never absorb the quantities available, this makes no sense. The gas argument was a pretext: each group had its own agenda. The tragic events of October, now dubbed 'The Gas War', sprang from much more deeply rooted issues, poverty and centuries-long social exclusion and discrimination. The 1952 revolution sought to redress that with very radical measures and at first succeeded, but that effort was diluted by years of military dictatorships (1964–82). The introduction of economic liberalisation policies in 1985, ... benefited a few but signally failed to improve the lot of ordinary, very poor, people.

An Oruro devil dancer, accoutred for the 'diablada' © Tony Morrison, South American Pictures.

'Morenada' dancers in the village of Amacaya in August 2008 © Peter Johnson.

The author marching with the Mayor and other dignitaries of San Pedro de Tiquina on Bolivian National Day, 6 August 2006.

Vista of La Paz © Tony Morrison, South American Pictures.

The author with former President Gonzalo Sánchez de Lozada and friends walking in the Yungas in August 1999.

The author with former President Víctor Paz Estenssoro in Tarija in May 1995.

The author with then President Hugo Banzer Suárez at the peacekeeping training exercise in La Paz in 1999.

The author taken 'hostage' during the peacekeeping training exercise in Honduras in 2000.

Fiesta during one of the author's visits to the Otavi hospital in the 1990s.

The author with staff at reconstructed Otavi hospital in March 2009.

Calle Jaén in La Paz © Peter Johnson, August 2008.

Mural in the swimming pool at Villa Margarita

Copacabana © Peter Johnson, August 2008.

Inca terraces on the Isla del Sol in Lake Titicaca.

The lower reaches of the road from La Paz to Yungas © Kimball Morrison, South American Pictures.

On Monday, 13th October, the Vice President, Carlos Mesa, distanced himself from the government. A day or two later one of the other parties in the ruling coalition did likewise. The writing was now on the wall, and the clamour for the resignation of the President became irresistible. On the evening of 16th October, by a curious coincidence, I gave a talk at Canning House, in London, entitled 'A Woman in Latin America', ... Naturally Bolivia figured large ... in my appreciation of the current situation in the region, and I could not be optimistic. Next day, 17th October, the government fell and the President went into exile in the United States. He and his family had to be taken by helicopter to the airport as the more extreme elements had publicly vowed to kill him and were gathered along the land route ready to carry out their threat. ... Carlos Mesa, as the Vice President, was quickly sworn in as the new President.

This cataclysmic dénouement has all the elements of a Greek or Shakespearian tragedy. In his first administration it was Goni who introduced sweeping measures to promote popular participation. Unfortunately, that principle, a cornerstone of democracy, and vigorously espoused by donors and NGOs, has been interpreted here as a vehicle for claiming rights and privileges, without any corresponding recognition of obligations and responsibilities. Another irony is that Carlos Mesa, who was brought into politics by Goni as his Vice-President, has now succeeded him, little more than a year after their joint inauguration in August 2002. ... He is charismatic and well-reputed as a former TV political analyst, but has no party political support or previous government experience and time is not on his side. His popularity is high now, but the dissidents have given him ninety days to meet their demands (some quite beyond Bolivia's means) and although only six weeks have elapsed since he took office, various protest marches are already in train.

The most disquieting aspect is that the whole democratic system is being called into question. This is a struggle between system and anti-system with unpredictable consequences...

I appreciate only too well that, to an Iraq-obsessed world, what happens here is considered to be of little consequence. Perhaps precisely because of that it is useful to write about it, for the events here are typical of problems and tendencies in other parts of Latin America, which can sow the seeds of serious instability for the continent in the future.

I described my state of mind at the end of my letter:

> ... the debâcle here, which I always knew to be an imminent danger, has hit hard. The phrase '*à quoi bon?*' re-echoes in my mind, not only as regards my work for Bolivia over four months of this year, but over the past forty-three years. I came back decided not to get involved again but inevitably find myself asked to help and cannot refuse. My allegiance has never been to any political party but only to Bolivia, and that is an addiction hard to shake off.
>
> I am not alone in my doubts. An old friend, and remarkable educationalist, Miguel Soler, ... recently wrote me a reflective letter about the state of education and the world generally, in which he mused, 'Will it be our lot to die seeing all our dreams for a better world disintegrate before our eyes?' He went on to say that, like me, he is not a pessimist, and retains all his old determination for the struggle, but that his scepticism grows dangerously.
>
> Walking in the Burghese Gardens on my October Sunday in Rome I came across the wonderful statue of Byron, with a quotation from his poem 'Childe Harold' beneath: 'A world lies at our feet, as fragile as clay'. He was writing of Ancient Rome, nearly two hundred years ago, but his words have a disturbing ring of actuality.

20

The Aftermath

To demonstrate United Nations support for the maintenance of democracy in Bolivia an official visit by UN Secretary General Kofi Annan had been planned for mid-November 2003. Although the government was overthrown a few weeks earlier, Bolivia was in even greater need of international backing and the visit went ahead.

In the new circumstances I had no stomach to be there and I had commitments elsewhere. Nonetheless I became involved peripherally in the preparations. The first call was nothing short of amazing. At ten o'clock one night the telephone rang in Knill. The caller was Lucho, the renegade builder of Villa Margarita, unseen for several years, and with whom I was in contact only through lawyers' letters, trying with signal lack of success to obtain repayment of his longstanding debt. Lucho, never abashed by such trivial considerations, went to the point straight away: 'Carlos Mesa wants you to come at once to organise Kofi Annan's visit. Your travel and all your expenses will be paid.'

When I had recovered the power of speech, I pointed out that there were plenty of people already doing that, both in the government and the UNDP office, and they certainly did not need me as well. Lucho was insistent and, as always, keen to show that he was on close terms with those in highest authority. Finally, I said, 'Look, Lucho, if Carlos Mesa really does want me to come, I am always ready to help, but I will only believe this if he or someone on his staff speaks to me personally.'

Needless to say, I heard nothing further from anyone on this. And as I put the phone down I regretted that I had not had the presence of mind to enquire of Lucho when he planned to repay me.

Then came another call, this time from the ambassador in the

265

Bolivian Foreign Ministry who handled UN affairs. Could I advise on the kind of help they should request from the secretary general? I suggested that the president should ask for an arrangement similar to that of 1982, when newly democratic Bolivia was struggling to right itself after years of military dictatorship. Then Pérez de Cuéllar had used his good offices with other member countries and international financial institutions to obtain flexible treatment for Bolivia. For that purpose he had named a senior official – myself in that case – to act on his behalf.

My proposed strategy was adopted and the Secretary General, Kofi Annan, appointed a Colombian Under Secretary General, José Antonio Ocampo, to visit La Paz.

I returned on 24 November and spent a month at Villa Margarita. One particularly nostalgic occasion was a Sunday barbecue with the old team from the ministry of finance with whom I had worked so closely and travelled round Europe before the Paris meeting such a short time before.

Everyone was in a state of shock. We had all been very conscious of the fragility of Goni's administration but no one had expected the overturn to be so violent, or the opposition to the government to become so personalised in intense hatred of the president. Goni's life had been really in peril. I found parallels with the events in Chile in 1973 that I had witnessed at first hand, when the downfall of the Allende government had been inevitable but no one had thought that it would take such a savage form or that the president would die. There the analogy ends: fortunately the trappings of democracy had been retained in Bolivia and there was no military coup, with the horrific consequences that Chile had endured.

Nevertheless, the aftershocks of the political earthquake that had rocked the country continued to be felt. Ironically the pink electoral slogans proclaiming Goni as presidential candidate, scrawled on walls and rocks all over the countryside during the 2002 campaign, still remained but now more sinister signs had sprung up alongside: 'Goni, *asesino*' ('Goni assassin'). The populist forces, especially Evo Morales, the leader of the *cocaleros*, were virulent in their attacks on the former president, now exiled in Washington. They even accused him of genocide. It was lamentable that between 50 and 60 people had been killed (there has never been agreement on the exact number) but this had been during the heat of the fray and could hardly be accepted, either in intent or numbers, as

266

conforming to the international legal definition of genocide. Moreover, the fatalities had been on both sides.

I had spoken several times to Goni by telephone, both during the last days of the crisis, when he and his family had been holed up in the presidential residence, and after his flight from the country. Not surprisingly he was traumatised by what had happened and the vertiginous manner in which he had been catapulted from power. He was also very bitter about Carlos Mesa, whom he had brought into government, and who he considered had precipitated the dénouement by distancing himself from the government a few days beforehand. But when I told him that overtures had been made to me about advising the new government on its international policies, as I had done for a succession of previous governments, he readily agreed that I should do so. He knew that my allegiance had always been to the country and its people, and that my services had always been provided *pro bono publico*.

While some might rejoice politically, the country's economic situation was now worse than ever. The deficit had increased, donors were hesitating to provide aid, and foreign private investors were alarmed. Onlookers were generally concerned that Bolivia had reverted to its old volatile habits of rapid changes of government and that the theme of our strategy paper in Paris 'Twenty Years of Bolivian Democracy and Reforms at Risk' had proved all too prescient.

The greatly fortified populist leaders multiplied their demands. They wanted higher salaries and greater benefits; rescission of Supreme Decree number 21060 of 1985 and economic liberalisation policies; and re-nationalisation of state enterprises, especially those dealing with natural resources. They were against many things: globalisation, the IMF, the USA and export of the country's huge deposits of natural gas, not only through Chile but anywhere at all. They did not seem to realise that such measures would be self-defeating, bankrupting the country further, and making the fulfilment of their economic and social demands even more impossible.

Carlos Mesa was enjoying unprecedented popularity and was regarded as the saviour of the nation. But it was obvious that continued public support for his fragile authority would depend on his ability to meet all the demands made on the government. He had named a cabinet of technocrats and, in his first speech, announced his intention to govern without the traditional political parties, which scarcely endeared him to them or to the Congress.

267

Evo Morales had emerged greatly strengthened after his leading role in the October events. It was alleged that he had received funds in the region of $US38 million from President Hugo Chávez of Venezuela to facilitate his successful efforts to bring down the government. He had frequently visited Chávez in Caracas and attended several antiglobalisation conferences in Europe, and so became known internationally. He was constantly visiting the new president and had great influence over him, for Mesa's fragile authority could only survive by giving into his demands. There were, however, signs of change in Morales' tactics. It looked as if he now aspired to become President of Bolivia through democratic means and this tempered some of the more outrageous actions that he had earlier favoured. Felipe Quispe, El Mallku, was reputed to have lost some ground but he was still strong in Achacachi and could bring the *altiplano* region around the lake to a standstill as he constantly threatened.

The ambassador in the foreign ministry who had called me in the UK now requested my advice as to how the fledgling new government could regain the confidence of the international community and so retrieve the benefits promised at the Paris meeting in October. I prepared key points for yet another international strategy (though in a very different context), and on 18 December the ambassador and I had a meeting with the new Secretary General of the Presidency at which I expounded them. He also waxed enthusiastic and insisted that I should have an urgent meeting with Carlos Mesa. But although the ambassador reminded him several times, nothing came of it. His renewed enquiries when I returned in March met a similar blank wall. It was hard not to conclude that I was being blackballed for having advised the previous government.

The UN Secretary General's office asked me to support José Antonío Ocampo, the Colombian emissary appointed by Kofi Annan to help Bolivia, but here too the relationship petered out at the beginning of 2004 and nothing very concrete resulted.

On 27 November Captain Villaroel, the current commander of the naval base at Tiquina came to lunch. It was a beautiful day and we ate outside on the upper terrace. The lake was calm and the mountains shimmering on the horizon girdled a scene of utter serenity, quite at variance with the turbulent affairs of the humans who dwelt there.

Aida had launched her own bombshell that morning. Only three days after my return she announced at breakfast that she no longer felt able, for health reasons, to work out at the lake at all, not even for the periods of my visits, as we had agreed only a few months before, or for the remaining weeks of my current stay. Her decision came right out of the blue. It was all immensely inconvenient but I determined it best to make no effort to persuade her to stay. She did prepare lunch for the commandant and myself and then departed, her suitcase already packed, making it obvious that she had been contemplating this move for some time. The whole of my little Bolivian world seemed to be changing all at once.

The commandant gave me a riveting account of the events that had culminated in the ousting of the president, particularly those of September on the road to Sorata. This region lay in his bailiwick and he had had to send troops to quell the uprising.

His analysis of what had happened and of future prospects made dismal listening. He was critical of Goni's handling of the crisis. Perhaps predictably, given his naval background, he thought that the president should have taken firmer action by sending in the military earlier. That way, he argued, the uprising could have been nipped in the bud and fatalities avoided. He also thought that the president had made a cardinal error by re-admitting Sánchez Berzaín into the cabinet as Minister of Defence. Sánchez Berzaín had flouted the tradition that civilians holding that portfolio should confine themselves to policy matters and not interfere in the day-to-day running of the military. He had been intensely unpopular with the armed forces. His gung-ho behaviour during the Sorata and Warisata standoff had, in the opinion of my guest, been the spark that led to the disastrous outcome.

I asked him if the military hierarchy was minded to take over the country. No, he replied. Since the return to democracy in 1982 they had kept strictly to their constitutional role, and would be very reluctant to do any such thing, except in the direst of circumstances. His greatest fear was that the historical tension between the poor indigenous highlands and the more prosperous lowlands, notably the Departments of Santa Cruz and Tarija, was now reaching the point of outright schism. The indigenous majority had proved their ability to bring down an elected government and advanced further along the road to political power. That reawakened traditional secessionist tendencies in other areas and could lead to a break-up of the country. If that were to happen there could even be a risk of civil war, in which case the military would be caught in the middle and suffer greatly.

When he had left I had to turn my thoughts to household problems. Johnny came to the rescue, suggesting that his half-sister, Nancy, could come and help out. That same evening she arrived by microbus from Le Paz. It was a very Bolivian solution. I could only hope that the same native wit could be applied to solving the problems of the country.

There was more bad news on the personal front. I had long been worried about the health of my old and dear friend, Roberto Jordán Pando. Fate had dealt him some severe blows in recent years, and now he was at death's door.

As recounted earlier, in 1998 he had been appointed Bolivian Ambassador to the United Nations. Many people, including myself initially, found it hard to understand why Roberto should have accepted an ambassadorial post from his old arch-enemy, General Banzer. I came to the conclusion that, Roberto's immense talents having been frustratingly caged for a number of years, he saw and seized an opportunity to serve his country in a tangible way. That he certainly did and, in my view, was the best Bolivian Ambassador to the UN for a very long time. At the United Nations in New York even a small country can exert disproportionate influence if it is represented by a personable and intelligent ambassador. During Roberto's tenure, Bolivia's voice carried weight.

This was no thanks to the foreign ministry whose instructions often not only arrived late but misconstrued the issue at hand. Roberto's forthright reactions to such instances were to lead to his undoing.

The incumbent Foreign Minister wanted to end his diplomatic career as Ambassador to the UN and, during the latter part of 2000, an amicable agreement was reached that the handover would take place early in 2001. In November a resolution on the Palestinian–Israeli question was to be voted to the Economic and Social Council. The matter was not of direct interest to Bolivia, but was of major importance to the United States. This time the ministry's instructions as to how to vote did arrive in time.

At the same time Roberto's wife, Willma, suffered a stroke and was in hospital. On the day of the vote, since the Bolivian position seemed straightforward and his wife was seriously ill, Roberto sent a member of his staff to register the vote while he hurried to the hospital. There the minister telephoned to instruct him to change the Bolivian vote as the result of a forceful démarche by the US Ambassador in La Paz the night before. Roberto pointed out that it was probably too late, as the vote was scheduled to take place at that very hour. He immediately telephoned his subordinate, but she had already voted according to the original instructions and had reaped an angry reaction from the American delegation. The US Ambassador presented a formal protest in La Paz at the Bolivian government's failure to honour its commitment of the night before.

Given the circumstances, one would have thought that the minister would have defended his ambassador, especially as he was soon due to leave the post. Not so: Roberto was dismissed with contumely and immediate effect. Banzer did nothing to protect his appointee. By coincidence, a group of Latin American ambassadors were due to visit Ambassador Richard Holbrooke in New York a day or two later, to express concern that the US exerted too much pressure on their national positions at the UN. Now they were able to point out, bitterly, that the head of one of their colleagues had rolled.

Neither Roberto's efforts, nor those of others, to redress this arrant miscarriage of justice ever produced any results. It was a tragic end to the career of a brilliant man who had never sought any other goal than to serve his country and its people. Willma's fragile health after her stroke did not permit her to return to the high altitude of La Paz. At first they went to Albuquerque in New Mexico where one of their sons was a professor. Almost exactly one year after Willma's stroke, Roberto suffered a similar attack. Now neither of them could live in La Paz.

Eventually they returned to Tarija, Willma's home town in the far south. I had not been able to see them but we spoke frequently. Roberto at first seemed to recover fairly well, but it soon became clear that his health was even worse than Willma's. Now, in December 2003, he had suffered another collapse and was in intensive care.

I immediately took a flight to Tarija. By this time he was at home but I could not believe the change in him. He came into the room leaning on a stick, with a nurse supporting him. He was a shadow of his former self, his sturdy frame reduced to a frail wraith, his normally ruddy complexion pallid. On seeing me he burst into tears. I had difficulty in restraining my own but did not want him to see how shocked I was by his appearance.

He wept again when I gave him my autobiography, *Never Learn to Type*, and we went through the references to him and our old times together. Someone who had never been lost for words or for a ready quip, he could hardly speak, but he smiled a lot. I left with a heavy heart, knowing it was our last meeting. Contrary to expectations he rallied for a few months, but I never did see him again.

Conversations with friends and acquaintances all had a common theme: appalled disbelief that matters could have got so bad and so sanguinary. There, however, the unanimity stopped. Some thought that Mesa's government was so precarious that it could not possibly survive to complete the presidential period, due to end in August 2007; others that it would, but at great economic cost with the country slithering ever further downhill to ruin. 'Secession' and 'regional autonomy' were phrases frequently heard. Even the words 'civil war' sounded on some lips, although others pooh-poohed the suggestion, arguing that Bolivians, though capable of violence, were not an intrinsically violent people. Some middle-class families were terrified because, during the October rampage, the mob had penetrated to the lower, more affluent, reaches of La Paz. They had plans for leaving the country rapidly if the balloon went up. There had been wild threats to kill all *blancos*; the class war now bore signs of becoming a race war as well.

I had seen Bolivia afflicted by many vicissitudes in the past forty-five years, but for over two decades I had witnessed, and been part of, a progression that, despite ups and downs, had seemed to consolidate democracy and stability. Now I felt as if we had fallen back, almost irretrievably, into the turbulent past.

The very future of the country seemed to have been prejudiced. Disposal of the fabulous gas reserves was now on hold, because the protesters were demanding that they should be nationalised and used only within the country. Eerily, their fears were echoing the thesis in our 1994 report for the Inter American Development Bank: that through the centuries the benefits derived from Bolivia's immense natural resources, from the silver of Cerro Rico of Potosí in the sixteenth and seventeenth centuries to the tin and rubber of the nineteenth and twentieth centuries, had all gone abroad. There seemed to be little understanding that these new resources far exceeded Bolivia's foreseeable requirements and that although Mexico and California were desperate for additional energy, there were other sources and they would not wait indefinitely.

The euphoria of those who had engineered the demise of Goni's government was far from being shared by all people of modest means. Johnny and his family, and Nancy, had their homes in El Alto, the epicentre of the final catastrophe. Their father Víctor, my old driver, had settled there years ago when the first houses had been built above the city and it became a desirable place of residence for lower-income families who had some prospects in life. Its character had changed with the flood of poor people and former miners. El Alto had rapidly exploded into a huge ghetto of over 800,000 people, many living in half-built homes, or shanties, without water or sewage systems.

In this smouldering volcano Johnny and his like had become outsiders. He told me how, during the October crisis, he and his family had been threatened if they did not join in the uprising, and described the subterfuges they had had to employ to avoid becoming involved. His anxiety was the greater because he was at the lake guarding Villa Margarita, while his wife, in frail health, stayed in El Alto, although they fortunately had grown-up children to help her.

Mateo was in a different category. He was Aymara, a *campesino* of limited education who had also settled in El Alto and some of whose children were attaining good educational qualifications. We had been amazed to discover that he had inherited from his parents fifty hectares of land near Viacha, not far from La Paz. How such a large plot had survived, when the break-up of the large latifundia in the agrarian reform of 1953 had mainly resulted in most landless peasants receiving small, scattered plots, was a mystery. So was the fact that Mateo chose to work for me rather than tend his farm, although a regular salary must be an incentive. Despite these privileged circumstances Mateo was a card-carrying, paid-up member of the MIP, El Mallku's party, as a sound insurance policy against having his land seized. In addition Mateo paid someone to join in the marches and demonstrations in his name, explaining that failure to be represented would result in a fine and threats of worse consequences.

273

We were a subdued little group at Villa Margarita, saddened by what had occurred and fearful of what might come next. The only one who was more ambivalent was Mateo, the wily *campesino* whose instinct for self-preservation would prevail if the worst came to the worst. But they all liked Goni, who, with his family, had frequently been a guest at Villa Margarita. With his characteristic *'don de gentes'* – a delightful Spanish phrase that roughly means an ability to get along with people of every kind – he had made friends of them all.

We were appalled, too, by the way in which the victors were singling Goni out for demonisation with their absurd accusations of genocide. Many people demanded that he be forced to come back and face justice and that his property should be expropriated. Some of my friends thought that he should never have left Bolivia, but settled in Santa Cruz. Others thought that this would have simply produced accusations that he was attempting to set up an alternative pole of power in a part of the country notorious for its secessionist tendencies, and that his life would have been in great danger. Quite a number felt that he should now come back from Washington to Santa Cruz to show that he had nothing to hide.

It was a terrible time. I swam every day and tried to enjoy my garden and drink in the peace and tranquillity of that incomparable view of lake and mountains, but even Villa Margarita had lost its lustre, together with all the dreams I had invested here and in Bolivia in general. I had planned to spend Christmas here, with Johnny and his family, for an al fresco traditional dinner cooked in the earth oven which we had at last got to function properly. At the last moment I could not face it. The memories of the previous Christmases I had spent with Goni and his family were too painful.

Just before Christmas the former US President, Jimmy Carter, arrived with his wife and entourage. In 2001 he had invited me to become a member of his newly formed International Council for Conflict Resolution. Up to now our concerns had centred on other parts of the world. Now attention was focused on my own chosen home. The US Ambassador David Greenlee gave a reception for the distinguished visitors and I invited President Carter and his wife to come out to Villa Margarita. Their official programme did not allow them to accept but we were able to have a brief talk.

Even he, with his remarkable optimism and faith in human nature, found it hard to be cheerful about Bolivia.

Immediately afterwards I flew to the UK, arriving there on Christmas Eve, and sought the solace of friends who knew nothing of Bolivia and its tragedies.

21

The Dream Fades

In 2004 my stays in Bolivia were shorter, for I found myself helpless to assist. It was a year in which more commitments than ever came my way in all the regions of the world and I was happy to bury myself in other work.

At the end of January Goni and Ximena paid a visit to London and I invited them to Knill. This was the first time I had seen them since the débâcle in October. On the face of it both were bearing up well, though inwardly deeply affected by what had happened. As one friend observed, Goni had all his life been successful at whatever he turned his hand to, be it in business, politics or public life generally. Unlike most of us he had never really had to face failure before and it was very hard to have to do so at this stage of his life.

To distract them from all these sad matters, I had planned a dinner with a few local friends having no connections with Bolivia. It proved an unforgettable occasion for unforeseen, and highly unwelcome, reasons. The weather on the Welsh Marches decided to celebrate the event with one of the worst winter storms of that year. Gale-force winds reached speeds of between seventy and eighty miles an hour, torrential rain drummed down relentlessly and the river burst into full flood. Trees and branches blocked roads and then an hour before the other guests were due to arrive the electricity was cut and remained cut for the rest of the weekend. With the lights went all water, pumped up from a well in the garden, the Aga cooker in the kitchen, as well as the electric cooker and the central heating on this bitterly cold night. My one open fire in the drawing room started to smoke heavily because of wind gusting in the chimney.

I couldn't help reflecting, perhaps too fancifully, that it was as if the elements had conspired to demonstrate, in the most dramatic

276

way possible, the dreadful fate that had befallen my chief guest, as if on the stage of a Shakespearian tragedy.

Like any country household we had candles, but not nearly enough candle holders and we had one kerosene stove, but no primus to heat the food. A copper oil lamp that had been used during the early years of my parents' marriage, and which was now merely a decoration, proved to be just that, for it had no wick. A despairing SOS call to the elderly gentleman in the nearest town, Presteigne, who for years had ferried me to and from to the airport, produced miracles. Now over eighty, he battled through the storm, negotiating fallen branches in Nash Wood, armed with an amazing array of candles and candlesticks, hurricane and oil lamps, and primus stoves. Setting himself up at the kitchen table he soon had all this paraphernalia in working order, the house lit by a myriad flickering candles, lanterns in the kitchen and primus stoves blazing away.

It was little less than a miracle that all my guests managed to arrive, although one couple had to make a detour through narrow lanes because a large tree was barring the main road. In spite of these inauspicious beginnings – or perhaps as a result – the evening was animated and deemed a memorable success by everyone present. Goni, with flashes of his old sardonic humour, remarked that he had thought he was coming to a developed country: this kind of thing, he asserted, tongue in cheek, could *never* happen in Bolivia. I promptly reminded him that such cuts happened all the time in Villa Margarita, even sometimes in La Paz, and that in June of the previous year I had had to seek his personal intervention when, for several weeks, the whole lake area had been bereft of energy on account of the criminal activities of El Mallku and his henchmen.

The most embarrassing aspect of all was that I had to request my two houseguests to desist from flushing the toilets, since there was only a limited amount of water in my storage tanks, and their ablutions had to be similarly constrained. It seemed a terrible comedown for a pair who had so recently been head of state and first lady but they took it in good part.

Next morning the three of us trudged through driving rain and mud to visit my nearest neighbours at Knill Court. Goni asked the lady of the house if she had ever been to Bolivia, to which she promptly replied without any nudging from me, or knowledge of Goni's joke of the previous evening, 'Yes, indeed. I once spent two days in La Paz after a trip to Peru. We couldn't do much because there was no electricity and there was a small revolution that kept us in the hotel.' For once Goni was reduced to silence!

It was not just the forces of nature that did their utmost to disrupt the visit. On the Saturday afternoon a friend rang from London to warn that the British Airways flight to Washington on Sunday afternoon, when Goni and Ximena were due to travel, was likely to be cancelled because of an unspecified terrorist threat. The same flight had reportedly been targeted during previous weeks and suspended more than once. Fortunately, the one service left functioning at the Walled Garden was the telephone and so, in the half-light of candles, we had been repeatedly fumbling to dial British Airways and get the latest news. One flight was cancelled, but fortunately the one on which they were booked was maintained. I was none the less relieved to receive confirmation that they had arrived safely back in Washington.

It seemed a curious coincidence that Goni was exposed to all these dangers even in places not remotely connected with Bolivia. Were one superstitious, it would be tempting to interpret this confluence of adverse portents as a further sign that Goni's star was not in auspicious orbit anywhere.

A peacekeeping training course for military personnel organised by the British government and its armed forces in Paraguay, a week or two later, gave me the opportunity to spend a few days at Villa Margarita in the last week of March 2003, mainly to make sure that all was well with the staff and the property. There had been suggestions from the ambassador in the foreign ministry who had contacted me earlier that the president's office still wished me to see Carlos Mesa, but once again the matter came to nought.

The witch-hunt against Goni was continuing unabated, with legal action threatened against him and Sánchez Barzaín, who had also fled to the United States, but with growing implications for other former ministers in Goni's cabinet who had stayed in the country. Some had returned to their elected seats in the Congress, among them Chacho Justiniano, former Minister of the Presidency, and one of the most honourable men I have known anywhere. He had been courageous in remaining in circumstances where revenge, rather than justice, seemed uppermost in many minds, but would not accept an invitation to Villa Margarita; his face was too well known, he said and it was too risky to go through El Mallku's territory.

As it turned out, none of my other friends ventured to visit me, except the newly appointed Ambassador to London, Gonzalo Montenegro, and his wife. I was nonplussed when some of my friends expressed the fear that I could be in danger and urged me to come into La Paz. Curiously, I felt no risk, because of my relations with the surrounding community that went back many years. Still, I did take the precaution of making the acquaintance of the new Naval Commandant at the base in San Pedro, and inviting him to lunch. In the past all the presidents had instructed the reigning commander to ensure my security. I doubted very much that this was the case now but was determined to maintain friendly relations.

In May I came back after a peacekeeping training planning mission in Central America, meaning to spend two weeks quietly at Villa Margarita, but fate was to decree otherwise. El Mallku was supposed to be losing popularity but he could still block the road to La Paz. I had not long arrived when he again threatened to do so, and for an indefinite period. So this time I travelled to the city a few days before my departure and stayed in a hotel, in order to be sure I could get to the airport. Infuriatingly, the blockade was called off at the last moment. That was good for Bolivia but I had unnecessarily lost precious days at Villa Margarita.

Protests, social demands and constant marches were still the order of the day and Carlos Mesa's administration teetered on a knife's edge. It survived mainly because the president bowed to virtually every demand and because people were alarmed by what the alternative might be. Fresh elections would provide a constitutional solution but there were fears that they could vote into power a 'coca' president in the person of Evo Morales, with predictable external repercussions, and a military takeover still seemed unlikely unless the country descended into anarchy or civil war.

One afternoon the American Ambassador, David Greenlee, came to tea at Villa Margarita with his wife, on their way back from a ceremony in Copacabana. Washington, he said, was extremely worried about the situation, as he was himself; US policy was to try to support the tottering administration in the interest of not letting the democratic process founder. When I asked his view about the prospects and the dangers of either anarchy or civil war, he was gloomy but thought that rather than these two outcomes the greatest risk was a state of 'anomie'. I had to ask for a definition. 'A state of nothingness,' he explained. It did not sound much better than the other two.

There had been cabinet changes and my old friend, Horst Grebe, had become Minister of Economy. A highly qualified economist, he had a thankless task for the financial situation steadily worsened as a result of the constant upheavals. Another Consultative Group had been hoped for but was impossible because the government could not meet the conditions laid down by the World Bank and the IMF without creating popular uproar. The populist leaders had the government over a barrel. Horst said that he would like my help, and I had told him about the earlier rebuffs. I reiterated my reluctance to take any initiative but he urged me to write a personal letter to Carlos Mesa.

I did so, and Johnny delivered it to the palace, and obtained an official stamp of receipt. I never received any reply or even acknowledgement. This seemed odd, even allowing for bureaucratic inefficiency, and stranger still on the part of a man whom I considered a friend, who had been a guest, with his wife, at Villa Margarita and who, when a television political journalist, had conducted a long interview with me, praising my forty years' service to Bolivia. Coming in the wake of meetings that had failed to materialise earlier in the year, it was impossible not to interpret this silence as a rebuff.

Populist voices were taking over at all levels. It was dispiriting to hear on the radio endless stories of authorities, prefects, mayors and teachers, being thrown out of office on the flimsiest of allegations, usually of corruption. Corruption was rife, but there was no attempt to subject the accused to the normal course of justice, perhaps because the justice system was also considered to be venal. One unfortunate rural mayor was lynched for having stolen communal funds. After his death it was discovered, too late, that he had been innocent.

My hospital in Otavi was also affected. In the UK I had had desperate calls from the doctor who had made such a good impression on me during my last visit. She had reprimanded the driver of the decrepit four-wheel-drive vehicle that was used as an ambulance, for driving when drunk, and the hospital porter for similar lapses. The pair promptly marched to Potosí and got their powerful syndicate to pass a resolution demanding her immediate withdrawal. The health authorities were so scared of the people-power now being exercised everywhere that they hastily acceded. This was happening all over the country. The people of Otavi wanted their doctor reinstated and I suggested that they, too, should present a resolution requesting this. Short of adopting the now favourite ploy of blocking the main road from Potosí to the Argentinean frontier, there seemed little hope of getting their voices heard.

In May I tried to intercede with the Ministry of Health to request a proper investigation. The minister could not see me and I was referred to the vice minister. She could not see me either and eventually I was received by her adviser. A medical doctor, he was sympathetic, but nothing came of it. It was all too clear that the odds were stacked against the Otavi doctor.

Meanwhile the arguments over the gas reserves still rumbled on. The big investors in the project, the Spanish company REPSOL and the UK companies British Petroleum and British Gas, were becoming restive. So were the inhabitants of the Department of Tarija, who stood to gain much from the export of the gas, supported by Santa Cruz, the other resource-rich region. Evo Morales and Felipe Quispe were ratcheting up their demands, however, insisting on total nationalisation of all hydrocarbon reserves, an increase of royalties on international gas and oil companies from 18% to 50% and arbitrary changes in signed contracts, as well as re-nationalisation of the state oil company, YPFB, which had been capitalised during Goni's first administration. The irony was that the programme we had taken to Paris in October 2003 was designed not only to quell their fears of the wealth going abroad once more but was also the only way to finance their long-outstanding claims for better health and education services.

Their request for a referendum on the hydrocarbons issue entailed many risks but once again President Mesa bowed to their wish.

I read the five questions for the referendum in the newspaper on the plane taking me to Miami on 20 May. They were so convoluted that I could not understand them and I doubted whether Bolivian *campesinos* would be able to either. They would, inevitably, lend themselves to varying interpretation.

I had planned to come back in August, but then a mission to Angola and other commitments intervened and I did not return until mid-November.

My sadness about Bolivia was compounded at this time by the news that my dear friend Roberto Jordán Pando had died in Tarija in August. After my visit in December 2003, he had survived to celebrate his birthday in February, but then there were circulation problems and one of his legs was amputated. He had lived on for several months, in great pain. It was a desperately sad end. I wrote in my annual letter:

Roberto was one of those men who remain faithful to their ideals and principles, come what may. Perhaps it was because of this that he never achieved the highest political office that should have been his, though military coups and military governments also played their part. He had unique understanding of the aspirations of the 'campesinos' and worked unremittingly to help them attain them. Perhaps if he had been able to play a greater role many of today's problems might have been obviated.

There were concerns over Villa Margarita too: in one of his weekly telephone calls Johnny told me that on two nights he and Mateo had been woken by lights around the perimeter wall. They thought there might have been five or six men but when they, too, shone torches the group dispersed. The great question was whether they might be followers of El Mallku wanting to invade Villa Margarita, or criminals bent on theft. General threats about invasion of property belonging to *blancos* had been made and I was the only person falling into that category around Tiquina. Peter McFarlane, son of American missionary parents, who had made Bolivia his home, had a larger property on the opposite lakeshore, nearer La Paz. There had been an attempt to enter his land but since my property was so small and rocky and not suitable for crops I thought the danger was not great. Burglary seemed the more likely explanation. Villa Margarita is very near the Peruvian frontier and it is well known that gangs of thieves filter into Bolivia, though more usually aiming for the richer pickings in La Paz.

On a later night Johnny saw lights again, this time on the promontory sloping down to the lake at the end of the cove on our south-western side. There were boats in the water, to which bulky objects were being carried down, presumably smuggled from Peru. We installed more lights and a system that would automatically switch on when anyone approached the perimeter wall. With the disappearance in the floods of the little house on the shore, that flank was not covered during the night, so Johnny installed a sensor connected with a siren that could be heard across the lake and as far as San Pedro. The trouble was that every time some living thing, however small, crossed the beam, this horrible screeching sound would rend the air and make everyone jump out of bed with alacrity. On one occasion Johnny went down with the dogs to investigate and found that the culprit was a guinea pig that had found a choice patch of grass and was running back and forth in the critical spot.

When a former commander of the base came to call one day we asked him about the smugglers.

'Oh yes,' he replied cheerily. 'When I was here our patrols used to see their lights all the time at the end of that bay.'

'So what did you do?' I enquired.

'Oh, looked the other way, of course. Much safer and I advise you to do the same.'

It was a reply that spoke volumes.

There was a sequel. Special lights were installed but broken by stones, presumably thrown by would-be intruders. Then, in February 2005, Johnny was awoken by the siren's wail at four o'clock in the morning. This time it was anti-drug police who apologised profusely, explaining that they were chasing drug traffickers, so perhaps that was the clandestine cargo that was seen earlier.

More alarming was the other news that our naval friend brought us: El Alto and other redoubts of the populist movements were awash with arms; a *barrio* in El Alto where all the residents were Peruvian, some of them reputed to belong to Sendero Luminoso, the 'Shining Path' guerrillas from Peru; and rumours that members of FARC, the guerrilla movement in Colombia had been spotted near Santa Cruz. We were living in a climate of uncertainty in which exaggerated fears could flourish, but some of these allegations were confirmed by other friends. One such, a former minister, told me that a left-wing lawyer advising leaders in the Alto, and who owed him a favour for some past service, had warned that he and his family should move to Santa Cruz. However, they had stayed put.

In October 2004 an all-party delegation of Bolivian senators and deputies visited the UK at the invitation of the Inter-Parliamentary

Union (IPU). I met them at a reception at the Bolivian Embassy and at a lunch at the House of Lords. This was followed by a meeting there with representatives of British Petroleum, British Gas and Shell. This gathering sought to provide a neutral venue for discussions of the gas question, in the hope of bringing about a mutual softening of positions. One of the lighter moments of this encounter occurred at the lunch, during a conversation between a conservative MP and the president of the Bolivian Chamber of Deputies, a member of MNR, for which I acted as interpreter. The MP, a woman, chuntered on at length and with great earnestness, about the immense advantages to be had from selling off council houses. The visitor listened with a polite but bemused expression, as well he might; for, as I eventually had to tell the over-enthusiastic proponent of this policy, Bolivia is a long way from having any social housing to sell off.

Evo Morales' party, MAS, had two representatives in the visiting group. The senator, a benign elderly gentleman, wore his trilby hat, standard *campesino* headgear, throughout the proceedings in the House of Lords, both at the lunch and the subsequent meeting. He smiled a lot but never spoke. Nor did his MAS companion from the Chamber of Deputies, but he did not smile and his silence was more sinister; it looked as if he was the genial old man's minder. Grim-faced, he kept getting up from the conference table to walk out of the room, or sit on the sidelines, as if to say, 'I am not part of this, nothing you say will change my mind.' The atmosphere of the meeting was cordial and the discussion courteous but underneath little had changed. The Bolivian parties represented all had different opinions, some anxious to preserve conditions attractive to foreign investment, others unwilling to settle for anything less than nationalisation and much higher royalties. The companies made the mistake of having a national of another Latin American country as their spokesman. Thinking to please, they achieved the opposite effect.

Arriving at El Alto airport on 15 November, weary and wilted after the twenty-six hour journey from Knill, I was not best pleased to find that all roads out to the *altiplano* were hermetically sealed by protesters. This time it was not El Mallku's indigenous group nor Evo Morales' *cocaleros* but inhabitants of El Alto who, dissatisfied with the services of a foreign company responsible for their water supplies, were demanding that the government rescind the contract.

Ominously, Johnny was not there to meet me but appeared a little later, having somehow managed to negotiate his way through the blockades. I remembered from many years before that there was an old road running along the lower flanks of the Cordillera which came out on the main road, well beyond the limits of the blockades. So we struck off towards the mountains, the Milluni mine and the towering peak of the Huayno Potosí. This meant traversing part of the Alto and we soon found that the blockades were not only on the main road, so had to make many detours to avoid their stone-throwing guardians. As if that were not enough, the rough, unpaved streets were scored with deep trenches on either side, presumably for water and sewage pipes. Some bright spark had evidently decided not only to dig everything up over a large area before laying the pipes and filling the holes, but also to dump the earth in the middle of the road at street intersections so that we kept finding ourselves blocked in an unsuspected cul-de-sac.

We emerged from this maze to ascend the barren, unpopulated uplands that lead to the lakes at Milluni, right under the crests of the mountains. But it was so long since I had been there that I could not find the entrance to the old remembered road. There was no one to be seen until two *campesinos* suddenly appeared over a bank and we stopped for directions.

'Señora,' said one of them pityingly, 'that road has not been passable for many years.'

We later found that this information was not exactly correct but at that moment there was no help for it but to return to El Alto, and try to find back ways that would take us past the toll station.

Time and again our chosen route brought us out too soon and the menacing sight of inebriated men waving sticks would make us urgently turn round and try another way. Even on the rough tracks we were following we came across a barricade, manned by some opportunistic young boys. They were not at all disposed to let us through but after some not very subtle negotiation and for the price of some sweets and small change, we managed to get past. At one point, a track having petered out, we found ourselves bumping over a plot of ploughed land.

In the end perseverance was rewarded and we emerged beyond

the toll station on the main road which, empty in our direction, was choked on the other side by a monumental queue of lorries waiting to go to La Paz. We reached Tiquina just in time before the pontoon ferries stopped for the night. The journey from the airport to Villa Margarita had taken six hours instead of the normal two.

One long-term resident of Villa Margarita was not there to greet me. Bandy, or Bandido, that lovely gentle dog, one of Perla's puppies, who had been with us since 1993, and used to accompany me in my walks over the hills, waiting impatiently at every bend for me to catch up, had died a few days before. He had been frail for some time and was eleven years old. Suri, the much less biddable dog who had replaced his twin brother Pedro, had never got on with Bandy, and Johnny thought that it was an attack by him that caused Bandy's death. In anticipation that Bandy would not last long Johnny had brought in a handsome young German Shepherd given to him by its owner, a lady in Tiquina. Christened Lobo (wolf) he had been an obstreperous puppy and I had not much taken to him. Now, however, he had blossomed into a beautiful dog, well behaved and a wonderful guard, although nothing could replace Bandido in my affections.

Otherwise, all was well at Villa Margarita. The same could not be said of the country at large. The referendum had taken place in July resulting in a 'Yes' vote, presumably because the majority of the *cocaleros* and *campesinos* had followed the instructions of their leaders. What this meant in practical terms was far from clear. The president and his staff prepared a draft law on hydrocarbons that did not satisfy Congress and that many people feared would frighten off foreign investors and harm the country's interests. Then Evo Morales, the MAS leader, and his cohorts in Congress produced an even more radical counter-proposal. The tangled negotiations that followed were so byzantine as to defy comprehension. I was told that the president wanted other parties in the Congress, particularly the MNR, Goni's party, to break the deadlock by proposing yet another version more palatable to external investors, and there were rumours of proferred concessions. The MNR, however, were determined not to pull the coals out of the fire for the president.

President Mesa's relations with Congress became even more strained. The tensions were exacerbated by the long-running controversy over bringing his predecessor to justice. After convoluted wheeling and dealing, it was proposed that the proceedings should encompass all the members of Goni's cabinet, which had contained members of other parties and some who had played no part in the crucial decision to deploy the armed forces. The legal intricacies were immense, and President Mesa's appointment of some judges to the Supreme Court in July was declared unconstitutional by the Congress, and alleged to have been intended to influence the court's decisions as the president wished.

Goni had been arguing for months that an internationally recognised commission should undertake a thorough independent investigation, adjudicating responsibilities for the deaths in October 2003 and for the abuse of human rights, but this was obviously going nowhere. There had undoubtedly been violence on both sides and it could be argued that the whole tragic episode had been instigated by those who started the protests, some of whom had resorted to violence and were certainly armed. They, however, had been exonerated by an amnesty declared early on by the Mesa government.

I met Chacho Justiniano and Carlos Morales. Carlos was in charge of preparing the defence of a group of ministers and I was electrified to hear that I might be called to testify that, during the conference call that the three ministers (Chacho, Carlos, the finance minister) and I had made to the president from Paris on 9 October 2003 at the end of the Consultative Group meeting, there had been no discussion about deploying the armed forces to quell the disturbances in El Alto. That was certainly true but I did not relish becoming involved.

The Otavi hospital had been without a doctor for several months. Aided by Fidet Guzmán, a professor of *campesino* origin who had been born in Otavi, I renewed my efforts to get the authorities to act. We saw the Director General in the Health Ministry and then Johnny and I went to see for ourselves. The long road through the mountains from Oruro to Potosí had at last been asphalted but in contrast to its modernity there was still ample evidence of stark poverty on the barren, beautiful highlands between the two towns. There seemed to me to be fewer people, however. Perhaps those who could escape had gone to the Chapare to cultivate coca, to Argentina to find employment, or to El Alto or other urban shanty towns in search of a better life.

In Potosí we had dinner with the ousted doctor. She had obtained employment with a non-governmental organisation but still longed to return to Otavi. We heard that the villagers had been so indignant with the drunken behaviour of the ambulance driver and the hospital porter that they had physically driven them out a few weeks earlier. They had proposed a highly respected local man to become the driver. He had been in La Paz, pleading his case, and we had brought him back with us.

Next day we drove to the hospital, taking with us the regional director of health. He refused to allow the doctor to accompany us, saying her reinstatement was out of the question because 'the syndicate would not agree'. At the hospital we found that a temporary doctor had arrived two days earlier, a young woman without experience who would have to leave the same day in order to complete her final examinations. As if by magic a new driver, nominated by the syndicate, arrived minutes before us, in order to pre-empt the appointment of the community's choice. It was clearly a set-up, hastily put in place for my arrival. The village officials could hardly contain their fury.

The hospital was badly in need of repair: leaking roofs, blocked toilets, overflowing septic tanks, and oxidised water pipes. I offered to finance the major part of the work on condition that the hospital was fully staffed and that the villagers would, as in the past, provide manual labour. The regional director assured me that medical staff would be provided but I found his manner evasive and doubted that he would keep his word. More to my dismay the village officials protested that they could not provide the labour. They had put in four months' work on the new basketball stadium, they complained. Later they proudly showed me this pretentious arena, much too large for this small community. It had, they equally proudly proclaimed, been the site of *olimpiadas* (Olympic games!) with neighbouring villages. The stadium had cost the equivalent of $US10,000, money obtained by popular vote from popular participation funds. Local priorities, it seemed, did not extend to the basic upkeep of their hospital.

On the way back we made a detour to the isolated village of Kepallo where, thirty years before, I had donated a health post, a subsidiary of the Otavi hospital, in memory of my parents who had once visited there with me. The commemorative plaque was still on the wall but it was now the home of the nursing auxiliary.

288

This was because a small, sparkling new hospital had been built, without community participation, but by some international organisation. The intentions were good, but the architect had forgotten to include a kitchen, and it hardly seemed sensible to spend money on new projects rather than build on what already existed. I could not help wondering how long it would be before this gleaming building would also fall into disrepair.

On my return to La Paz I despatched Johnny's brother, Edgar, to Otavi to cost the basic repairs. He came back with an estimate of $US4500 and the dispiriting information not only that the community was adamant about not providing labour but that most of the repairs needed were the product of negligence and lack of maintenance and proper cleaning. It was hard to know whether the community's attitude, so different from their parents' enthusiastic cooperation when the hospital was built, stemmed from becoming too accustomed to many hand-outs over the years or from disillusion with the health authorities.

I nonetheless wrote to the director general of health, reiterating my willingness to provide money, as long as some local support was forthcoming, as well as from the ministry, and reminding him of his earlier promise to equip the hospital with a new ambulance. Fidel Guzmán told me that the director general had been delighted to receive my missive.

'An admirable letter!' he was reported to have exclaimed, 'How well she writes!'

Unfortunately his enthusiasm did not extend to sending me a reply, nor was the promised ambulance forthcoming.

On Sunday 5 December the whole country voted in municipal elections. Everything came to a standstill. Travel between departments was forbidden and no private vehicles were allowed on the roads. Violence had been feared but a generally peaceful atmosphere prevailed. New procedures were introduced whereby individuals and civic groups could present candidates, as well as political parties.

For San Pedro and San Pablo de Tiquina, with about 900 inhabitants each, no fewer than 59 men postulated their candidatures for the post of mayor. One hoped that they were inspired by an overwhelming sense of civic duty but the pickings were tempting.

289

The history of the previous mayors of Tiquina had not been a happy one. One had stolen substantial sums of money from popular participation funds, had fled on one occasion, been booted out by the populace on another, threatened with lynching, and spent time in gaol, but then been voted in again, no one knew quite why or how.

The national election results showed that all the traditional parties had lost heavily. Even Evo Morales' popular MAS had not done as well as expected. It was the individuals and the civic groups which made the most gains, further evidence that Bolivian politics were becoming more and more fragmented, reflecting widespread disillusion with traditional political structures.

The one bright spot in an otherwise sombre scene was that no major structural repairs were required at Villa Margarita and everything was functioning well. My property had not been invaded, and there had been no further nocturnal marauders. Even so, as I boarded the plane bound, as I thought, for a hip operation and three months' recuperation in the UK, I could not help wondering what I would find when I next returned in March.

22

A Nightmare Scenario

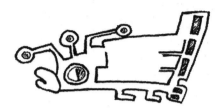

My hip operation did not take place. At the last moment the surgeon decided that it was premature. I did not change my plan to defer coming back to Bolivia until March 2005 but did keep a close weather eye on developments. The news continued dispiritingly bad. Once again, as soon as the festive season was over – protests and even revolutions invariably come to a halt in Bolivia for high days and holidays – the turmoil started up again. Every group, large or small, clamouring for satisfaction of their various claims, or objecting to some part of the government's policies, invariably accompanied their demands with the threat of '*medidas de presión*' (pressure measures). These mostly took the form of blocking roads, a method of proven effectiveness.

Even more disturbing developments in January pointed towards further dissolution of the body politic that had existed up to now. At the year end the central government had been obliged to raise fuel prices. In January this measure incited strikes not only on the part of the nationalistic, anti-globalisation residents of El Alto but also in Santa Cruz, the economic engine of the country, where sympathies are pro-capitalist. President Mesa was forced to rescind the increases and Santa Cruz won an important victory in their fight for regional autonomy, with the concession that voters could henceforth elect the department's highest official, the prefect, an office until now in the gift of the president. This led to calls from civic groups in the highland departments for the right to elect officials who were previously appointed and to another referendum being scheduled for July. Despite endless heated debate the passage through Congress of the hydrocarbons law remained in a state of suspended animation during the first two months of the year.

Amidst all this gathering doom and gloom it was a relief to attend a joyful Bolivian occasion in London, on 1 February, when a performance of Bolivian baroque music from the Chiquitania was given at the Wigmore Hall. The Chiquitania is a remote region in the eastern part of Bolivia administered during the Spanish colonisation by the Jesuits. They discovered that the tribes there had their own musical traditions and instruments to which they added their own music brought in from Europe. The Jesuits encouraged the musical development of the indigenous inhabitants, and trained them to make their own instruments, as well as building some beautiful churches of unique design. This flourishing cultural experiment came to an abrupt end when the Jesuits were expelled from Spain in 1767 and simultaneously from all its colonies. The churches fell into desuetude, and with them the music, which was mostly of a religious character.

In the 1960s I had tried to visit the Chiquitania but it was so remote and inaccessible that I never found sufficient time to make the journey. That has all changed since, with the development of roads. In the latter part of the last century a resourceful and energetic priest set about restoring the churches and salvaging their lost treasures, untouched for over two hundred years. These included the exciting discovery of substantial quantities of church music.

With the help of a special foundation, bi-annual festivals are now held in the Chiquitania, to which music lovers flock from all over the world. They included the British baroque music group Florilegium, which incorporated some of the music into its own repertoire. At the beginning of 2005 a tour was organised through Vienna, Amsterdam, London and Berlin. Four Bolivian singers were invited to join the group, three women and one man. Wherever they went they invariably brought the house down. It was a joy to see the delight in their faces that they were being applauded so enthusiastically by connoisseur audiences in some of the greatest European concert houses. The man, with a lovely tenor voice, could not stop smiling his joy. He was obviously of Andean Indian extraction and I learned later came from El Alto, the *barrio* not usually noted for generating harmony.

The event also had another unexpected significance for me. Chatting to the First Lady, Doña Elvira, who had come to London especially for the occasion, the conversation turned to the situation back at home and the tribulations of her husband – they were both, after all, friends of mine. In the course of our talk my own possible role came up and I had perforce to relate the apparent rebuffs that

292

I had suffered. Elvira was aghast and insisted that there must be some mistake.

That chance meeting in London had a sequel. One Friday afternoon a few weeks later the telephone rang in Knill. It was President Mesa to tell me that the Secretary General of the Presidency had never advised him of the various proposals for a meeting and, even more incredibly, that he had never even seen my personal letter. One could not help wondering at such a degree of disorganisation in the palace bureaucracy or how many much more important documents might have gone astray. The president went on to apologise and expressed the hope that I would continue to help and visit him when I returned to Bolivia two weeks later.

In the meantime, I had a number of speaking engagements, including a lecture at Nottingham University with the provocative title 'Democracy at Risk in Latin America?' during which, as may be imagined, I gave prominence to the current goings-on in Bolivia. When I arrived in Vienna to be keynote speaker at a ceremony celebrating International Women's Day, I learned that Carlos Mesa had tendered his resignation on 6 March, accompanied by a blunt statement that the country was 'ungovernable'. This was obviously a ploy, in an attempt to bring people to their senses and muster support. When the president appeared on the balcony of the palace delivering a histrionic speech and waving a Bolivian flag, massed crowds in the Plaza Murillo below cheered him on. The Bolivian Congress, no doubt seeing an abyss yawning before it, rejected his resignation a day or two later. For a while it looked as if a more harmonious relationship could develop between the executive power and the main parties in the legislature, but news that a meeting between Carlos Mesa and Evo Morales of MAS had broken up in disagreement had a very ominous ring.

From Vienna I flew to Madrid to attend the summit on 'Democracy, Terrorism and Security' organised by the Spanish government and the Club of Madrid, on the first anniversary of the horrendous train bombing perpetrated in March 2004, where I was to be the moderator of a high-level panel on the subject 'From Violence to Voting'.

As a member of the Club of Madrid (composed of democratically elected former presidents) Goni was also in Madrid, the first time we had met since the accident-prone weekend in Knill. He was naturally depressed that he had felt obliged, for reasons of precaution, to sell his mining company, not only because he had had to do so for less that its real value, at a time when international mineral prices were rising after a long spell in the doldrums, but because it was his life's work. He was also concerned about the prospects for his trial. A few weeks before, the Bolivian 'Fiscal General', or Attorney General, had formalised the charges against him, although without requesting him to make a prior declaration as would normally be the case. At this point matters had descended into farce: the Fiscal, in his haste, had referred to the wrong article in the country's Penal Code. Instead of citing the one relating to genocide, and accusing the former president of being guilty of that, 'with the complicity of his Ministers' – in itself a totally absurd imputation – he had cited another – in effect accusing Goni of 'committing *rape*, with the complicity of his ministers'! The imagination boggled. Even Goni had to laugh at this egregious instance of black comedy.

Above all, he was depressed by the state of the country, and the possible destruction of all that he had worked for to make Bolivia a viable player on the international stage. We discussed Carlos Mesa's pseudo-resignation and Goni was almost sympathetic: 'He is in a very similar situation to that in which I found myself eighteen months ago,' he commented, 'except that he has publicly declared that he will never use force to impose the government's authority.' He remained convinced, however, that Mesa had become his sworn enemy and was behind all the moves to bring him to trial on trumped-up grounds. It was impossible to persuade him otherwise.

When I returned to Bolivia on 16 March, more dramatic developments greeted me. While I was flying over the Atlantic on the previous night, President Mesa presented another bombshell. He sent a message to the Congress proposing that the date of the next elections should be advanced from June 2007 to 28 August of the current year, 2005. Evidently he did not feel that his resignation of ten days before had produced the desired effect and still considered the country to be ungovernable. In the intervening days he had been dealt two blows. The first was a ruling from the same accident-prone fiscal general and his colleagues, the other *fiscales*, declaring that not only freedom of expression and peaceful protest marches were legal under the Constitution, but also the blocking of roads.

Secondly the Chamber of Deputies had approved a new version of the hydrocarbons law. Deaf to the president's pleas for moderation they had included very radical elements likely to discourage current and future foreign investors. The MAS demand that royalties from foreign companies be increased from 18% to 50% had not been accepted as such; instead 32% taxes would be levied on top of the existing 18% royalties, which came to 50% in all, the argument being that the government could vary taxes at will. Other troubling articles permitted the so-called 'obligatory migration of agreements' (which means that Bolivia could unilaterally modify signed contracts) and stipulated that local indigenous communities must be consulted before exploration could begin which, in certain circumstances, could amount to giving them a virtual veto.

People near to the president put it about that if Congress rejected his proposal for August elections he would resign forthwith, this time irrevocably. If he did so, the Constitution decreed that the president of the Senate, a member of Jaime Paz Zamora's party, should succeed, but he was not well liked. Next in succession came the president of the Chamber of Deputies and then the president of the Supreme Court.

On the day after my arrival Congress debated for several hours and, as widely predicted, rejected the president's proposal for August elections as unconstitutional. An additional argument, unuttered, was that they would all have to give up their seats and their comfortable living. Chacho Justiniano and others told me they fully expected that we would have a new president before the day was out.

Everyone waited with bated breath amid apprehension that major trouble would break out, with incalculable consequences, if Mesa resigned. The hours passed, journalists picketed the Palacio Quemado, but tight-lipped secrecy was maintained by the presidential entourage. It was not until nearly midnight that the announcement came: to the surprise of many, who believed that the president did not want to stay, he decided to do so. Among those who conferred with him during those fraught hours were the top military commanders. It was reliably reported afterwards that they asked him to remain in office, perhaps fearing that they might not be able to contain the situation if he went. Theirs may well have been the deciding voice.

The immediate crisis was over but the president emerged greatly weakened. Two unfulfilled threats of resignation within ten days hardly bode well for a country's stability. Fortunately a few days later saw the beginning of Holy Week and its accompanying religious rites. This, combined with the time-honoured custom of suspending conflicts during festive days, gave rise to a welcome breathing space. But for how long? The festering problems of the hydrocarbons law, the proposed Constituent Assembly to modify the constitution and a myriad other bones of contention, still remained to be tackled.

My premonitions were not much eased by an hour-long meeting I had with the president on 22 March. I saw before me a very different man from the one I had last met in September 2003. He had aged noticeably, his handsome face drawn and haggard and his complexion unhealthily sallow. What was perhaps meant to be designer stubble conveyed instead the impression that he had neither the time, energy or inclination to shave properly. I had the overwhelming sensation of listening to someone who was caught in a trap and saw no means of escape, like an animal in a cage.

He was very anxious to talk and did so with a frankness that indicated, more than anything else could, that he recognised that my fundamental allegiance was to Bolivia and not to any particular person or party, although he understood my long-standing friendship with Goni. Perhaps because of that he felt it necessary to rehearse the events of October 2003 and his reasons for accepting the presidency, which many had construed as a traitorous act.

He also went over the happenings of the previous fortnight, saying that he had felt he had no option but to remain. I did not get the feeling that this was a willing decision on his part and, indeed, the depressing picture he painted of the immediate and future prospects for the country bode fair to validate that interpretation. His primary preoccupation was the embattled hydrocarbons law which the Senate was that day beginning to consider. He saw no good coming from this debate, predicting that the upper house would make no modifications to what he deemed to be a disastrous draft as approved by the Chamber of Deputies. Then it would go back to the latter before being referred to him for final approval and promulgation. People talked of his veto, he complained, but in fact he had no veto. He could only make observations and when these went back to the Congress they could simply reject them and promulgate the law. If a law was passed in the terms that he feared, he went on, the adverse consequences for Bolivia would

296

be incalculable, the country isolated, and foreign investment, on which the country depended so heavily, would be severely affected.

The president made clear that one of the purposes of the meeting was to tell me that he would like to make use of my services to improve relations with donors and facilitate external development finance when the time was appropriate. We both had to agree that that was not the present moment. A World Bank Consultative Group meeting had already had to be postponed more than once because donor attitudes towards Bolivia were not propitious in the current atmosphere of acute uncertainty. Not until the hydrocarbons law was finalised could the way ahead become clear, and all would depend on the nature of the final text.

Mesa was bitter about Goni, whom he accused of trying to destroy both him and the whole country. I told him that I had just seen Goni in Madrid and that on the basis of my conversations with him, I could not believe this to be true. The president was not to be convinced, insisting that Goni had financed MNR deputies and instigated the passage of a draft hydrocarbons law that would bring the country to its knees and make the president's own life impossible. He knew Goni thought that he had personally pushed for him to be brought to trial but this was totally untrue: he had a million other things on his mind, and the judicial process had been mooted and approved by Congress, while the attorney general was a nominee of Evo Morales and his MAS party as part of a deal on the distribution of legal posts.

It seemed ironic and sad that, in the brief interval of ten days, I found myself trying, and failing, to persuade two men who had once been so close that their judgements of one another were mistaken. The prospect of the two of them, each remarkable in his own sphere, locked in a struggle that neither could win, inevitably brought to mind, yet again, analogies with Greek and Shakespearian tragedy. It was all the sadder remembering their joint electoral triumph two and a half years earlier and the happy day in August 2002 when they came together to Villa Margarita, swam in my pool and enjoyed a convivial barbecue.

During all these upheavals life at Villa Margarita with Johnny, Mateo and Nancy followed a more or less normal course. Nancy had met me at the airport with Johnny, bursting with enthusiasm over the things she had learned at the cookery classes to which I had sent her during my absence.

'Señorita, I can now make lemon foot,' she announced triumphantly, adding for good measure, after a moment, '*and* apple foot!'

'Foot?' I asked, bewildered, still feeling the effects of the long journey.

'Yes, foot!' Nancy insisted.

At last the penny dropped in my sluggish jet-lagged mind.

'You mean *pie*!'

The mystery was solved. In Bolivia the word 'pie' has never been translated into Spanish but simply adopted as it is and pronounced as in the original English. If you pronounce it the Spanish way, with an acute accent on the 'é', it comes to mean 'foot'.

Johnny and Mateo had many things to show for their efforts. There were new stone terraces, additional flowerbeds and a bird table with a red roof of tiny tiles just outside my study window so that I can see the birds feed as I work at my desk. Johnny had also hired a gardener to come for one week a month. Eusebio worked part-time with the municipality of La Paz, and the effects of his expertise were already visible. Neither Johnny nor Mateo profess to be gardeners, although they, along with Alejandro, have done wonders with a very barren site. Mateo, however, is prone to accidents of the most bizarre kind, and should never really be allowed out with a pick in his hand. This time he had managed to slice through one of the main irrigation pipes; break the lid of an appurtenance in the swimming pool, for which no replacement is available in La Paz; and, worst of all, eliminate my favourite kiswara tree, which had seeded itself in the lee of an outcrop of rock, and which I had commended to everyone's special protection.

Once again a familiar four-legged friend was missing: this time it was Lobo. Both he and Suri regularly escaped on courting excursions but this time Lobo had really disappeared. Johnny had acquired a new little black puppy, not dissimilar to Bandido, but he was still very small. Since Suri had now taken to visiting us just for meals our canine defence corps was severely depleted.

When I expressed my concern Johnny said, 'But I know where Lobo is.'

'How?'

'Well, I called in the *yatiri* and he read in the coca leaves that Lobo had been stolen but is not very far away.'

This time, it appeared, a third *yatiri* had come, one rejoicing in the name of Eleuterio. He lived away in the hills behind San Pablo on the other side of the straits. On the basis of this rather flimsy evidence, and other intelligence he may have gleaned in San Pedro, Johnny found out that the daughter of the previous owner had stolen Lobo.

The daughter has a butcher's stall in the Copacabana market and so one Saturday we paid her a visit. The butcher, a tall buxom girl, could not have been pleasanter. They needed Lobo, she said, because there were many thieves in Copacabana, especially in Holy Week, which was just about to begin. When I asked why they hadn't talked to us instead of just taking him she wiped her hands on her blood-stained apron and gave an equivocal reply.

'Can we have him back, please?' we asked, and Johnny added, 'I'll get you another dog to replace him.'

'Not until after Easter,' said the butcher, evasively. 'The robbers will have moved on by then.'

She smiled as she spoke but neither Johnny nor I was very convinced that she meant what she said.

We had asked to see Lobo and after two hours' wait he was brought to meet us by the lady's husband, on a makeshift lead of white tape. When still several yards away he sensed Johnny's presence and went mad with joy. It was hard to leave him, eagerly panting and obviously thinking we were about to bring him back to Villa Margarita and the freedom of the garden. Negotiations continued for some time but he was never returned.

The matter of security remained a priority, the normal risk of ordinary robbers now widened to include possible invasions and occupations as well as sporadic violence. The new Comandante Naval, Captain Agramonte, came to lunch and we discussed the matter. On the general situation he was as gloomy as everyone else, and repeated the fears expressed by his predecessors that things might deteriorate, if not to civil war then to a state of anarchy so acute that the reluctant military would have no option but to restore order and authority.

As for the security risks at Villa Margarita, the captain considered the population around here to be moderate in their views and to regard me as a good neighbour. How much that counts for in an enraged and drunken mob was open to question. Moreover, the captain warned that there was a focus of radical opinion in Tito

Yupanqui. The road above my house takes 17 kilometres to get there, winding along the shores of the Lago Menor, but for nimble feet or crows it is a much shorter distance over the tops of the hills.

The captain thought that radio connection was the answer, an idea he followed up with some alacrity, testing the capacity of various types of radio to call the naval base from different locations in the tortured geography of this promontory. It was a relief to learn, shortly after I left Bolivia again for Europe, that the radio network was installed and working well.

Johnny, as usual, was full of imaginative ideas for new projects to beautify Villa Margarita but, like so many others, I thought it unwise to indulge in new investment until the outlook was more certain. The fear that Villa Margarita might be over-run, and the work of so many years destroyed, was a constant nightmare.

One project, long in gestation, was the painting of a large mural on the end wall of the swimming pool. My original idea had been for a simple landscape of mountains and lake but Johnny had produced an acquaintance who proved to be quite a considerable artist. Don Alberto had presented an ambitious design, a veritable kaleidoscope of Bolivian life, richly coloured, and teeming with life and energy. I had been carried away with enthusiasm and commissioned the work right away, providing Don Alberto with a sizeable advance to spur the work on. ('Will you never learn?' one of my Bolivian women friends exclaimed incredulously, some time later.)

That first encounter had been lost in the mists of time. So, too, unfortunately, had Don Alberto, who all too evidently did not incorporate in his own person the life and energy that pulsated in his work. Johnny eventually tracked him down on a remote hilltop above La Paz, and extracted a promise that the work would be finished before my arrival in March 2005. The problem, it transpired, had been the break-up of his marriage, which had also gobbled up the advance.

On my return I had found Don Alberto's grand design sketched out on the wall, but with no colouring and far from finished. It was nonetheless impressive, and tantalising in the glimpses it gave of what it might eventually become. It was not only a social panorama of Bolivian life in all its aspects – urban, rural, rich and poor – set against a backcloth of the Sacred Lake and the Cordillera Real and the looming figures of Manco Capac, Mama Ojllo and other ancient gods, but also a political commentary in the Mexican style. Peasants ploughed their fields among ruminating cows, sheep and llamas; a street seller plied his wares, while another boy pulled the plaits of a young girl; folk-lore dancers pranced through the crowd which included a group of rowdy, carousing drunks; bowler-hatted, bell-skirted *cholitas* under makeshift canvas shades proffered their meat and fruits and vegetables; and there was even a discreet back view of a portly man relieving himself against a wall, an all too frequent sight – and smell – in La Paz. (I had not noticed this figure until one of my Sunday *parrillada* guests, slightly shocked, pointed it out.) And there, bang in the middle of the foreground, were three large figures chatting together: a sanctimonious-looking bishop, complete with mitre; a fat general, strung around with medals and sporting a large posterior; and an unmistakeable oligarch, bowler-hatted (but not the kind of bowler the *cholitas* wear), his status confirmed by an ostentatious watch and chain wreathed around his prosperous paunch. In short, the traditional perpetrators of Bolivia's history, though seen through the prism of the 1952 revolution rather than the realities of half a century later.

Don Alberto, run to earth again by Johnny, came to see me just before I left. He was a most unlikely-looking artist, short, with rather heavy features in no way enhanced by one large and rather wobbly tooth, which tended to dominate his listeners' attention.

'I beg you not to blame me,' he said apologetically, 'but my wife and I have parted, and now sometimes she has our two children and sometimes I have to look after them and cannot work.' The lone tooth bobbed up and down in a clear signal of emotional distress. 'You see, Señorita, I am an artist.' And indeed he was, for all his unlikely appearance, as even the faint outlines of his mural most amply showed.

We parted amicably, Don Alberto effusively promising that the mural would be finished by May, I fervently and silently hoping that it might be done by my return in July.

I was looking forward to meeting Johnny's other acquisition, the new part-time gardener Eusebio, who was due to spend the last week of my stay at Villa Margarita. That was to be another frustrated aspiration, although there were promises that he would come 'soon', a word of imprecise definition in Bolivia.

We did not fare better with Eleuterio, the third (and, according to Johnny, best) *yatiri*, the one who lived on the other side of the hill on the opposite shore of the lake. I decided that I would like to get this marvel of divination to read the coca leaves for me as well. Johnny and Mateo set off on the ferry across the straits and then separated to encircle the hill, as they foresaw that Eleuterio would not be at home but pasturing his sheep on one of his small plots of land. In the midst of this expedition Johnny suddenly remembered he had left a pump functioning in the swimming pool that had to be turned off at a certain hour and returned, post haste, leaving Mateo to deliver the message. This was not a good omen, Mateo being a less than reliable conveyor of information.

However, he returned with the news that Eleuterio would visit us at 5 pm on the following Tuesday afternoon, and a list of the things we had to acquire before the ceremony. Johnny duly purchased these at one of the *boliches* in San Pedro. Besides a plenitude of coca leaves they included sweets, and a lot of Wills cigarettes which, I was alarmed to learn, I would have to smoke at a certain critical moment in the ritual.

I need not have worried. We waited expectantly on Tuesday at 5 pm and, indeed, until late at night, but no *yatiri* appeared. Next day Johnny and Mateo speculated that it was because we had not committed his services with an advance payment on account. Since Eleuterio lived a very long way away and did not possess a cellular phone, which nowadays seems to be the inseparable companion of every *campesino*, however poor, we never did find out what happened. Presumably he relied on some less worldly form of communication to which, alas, we did not hold the key.

And I was left with no inkling of what the future might hold for me or Villa Margarita, much less Bolivia.

On my afternoon walks I tried some probing of a more down-to-earth kind. One day, strolling towards Camacachi, I met Don Arturo striding towards San Pedro with a purposeful air, his dog scampering along at his heels. Don Arturo is a spry 86-year-old Aymara, a widower living alone in an unusually big house. He was well dressed, wearing a tweed jacket that, though old, was obviously of good quality, and a smart trilby hat perched at a jaunty angle above dark eyes that sparkled in the furrowed wrinkles of his face.

He was carrying spring water to sell in San Pedro, he told me, an entrepreneurial venture of which I had never previously heard.

Despite his prosperous air, he did not appear to have any source of livelihood other than his land, but perhaps he had inherited larger plots than those of his neighbours. He had always lived in Camacachi, yet he had educated his three sons to university level. One of them had a high position in the ministry of education while the others had good jobs, one in Italy, the other in the United States. Perhaps, then, his income was augmented by remittances from abroad.

Despite this evidence of upward social mobility, his views on the political situation were of the unredeemed local and radical variety. I was treated to a diatribe on the iniquities of 'transnational companies', expressions of total support for the most extreme form of the hydrocarbons law, and, inevitably, an attack on Sánchez de Lozada, in some key instances not borne out by the facts. When I gently pointed this out Don Arturo retorted, 'But I heard this on the radio, so of course it must be true. I listen every morning.' Not for the first time I pondered the impact of modern communications on political attitudes, through the messages transmitted every day in machine-gun Aymara on a myriad different stations. Don Arturo had no time either for Carlos Mesa, and it was not easy to discover what solution, if any, he saw for the country.

On my way back home I met Don Arturo again, returning at a spanking pace quite unaffected by his long walk, and the steep uphill climb from San Pedro. He looked as indestructible as the distant mountains and there seemed little doubt that that went for his opinions as well.

Shortly afterwards I passed the time of day with a younger man, in working clothes, en route to Camacachi, where he too had been born and bred. He was, he told me, a civilian carpenter working at the naval base at Tiquina. His views could hardly have been more different, although the origins of both men were so similar. He was totally against the radical movements and actions of Evo Morales and El Malku.

'These road blocks, señorita,' he exclaimed, 'are against the interests of everyone, especially those of us who live here, and of the same *campesinos* who set them up.'

Presumably his views had been stimulated not by the radio but by his work with the naval base. But he did not have a good word to say for Carlos Mesa either.

'The president should *govern*, and exert his authority,' he proclaimed.

On my last afternoon I climbed the hill behind the house, taking the rough foot trail that leads over the summit or *cumbre* and so down to the village of Chicharro. If one were to read the signs in stones and rocks the message was stark and menacing.

'Repent at once!' screamed the wobbly white painted letters threateningly, 'Christ is coming!'

All along the way the same apocalyptic message was repeated, in varying forms, but with the underlying theme and certainty that eternal hell fire awaited those who did not heed the warning to amend their ways, and that the descent of an avenging Christian deity was imminent, perhaps even around the next bend.

Whatever fervent evangelist, had passed that way, the white paint was still very fresh. At the *cumbre*, where I sat on my familiar stone and gazed at the breathtaking view of the Lago Menor and the hills stretching to the nearby frontier with Peru, more faded and more mundane messages could be discerned on surrounding stones, dating from the elections of two and half years earlier. One said, 'Evo for president!' The other, 'El Mallku for president!'

Sitting there, drinking in one of the most beautiful panoramas in the world, and wrapped in a cloak of tranquillity and almost complete silence, broken only by the faint braying of a donkey or a dog barking on the other side of the deep valley in which Chicharro lies, I could not find comfort in either of these portents for the future of Bolivia.

Perhaps only divine intervention could produce a solution, or some other 'act of God', (against which my insurance company so thoughtfully provided protection, both for me and Villa Margarita,) but I couldn't quite envisage that for my adopted country either.

Only time would tell whether the dreams or the nightmares would prevail.

23

Back From the Brink

During the weeks after I left Bolivia on 8 April the situation grew steadily worse and President Carlos Mesa, who not so long before had enjoyed more popularity than any other recent president, became increasingly beleaguered.

In May, after much travail, Congress finally approved the controversial Hydrocarbons Law, and sent it to the president for his endorsement or observations. The president had let it be known that he considered it 'confiscatory' and threatened to veto it. But when the moment came he simply appeared on television to express his 'conceptual' disagreement with the law, a position that had no judicial basis but saved him using his veto. That would have put him in confrontation with many social sectors in the country which had already labelled him as being on the side of the oil companies. But this evasion merely infuriated everyone and invoked a shower of criticism. In the end Mesa decided not to decide and sent the law back to Congress, without observation, for them to promulgate.

As was to be expected, the oil companies were not at all happy with a law which increased their financial obligations from 18% to 50% (18% royalties and 32% taxes) and authorised the unilateral 'migration', or modification, of existing signed contracts. Once again, dire warnings of legal action and, more broadly, of a steep decline in external investment, began to be rumoured.

On the other side, more bizarrely, what one might think could be a famous victory on the part of the radical proponents of the bill was not interpreted as such. The day after the promulgation of the law on 17 May, Evo Morales and his MAS supporters came out in protest that the law did not go far enough and joined forces with the more extreme elements of the Bolivian Workers' Federation (COB), and the neighbourhood groups of El Alto, in demanding total nationalisation of the country's hydrocarbon resources.

305

Demonstrations and the ubiquitous roadblocks spread like wildfire across the country. Soon 80% of the country was affected, more than a hundred centres were cut off, and the city of La Paz found itself living in a virtual state of siege, invaded by 20,000 *campesinos* according to some estimates, but many thousands more according to others. The streets were clogged by daily marches, food and gas supplies began to run out, water and electricity cuts were frequent, and groups of citizens, seized by panic, began to organise themselves in self-defence against the *campesino* invasion. On the other side, El Alto declared itself on indefinite strike and was fully mobilised for action. It was October 2003 all over again, but this time far worse. In reaction to the uprisings instigated by the western highlands, the clamour for more autonomy, and perhaps even secession, on the part of Santa Cruz and Tarija became ever more vociferous. The danger of the country breaking up in anarchy, or even civil war, loomed more menacingly than ever before.

The president's initial reaction was to ignore the protests, assuring the public that the country was 'tranquil'. He had painted himself into a corner by announcing at the outset of his presidency that he would never use force, a reaction to the sanguinary events of October 2003. Force should always be a last resort, but any government must have that back-up position if it is to maintain any semblance of authority. In Bolivia the masses had been able to take things entirely into their own hands and by now it was clear that the country was totally out of control and the government powerless to regain any authority.

The radical populist protesters were now calling not only for the nationalisation of the hydrocarbon resources, but also for an immediate Constituent Assembly to revise a Constitution that they felt did not properly reflect the interests of the indigenous majority. The businessmen in Santa Cruz and elsewhere were beginning to demand the president's resignation, as well as greater autonomy, on which a referendum was planned. The conflict between the eastern and western parts of the country was nearing a dangerous conflagration point.

Villa Margarita could not remain immune from the general disruption. For several weeks Tiquina was totally cut off from the rest of the country. Nothing and nobody could come in or out, including food, water and vital supplies of cooking gas. Johnny and Mateo were holed up in Villa Magarita, along with Eusebio,

306

the part-time gardener, whose fortnightly visit had coincided with the explosion of popular rage. Johnny and I spoke by telephone every few days, but there was little I could do from far-off Wales. I did tell him to raid all the provisions in my freezer, only to learn that they had perished earlier as a result of a lengthy electricity cut.

There were even more imminent risks. One day Johnny told me he had received visitations both from San Pedro and Camacachi, the village farther along the lakeshore. A fierce argument had arisen between them as to which of them Villa Margarita 'belonged'.

'I thought it belonged to me!' I wailed rather pathetically.

But of course these interventions intensified earlier fears of an invasion or forced occupation. Later news was a little more reassuring. The real bone of contention, it seemed, was that Villa Margarita was not taking part in the protest movements and the argument was as to which village group it should adhere.

Johnny and I decided that discretion was the better part of valour and that Mateo, an Aymara, who already had formed affiliations with El Mallku's movement as a matter of self-protection, should be deputed to represent Villa Margarita at ongoing events.

'But tell him very clearly,' I enjoined Johnny, 'that he is not to "rape and pillage"; or anything violent of that ilk, but merely to be there as "an act of presence".'

That proved to be the right pragmatic solution. But another more tragic problem had no solution. Johnny told me with sorrow that both our dogs, Suri and the delightful new acquisition Nerón, had fallen seriously ill with a mysterious disease. There is no veterinary service nearer than La Paz. Johnny consulted one by phone and was told it was probably some fulminating flu virus. Medication was prescribed but Johnny could not travel to La Paz to buy it. Nerón died, and Suri very nearly followed him. When the blockage was lifted Johnny purchased two puppies in La Paz, who for the first time came equipped with veterinary certificates, describing them as being *mestizo*, that is, of mixed race, an appropriate qualification in a country where the *mestizo* abounds. But one of those puppies also fell ill of the same dread disease and died, the second canine victim of the uprising.

On 3 June Cardinal Julio Terrazas and the Episcopal Conference agreed to try to mediate in the conflict, a role they had been reluctant to assume since a failed attempt to do so two years earlier, just before the fall of Goni's government. They had hardly begun their work when, three days later, President Mesa, who had called on them to help him resolve the crisis, suddenly announced his 'irrevocable' resignation. The timing was curious, to say the least, and it was the third time in as many months that he had resigned.

This time events moved speedily to a dénouement. The constitutional succession now lay in the hands of Congress. The president had resigned on a Monday, and they were to convene to resolve the issue on Thursday. According to the Constitution the successor, in the absence of a vice-president, should be the President of the Senate and, after him the President of the House of Deputies and then the President of the Supreme Court. Events took on a dangerous and dramatic dynamic of their own in the intervening three days. The President of the Senate was not popular in many circles and new marches now took place to prevent his succeeding.

The outgoing president also played an ambiguous role, first appearing to vacillate yet again over his 'irrevocable' resignation and then indulging in some devious manoeuvres, including a violent denunciation of the President of the Senate to prevent him from taking power. He also facilitated the incursion of miners into Sucre to prevent Congress from sitting (the session had been transferred to Sucre because of the impossibility of meeting in besieged La Paz). At this point the armed forces took a stand, indicating that they would be prepared to intervene to defend the unity of the country and democracy: they would respect the constitutional succession but underlined that this option should 'interpret' popular feeling and be by consensus.

Things came to a head with the death of one miner in a confrontation with the military. Then, in quick succession, the presidents of the Senate and of the Chamber of Deputies renounced their right to the presidency. This opened the way for the Congress to be hastily convened, in the most precarious circumstances, to appoint the President of the Supreme Court, Eduardo Rodriguez Vertzé, a highly esteemed and respected lawyer, to succeed Carlos Mesa.

Thus Bolivia lost its second president in less than two years. This time the country had trembled on the very cliff-edge of civil war and had only drawn back in the nick of time. As part of the eleventh-hour deal that was reached the presidential and congressional elections, due in 2007, were to be advanced to December 2005.

Thus President Rodriguez's mandate would be a provisional one, to tide the government over until a new president would assume power in January 2006. His government would therefore be one of transition or, as some put it, of 'truce'. It was further stipulated that the election of departmental prefects (formerly appointed by the head of state) would also take place in December, and that there would be more elections in July next year for a Constituent Assembly to decide on a new Constitution, as well as a referendum on autonomy for the regions.

With this the *campesinos* left La Paz, the roadblocks were lifted, and the country calmed down into an uneasy truce, expected to last until the elections. But everyone knew that this would be only a temporary lull, that the fundamental issues had been put on hold, not resolved, and that what would happen during and after the elections, when the opposing sides were so tightly drawn, was anybody's guess.

I was following these events closely from Wales and in constant touch with the Bolivian Ambassador in London, Gonzalo Montenegro. Over lunch in London, he urged me to help the new president, especially with regard to possible United Nations support for the December elections. Those polls would clearly play a pivotal role in determining Bolivia's future and it was essential that they should not only be free and fair, but generally perceived as such. Not long after, the ambassador informed me that the president wanted to see me as soon as possible.

Coincidentally I was attending a conference in London on elections in Angola at the same time. There a representative of the UN asked me to assist an exploratory mission of two electoral advisers who would be visiting Bolivia in August. In addition an Inter-Parliamentary Union visit by three members of the House of Lords was planned for the end of that month.

The convergence of all these happenings made the timing seem good and I arrived back in La Paz on 26 July. In this new period of peace I had looked forward to ending my long journey with an uneventful ride from the airport to the lake, but it was not to be. Two lakeside villages, Huatajata and Chúa, were having a local squabble as to which of them was to be the site for a new mayoral office, and so had blocked the main road between them. We had to turn off at Huanuni, up into the foothills of the Cordillera, through Achacachi, that town of deserved ill-repute, on that day mercifully but somehow ominously deserted, and then take a rough track through parched and barren hills where several buses had expired, leaving their hapless passengers to push them or trudge along behind. With our lighter load we were luckier, but the detour added another hour to the trip and a great deal of dust to our persons. But I had long ago decided that Robert Louis Stevenson's adage – 'To travel hopefully is better than to arrive' – has a peculiar applicability to Bolivia.

At Villa Margarita many pleasant surprises greeted me. Johnny, Mateo and Eusebio had made good use of their enforced confinement during the troubles of May and June. A new flight of steps had been built down one side of the hillside, along the rocky path up which I used to scramble from the swimming pool. It was not exactly what I wanted aesthetically but I could not fault the good intentions behind an excellent job of work over difficult terrain. Johnny had hired some locals to help and it was possibly the sight of these men working diligently when elsewhere everything had come to a standstill that had roused the ire of the protesting *campesinos* in Camacachi and San Pedro.

I made the acquaintance for the first time of Eusebio, also known as Pastor, because in his free time he is an evangelical preacher roaming all over the countryside. His efforts to sermonise Johnny and Mateo landed on very stony ground but he had done wonders with my rocky garden and there were new borders and terraces everywhere.

There had been a message from the president's office at the airport when I arrived and two days later he received me in the Palacio Quemado. Eduardo Rodriguez was the nearest thing to a *deus ex machina* that Bolivia could have hoped for to save it from the abyss. Fairly young, and belonging to no political party, he is known as a man of probity and intelligence, a stickler for justice and the rule of law. These qualities are enhanced by a most pleasant and accessible personality.

We had met briefly years before when he was a member of a Bolivian delegation that had visited me in Vienna, when I was Director General of the UN office there. On this re-encounter I was struck by his decisiveness, his calm and thoughtful analysis of the unique yet limited nature of his mandate and his rational assessment of the things that could be done in the brief time allotted to him.

310

He wanted my advice on a number of issues: preparatory discussions with concerned parties to help clarify the matters that would be the subject of the Constituent Assembly and the referendum on autonomy; negotiations with the foreign oil companies which had already given notice of their intention to go to arbitration, a matter that he thought should be postponed until a newly elected government assumed power; and a number of questions related to the UN, including the desirability, or not, of attending the Summit of Heads of State in New York in September. I urged him to go and, at his request, subsequently prepared some ideas for his speech there, as well as responding to his other requests as best I could.

He agreed with my proposition that the most important thing over the next few months was to ensure transparent and genuinely free and fair elections, but at first demurred at the idea of support from the UN, on the grounds that Bolivia had long experience of holding elections and its electoral count was technically competent. This was undoubtedly true but when I explained that the idea was not to provide technical advice, but rather, through observers and mechanisms such as the 'quick count' used by the UN with singular success elsewhere, to reinforce the electoral count's final verdict, he readily saw the advantage: given the fragmentation of Bolivia's political parties, the results were bound to be extremely close and there would undoubtedly be claims of fraud from any who lost by a narrow margin.

Soon afterwards preparations were in full swing for the celebration of Bolivia's national day, 6 August, that year marking 180 years of independence. Official ceremonial was rather low-key but the general festivities in towns and villages all over the country went ahead with a swing and lasted until the day of the Bolivian flag, 17 August. Day after day there were bands and civic parades, folklore festivals and dancing in the streets, all notions of protests, blockages, hydrocarbons, autonomy and elections set aside for a blissful few days of merrymaking and revelry, liberally lubricated with beer and *chicha*.

The villages clustered around the lake were no exception. Things began soberly enough, with a proper sense of decorum. August 2 was 'El Día del Campesino', the day of the peasant farmer or countryman. On my arrival a missive was awaiting me from the dignitaries of Camacachi, nominating me 'Godmother of School

311

Materials' which meant that I was expected to donate school supplies to the children. So, on the appointed day, Johnny and I set off with sixty bags stuffed with notebooks, pens, paper and coloured crayons. The big field which serves as Camacachi's main square or meeting place was suspiciously empty, except for a few benches and a loudspeaker system. Soon, however, a straggling procession hove into sight, carrying banners and flags and led by the children, some very small and obviously flagging after much too long a walk. Then there were even longer speeches, led by the Secretary General of the community, a redoubtable lady called Elvira Calle Ventura, resplendent in a voluminous and heavily tucked purple velvet skirt and a bright red shawl; the national anthem sung slightly out of tune; more songs; and poems dramatically declaimed by small boys and girls with a wealth of expansive arm gestures that tended to get entangled with the microphone (it is no wonder that Bolivians of every class turn out to be born orators!).

The published programme was already three hours behind schedule and I was beginning to wonder when we would ever be able to distribute the goodies. Doña Elvira and some of the local authorities were anxious that we should leave them to be handed out later, but the teachers insisted that I should do it personally, intimating privately to Johnny that they feared the supplies might otherwise never reach the children. It was sad to see that the prevailing atmosphere of suspicion about one's neighbour's probity reached down even to a small rural community such as this. But such feelings were more than compensated by the sight of the joy in the little faces, ruddy from the effects of *altiplano* wind and sun, as they reached out for something that would appear a poor gift for a child in a more affluent society, but to them marked a rare moment in their deprived little lives.

At home another missive was awaiting, addressed to 'The Most Distinguished Señorita', embellished as always by a flurry of signatures and official stamps. This was from the mayor and other dignitaries of San Pedro and invited me to attend the civic act and procession that would mark the national anniversary on 5 August (since the actual day, 6 August, fell on a Saturday). I thought this would mean sitting on an uncomfortable bench under a blazing sun while the event unfolded before me.

Not a bit of it. When I arrived, on time (a cardinal error to begin with) and armed with a large straw hat, I found I was expected to take an active part in the proceedings and was pressed into service by the mayor and his cohorts.

The Bolivians share with the British a taste and a talent for organising ceremonial events with all the trappings of bands and pomp and circumstance. In San Pedro we have the privilege of a naval band as well as the ubiquitous local brass bands, common to every region. Bolivians, even those with no military connection, love to march and are very good at it. A cynic would argue that they have plenty of practice in the daily marches through the streets of La Paz, and elsewhere, in protest against whatever the gripe of the moment may be. But on civic days it is a very different matter, and no self-respecting Bolivian would abstain from participating in these solemn precursors of the dancing, drinking and general revelry that will follow.

It was an imposing array that confusedly assembled at the top of San Pedro's main street and eventually set off only forty-five minutes late. This was because we waited in vain for the Comandante Naval to join us but he did so only later, in the plaza. Despairing naval officers hurried hither and thither, trying to instil some sense of order. I found myself, a rather incongruous figure, leading the march alongside the mayor and another local official.

In front of us part of the naval band blew mightily as we moved off at a smart pace, while the rest of the band marched behind our advance party to give encouragement to the serried ranks following on behind. To be honest there was hardly anyone to watch our splendid parade, apart from a few bemused tourists waiting for their bus to arrive on a pontoon from San Pablo, as everyone who was anyone in Tiquina – 'le tout Tiquina' as one might say – was taking part.

Down to the square we marched, the mayor a stickler for our front line to stay in step and keep the right distance from the band in front and between ourselves (perhaps he had once been a military conscript). Then we went round the square, making very neat corners, to the lake side, where tramlines had been drawn to keep us on the straight and narrow, and then onto the raised part of the plaza. The band assembled itself in front of the market, and played in the other contingents as they drew up in formation in front of us.

First came the *barqueros*, the men who manoeuvre the ungainly pontoons across the straits; then the *transportistas*, who drive the trucks and mini-buses; then huddled ranks of identically brown-shawled ladies – the *pescadoras*, who clean and sell the fish that we can never find, and the market ladies who keep the rickety kiosks along the shore or cook meals in the covered market place. Finally in marched the children, the primary schoolchildren rather raggedly, then the smarter secondary school, complete with a band of drums, mini-skirted 'majorettes' owing more to imported American culture than to Andean tradition, and a swaggering, goose-stepping band leader, expertly twirling a *bastón de mando* (staff of command). Last of all, to show up all these amateurs, the naval ratings brought up the rear in a stirring quick march to the tune of a souped-up folk dance played at a rollicking pace.

All of this was accomplished with commendable dignity and formality as were the interminable speeches and tributes to the heroes of the Independence – Bolívar and Sucre, with a few offhand references to Santa Cruz – that followed, when anyone who was anyone felt obliged to hold forth (I was fortunately spared). But through it all ran a thread of insouciance, that leavening element of informality and cocking a snook at authority that also conveys an unmistakably Bolivian national trait. Ecstatic stray dogs ran in and out of the legs of the marchers, threatening to bring the whole parade crashing down; two grubby-looking little girls lounged on the seats meant for the VIPs; and an early drunk relieved himself against a wall at the corner of the square.

When the speeches at last dried up I thought release was near, but no. The episode was taking on aspects of the old song about the 'grand old Duke of York': everyone was marched back up the hill again, then down, and once more round the plaza. At the most discreet moment I could find, I slipped quietly away.

Apart from such excitements, life at Villa Margarita continued on a very even keel, with daily swimming, writing and lunch on the upper terrace above the lake with the mountains shimmering in the distance. For a whole month the sun shone out of a cloudless sky, the garden and the surrounding hills daily becoming more parched and sere. Nights were cold and still, the sky hung with stars and, for a while, a full moon beat a silver path across the dark waters beneath my balcony.

Doña Perpetua and her husband continued to tether their unfortunate

314

donkey on bare patches of hillside, without water, for days on end, or down by the lake on a leash just too short to allow the poor beast to reach the water's edge or the juicy totora reeds. Surreptitiously, whenever they were not around, we would rush buckets of water to him and he came to recognise Mateo with such vociferous braying that we feared the whole neighbourhood would be alerted. Once, greatly daring, Mateo moved the donkey to a better patch of *paja brava*, but luckily Doña Perpetua did not notice. Their dog was no longer chained to the makeshift kennel to keep guard over the now empty hen-house, but my relief at his release was tempered by the news that he was now dragging his atrophied back legs round the plaza of San Pedro, emaciated and looking desperately for food now that we were no longer able to feed him. I could not help reflecting that fate would have been much kinder had it carried him away with the mysterious disease that had killed our well-cared-for dogs.

Don Saturnino the local *yatiri*, a kindlier owner, brought his two brindle cows past the house every morning on his way down to the cove where they browsed all day among the totora, knee deep in the brackish water until evening when they were led back up the hill to the village. Don Pedro, my gentle nearest neighbour, tended his bean holms, now ready for harvest, but adamantly refused to sell me the twenty-centimetre fringe of land I needed along the boundary wall to construct a drainage system that would avoid another flooding of the swimming pool when the rains returned. Predictably, Don Alberto, the gap-toothed painter, had not finished the mural by May, as he had faithfully promised, nor even by the end of July. Now, however, at last galvanised into action, he was a daily fixture, a melancholy figure working under an impromptu awning rigged up by Johnny, his one tooth wobbling in concentration, and speaking only to mourn his lot, the iniquities of his estranged wife and the complications of his two children who, it seemed, did not study unless he was around to goad them into doing so.

'I shall not be able to sleep at nights until this work is finished,' he kept lamenting.

Since it was at least two years since it was first commissioned that sounded like a long period of insomnia. But then, two days before my departure, hey presto, it was done! Well, apart from a couple of flags and a few more details, promised for a later date. But it is a magnificent and striking addition to the swimming pool.

Eusebio, the part-time gardener, proved to be a cheery little gnome of a man, always smiling, very hard-working and obviously a man of many parts. He was once a miner and now his services as a preacher were also in great demand all over the highlands, messages constantly arriving to call him away. He seemed to have settled himself in Tiquina with his wife and four children and his sister-in-law came at weekends to sell things in the market. She was working on a thesis at one of the many universities and left me speechless when she arrived unannounced one day and asked me to brief her on 'concubinage in the United Kingdom'!

Once a week I went shopping in La Paz, and to meet friends, a whole day excursion, and at weekends visitors came from the city for Sunday barbecues. One weekend it was the electoral mission from the UN in New York, the next, three members of the House of Lords, on an Inter-Parliamentary Union mission, equally keen to 'help Bolivia'. They arrived nearly three hours later than my other guests, on a very slow naval boat from Huatajata where an over-enthusiastic chief of protocol in the Bolivian Congress had injudiciously organised a prior reception in two *altiplano* communities, a sure recipe for kilometric speeches, much dancing, feasting and carousing, not to mention disruption of any planned programme. They also brought with them some unexpected additional guests, including the MAS senator still inseparable from the hat he had doggedly worn during the lunch and meeting in the House of Lords a few months earlier, as well as a horde of hangers-on, drivers, security men and the like who fell hungrily on the *salteñas* and other culinary delights before the real guests could get a look in. But one of the delights – and challenges – of Bolivia is that you have to be ready to rise to all sorts of unexpected eventualities and the impromptu and unplanned often turns out to be the most enjoyable, as was the case on this occasion.

A less enjoyable intrusion into the normally calm tenor of our days was the discovery that the guest bathroom toilet was blocked. At first deemed a merely temporary inconvenience it turned out to be more serious and a plumber was hastily summoned from La Paz. The only day he could come was on the national day itself, Saturday 6 August. The full scale of the disaster soon became clear: the pipes were clogged up with the roots of two eucalyptus trees near the house that had been lopped but not felled. Soon a large part of the bathroom floor was up, then wide areas of the front patio, and later, as the problem was traced through the very foundations of the house, the floor tiles in the colonial colonnade on the front had also to be lifted and deep holes dug. With Johnny helping, the work continued by lamplight until after midnight, long, snake-like coils of slimy black gunge being pulled out by the yard. Next morning early, Juan, the workman from across the lake, was called in and by lunchtime everything was back in place, as if nothing had happened.

This is something else that reconciles you to some other drawbacks of living in Bolivia. Untoward, and possibly unnecessary, things are always happening but when disaster really strikes, it is a case of all hands to the pump (literally in this instance) and near-miracles are performed. Of course, in this case, as often, the solution was only temporary: the eucalyptus trees had to be felled and their roots removed which meant tearing up the paving stones all over again. And who knows whether the foundations of my fragile adobe house have been irretrievably undermined?

It is hard to avoid the analogy with the country as a whole. There was a period of truce, things on the surface are calm, despite occasional local skirmishes that inevitably culminated in road blockages, mercifully on a local scale rather than countrywide as a few months earlier. (This has become a national pastime: were rapid road blocking to become an Olympic sport, Bolivia would surely bear off all the gold medals.) But the basic problems had not been dealt with, but just papered over for the time being, lying dormant until the next major test of the December elections and later the Constituent Assembly.

In the last few years Bolivia had seen some earth-shaking changes. The fundamental question remained: Had the very foundations of the nation's fragile democratic structures, painstakingly built over the last decades, been irretrievably undermined?

24

The New Bolivia – and Farewell Villa Margarita?

In October 2005 I was back in Bolivia to receive friends from the UK who were taking the classic Andean tour – Lima, Cuzco, Macchu Picchu, and thence by train to Puno and across the lake into Bolivia.

I arrived on 4 October and the next day was received by President Rodriguez. The country was in even greater turmoil with electoral fever mounting as voting day, 12 December, drew closer. Every faction, interest group and political party, and even individual politician, was striving to wrest maximum advantage from a fluid situation, unmindful of the overall national interest. Yet I found Eduardo Rodriguez as serene as before, logically analysing the situation and retaining his sense of humour.

Probably the most serious of the mind-boggling problems facing him concerned the distribution of congressional seats among the different departments and regions. These had been set on the basis of a previous census, but a more recent one gave a different result. Owing to substantial migration from the *altiplano* to the lower and more prosperous regions of the country, additional seats should be assigned to those departments, to the detriment of the *altiplano*, where the majority of the population is indigenous and Evo Morales' party, MAS, has its major base. The furore that this occasioned among the latter can well be imagined, and tense negotiations were still going on.

Members of Congress were muddying the waters further by pressing for the elections to be postponed, perhaps even until 2007, the year in which they would have taken place had two presidents not been thrown out. United for once, they wanted to hold on to their seats and the perks that went with them. Given the low esteem in which all traditional parties were now held, and the cataclysmic political changes taking place, they had scant hope of retaining their posts after the elections.

The president effectively stymied this move by repeatedly proclaiming his irrevocable intent to step down on 22 January 2006, the date on which the new government was to take office. It was a signal example of lack of self-interest when most others prominent on the scene were grabbing for power. In the end, the dire prospect of the vacuum that would open up if there was no legitimate government to succeed him made wiser counsels prevail.

I had planned to meet my friends in Puno but communications proved so difficult that I eventually gave up. Instead I greeted them on the quayside at Huatajata on 15 October, and drove them back to Villa Margarita. I had planned several sight-seeing trips but all involved long drives on rough roads, so we settled for a couple of relaxing days by the pool, and cosy evenings by the fire, interrupted only by a *parrillada* with friends from La Paz, including the American and British ambassadors, and a visit to Copacabana.

Another hazard loomed over our drive to La Paz on 18 October, prior to their departure for London next day. An acute shortage of domestic gas on which the majority of the population depend for cooking had reached crisis proportions, causing widespread protests and blockages of city streets and main roads. Even the Commander-in-Chief of the Navy had been delayed two hours in arriving at the annual anniversary parade of the Tiquina Naval Base on 14 October, leaving the assembled audience, including myself, shivering in review stands inappropriately set up in the shade on a less than clement day. All went well until we reached El Alto, where angry housewives, and a few men, banging gas canisters, blocked the roads down into La Paz. Johnny knew all the byways to avoid the obstructions but even his ingenuity was tested. We climbed pot-holed streets spiralling up the mountainside in *barrios* that I didn't even know existed, twisting and turning, but every time were brought up short by another noisy protest. At one crossroads a taxi driver tried first to persuade and then to argue his way through. The reaction of the assembled throng, under the impassive gaze of a helpless policeman, was so violent that we beat a hasty retreat. It must have taken a couple of hours or more to reach our hotel for a very late lunch. For my friends it was an interesting insight into 'people power' in today's Bolivia.

They left at dawn next day. Later I attended a small lunch at the spanking new – and highly fortified – residence of the American Ambassador David Greenlee and his wife. Another guest was the representative of the Inter-American Development Bank. The conversation naturally turned to politics and the prospects for the coming election. The Embassy still thought that Jorge Quiroga Banzer's former vice president, and briefly president after Banzer stepped down through ill health, could win the presidential race, though by a very small majority. The IDB representative's money was on Evo Morales.

Another subject was the brewing row in the media and among some politicians, over the export of missiles for destruction by the US armed forces. The ambassador explained that this was a routine matter: the missiles were obsolete and dangerous, Bolivia did not have the technology to destroy them safely, and so this was being done by the Americans with the agreement of the government. Any thought that this was a storm in a teacup that would quickly blow over was to prove sadly wrong.

I left for the UK on 21 October and spent the previous night in La Paz. As we coasted down into the city I telephoned the palace to leave a farewell message for President Rodriguez. Knowing that he was closeted in last-ditch talks with the parties about the distribution of seats, I asked his private secretary not to disturb him, but simply to convey my good wishes. To my surprise the president emerged from his meeting to speak to me, a characteristically courteous gesture. Things were very difficult, he told me, then adding, with his customary quirky sense of humour, 'I think I am going to take a solomonic decision and threaten to kill the baby!' Once again I marvelled at his unruffled equanimity in the face of circumstances that would daunt even the most valiant.

I had explained to the president that I would not be able to return to Bolivia until February as I was taking a long holiday in Australia and New Zealand, including an expedition cruise to Antarctica on a Russian icebreaker. By that time, if all went well, a new government would be installed. There was little I could do to help in the interim, but if at any time he felt that my assistance might be useful, he had my telephone contacts.

When I boarded the plane the next morning I was blissfully

unaware that nine months would elapse before I saw Villa Margarita again, the longest I had ever been away.

In early December 2005 I was in Bucharest for a peacekeeping training exercise organised by the British Foreign Office and the Joint Services Command and Staff College for senior military and other personnel from Russia and Eastern Europe. All went well until, late on 7 December, I caught my heel on an uneven step and precipitated myself onto a marble floor, knocking myself unconscious. There followed a memorable twenty-four hours in a Romanian hospital where it was discovered that, in addition to a deep wound on my forehead, I had fractured my face in three places.

Back in England the repercussions of that accident were to limit my activities for many months. When the dreadful bruising subsided, serious damage was diagnosed in my left eye, which had been pushed back into my head. That required two operations and a period of enforced rest when I could not read or write, and air travel was proscribed because of damage to my sinuses. That ban was lifted in March 2006, and I was able to travel to Kenya for a peacekeeping exercise for Africa. On my return a chest infection caused me to postpone travel to Bolivia yet again and summer months brought many commitments in the UK. So it was not until late July that I came back to Villa Margarita, despite new complications that might require two further eye operations. If the condition worsened while I was in Bolivia, I was to take the first plane home for emergency surgery.

While I had been in hospital in London, presidential and congressional elections had taken place remarkably peacefully in Bolivia, on 18 December 2005, together with the direct election, for the first time, of prefects for the nine departments. In the final run-up it was widely predicted that the result would be very close, with the betting on Quiroga winning by a very slim majority. The main concern was whether Evo Morales, who was confidently predicting victory, would accept such a result or whether there would be further social unrest and civil strife.

That concern proved to be totally misplaced. Morales won 54% of the popular vote, nearly double that of his nearest opponent, thus becoming the first Bolivian president to be elected outright in many years. Several large traditional parties suffered badly: MIR practically disappeared, and MNR, the architect of the 1952 revolution, was reduced to its lowest representation since its creation. The people had spoken, and with a vengeance. It was a true revolution. Morales and MAS had received support not only from his indigenous followers but also from some surprising areas of the country and La Paz. The assumption was that many of the latter hoped thereby to see an end to the endless marches and road blockages that were making normal life virtually impossible.

Before assuming the presidency on 22 January 2006, Morales took a whirlwind tour, first visiting his close friend President Hugo Chavez of Venezuela and Fidel Castro in Cuba, and then travelling on to Europe, China and South Africa. The trip caused a sensation: here was a charismatic Amerindian leader whose populist style and policies gave rise to immense speculation, and who throughout the trip wore the same woolly jumper, striped in red, blue and white. Pictures of Evo sporting this casual attire alongside stiffly suited heads of state and other dignitaries were splashed across the front pages of newspapers and television screens all over the world. Evo's *chumpa* seemed set to acquire the same iconic stature as Mao's jacket, Castro's beard and fatigues, and Ché Guevara's beret.

His inauguration as president bore similar iconoclastic features. The main ceremony took place among the pre-Colombian ruins of Tihuanacu, on the shores of Lake Titicaca, and was attended by Indian groups from all over the country as well as the region, some coming from as far away as Ecuador in a show of Amerindian solidarity. There was an honour guard of *campesinos*, sacred promises to the Pachamama, the ancient Andean earth goddess, and a barefoot homage to the pyramid of Akapana. The formal traditional transfer of power in Congress was relegated to second place.

Unorthodoxy was to be the hallmark of the new presidency. No one knew quite what to expect. There was fear in many quarters – the political élite, the middle classes and the *karas* or whites – and, among the jubilant indigenous majority, euphoria. Evo's public statements were a fiery cocktail of nationalism and anti-Americanism but there were puzzling contradictions. Some actions were laudable: he declared a war on corruption, halved his own salary and cut those of politicians and civil servants, saying that he wished to use the savings to employ more teachers. Modest rises for teachers and health workers were authorised. For the armed forces, the president adopted draconian measures. He appointed a new High

Command, leap-frogging two entire *promociones*, and forcing 27 senior generals into retirement.

Other messages on key planks in his electoral platform such as coca, agrarian reform and the nationalisation of gas reserves were mixed. Some considered it a conflict of interest when Evo retained the post of Secretary General of the Coca Growers Federation. His slogan was '*NO* to zero coca but *YES* to zero cocaine'. He appealed to his fellow coca growers to limit themselves to one legal *cato*, an area of 40 square metres. For coca exceeding subsistence needs he had an ambitious plan of industrialising and exporting coca in the form of tea, medicines, herbal treatments and even toothpaste. Such proposals had been made before and it was unrealistic to think that they could mop up the enormous amounts of coca being produced.

His policies would entail modification of Bolivia's adherence to the UN Convention on Illicit Trafficking in Narcotic Drugs and Psychotropic Substances, which I helped to negotiate in Vienna in 1988. At the 2006 meeting of the UN Commission on Narcotic Drugs the stance of the Bolivian delegation inevitably caused some consternation.

For the first few months Morales was silent on the main platform of his political ascendancy – the nationalisation of Bolivia's oil and gas reserves. Those already concerned by the passage of the hydrocarbons law in 2005 were lulled into thinking that the new government's policy in this area, so vital for foreign investment, would not be as radical as had been feared. They were wrong. Choosing the symbolic date of 1 May, Morales struck with characteristically dramatic effect. Wreathed in triumphal garlands he personally led armed troops into the San Alberto gas field, near Talija, operated by Petrobras, the Brazilian state oil company, and Bolivia's principal customer. The troops hoisted a banner proclaiming the site to be 'The nationalised property of the Bolivians' and a soldier hoisted a Bolivian flag on top of the gas facility. Taking the microphone, Evo Morales personally issued a presidential decree ordering foreign companies to hand over gas production to Yacimientos Petroliferos de Bolivia (YPFB), the state oil company. Simultaneously, units of the armed forces seized fifty-six other gas and oil installations elsewhere.

The decree gave foreign companies 180 days to sign new operating contracts or leave Bolivia. 'This is just the beginning,' declared

323

the president. 'Tomorrow it will be the mines, the forest resources and the land.' YPFB, greatly weakened by the 'capitalisation' process some ten years earlier, was to be reorganised so that it could take charge of the negotiations and of production and export.

It was not clear why the president had waited until May to take this much-heralded step. The reasons for doing so now appeared to be mainly political. There were growing murmurs among his most radical followers that the president was not fulfilling the promise of drastic change on which he had won his overwhelming electoral victory. Even the rank and file of ordinary *campesinos* felt strongly about nationalisation, although they barely appreciated its far-reaching implications. Moreover, two new elections loomed in early July: one for a Constituent Assembly mandated to make radical reforms to the Constitution; the other a referendum on greater autonomy for the prefects of the nine departments, who had for the first time been elected in December 2005, instead of being appointed by the president.

The 255 members of the Constituent Assembly were duly elected, but the president's party, MAS, won only a simple majority and not the two-thirds that the president had expected. As to autonomy, the president, who originally favoured the proposal, changed his mind and urged his followers (mainly in the highland regions) to reject it, which five departments obligingly did. But four – Benl, Pando, Santa Cruz and Tarija (known as the 'Half Moon', because they curve round Bolivia's northern, eastern and southern frontiers) – voted in favour, increasing the dangerous rift between *altiplano* and lowland regions.

This was the situation when I returned to Bolivia at the end of July 2006. I travelled with Johnny Vera, my majordomo, whom I had brought to the UK in May for medical treatment for his badly swollen and discoloured right leg. In Bolivia it had proved impossible to get a convincing diagnosis, much less successful treatment, and amputation had even been suggested. Consultations with a top-notch vascular surgeon in London dispelled that disturbing idea, and provided the diagnosis that originally Johnny must have suffered a deep-vein thrombosis. Unfortunately no operation or cure was possible, the only solution being to keep the problem under control with fitted medical stockings. Armed with a stock of these and the reassurance that Johnny's condition was not life threatening, we embarked on the long trip back to Bolivia.

The country was becoming ever more isolated, as the 'milk-run' flights up into the Andes from Brazil were further reduced. Both the Bolivian airline, Lloyd Aéreo Boliviano (LAB), and Varig, Brazil's national airline, had ceased operations owing to financial woes. Aerosur was flying still, but we had to wait ten hours in São Paulo, in an airport terminal that seemed more like a morgue, without passengers or aircraft, or even a place where one could get a decent meal. The omens were not good for catching the first aircraft out if something went wrong with my eye. Having left Knill on Thursday afternoon, we reached La Paz late on Friday night. There Johnny's family gave him a rapturous reception. He had never been out of Bolivia before, and still did not speak a word of English, but he had taken to life in the Welsh Marches like a duck to water.

Next day we shopped for essentials before driving to Villa Margarita where one of Johnny's sons had been holding the fort, along with Mateo. Everything was in order, apart from a broken pump, victim of Mateo's over-enthusiastic hauling on a cable, but the pleasure of a tranquil homecoming did not last for long.

In San Pedro, on Sunday morning, Johnny ran into the new mayor, or 'alcalde', who said he wished to see me urgently and would call at 6 pm. True to form, he arrived after 7 o'clock, when I was longingly thinking of a quiet evening by my log fire. His name was Gregorio Argaña, and I had met him briefly while marching at his side in the patriotic national day parade a year earlier.

I had got on well with his predecessor, Milton, and it was not clear why his five-year tenure in the mayoral office had been curtailed. It was obviously not something venal, for he was still a *Concejal*, so political manoeuvring seemed more likely. Argaña was a different kettle of fish, as his glowering demeanour alerted us as soon as he arrived and grudgingly accepted a cup of coffee. He had told Johnny that he wanted to talk about Christmas toys for the children of all the surrounding communities and the local taxes that I had been trying unsuccessfully to pay for many years. These subjects did come up but he had more pressing things on his mind.

This was not the first time he had come, he began. By ill fortune it must have been just after Johnny left. He had not been well received, he went on, his brow darkening further. The young man

325

had been all right – bearing in mind what young people were like nowadays – but there had been an old man who had been insufferably rude. Who could that be? Johnny and I wondered aloud, disingenuously. Just at that moment Mateo injudiciously hove into view on the courtyard outside.

'That's him,' cried the mayor, jabbing an angry finger in Mateo's direction. 'He had the nerve to ask what I thought I was doing here.'

Heaping coals on the fire Mateo had asserted, 'We belong to Camacachi, not San Pedro.' There was an ongoing dispute between the two as to which village the land around Villa Margarita belonged and Camacachi had included us in their recent census.

We hastened to apologise, but our encounter had got off to a poor start. It was hardly a diplomatic way of greeting the mayor of San Pedro.

'I have come to give you a friendly warning,' he went on, though his manner looked anything but friendly. 'There is talk in some communities – Tito Yupanqui, Santiago de Oja and others – of occupying this property.'

Several properties in the vicinity had already been occupied – the trout farm in the next bay at Curiwaya and some church lands in Copacabana – so this sent a chill down the spine.

'On what legal grounds?' I asked feebly. 'I have all the titles to my land, and it is only half a hectare of rock, not productive land.' (The Morales government had issued a decree authorising seizure of properties of over 50 hectares that were not being used productively.)

'I know,' said the *alcalde*. 'One of the people you bought it off was my father.' But he waved his hands about airily to indicate that such niceties had no value in the new era just beginning.

'What can we do?' I asked. Very little, it appeared. Once again, and now definitely protesting too much, the *alcalde* was at pains to stress that he had no say in the matter and was simply 'a friend' tipping us off. If they came (or rather, when), he explained kindly, we would have to leave immediately, taking nothing with us. While we struggled to digest this unwelcome piece of information he dropped another bombshell.

'By the way,' he said, almost conversationally, 'you are illegally occupying the land on which your access road is built. One of the main principles guiding my tenure of office' (he spoke as if quoting an administrative guideline or political tract), 'is to rid this municipality of all traces of the corruption and incorrect practices that have bedevilled it for so many years.' At this, a sanctimonious smile spread across his face.

'Wait a minute,' I protested. 'I paid for that strip of land. There was a community meeting one Sunday morning and the then mayor told me that I could purchase the land belonging to the municipality by arranging for the bulldozer that would make the road to level the football pitch in San Pedro. The town council sent a letter to me in Vienna, confirming this arrangement, complete with official stamps, signatures and fingerprints. Afterwards I had the football pitch levelled.'

'I have been through all the papers,' said the mayor, now positively gloating, 'and there is no trace of any such documentation. What's more there is no football pitch. We are only now beginning to create one for San Pedro.'

This was mind-boggling stuff, to which there was no ready answer. I remembered with misgiving that the letter from the earlier town council was almost certainly in the UK.

'So,' said the *alcalde*, with all the steamrolling authority of the bulldozer that had disappeared from the municipal annals, 'we are going to recuperate the land on which the road is built.'

'Recuperate?' I asked, bewildered. 'What do you mean, "recuperate"? Are you going to tear the road up? It's a sound concrete surface that cost US$11,000, in addition to the cost of bulldozing the football pitch. Lots of members of the community use it. They bring down their animals to the lake shore and Don Heliodoro [he of the chicken houses] sometimes has lorries come with feed for the hens.'

But Don Gregorio remained adamant.

'There must be some solution,' I expostulated. 'I shall look out my papers, but if there had been some error, or incorrect procedure, what can be done to ensure my access? Do you wish me to "re-purchase" the land?'

Don Gregorio was not to be drawn and my remark was to prove inadvertently injudicious. We went on to talk of taxes. Municipal councillors had told Johnny that four to five thousand bolivianos would cover the current and all previous years, and I declared my intention to pay that week.

'Not so fast,' said the mayor. 'My topographers have to measure the property and make a plan.' I forbore to point out that that was precisely what I had been requesting for several years, and meekly agreed to receive the topographers on Tuesday. 'I shall come with them and we can continue our discussion,' said the mayor ominously.

As a parting shot he reminded me about the need for Christmas toys for the children. After he had left, Johnny, Nancy and I collapsed into armchairs round the fire and considered the situation. Over some comforting whisky initial panic subsided somewhat. 'It's intimidation,' we consoled ourselves, not very convincingly. 'He can't really do anything. Probably just wants money.'

Brightening considerably, I remembered that my insurance policy, reflecting hazards peculiar to Bolivia, included coverage against 'political risks', 'mutinies' and 'civil unrest', which summed up pretty well what we were facing. 'Let them come,' I said, 'and I shall just take the money and run.' But this cheery mood did not last. The insurance company would almost certainly find some small print letting them off the hook. And in my heart of hearts I knew that I could not bear to lose Villa Margarita. It meant a lot more than money.

The friends in La Paz whom I called for advice, and help if possible, were all horrified, but not surprised. 'This is the new Bolivia' was the constant refrain. They had all held ministerial positions previously, but now they were yesterday's men. Some had contacts in the new administration but of doubtful value. One rang his close friend, the prefect of the Department of La Paz, and the prefect promised to demand a report from the municipality of Tiquina. This was only marginally reassuring, as the radio had reported a move to unseat him from the post to which he had been elected only seven months previously. Everyone agreed that it was important that the meeting I had requested with President Morales should take place as soon as possible. That request had been made for quite another purpose: to offer my services to the government as I had done for all the previous administrations and also, if desired, those of a newly formed non-governmental organisation, Independent Diplomat, whose purpose was to provide objective diplomatic advice to governments with little experience. I was loath to use the occasion to speak of personal problems, but the general advice was that only Evo Morales could sort matters out.

On Monday morning help came from an unexpected quarter. An

early visitor was Don Tito, *el mallku* (or chief) of Camacachi. Awaiting me on arrival there had been an official missive from him and his dignitaries requesting me to provide a computer for communal use. I told Don Tito that I was ready to do so, provided someone could be trained in its use, but added, 'Of course, if Villa Margarita is occupied and I am forced to leave, I shall not be able to go ahead.'

Don Tito's reaction to the mayor's visit was also one of horror. How could this be, he thundered, when I had for many years been a respected *vecina* (neighbour)? Anyway, I was not a resident of San Pedro, but of Camacachi and they would defend me.

'That goes for the access road as well,' he went on. 'The old cemetery alongside is *our* cemetery. The *alcalde* wants to include it all in San Pedro as an urban area, and charge higher property taxes. As part of Camacachi you should pay only the rural rate. We have documents to prove this and are going to fight it out.' I was not sure I wanted to get into this local embroglio.

Everyone seemed to be beating a path to my door. Next came Don Heliodoro, husband of the formidable Doña Perpetua. He was restarting the mass production of chickens and eggs in his ramshackle hut in the cove below. On my first morning I had wakened to the sound of hundreds of birds and had rushed to the window hoping to see some great gathering of water birds, until a triumphant cock-crow alerted me to the reality. Don Heliodoro was here to reiterate his claim for electricity from my transformer. He was quite belligerent about it. Johnny and I told him that we would consider it, but he must present an authorisation from the electricity company.

The evening brought back Don Tito, this time accompanied by three of his cohorts from Camacachi's administrative hierarchy, each endowed with an imposing title, and all but one, I noticed with some bemusement, boasting 'Argaña' as their maternal surname.

'Are you all related to the mayor?' I enquired.

'Oh yes,' they chorused, 'the Argaña family all come from Camacachi.' Rather than a quarrel between two rural communities, this was taking on all the aspects of a family feud.

They had brought maps dated 1969, officially stamped, and showing Wila-Wila, where Villa Margarita now stood, the old cemetery and the land crossed by my access road, as rural areas forming part of Camacachi. The snag was that a topographer from the Agrarian Reform Institute had to verify this and that cost money.

And there were the fares of those members of the community who had to go to La Paz to negotiate all this...

We would soon be awash with topographers, I reflected. For the visit of those establishing the basis for San Pedro's taxes, we invited Johnny's brother Edgar to be present since he was well versed in the rules and regulations and could defend us against excessive demands. To give him more gravitas, we endowed him with the temporary and honorary title of *Ingeniero* (Engineer).

The '*Ingeniero*' promptly turned up at 9 o'clock, but not so the official topographers. After a wasted morning Johnny and Edgar departed disconsolately for lunch in San Pedro, after which Edgar would return to La Paz. Hardly had they gone when two figures came ambling down the road – the official topographers. I sent Mateo post-haste to the village to summon Johnny and Edgar back, and meanwhile showed the topographers the legal documents, which clearly stated that my property totalled 5400 square metres, just over half a hectare.

'Take a note of that,' said the man from La Paz officiously to his local minion, who duly put pen to paper. They then went down to the swimming pool and when the others returned they decided it was time for lunch and said they would be back at three o'clock. Of course they weren't, and when they did appear, the man from La Paz said it was all very complicated and we might be well advised to hire our own topographer whose findings they would then review. Edgar left for the city, promising to engage a friend for that purpose.

This saga continued for weeks. One of Edgar's friends fell by the wayside, then another was found, who came twice but presented his work only a couple of days before my departure, when we submitted it to the municipality. In the meantime, Johnny tried to break the logjam by paying the 4000–5000 bolivianos originally quoted. 'But,' said the same councillors who had originally requested this amount, 'it is an exceptionally beautiful place. It is worth much more than that.' And they began to pull figures out of the air. We decided to await the official appraisal based on our topographer's calculation. The municipality's topographer from La Paz, with his San Pedro sidekick, was supposed to turn up daily but never did. Neither did the mayor.

We lived in a kind of limbo, never sure whether an occupying force would appear and turn us out. I advised Johnny, Nancy and

Mateo to have a small bag ready with their important belongings and did the same myself. Two nights after the mayor's visit the dogs set up an alarming racket at one o'clock in the morning (we now had three; still the recalcitrant though partially reformed Suri, and two delightful new young dogs, Negrón and Coco). Waking from a deep sleep I flung on a dressing gown and flew downstairs. Outside the glass front porch a dark figure stood. A few minutes of palpitating panic ensued before I made out that it was Mateo. Then the alarm siren sounded shrilly down by the lake shore and more anxious time elapsed before we discovered that it had been set off by Johnny and Nancy who came panting up the steps. There was no intruder, but it was a sleepless night for all of us, and there were more to follow.

No appointment with the president was possible during my first week, as 6 August was Bolivia's National Day. This year it was celebrated in the capital, Sucre, where, in addition to the usual ceremonies the Constituent Assembly, was formally inaugurated. Representatives of indigenous peoples from all over the country, and from neighbouring Andean nations, converged on Sucre, as well as the customary array of ambassadors and ministers. Some 39 Bolivian ethnic groups paraded alongside the goose-stepping and scarlet-coated soldiers of the Colorado Regiment. It was a deeply moving sight, a colourful symbol of the new Bolivia.

Other signs and portents were less reassuring. In a rambling rhetorical speech lasting an hour and thirty-five minutes, the president unleashed a virulent attack against the Catholic Church and against Eduardo Rodriguez, his predecessor in the presidency. The man whose honesty and statesmanship had saved the country from civil war and made possible the elections that had voted him into power he now accused of the vilest crimes of treachery and corruption. The hapless object of his ire was sitting in the front row, under the full blaze of the cameras focused pitilessly upon him.

I had met Rodriguez soon after my arrival and listened with dismay to the misfortunes that had befallen him. The accusations revolved around the destruction of the missiles (originally a gift to Bolivia from China) that had been the subject of conversation during my lunch at the American Ambassador's residence nine months earlier. The embattled former president gave me an aide-memoire recounting his version of events. Approached by the US Ambassador with an offer to destroy these obsolete weapons, which had been banned worldwide by the United Nations as a potential threat to commercial aircraft if they fell into the wrong hands, Rodriguez had agreed in principle but with the caveat that proper legal and military procedures should be followed.

During the president's absence at a heads of state meeting in September 2005 a US Hercules plane landed in La Paz with specialist US forces who, with the connivance of some senior military officials, flew the missiles to the United States without the knowledge of the president, the only person authorised to order the intervention of the special Bolivian anti-terrorist forces involved in the operation. He was not even informed of the transfer of the missiles on his return, which led to his inadvertently assuring political leaders, including Evo Morales, that they were still in the country. It was only when news broke in the media that he discovered what had happened.

Rodriguez had ordered an investigation which revealed that members of the US military mission in Bolivia had negotiated an agreement with the Ministry of Defence for the removal of the missiles, including the promise of a financial transfer. On receiving the report in January 2006, shortly before he stepped down, the president accepted the resignation of the minister of defence, dismissed the commander in chief of the army, instituted proceedings against other generals involved and called in David Greenlee, the US Ambassador, to protest against the abuse of Bolivian sovereignty and of his own authority. The foreign minister followed this up with a formal diplomatic protest. Rodriguez recounted all this to Evo Morales on the eve of the latter's installation, and had been assured of his understanding.

Notwithstanding, in March 2006, when Rodriguez was away in China, the attorney general formalised an accusation against him, the former defence minister and the commander in chief of the armed forces, listing a long litany of crimes: submitting the nation to foreign domination; espionage; revelation of secrets; and breach of the Constitution and the laws of the country. The generals responsible for the transfer of the missiles were not included, nor were due legal processes followed: Rodriguez was not advised of his rights nor allowed to present his explanation. He resigned from the post of President of the Supreme Court of Justice, to which he had returned after relinquishing the presidency.

Rodriguez was in a very serious situation: the penalty for the crimes of which he was accused was thirty years in prison. Most disturbing of all, he seemed to be considered guilty until proved innocent. The undercurrents to this murky affair gave rise to suspicions that there was much more to it than the matter of the Chinese missiles – a desire to precipitate his departure from the Supreme Court perhaps? Or some obscure revenge for past judicial acts in that court, where he was renowned for showing the same objectivity and incorruptibility that had characterised his brief tenure of the presidency? The ambassadors present in Sucre were appalled by the public humiliation of the man who had saved the country from disaster.

Rodriguez enjoined my help in arranging for him to meet the Secretary-General of the United Nations. The previous year, when he had visited UN Headquarters officially as president, I had been successful but now that a new president was shortly to attend the General Assembly in New York, the appointment proved elusive.

On the weekend following the Sucre celebrations Eduardo Rodriguez and his family came to Villa Margarita for a *parrillada*. The other guests included David Greenlee, the outgoing US ambassador, and I took the precaution of asking Eduardo whether he would find the encounter embarrassing. 'Not at all,' he assured me, and a cordial atmosphere prevailed, not least because of Rodriguez's gentlemanly behaviour.

Later in August Rodriguez's case was submitted to Congress. There were hopes that it would prove impossible to obtain the two-thirds majority in the Senate necessary for an indictment. He was not the only former president in difficulties. Accusations of genocide against Gonzalo Sánchez de Lozada relating to events in 2003 were still being pursued and the new ambassador to Washington proclaimed that the principal mandate of his mission was to obtain his extradition. There were also accusations against Carlos Mesa (2003–5) and Jaíme Paz Zamora (1989–93). In fact, every former president still living except one (the only woman) was under indictment. It seemed you had to be dead to escape. But perhaps this was the administration's way of expressing their belief that everything that preceded them had been corrupt and evil.

Another cloud on the horizon was a long-rumbling row between the church and the government over a proposal to exclude religious teaching from school curricula. That was patched up, but an even greater controversy was set in train by the education minister's proposal for new education reforms giving much more emphasis to Aymara and Quechua, which were bitterly opposed by urban teachers but supported by their rural counterparts. Meanwhile scandal was brewing over the alleged mishandling of the export of a consignment of gas by the state oil company, YPFB, through the illegal use of a private company, and there were calls for the resignation or dismissal of the YPFB President, Alvarado, on grounds of corruption. Despite Morales' initial refusal both Alvarado and the minister of hydrocarbons were obliged to go in September.

An even more serious question was YPFB's failure to manage the nationalisation of oil and gas resources. It had not been restructured, nor had it received the money needed to discharge its enlarged functions. The decree of 1 May had specified that, during the 90 days immediately following, audits would be carried out, and that in the subsequent 90 days new contracts would be negotiated with foreign multinational companies. After nearly four months no progress had been made. The flamboyant decree of 1 May had remained just that.

Bolivia's image abroad had suffered, particularly among actual or potential investors. Some smaller companies had pulled out. The larger ones were staying for the time being but freezing all planned new investment. Negotiations with Brazil over a new price for Bolivia's gas became exceedingly acrimonious. To add even more salt to the wound, Petrobras announced sizeable new investments in Peru, and in Venezuela, whose President Chávez was reputed to have persuaded Morales to take the plunge into nationalisation.

Relations had deteriorated with most of the surrounding countries, besides Brazil, Bolivia's most important neighbour. President Lula came from a background not dissimilar to Morales', but had tailored his populist background to the realities of the situation he found when he came to power. Morales had made no secret of his preference for the populist Peruvian presidential candidate who had been defeated in the polls by Alán García. At the inauguration of President Bachelet in Chile, Morales had promising conversations with his counterpart but soon afterwards, to celebrate Bolivia's 'Day of the Sea' in March, he issued an inflammatory anti-Chilean declaration and the old problem of access to the sea remained a candescent issue. With Argentina there were problems relating to the export and pricing of Bolivian gas, some of which Argentina was re-exporting to Chile, a destination that was anathema to the Bolivian government. As for Paraguay, Bolivia had roused the government's ire by protecting two men accused of assassinating the daughter of a former Paraguayan president.

From the outset, Morales had adopted a strong anti-American stance, allying himself with President Chávez and Fidel Castro and making distinctly uncomplimentary remarks about President Bush. These were to come home to roost in negotiations over the renewal of an important agreement on trade and drugs, due to end in December 2006, which facilitated Bolivian exports. Many small industries depended on it especially in El Alto, the satellite city above La Paz where there is poverty and high unemployment, and as many as 100,000 jobs could be at risk. An official delegation, headed by Vice-President García Linera, was hastily despatched to Washington but came back empty-handed. Some media comment suggested that this was partly because the vice-president allowed himself to be lured away to Los Angeles to attend the Miss World contest, in which Miss Bolivia was competing. But the real reasons were more deep-seated.

The most important event was the Constituent Assembly, convened to change the political face of Bolivia for ever. Its deliberations were to culminate in the adoption of a more representative and inclusive constitution in a period of not less than six months and no more than a year. Its beginnings were not auspicious. First the buildings were not ready. Then, when delegates were able to meet under the presidency of an indigenous lady, much time was lost in endless wrangling over procedures and a few even resorted to fisticuffs.

The greatest tension arose over voting requirements. The law establishing the assembly required a two-thirds majority but, as MAS had not won two-thirds of the seats, President Morales demanded that the rules be changed so that a simple majority would suffice, thus ensuring that MAS views would prevail. The other parties denounced this manoeuvre as undemocratic.

Further concern was caused by President Morales' declarations that the Constituent Assembly was supreme and could exercise its authority over all other institutions, including Congress and the president. Alarming conspiracy theories began to circulate. The Constituent Assembly, it was speculated, could dissolve the Congress, President Morales could then resign and the assembly appoint him as Head of State for an indefinite period. One could only hope that such suppositions were exaggerated.

*   *   *

335

In a curious way ordinary daily life went on unhindered. Every day, as the previous year, Don Saturnino the *yatiri* brought the same two brindle cows down to the cove below to feast on totora reed, their number now increased by two calves; Don Pedro was harvesting a new crop of bean holm; the same poor donkey was tethered either far from water or frustratingly just out of reach of the lake's edge, with Mateo providing buckets of water whenever Doña Perpetua and Don Heliodoro were not around.

All political unrest was suspended for celebrations of the national holiday of August, which went on for a week. My invitation to Camacachi's commemoration of the 'Día del Campesino' arrived so late that I missed such delights as the men's regatta, the ladies' rowing race, the donkey race (appropriately, Don Tito's donkey won) and – even more keenly regretted – the ladies' sack race (do they keep their bowler hats on, I wondered). Perhaps predictably, I was not invited by the mayor to march in San Pedro's civic parade.

The main festivities took place in San Pablo, whose inhabitants are always more ready to engage in festivities than the more frugal denizens of San Pedro. Day after day, night after night, the bands boomed out and the drums throbbed rhythmically on the other side of the lake, where local folk danced and drank themselves into a stupor.

Every night before going to bed I went out onto my balcony to listen to the distant revelry and gaze at the stars. A week later there came a time of full moon, magical nights at this season, when it rises nearer and nearer to the Illimani. There was a poignancy about those nights: a faint breeze ruffling the plumes of the eucalyptus grove down on the lake shore and wafting up faint traces of their scent; the sound of small waves lapping the stony beach; an occasional frog croaking and sometimes even the shrill chant of cicadas; and, far on the other shore, the distant bark of a dog. There was also majesty and mystery. The scene before me was awesome: the moon, climbing a firmament of stars, brought the sinister darkness of the sacred lake into luminous life. Rimming the pale horizon the ghostly moonlit peaks of the Cordillera Real gave the ancient legend of the Achachila, the gods of the mountains, a new and present significance. The telluric power of this mythological landscape was overwhelming. But through it all there ran an elegiac sense of irrevocable parting, of exclusion even. For the first time

I felt that I was gazing on all this beauty almost as an outsider, that I was silently saying farewell and would soon be gone.

The pressures were mounting. Don Heliodoro returned, bearing a tattered piece of paper purporting to be an authorisation from the electricity company for the installation of the cable that would provide power to his hen-house. Johnny was away in San Pedro. His sketch showed the connection halfway down my cable and not from the transformer, as agreed. Playing for time, I said I would give a decision when Johnny returned, adding as a palliative that I was agreeable in principle provided our conditions were met.

But Don Heliodoro was unimpressed and flew into a rage. 'Oh, so Johnny knows more than you do,' he sneered, using the over-familiar '*vos*' instead of the respectful '*Usted*', and stumped off in fury.

Johnny and I found that the supposed authorisation was dated 2002 and that the signature was almost certainly a forgery. We also noticed that Doña Perpetua's maiden name showed her to be yet another member of the ubiquitous Argaña clan.

From the mayor there was an ominous silence. Then, on Sunday 20 August, only six days before my departure, Johnny met him when he visited his office to leave our topographer's work and make another attempt to pay the taxes. The mayor was in a filthy mood and waved all these papers aside.

'I am going to build a wall across your road,' he shouted angrily, 'so that the Señorita can't get out and, if she does, won't be able to get back in again.'

Suiting the action to the word, he instructed a minion to erect the wall that very morning.

When Johnny came back we considered our options. We could leave by launch across the lake but could not take the jeep, although Johnny was already planning how he could build up the jetty so that a pontoon could take the vehicle along with ourselves. He also brought the news that the person stirring all this up was none other than Don Heliodoro, though how he thought this would further his request for electricity was hard to fathom.

More encouragingly, Johnny had located the man who had been mayor in 1988. He had promised to come that evening.

That Sunday morning Don Tito appeared to finalise arrangements for the computer, which I promised to deliver on Thursday. He was reassuring when we told him about the mayor's threat.

'Don't worry,' he consoled us, 'as soon as that wall goes up we will come from Camacachi and tear it down.'

Gratifying as this show of solidarity was, I was not happy at the prospect of finding myself in the midst of a civil war between two Andean communities. On top of the existing quarrel as to whether we belonged to Camacachi or San Pedro, our situation was rapidly resembling that of the proverbial ham in the sandwich.

The visit of the former mayor, Luís Poma Yucra, was like a breath of fresh air. He had twinkling eyes and a reassuringly open countenance.

'Of course I remember our arrangement,' he said. 'There was a town meeting one morning and we wrote to you in Vienna, asking you to make the football pitch in exchange for the land. There ought to be a copy in the mayor's office. And the football pitch exists, but now it's used only by the school. We should have drawn up a document recording the transaction. But that is easy to remedy. Leave it to me. I'll be back in the morning. You are not to lose any more sleep over this,' he added, with almost avuncular concern. I was indeed enduring wakeful nights, worrying about what was going to happen.

Next morning at half past seven he was back, bearing a flimsy piece of paper. The letters were faint, typed on an ancient typewriter with an ageing ribbon, but the record of our agreement was impeccably couched in legalistic language and authenticated by a flurry of official stamps and seals. It bore a date in early 1989. We both signed it. That night I at last slept well.

During my last week the palace admitted that my audience with President Morales was not going to happen, as he had gone on another of his frequent unscheduled trips. Friends warned me that I was highly unlikely to see the foreign minister either, as he seldom received even ambassadors.

Then on Wednesday I received a telephone call advising me that Minister Choquehuanca would receive me next morning at eight o'clock. I drove to La Paz, where I spent the night before presenting myself at the ministry with the UNDP Representative, Antonio Molpeceres.

I had been there so many times, visiting more foreign ministers than I could remember, but this was to be a visit like none other. We arrived early, but the minister was already there and we were ushered in before the appointed time, giving the lie to friends who had warned that I would have to wait a long time.

The minister told us he had already met with the president at five o'clock, well before dawn. Being rural folk they still kept the early hours to which they were accustomed. I liked his simple open manner and he listened attentively as I summarised my long association with Bolivia, and the ways in which I had tried to help previous governments, in external matters, and rural development.

'I know who you are,' he interrupted. 'I was born on Lake Titicaca, not far from where you live. And I know that in San Pedro de Tiquina they say, "Up there, on the hill, lives Margaret Thatcher".'

We both laughed, and I told him the story of my visit to the Otavi hospital when a drunken *campesino* had launched an impassioned toast proclaiming that my name was engraved in the community's memory, but then inconveniently forgetting it, eventually finding inspiration in 'Thatcher', the inevitable combination with 'Margaret'.

This exchange got us off to a good start. I offered my continued voluntary services, and handed him the letter from Independent Diplomat which he promised to give to the president. His response to my offer was sibylline:

'In 1993,' he began, 'we took a policy decision not to read any more books.' There was a pregnant pause that I found impossible to fill with any suitable comment. He went on: 'You see, we have always been governed by people who'd had university educations, and look what a mess they made of it! So we are resolved to learn from our elders, our Aymara and Quechua elders. We will look into the wrinkles of our grandparents and learn from them.'

Once again I was stumped for words. It hardly seemed appropriate to enquire how well Aymara and Quechua elders would be able to advise on negotiations with powerful multinational companies, or policies to attract foreign capital. The foreign minister had made a similar statement on his appointment seven months before, along with the dictum that all Bolivian ambassadors must be able to speak Aymara or Quechua, but afterwards a *démenti* had been issued. Now, however, he had said it to me, and I subsequently heard that he had given the same message to others.

Most disconcertingly, as he spoke his gaze was fixed on my

face. I concluded that I had received as positive a reply as could be expected, albeit an indirect one. Afterwards I could not help asking a friend, 'Do you think I need cosmetic surgery?'

The rest of that morning was spent in a mad rush to collect the new computer and the two trained technicians and get back across the lake to Camacachi by one o'clock. We arrived only fifteen minutes late. I had entreated Don Tito not to make a fiesta of the event, but limit it to a small group.

I ought to have known better. To ask an Andean community not to have a fiesta was to fly in the face of all the accumulated wisdom of the Aymara elders. A goodly crowd of them soon gathered, mostly ancient ladies who huddled on the floor in one corner, their voluminous and vivid skirts arrayed around them like fallen autumn leaves. I could not discern what ancestral wisdom emanated from their wrinkled, attentive faces. They made not a murmur until the computer sprang into life, a voice sounded from it and was immediately echoed by a collective 'A-a-ah' of appreciation. Elderly men who could not crowd into the small room clustered outside the windows, mouths open in wonderment.

It was difficult for the technicians to give much training. The number eager to learn was far too big. Then there was lunch. Trout caught that morning were piled on huge mounds of rice, potatoes and salad. It was too much for me and to my embarrassment the old ladies, now seated outside on the ground alongside our table, were partaking of more frugal fare, mostly dried broad beans laid out in piles on colourful *aguayos*.

Inevitably the local band appeared, Don Tito banging away at the drum. There was no escape. I was expected to open the ball, and a man in a stylish trilby hat led me to the middle of the floor amid general applause. Then the stout elderly ladies sprang to their feet and began dancing with unexpected nimbleness, some with one another, bowler hats bobbing in unison, some with men from the village.

The musical numbers that followed one another sounded remarkably similar, all requiring the same rather monotonous but exceedingly energetic steps. I pleaded exhaustion and sat down, whereupon the ladies advanced, showering us with confetti, rubbing it ruthlessly into our hair to ensure that it would stay with us for a long time. The technicians had been made to dance too, so little training was done, and one of them had to return next day.

340

The computer was very visible through a many-windowed room, but the community promised us that they would erect iron bars to deter thieves. Meanwhile they draped it in a *wilpaya*, the indigenous flag now adopted throughout the Andean region, which some say has Aymara origins back in the mists of time but others claim to be of much more recent invention. It seemed a fitting symbol.

When we got back to Villa Margarita any hope of putting my feet up evaporated when Johnny informed me that the mayor had arrived unannounced. I did not want to see him, but Johnny insisted that it would be wiser to do so.

A very different man from the aggressive bully we had encountered before, he came as near to eating humble pie as his pride would let him, but not so near as making an apology.

'There have been some misunderstandings, Señorita,' he began (an understatement if ever there was one). 'I want to assure you of my full cooperation. There will be no more problems.'

I assumed that Luís Poma, the former mayor, had shown him the document officialising the football pitch transaction, but when I presented him with a copy, as well as the receipt for thirty-five hours of bulldozer operation, he said it was the first time he had seen them. Why he had changed his mind was a puzzle but I thought it prudent not to ask, and merely thanked him, with as much cordiality as I could muster. He *had* seen the topographer's work, however, and the news on the tax front dimmed my initial relief. 'The tax will be at least 11,000 bolivianos' (nearly three times the first assessment given to us), he announced in a rapid return to his old self. 'Of course, this has nothing to do with me,' he hurriedly added. I reiterated my willingness to pay my dues but requested an official calculation.

In the evening the Junta de Vecinos (Neighbours' Association) of San Pedro came. There were three of them: the president, the secretary of finance and the 'Corregidor'. There was not an Argaña among them and the Corregidor was Luís Poma. They had come to pledge the support of San Pedro, to assure me that I was a valued member of the community and to invite me to a meeting of the whole village the next evening. In passing they mentioned that fifty bags of cement for the new football pitch would come in handy. Football pitches were beginning to haunt me.

341

The reason for the Mayor Argaña's transformation became clear when Luís Poma launched into a monologue: 'You see, Señorita, the president of the town council is my son, and the president is one step above the mayor. I told him I was ashamed to have a son who condoned injustice and disrespect to such a distinguished *tiquinense* who has done so much for San Pedro...' He went on in this vein, the general message being that he would disinherit his son if he didn't rectify this monumental wrong. It obviously had an effect, for the son had called a crisis meeting of the Municipal Council, which soundly chastised the mayor and called him to order.

That night I went to bed happy. The concerted action of two Andean communities, Camacachi and San Pedro, had dispelled the nagging fear that I was about to lose Villa Margarita for ever and my heart was touched by the loyalty and decency of the people who had risen in my defence.

Next day Don Heliodoro came, with a new sketch showing the electricity connection correctly, and I gave him a letter agreeing to the arrangement, subject to some conditions, which he accepted.

The tumultuous events of the previous four weeks seemed to have reached an almost storybook happy ending, just in time to allow me to leave with a tranquil mind. But life is never as simple as that, and certainly not in Bolivia.

My lawyer thought that I could probably survive attempts to seize my property during my lifetime, but the very moment that I popped my clogs, Villa Margarita would be taken over by the local community or the naval base, whatever my will said. I was less pessimistic, but he said that he could no longer execute the will that I had drawn up in the early 1990s, which had provided for Villa Margarita to be sold to the highest bidder. Part of the proceeds were to go to the Otavi hospital, through UNICEF, and the rest distributed among my employees. Now I realised that, in present unpredictable circumstances, it would be difficult to find a buyer for the property.

We reconsidered an earlier suggestion of my lawyer's that I should put Villa Margarita into the hands of a foundation that could defend it after my death. I had never liked the idea but during these fraught weeks I approached the local director of UNICEF.

He was interested and submitted a proposal but my lawyer did not think it would solve the problem. I was also dismayed to learn that UNICEF's regulations had changed since my will was drawn up, and that even if I specified that funds channelled through them were to go to the hospital they could use them anywhere in the world, even for administrative expenditures in New York.

My lawyer, more confident than I that a sale was possible, approached a Bolivian friend who loved the lake, proposing that he should buy it and give me life tenure. Unfortunately on this I was proved right: the friend was interested but not ready to risk his money in the prevailing political climate.

All the other options entailed my relinquishing the title to Villa Margarita in the near future. Although I would, in every case, be allowed to live there for the rest of my life, I could not overcome the ominous feeling that, while nothing would be changed outwardly, things would never be the same again. I had won the battle of those weeks but perhaps lost the war.

The dream I had cherished for so long was fading. So much had gone into the creation of this unique and magical place, love and imagination as well as hard work. But the sense of loss was even deeper than that. Perhaps it was a romantic hallucination, emanating from the strange powers of the Sacred Lake, but I had always felt, in some instinctive way, that the destiny of my venture was caught up in the destiny of the country. Now I was deeply worried about where its unfolding history was leading. It was right and proper that the people who had inhabited these lands from time immemorial should play a major role in the affairs of state. The change should have taken place long before. But it was important that it should be successful and there had been many signs and portents during the first eight months of 2006 that filled me with foreboding.

Yet there was a consoling thought that sustained me, as I said farewell to the mountains and the lake. The *campesinos* of Camacachi and San Pedro had demonstrated by their loyalty and sense of justice, the very essence of the qualities of the 'ordinary' people of Bolivia that had drawn me to make my home with them. I could only hope that these same qualities would infuse the body politic.

Epilogue

Over two years have elapsed since I wrote those words and, while my direst fears have not materialised, the political situation has become increasingly precarious and unpredictable. As a friend quipped: 'Anyone who says he knows what is going to happen in Bolivia is ill-informed'. Tension escalates as new Presidential elections loom in December 2009. In April Evo Morales denounced an alleged plot to assassinate him, involving several foreigners. Significantly, this followed on the discovery of a bomb outside the residence of Cardinal Terrazas, the Catholic Archbishop of Boliva, who has been an outspoken critic of the President.

Villa Margarita has not remained immune from these upheavals. The latest scare came during my most recent visit in March 2009. A few days before my arrival radical elements among the 'campesinos' seized the house of Víctor Hugo Cárdenas, on the lake shore about halfway along the road between La Paz and Tiquina. Víctor Hugo was the well-respected Vice-President during Sánchez de Lozada's first government from 1993–7 and the very first indigenous person to hold high public office in the country. While this was by no means the only instance of property seizure on the *altiplano* it broke new ground because the ousted owner was not a member of the former oligarchy, nor a non-indigenous person, but himself an Aymara born and brought up on the shores of Lake Titicaca, among the very people who had commandeered his property, the difference being that he had managed to better himself through higher education. Public outrage escalated among MAS opponents when it became clear that the government had no intention of intervening to recover the property and the police stood by at a safe distance, doing nothing. International protests joined those within the country, not only because of the high regard in which the victim is universally held but also because it was now clear that private property, legally held, no longer had any guarantee, a further disincentive for much-needed foreign investment.

A week later, on the day after my arrival, the wife of my Aymara employee, Mateo, crossing the straits of Tiquina on a launch, on her way to La Paz, overheard a group of men saying, in Aymara, 'The next house we have to seize is that of the Señorita,' as they pointed to Villa Margarita silhouetted on the headland. This sparked off new alarm bells as such actions usually took place at the drop of a hat and property once occupied was not only difficult, if not impossible, to retrieve, but was likely to be looted and vandalised. I immediately took preventive action, speaking to the Bolivian Ambassador in London (a close friend of the present Vice-President, and the British Ambassador in La Paz), as well as getting a message to the Foreign Minister pointing out that confiscation of my house could well have very adverse consequences not only for me but also for Bolivia, internationally, as well as within the country. The UNDP Resident Coordinator also wrote an official Note to the Foreign Ministry, receiving an assurance that the matter had been referred to the Ministry of Government for appropriate action. For good measure I also had the new Commandant of the Naval Base at Tiquina to lunch and he promised that, should anything occur, his troops would be promptly on the scene.

What would actually happen in the event of an invasion is open to speculation but, for the time being, Villa Margarita is still in my possession and it is my hope that, when I die, Johnny will become the owner of the land he has for so long cherished. He has all sorts of plans and hopes to make it a special small hotel for discriminating tourists visiting the lake. This will mean building one or two cottages on the terraces. Given his entrepreneurial gifts and capacity for hard work I am hopeful that he will be able to carve out a better life for himself and his family, provided his health and the political circumstances allow him to do so.

My visits to Villa Margarita have become less frequent. Apart from my latest stay in March 2009, in each of the last couple of years I spent a month here over Christmas and New Year and another in late July and August. One reason is connected to my own health, as my travel was restricted by several operations in the UK: a third one in 2007 to deal with the aftermath of my disastrous fall in Bucharest; and two more in 2008, one on my knee in March and the other a hip replacement in December, 2008.

346

The main reason, however, was the lack of any opportunity to continue working for Bolivia, as I had done for so many years, while my engagements elsewhere increased.

In the last few months of 2006, following our unusual first meeting, Foreign Minister David Choquehuanca kept assuring me that both I, personally, and the organisation Independent Diplomat, could provide much-needed assistance. Meetings in London with the Bolivian Ambassador resulted in a list of projects, ranging from reorganisation of the Foreign Ministry to training courses for the new Bolivian ambassadors abroad, most of whom had no previous diplomatic experience. On 21 December 2006 I discussed all this with the Minister and presented him with a draft agreement between the Ministry and Independent Diplomat. He was enthusiastic to move ahead as a matter of urgency and requested that the head of Independent Diplomat, Carne Ross, come to Bolivia in early January to sign the agreement. He fixed an appointment for 7 January at 5 p.m., the day before I was to leave for Wales. It also happened to be a Sunday, but that was in keeping with the unusual hours kept by the members of the Morales' administration and their pride in working all day and every day. Nonetheless, I took the precaution of reconfirming it several times.

It was also very short notice but Carne Ross suspended his other appointments and rushed out to Bolivia by a circuitous and tiring route, all that he could arrange at that peak travel period. We had some preliminary meetings with Ministry officials and others but when we presented ourselves at the appointed time on the Sunday, we found the Ministry door locked and guarded by a very aggressive, armed policeman who believed not one whit of our story and threatened us with all sorts of dread reprisals if we did not move on and that pretty promptly! Fortunately, a Ministry official who was to accompany us to the meeting, turned up, late of course but just in the nick of time to rescue us. Equally nonplussed, he phoned the Minister's mobile phone, and found he was somewhere far off on the *altiplano*, drumming up support for the President on the latter's orders – a strange function for a Foreign Minister, the more so as support for the President was rock solid in the countryside, still hovering around 90 per cent! As both Carne and I had fixed tickets we had to leave next day and his mission was aborted. Later a verbal apology and a renewed expression of interest were received through the Ambassador in London but by then the enthusiasm of Independent Diplomat had been severely dented. Our experience was not exceptional, the senior representatives of at least one major European donor government having received the same cavalier treatment.

A glutton for punishment, I nonetheless pursued the matter again with the Minister on my next visit in July 2007, presenting him with an Aide Memoire and another copy of the agreement (the Ministry had lost the papers). The same enthusiasm was reiterated and this time I took some heart from the fact that another official was present, which perhaps gave some better guarantee of follow-up. Indeed, he was instructed to provide comments on the documents for further discussion before I left Bolivia in mid August. My hope was misplaced: despite constant telephone reminders I never heard anything more, either then or later through the Ambassador in London.

Sadly this insouciance seemed to be par for the course. In August 2006 I had been asked for assistance by the German Embassy in La Paz, which was advising the Ministry of Planning on the mobilisation of external finance and, in particular, on the organisation of another World Bank Consultative Group, which I had often done for Bolivia. At their request I attended various meetings with the Ministry of Planning but then the Minister was changed and there was a lull. Later the Germans asked me to go to a meeting in Berlin in November, 2007, to which they had invited the new Minister and his team, with all their expenses covered. I accepted but once more heard nothing further until I returned at Christmas, when the German Embassy told me that not only had the Minister not gone to Berlin but he had not even bothered to reply to the invitation!

So it was not only I who was finding it difficult to help Bolivia. It was hard to know whether the government's inexplicable behaviour was due to inefficiency, inexperience, or downright rudeness. One reason could be that the Bolivian economy was riding high, with gas exports booming at ever higher prices, the national budget in the black for the first time in living memory and money pouring in from President Chávez and Venezuela. In such circumstances they perhaps felt they could scorn assistance from other donors, of whom they were in any case very suspicious.

*   *   *

Another reason might be the complications of governing an unruly country and dealing with internal politics which allowed scant time for attention to international relations. The Constituent Assembly had started badly, wrangling over voting procedures, and now things went from bad to worse. There was clamour from Sucre, the legal capital of Bolivia, where its deliberations were being held, that the executive and legislative arms of the government should also be transferred there from La Paz, thus making it the capital in the fullest sense. Simultaneously the richer lowland Departments, where most of the exploitable national resources are located, became increasingly vociferous in demanding autonomy from the central government.

This growing rift between the western, indigenous regions of the *altiplano* and high valleys on the one hand and the tropical lowlands on the other, posed a dangerous threat of splitting the country in two. Even on the *altiplano* the government was facing mutinous reactions from its own more radical supporters, disappointed that the exaggerated promises of a better life did not materialise overnight. Their protests adopted the well worn practices that had proved so successful when Morales had been in opposition and had brought down two Presidents in succession: strikes, demonstrations and the notorious roadblocks that could quickly bring whole regions and even the entire country to a standstill. The President was understandably furious, and his anger was in no way appeased when the aggrieved perpetrators of these affronts pointed out that it was he who had taught them how effective roadblocks could be!

Once again roadblocks disrupted our lives. On one occasion, returning from our weekly shopping in La Paz, we arrived at the tollgate on the outskirts of El Alto just as the hordes swarmed in to bar the road. As usual we took evasive action along rutted tracks across the *altiplano* but there were so many diversions that even Johnny's normally unerring instinct failed him and we got lost. Eventually finding ourselves on the road to Guaqui I had the bad idea of suggesting that the only way to get home was to circle the other side of the lake and return through Peru. We had not bargained for the unbelievable bureaucratic impediments to taking a car across the frontier nor that, when we at last reached the small border post at Tito Yupanqui, the nearest point to Villa Margarita, it was to find that an impassable trench had been dug on the Bolivian side.

349

By the time we had retraced our steps and arrived at the main border post at Karasani it was nearly midnight.The Peruvian guards were still on duty but we had to wake a disgruntled customs official to get the last gate unlocked. He only did so after I had made an all too convincing imitation of an aged and ailing lady who might expire at any moment. But then the barrier on the Bolivian side was also locked, making it impossible for a vehicle to pass through, although smugglers on foot or bicycles could easily do so through gaps at the side, unimpeded by any guards since they were all fast asleep. No amount of shouting and banging on doors or blowing the car horn could stir them from their slumbers. The only hostelries where we might pass the night were behind us, on the Peruvian side, but we dare not brave the wrath of the Peruvian customs man, who was probably once again asleep by this time, and so were caught in No Man's land between the two countries, facing several hours of freezing cold and hunger in the jeep – we had not eaten since lunch taken twelve hours before. Johnny rose to the challenge and after some time cajoled two locals into showing him a precarious smugglers' track which avoided the main barrier. It was blocked by huge rocks and our noisy efforts to remove these finally roused a customs officer who then tried to stop us. After further pleas of age and infirmity on my part – I was getting all too good at it by this time – he agreed to help us for a consideration: 300 Bolivian pesos which he tactfully described as 'customs fees'. Even so, the jeep could only negotiate the track tilted at such an alarming angle that I wanted to get out, until Johnny pointed out that it was only my far from frail weight that was stopping the vehicle from toppling over! It was 2:30 a.m. before we eventually reached Villa Margarita, exhausted after a journey that had taken twelve and a half hours instead of the usual two and a half.

Predictably, the Constituent Assembly was unable to come up with a new constitution by the scheduled date of 6 August 2007 and was given an extension until 15 December. Its deliberations continued to be beset by problems, and even violence, and the document that eventually emerged in December had to be produced in secret in a military barracks guarded by the army, in sessions attended mainly by the government party, MAS, as most of the opposition stayed away in protest. Nonetheless President Evo Morales received the new Constitution in a flamboyant ceremony before an immense multitude of his supporters in the Plaza Murillo in La Paz on 15 December. Ominously, on that same date the dissident departments, by now known as the *Media Luna*, or Half Moon, because of their configuration on the eastern side of the country, launched their statutes of autonomy with similar fanfare in their respective capitals.

The proposed new Constitution was a huge, unwieldy document that very few people had studied in any detail but rumours of what it contained caused alarm and consternation in some quarters. Morales' party, MAS, claimed its policy to be 'Democratic Revolution' and the general purpose of the constitution was to give greater participation in the affairs of the nation to the indigenous population, a principle to which no one could object. But there were ominous implications in specific articles, one of which provided for the repeated (and perhaps indefinite?) reelection of President Morales. Many detected worrying signs of creeping authoritarianism and of movement towards a one-party state and a general erosion of democracy.

During 2008 the confrontation between the government and the departments comprising the *Media Luna* escalated month by month and the latter's provocative acts of brinkmanship became bolder than ever. On 4 May the Department of Santa Cruz – the most important one by virtue of population size and the richness of its resources – voted overwhelmingly for autonomy from the central government, amid general jubilation. The other renegade departments, Tarija, Beni, Pando and Chuquisaca, soon followed suit.

Morales' riposte was to denounce the referendums as fraudulent and organise yet another one of his own, nationwide, on 10 August. The question posed to the populace this time was whether he and the prefects heading all nine of the country's departments should continue in their posts or be 'recalled'. In a sense it was gambling for high stakes but the President's confidence in his continuing popularity among the mass of the people was vindicated when he was confirmed in his post by a national majority of 68 per cent, several points higher than his electoral victory in 2006. This apparent triumph was marred by the fact that the prefects of the rebel departments of Santa Cruz, Tarija, Beni and Pando were also endorsed with majorities higher than in the general election (Santa Cruz with 64 per cent). The prefects of La Paz and Cochabamba lost their seats, while those of the *altiplano* regions of Oruro and

351

Potosí held their own. Chuquisaca was suffering its own problems, with opinion divided between the capital, Sucre, and the pro-government countryside.

Thus the so-called 'recall' referendum, far from resolving the problem, merely served to widen the gulf between the highlands and lowlands, and spur the *Media Luna* departments on to further defiance. The government was rapidly losing control over those areas, where pro-autonomy civic groups seized public institutions and even airports, that of Santa Cruz for a while causing the suspension of such international flights as were still serving the country. In response, the government organised massive marches and demonstrations of its own supporters, leading in some cases to violent clashes. Neither side would admit outside mediation to resolve the conflict.

Matters came to a head on 11 September, of all symbolic dates. In Cobija, the capital of the Department of Pando, a thousand ' campesinos' on their way to join a pro- government rally, were ambushed by paramilitary groups and a number of them were brutally killed. The government accused the prefect, Leopoldo Fernandez, of masterminding the attack and declared a state of siege in Pando. Fernandez at first urged his supporters to take up armed resistance but the Bolivian army remained loyal to the President and occupied Cobija. Fernandez was arrested and taken to La Paz, where he still languishes in prison in April 2009, so far without trial.

For a few days the spectre of civil war once again loomed large, as well as the possible secession of key areas of the country. President Chávez went so far as to volunteer Venezuelan troops to defend his friend's government but this offer was rejected by the Bolivian military. As so often before, wiser counsels prevailed at the very last moment, when all seemed to be lost. On 18 September 2008 talks between the other renegade prefects and the government began in Cochabamba. Neighbouring countries had also grown increasingly alarmed by a conflict that could all too easily overspill Bolivia's frontiers and an emergency summit meeting of the newly formed Union of South American Nations (UNASUR) was convened in the Chilean capital, Santiago.

Mediation efforts followed in which UNASUR was joined by the Roman Catholic hierarchy in Bolivia, the United Nations, the Organisation of American States and the European Union. These endeavours culminated in a meeting of the Bolivian Congress on 21 October at which agreement was reached to hold a referendum on the disputed new Constitution. In return for their support the opposition parties obtained concessions on some of the more extreme provisions of the draft, notably that, while Evo Morales could be eligible for reelection to the presidency immediately following his first term (something not allowed under the existing Constitution), this would be for one further five year period only, and not an indefinite prerogative. New presidential and legislative elections were to be advanced to December, 2009, two years ahead of the scheduled date of 2011.

The new referendum duly took place on 25 January 2009 in a generally calm atmosphere. Apart from authorising a second five year term for the President, if elected, the main underlying principle centred on the prerogatives of the indigenous majority of the population, affording 36 ethnic groups the right to their own territory and language and to their own form of community justice. The referendum also limited the size of land holdings, which, in the eastern part of the country, had not been curtailed by the incomplete agrarian reform of 1953.

The referendum results showed a majority of just over 61 per cent of favourable votes, and so the new Constitution came into force. Once again, however, the overall average masked the same regional discrepancies, the negative vote strongly evident in the *Media Luna* departments, while the *altiplano* was almost universally in favour. Opposition figures were also quick to point out that the majority vote was somewhat less than the 68 per cent registered in the 'recall' referendum of August, 2008. That difference may well not be significant in relation to the general elections at the end of 2009 which, on present showing, Morales is virtually certain to win, not least because the political parties opposing him are weak and divided. The distribution of the vote is nonetheless an ominous sign that the underlying problems dividing the country have not been addressed during the current truce. 2009 looks likely to be a turbulent year, as well as perhaps a definitive one.

Externally the government's main emphasis was on anti-American rhetoric, echoing the policies of their chief ally, Venezuela, and relations with the United States progressively declined. In September

2008 the government declared the US Ambassador, Philip Goldberg, to be 'persona non grata' and in sympathy the Venezuelan government expelled the American Ambassador in Caracas.The immediate pretext was that Goldberg had met some of the dissident prefects but the real reason was probably more fundamental. The U.S. government had for many years made its aid conditional on effective drug control and restriction of coca production. Under the Morales' government it had increased and so President George W. Bush decertified Bolivia as ineffective in the drug war and suspended its trade preferences under the so-called ATPDEA programme. Morales retaliated by ordering the US Drug Enforcement Administration to leave Bolivia and the last DEA agents departed in January, 2009.

With the election of President Barack Obama there were signs of a softening of attitudes on both sides. President Obama congratulated his Bolivian counterpart on the results of the January referendum on the Constitution while Foreign Minister Choquehuanca declared that Bolivia was seeking to renew its ties with the United States and would be ready to accept a new US Ambassador.

Amidst all this turmoil life at Villa Margarita went on much as usual. For the most part, despite occasional scares and mishaps, Villa Margarita, located far out on the *altiplano* and surrounded by indigenous communities, was a haven of tranquillity compared to what was happening in the rest of the country. My household still consists of Johnny, Mateo, Nancy, Eusebio and the dogs; among the latter there have, alas, been more fatalities, the saddest, a beautiful dog called Coco, found dead along the shore, another case of poisoning by a neighbour. For a while his companion, Negron, was inconsolable but has now found consolation with two new puppies.

In late 2007 a new member joined our little community: we managed to persuade our pugnacious neighbour, Don Heliodoro, to sell us his maltreated donkey, to which we had surreptitiously given water for years. We christened her Mafalda, after a famous Latin American cartoon character, but, despite the improvement in her quality of life, her character proved to be unruly and her presence a mixed blessing. We had thought she might keep the grass on the many terraces cropped but she turned out to have a great penchant for roses – blooms, leaves, thorns and all – so she had to be confined to the lake shore where we hoped she would lead a contented life, munching *totora* reed, with water constantly in reach. Not a bit of it. She developed a capacity for freeing herself from her tether – something she had never achieved in her former existence, when tied for days on a barren hillside, with scant pasture and no water. In the middle of the night she contrived to clamber up the hundred or so steep steps to bray lugubriously outside Johnny's door. Occasionally taken by Eusebio to graze on the fresh pastures of his property, she invariably escaped and was found sometimes in the main plaza of San Pedro and on one memorable occasion on the football pitch of the naval base!

We had no idea how old she was but Johnny and Mateo, ever-optimistic, decided that it would be nice to have the patter of tiny donkey feet around the place and entered into a contractual arrangement with the owner of a male donkey in Camacachi. Mafalda was duly taken there for a week. But after three days the owner of her intended mate, grim-faced and furious, returned her to Villa Margarita: a reluctant bride, she had beaten up an over-eager suitor and left him very much the worse for wear. The final dénouement, just before my last visit, was sad. Mafalda disappeared again, in mysterious and still unexplained circumstances, and this time was never found. The awful speculation is that she was stolen and taken to Peru, where she would most likely be turned into donkey meat, a tragic end to a well-meant attempt to help an animal in distress.

One constant source of preoccupation has been the precarious state of Johnny's damaged leg. After his visit to the vascular surgeon in London in 2006 everything went well for some time. Towards the end of 2007, however, dreadful ulcers broke out and festered into an open wound. Once again I worried about gangrene and a possible amputation. During my stay I took him to the best Bolivian vascular specialist I could find in La Paz. The leg briefly improved but after my return to the UK its condition deteriorated alarmingly and Johnny was for a period hospitalised. The only solution was for him to see the same London surgeon who had attended to him before and so Johnny travelled to the UK in May, 2008. Up till then the reports on the leg had been uniformly bad but on his arrival Johnny cheerfully informed me that the lesions had miraculously and suddenly healed owing to the ministrations of a

355

yatiri, or witch doctor, just the week before. This personage had thrown a few coca leaves around and made some incantations and libations to the Pachamama (the earth goddess) but, more importantly, had applied a poultice of Andean herbs with almost instantaneous results. I quailed at the prospect of telling an eminent Harley Street specialist that his distinguished services had been preempted by a purveyor of black magic but he graciously took it in his stride, remarking that most modern medicine had evolved from traditional practices and that the herbs had probably contained antibacterial properties. He expressed the hope that Johnny had brought some of them with him for analysis but happily he had not: he had already had quite a difficult enough time with the immigration officials, despite having all the requisite guarantees of financial support and return booking, without having possibly suspect plants in his possession.

This time, the respite has been shorter. Over Christmas 2008, when I could not be in Bolivia because of my hip operation, Johnny's foot was struck by a loose rock and the wound opened again. Unable to travel I could only listen to the telephone bulletins that seemed anything but reassuring.

'How about the "*yatiri*"?' I anxiously enquired.

'I have sent a message,' said Johnny 'but he is a long way away, very busy, in Charasani. So many people want him'.

Eventually help came from Cuban doctors stationed at Amacari, a small health centre not far beyond the hills behind the house. Relatively recent arrivals, they are products of Evo Morales' close friendship with Fidel Castro. This programme has been bitterly criticised by the government's opponents but in Johnny's case, at least, their expertise and willingness to help proved a godsend.

Mobility problems of my own have curtailed my solitary excursions over the rocky hill paths above the house, although I hope only temporarily. Ever thoughtful, Johnny has found an old mountain track only ten minutes' drive away in the jeep. It winds through the hills, each curve opening up a new and romantic view, sometimes of the whole glittering chain of the Cordillera Real, at others of the Great and Small Lakes of Titicaca. Very occasionally an ancient and battered taxi bounces by, ferrying passengers between Tiquina and Amacari. But mostly the only traffic is of *campesinos* trudging to and from market, with a loaded donkey in tow, or herding their animals back to the corral as evening approaches. There are few enough of them in this almost deserted countryside, their frugal brown homesteads barely discernible on the hillsides or in the folds of the valleys. Some of them are already abandoned, their roofless shells encased by crumbling adobe walls. Johnny and I walk there so often that we have become well acquainted with the few men and women bent over their agricultural tasks in the tiny stone-strewn fields along the way. In March those hillsides, normally sere and drab, were brightened by drifts of wild pink cosmos. Nearer at home relations with the two neighbouring communities, San Pedro and Camacachi, have followed their familiar course, marked by intense rivalry and competing requests for me to become *'madrina'*, or godmother, of this or that. This benign sounding term is not honorific but a scarcely veiled command that you are expected to finance the activity in question. Camacachi never got around to barring the windows of the small room housing the computer that I had given them. Miraculously it was not stolen but when I next visited the village I was taken aback to find it almost awash with technology. President Morales had used the largesse of Venezuela to provide a computer to every rural community and Camacachi had been favoured with two, far in excess of their needs and capacities. All three computers had now been transferred to a new adobe building, still only half built and roofless, so of course my contribution was then demanded in order to ensure the protection of the machines! Before this could be completed, however, some bright spark managed to make a wrong connection and all three computers were burnt out ... !

After the many disappointments of the last few years, there were more encouraging developments at the Otavi hospital, in the Department of Potosi, to which, for my sins, my name had been given over 40 years ago. The devoted woman doctor who had been ousted by the political machinations of the drunken watchman and the chauffeur was followed by some unsatisfactory replacements who did not last long, but then an equally committed male doctor was appointed. Better still, he was promoted to be the regional director, based in Puna, and used his greater authority to procure the ambulance that Otavi had so long been promised – a spanking new one at that. About the same time the planned reconstruction of the hospital with financing by a European non-governmental organisation, also promised for many years, at last began to take shape. In August 2007, with my dear Chilean friend, Maria Angélica Junemann, and the indispensable Johnny, we made an eventful 1600 km round trip by road to check on progress. We were dismayed to find that they had torn down the old hospital first so that its services had to be provided in makeshift circumstances in the market. But work was obviously going on apace and the planned structure was ample and ambitious, though I was disappointed that it did not contain an operating theatre, which had been an important feature of its predecessor. There was the usual rustic lunch, music and dancing with the Mayor and other local authorities and general jubilation.

'It will be finished by Christmas' they cried. 'Come back then for the inauguration and a great fiesta!'

But when I got back at Christmas it was to learn that construction had been halted for no clear reason and that the doctor was being replaced. Long experience should have braced me for something like that but for once I had dared to think that things were going smoothly.

It was a year later, in August 2008, when the news came that the hospital was at last ready and I was invited to attend the inauguration. I had a British friend staying for a few days who had not visited Bolivia before and we planned to drive to Potosí and Otavi by road and then take a circuitous route back through the mountains, via Sucre and Cochabamba. But then came the 'recall' referendum of 10 August and the accompanying political turbulence raised fears that the roads might be blocked and we could get stuck for days on some remote mountainside. So it was not until March 2009 that Johnny and I undertook the long trip to Potosí and Otavi. Even then the hospital had been functioning for only a few weeks. We were taken round its sparkling new facilities by the young woman doctor, who seemed very committed, and we marvelled at the addition of running water and functioning electricity, unattainable for so many years. But there were some flies in the ointment: the number of patients in the hospital's catchment area had declined markedly, owing to the dire economic situation and the migration of young people to Argentina and even farther afield. Another disturbing element was the attitude of the local community, especially one or two elders. One of the most attractive features of the new hospital is the provision of living quarters on the premises for the medical personnel, complete with showers and toilets but the villagers oppose their moving in because 'they may spoil them'! Given the conditions in which most of them live, and evidence already that locals using the patient's bathrooms are not leaving them clean, this refusal is incomprehensible. Because my visit was unannounced, I was able to remonstrate with only some of the younger and less influential community leaders. They promised to take action, as did the regional director of health, with whom I also raised the problem but so far I have heard nothing. Meanwhile the personnel continue to live some way away in sub-standard housing without water or sanitary facilities, making a speedy response to night-time emergencies difficult.

There are always interesting alternatives to explore in Bolivia and when my friend and I were unable to go to Otavi in August 2008 we visited instead all the local places of interest, including the island of Suriqui, where the ancient 'totora balsas' are still made and had a bleak picnic in a snowstorm on an open boat. Then, warmer climes called and we decided to go to the Yungas, the subtropical valleys that careen down from the Eastern Cordillera, where the situation was reportedly calm.

I had not been there for several years and found it much changed. The old dirt road down to Coroico, once the only access to North Yungas, is far better than when I used to travel it in the early 1960s and less prone to sudden landslides. Virtually unknown then, it has become notorious as 'the worst road in the world' and foolhardy cyclists flock in from all parts of the globe to claim the dubious trophy of having ridden it – and sometimes do not live to tell the tale. It is still a narrow corkscrew spiralling vertiginously down to the lowlands, fringed with bottomless precipices and bristling with crosses commemorating hapless travellers who failed to make it. For the less adventurous there is a modern, asphalted road which takes a more roundabout but no less picturesque route. The road up to the Cumbre, the highest point before the descent, which I remember as passing through tundra inhabited only by flocks of llamas, is now bordered by straggling houses, an ugly overflow from La Paz. On the peak we had another frigid picnic amid the snow-covered mountain crests before descending through swirling mists that occasionally revealed glimpses of sheer rocky cliffs on either side of the valley and of whitewater streams tumbling headlong far below towards the distant Amazon and the Atlantic Ocean. So rapid is the descent that the vegetation changes with amazing speed and soon we were in an exuberant green paradise, a world far removed from the cold frugality of the *altiplano*.

We stayed at a self-proclaimed five star hotel perched on the steep banks of another rushing mountain torrent at the bottom of a deep ravine, a long string of bungalows surrounded by lush gardens of bougainvillea and other exotic plants. We were almost the only residents in this tropical paradise, marred, however by a few inconveniences, such as no hot water and a complete blackout in the middle of the night, without even a torch or candle to hand. Not one of the putative five stars shone out to help one grope one's way to the bathroom. We visited Coroico, still a small town clinging perilously to the top of a hill far above, its whitewashed houses leaning companionably over narrow cobbled streets, their rickety balconies almost touching. The new road ends there and for a return trip we took a longer route along the unpaved road that leads across the mountains to Chulumani. Hour after hour a succession of breathtaking views unfurled before us as we passed from one narrow valley to the next, sheer rock faces yawning below on one side or the other. Most of the hills above were lushly green, their terraced slopes planted as far as the eye could see with coca, the 'green-gold' of the Yungas. The Incas came here in search of gold – *Coro*, which prefixes so many place names here, is the Quechua word for gold – as well as coca for ritual use, but the extent of these plantations now bears witness to an expanding international market for quite other purposes. The homesteads of the small farmers who tend them are few and far between but every so often, as you round a bend, a hilltop village appears in the distance, a cluster of white and adobe houses looking for all the world as if they are suspended from the sky over the rim of the abyss. On mountainsides too steep even for coca to grow, stands of rainforest flourish, their unrelenting green punctuated at intervals by the scarlet flash of a flame tree, and silvery threads of water cascade down from the heights to the river coursing along the boulder-strewn gorge far below. As we made the long ascent from Chulumani to the Cumbre the landscape became increasingly sere and forbidding, the weather worsened and we struggled through thick fog until at last we broke through the clouds into the limpid sunshine of the *altiplano*.

That trip was invigorating in more ways than one. Besides bringing back memories of long ago it was for me a salutary reminder of the immense grandeur and beauty of Bolivia, its infinite variety and boundless resources, that helped to put the present violence in a wider and timeless perspective. It made me realise that whatever happened, and however disillusioning the political manoeuvrings might be, the emotion that binds me to Bolivia stems from far deeper springs and will remain a lifelong passion.

Towards the end of that visit of August 2008, alone again in Villa Margarita and reflecting on all of this, something else occurred that warmed my heart. I have related in these pages the various occasions when I seemed in danger of losing Villa Margarita, and was saved by the support that I received from my Aymara neighbours. The Mayor of San Pedro who had given me so much grief was eventually chased out of town. Several of his successors did not last long, either because they were alleged to be venal, or in some other way did not meet the expectations of the local communities On my last Sunday Johnny returned from the *feria* in a state of suppressed excitement, wearing an expression best described in that untranslatable Spanish phrase *'una cara de circunstancia'* (literally 'with a face of circumstance'). Several of the *campesinos* had told him that they wished me to stand for election to the post of Mayor of San Pedro at the next election! I allowed myself a wry smile at this turn of events, not least at the irony of a population obsessed by the supremacy of indigenous ethnicity wanting to resort to the only non-indigenous member of the community to be its leader. In its way it was an honour and I was touched by such an unexpected expression of confidence and friendship. But I did not need to ponder long over my reaction. The offer had all the trappings of a *cadeau empoisonne*.

Not for the first time I found myself recalling that old Spanish proverb: *Hay amores que matan* – 'There are loves that kill'.

Villa Margarita   April 2009

361

List of Acronyms

ADN:	Acción Democrática Nacional – Bolivian political party
COB:	Central Obrero Boliviano – Bolivian Workers' Federation
DEA:	US Drug Enforcement Administration
ECLAC:	UN Economic Commission for Latin America and the Caribbean
GDP:	Gross Domestic Product
IADB:	Inter-American Development Bank
IBRD:	International Bank for Reconstruction and Development, also known as the World Bank
IMF:	International Monetary Fund
MAS:	Movimiento al Socialismo – Bolivian political party at present in power, led by President Evo Morales
MIR:	Movimiento Izquierdo Revolucionario – Bolivian political party
MIP:	Movimiento Indígena Pachakuti – Bolivian political party led by El Mallku, Felipe Quispe
MNR:	Movimiento Nacionalista Revolucionario – formerly the main Bolivian political party
NFR:	Nueva Fuerza Republicana – Bolivian political party
OAS:	Organisation of American States
PRSP:	Poverty Reduction Strategy Paper required by the World Bank as a pre-condition for financial aid
UN:	United Nations
UNCTAD:	UN Conference for Trade and Development
UNDP:	UN Development Programme
UNESCO:	UN Educational, Scientific and Cultural Organisation
UNICEF:	UN Children's Fund

Glossary

Sp. – Spanish; Aym. – Aymara; Qu. – Quechua

(The meanings given relate specifically to the context in which the words are used in this book)

Achachila (Aym): the gods of the mountains
aguayo (Aym.): woman's shawl used for carrying baby, or produce, on back
aguinaldo (Sp.): one month's extra salary paid at Christmas
aliscafa (Sp.): hydrofoil
altiplano (Sp.): Andean high plateau
ayllu (Aym.): Aymara community or extended family

bailecito (Sp.): an Andean dance
balsa (Sp.): traditional totora reed boat used by Andean fishermen on Lake Titicaca
barcaza (Sp,): pontoon or barge
barquero (Sp.): boatman
barrio (Sp): town or city district, or quarter
bastón de mando (Sp.): staff of command used by community leaders
boliche (Sp.): small bar or café
bombo (Sp.): drum

caimán (Sp.): crocodile, also colloquially used to describe a military lorry
calamina (Sp.): corrugated iron
camba (Sp.): native of lowland area around Santa Cruz
campesinos (Sp.): peasants, country-folk
cañahua (Qu.): cereal native to the altiplano
carabinero (Sp.) policeman
carnavalito (Sp.): an Andean dance

365

cato (Sp.): traditional plot of land measuring 40 sq. metres

caudillo (Sp.): leader, often with charismatic qualities

chacra (Sp.): small-holding

chairo (Aym.): spicy altiplano soup

ch'allar (Aym.): ancient Aymara custom of pouring libations on the Pachamama, the earth goddess

chapaco (Sp.): native to Tarija in the south of Bolvia

charango (Qu.): small stringed instrument, traditionally made from carapace of armadillo

charlar (Sp.): to chat

chicha (Sp.) beer made of fermented maize

cholo, chola (Sp.): man or woman of mixed Indian and Spanish blood

chuña (Aym.): dehydrated potato (black)

cocalero (Sp.): a coca farmer

comparsa (Sp.): group of musicians and dancers

conejo de las Indias (Sp.): guinea pig

conquistador (Sp.): conqueror, word usually used to describe the Spanish colonisers of Latin America

cordillera (Sp.): chain or range of mountains

criollo (Sp.): someone born in, or something typical of, the former Spanish colonies

cruceño (Sp.): a native of Santa Cruz

cueca (Sp.): traditional courtship dance (Spanish in origin)

cumbre (Sp.): summit

curandero (Sp.): witch-doctor

deshaucio (Sp.): separation payment on leaving employment

diablada (Sp.): the devil dance of the Oruro carnival

don de gentes (Sp.): expression used to describe a congenial person with a knack for getting on with people

fiesta (Sp.): party, celebration

gringo (Sp.): foreigner (often specifically a North American)

gremio (Sp.): guild, trade union

hacienda (Sp.): farm, estate

huayño (Aym.): Indian mountain dance, typical of Bolivian altiplano or Peruvian sierra

kallawaya (Aym): witch-doctor
kantuta (Aym.): national flower of Bolivia, native to the altiplano
kara (Aym.): non-indigenous white person
katja (Aym.): mysterious disease caused, according to the witch doctors, by failure to pay sufficient tribute to the Pachamama or earth goddess
kena (Aym.): tree native to altiplano
kiswara (Aym.): tree native to altiplano
kolla (Qu.): native of the highlands

lluchu (Aym.): pointed woolen hat with earflaps, typical male Indian headwear also known as chullo (Qu.)

madrina (Sp.): godmother
mallku (Aym.): chief, leader, headman
manifestación (Sp.): street demonstration
maraqueta (Sp.): typical Bolivian bread rolls
mesas (Sp.): ceremonies carried out by witch doctors
mestizo (Sp.): a person of mixed Spanish and Indian blood

parilla, parillada (Sp.): barbecue
paro (Sp.): strike
paja brava (Sp.): *ichu* grass, the stiff, spiky grass native to the altiplano
pejerrey (Sp.): succulent white freshwater fish
pescadores, -as (Sp.): fishermen, fisherwomen
pisco (Sp.): type of grape brandy commonly drunk in Bolivia, Chile and Peru
pollera (Sp.): the full, fluted skirt worn by Andean women

quena (Qu.): Andean flute
quínua (Qu.): highly-nutritious millet-like cereal, native to the altiplano

sajta de pollo (Qu. and Sp.): highly-spiced Bolivian dish, made of chicken
salteñas (Sp.): spicy meat pasties, typically eaten in La Paz
sebo de llama (Sp.): llama fat
sierra (Sp.): mountain, hill
socio (Sp.): member

367

sorojche (Aym.): mountain or altitude sickness
sullu de llama (Aym. and Sp.): llama foetus
supay, supaya (Qu.): evil spirits living in the earth, who have to
    be appeased

taquirari (Sp.): typical Bolivian dance, especially in the lowlands
tarka (Aym,): square, wooden Andean flute
tarwi (Aym): a form of wild lupin, widely cultivated on the altiplano
tío (Sp.): literally 'uncle' but among Bolivian miners used to
    describe the spirit of the mine, a clay or stone idol at the entrance
    to which they pay tribute
tiquinense(Sp.): inhabitant of Tiquina
totora (Aym.): reed growing in Lake Titicaca, from which the
    traditional reed boats are made
transportista (Sp.): lorry driver

vecino –a (Sp.): neighbour (male and female)
villancico (Sp.): Christmas carol
viscacha (Sp.): a rodent found on the altiplano

wuipala (Aym.): rainbow-chequered flag claimed by the Aymaras
    and the MAS party as the age-old flag of their indigenous nation
    but whose origin is disputed by others

yatiri (Aym.): Aymara medicine man, or witch doctor
yungueño (Aym.): cocktail of pisco and fruit juice

zampoña (Sp.): reed pipes, resembling the pipes of Pan
zapateado (Sp.): fast and spirited finale of the cueca dance, involving
    much stamping of feet by both partners